PLATFORM
for
CHANGE

PLATFORM
for
CHANGE

a message from
STAFFORD BEER

JOHN WILEY & SONS
Chichester · New York · Brisbane · Toronto

First published 1975, corrected reprint 1978
Reprinted in Stafford Beer Classic Library 1994, reprinted May 1995

Copyright © 1975, 1994 by John Wiley & Sons Ltd,
Baffins Lane, Chichester,
West Sussex PO19 1UD, England

National 01243 779777
International (+44) 1243 779777

Other Wiley Editorial Offices

John Wiley & Sons, Inc., 605 Third Avenue,
New York, NY 10158-0012, USA

Jacaranda Wiley Ltd, 33 Park Road, Milton
Queensland 4064, Australia

John Wiley & Sons (Canada) Ltd, 22 Worcester Road,
Rexdale, Ontario M9W 1L1, Canada

John Wiley & Sons (SEA) Pte Ltd, 37 Jalan Pemimpin #05-04,
Block B, Union Industrial Building, Singapore 2057

Library of Congress Cataloging in Publication Data

Beer, Stafford.
Platform for change

1. System theory.   2. Operations
research.   I. Title
Q.295.B28 003'.08 73–10741
ISBN 0-471-94840-3

British Library Cataloguing in Publication Data

A catalogue record for this book is available from the British Library

ISBN 0-471-94840-3

*a new sort of book
for a new sort of world*

a new sort of book
for a new sort of world

What's going on?
Is there anything
to be done about it?

Stafford Beer says yes
even though he thinks that we
society
may well go over the cliff.

Many people
especially that mere half of the world
that is less than 25 years old
see the edge of that cliff
all too clearly.

But by using the legacy
of mankind's ordered knowledge
called science
something may yet be done.

Let us not be turned off science
for the wrong reasons.

Modern science talks
about systems
and proposes a new outlook
on the world.

It is all here.
The book itself is a system.
It interlocks a narrative – yellow
with arguments of change – white
and comments in a META language – gold
to generate a thesis – blue.

These chunks interact
at every level
and are enlivened
by DIAGRAMS of system
so that the eye
the pattern-recognizer
can piece the new outlook together.

Half the book
is written
in this style.

Maybe
you already see why.

don't bite my finger—
look where it's pointing

WARREN S. McCULLOCH

HELLO

I would like to talk to you

       if you have the time

in a new sort of way
about a new sort of world.

That's because I reckon the world we have
is in very deep trouble :
and I don't just mean

       wars
       rumours of wars
       pollution
       exhaustion of natural resources
       violence

you can go on with that list :
it is all on the menu
for what's left of the century

       if we get that far

No
there is something more fundamental
of which the items we were listing
are merely symptoms

       treating symptoms
       gets you nowhere
       if there's something really wrong.

We are getting nowhere
with the disease itself
not even recognizing it.

You will find out
why my talk takes so long

       I am sorry about that
and I have found a way
to make it very much shorter
       as you will see.

The trouble is
I don't think the short talk

COLOUR CODE : YELLOW
Narrative

        which is embedded in the long one
is comprehensible on its own.

Next
you'll be wondering
why I am writing like this.
No, it isn't meant to be poetry

        I do write poetry
        and this isn't it.

The fact is
I have published four books already
in the approved style.
They look like novels
        but they aren't novels.

It is the business of words to communicate
but the more is not the merrier.
Some people
notably poets and mathematicians
use other tricks than words themselves can play
to convey meaning.
Grouping is one of them

        it cuts down verbiage
                punctuation
                parentheses
                circumlocution
        and pinpoints ideas.

So I'm trying that in this message.
If it's tiring at first
        sorry
the reason is
that reading habits are hard to break
and that's not all
        reading habits
        thinking habits
        running-the-world habits
they are all hard to break.
And that's where we came in.

I was talking about
what's on the menu
for what's left of the century

        if we get that far.

COLOUR CODE : YELLOW
Narrative

As the world staggered into the seventies
I took a personal decision.

        The style of this page is indeed
        for the personal bits.
        Grouping again.

Although I have always done
a lot of other things as well,
my employment since leaving the army
        1948
        India, dear India
        जै हिन्द
was always salaried work
mostly for industry.
I had come to the end of the road
in my latest job
        1969
        twenty-one years
        of that stuff
and re-appraised the situation.

What was the use
of seeking another such job
        all safe and sound
        pensions
        all that
from which haven to speak and write
as I had done for years
about the desperate need
for drastic change
        and how to do it
in a sick world?
        Not even ethical.

How to begin?
It was almost 1970.
A decade
opened its doors for business.

There were speeches to be made
already committed
throughout that first year
and I must see them through.

What's more
these platforms gave me the opportunity
        if I could only seize it
to collect my thoughts for the new life
and to propound

ARGUMENTS OF CHANGE

of rather than *for*
in the mathematical sense
to speak of matters
on which change *depends*.

But the platforms were spread
all over the place.
I might succeed
in making a year's coherent thinking
but no-one would know
except me
the continuity man.

The first instinct was to breathe a sigh of relief.
After all
              and it's been done before
one could use the same stuff . . . . .

But what a waste.

Then came the idea embodied in this book
which may be misrepresented
              reviewers don't always
              actually read the thing
              you know
as a collection of speeches.

They are here you will find
but they were designed
to constitute a system
              which is to say a whole
              recognizably different from
                          perhaps more than
              the sum of its parts.

The speeches record what I actually said.
This book exists to say
what I actually meant.

Simultaneously
I started working seriously
on the process of how you can possibly change things
and also trying to do it.

Pausing for breath
              a year later

COLOUR CODE : YELLOW
Narrative

I made a new speech
trying to pinpoint the disease
that's here too.

And another year on
I tried to tell the story
of a great adventure
in real life
as far as it's gone
which ends this message.

Well
that explains the title

PLATFORM FOR CHANGE

but I have yet to explain
why this seems to be the moment
to go public
after all
the platform's still there
and the action is getting hotter.

The reason is
because there isn't much time left

and I hope someone will find
in this message
a springboard for leaping gladly
into what's left of the century

if we get that far.

Enough of motivations
and we can leave for a while
the narrative format
in which the personal story is told.

✳ These colours and formats
manifest the structure of the book
which is also a system.

THE NEXT COLOUR COUNTS AS EXPLANATION

When you see *this* colour again
you are back to the narrative
to personal bits.

In the original edition, these pages
were printed on yellow paper.
For this Classic Library edition
yellow pages are printed on white paper
COLOUR CODED as below.

✱

COLOUR CODE : YELLOW
Narrative

6

Skip them if they bore you
        I really don't want to indulge myself
        at your expense.

But equally
I am fed up with hiding myself
        an actual human being
behind the conventional anonymity
of scholarly authorship.

COLOUR CODE : YELLOW
Narrative

This is my explanatory colour
I seek to explain a technical term
that I have not been able to manage without.

The term is

METALANGUAGE

—a language
meta— $\mu\epsilon\tau\alpha$ —
'the next after'
'over and beyond'
the language we are using at the time.

Why should anyone need a metalanguage?
There would be no point
unless the language we were using were defective.

All languages are defective.
In what special sense?
Simply that there are always propositions
about the language itself
that cannot be expressed *in* the language.

This discovery was made by theoretical logicians
(sometimes called metamathematicians)
and is generally regarded as 'academic'.
I do not think it is.
We can bring the idea down to earth :

> The barber in this town shaves everyone
> who does not shave himself.
>
> Who shaves the barber?

It isn't that the barber has a beard.
The language—meaning the logical structure of the talking—
is snarled up in itself.
There is no direct answer to the question.
More particularly, there is no way of discussing
what has gone wrong *using the language*
—because the language is in general perfectly all right.
You just find that you cannot talk about the barber himself
without contradicting yourself.

But we are already managing to discuss the problem

COLOUR CODE : GOLD
Metalanguage

and we could soon sort it out.
Bertrand Russell did it first, and the key thought is
about the class of classes that are (or are not) members of themselves.
The key thought is nothing to do with either barbers or shaving.

Never mind the logical theory :
we are already speaking a metalanguage—
and I am sure you see why.

But everything we say—
and everything we even think—
is expressed in propositions having a logical structure.
If we have no formal way of questioning the *validity*
of saying any such thing as we say
we stand to be caught in this trap.

If the barber shaves himself, he cannot shave himself :
if he does not shave himself, he shaves himself.

The trap is very different from the thinking traps
of which we normally take account.
It has nothing to do with
                getting the facts wrong
                drawing false conclusions from the facts
                or taking too narrow a view.

People are prepared for those traps.
And unfortunately they are inclined
to equate the problem we have raised
(which is called undecidability)
with taking too narrow a view.

This mistake, put in another form, says
a metalanguage offers a more embracing perspective
than the lower-order language.
It does do this—but the whole point is missed :

                a metalanguage is competent
                to discuss undecidability
                in the language.

Just now we had a brief metalinguistic discussion
about the barber example, and spoke of
class inclusion.
Now we are in a position to construct
a new language for talking about this barber.

COLOUR CODE : GOLD
Metalanguage

Look at these classes :

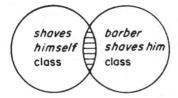

It is evident that the hatched area
IS the barber.
The language we started with is so constructed
that the two circles are *necessarily* kept apart.
That language actually DECREATES the barber.
No wonder we felt trapped.

Note that the second language is not a metalanguage,
but that we had to move into a metalanguage
to provide the logical vantage point from which
to perceive the nature of undecidability in the first language
and to design the second.

This understanding will be needed for further explanations later.
The purpose of explaining the term metalanguage now
in the context of the structure of this project and book
is to be able now to say :

> whatever is written in this explanatory colour
> is speaking the book's metalanguage.

Let us carefully consider the practical problem
presented by the project

PLATFORM FOR CHANGE

—which is interesting mainly because it exemplifies
the much more general problem of promoting change.

Any Argument of Change is put forward
in a specific context.
One can always wriggle out of the context, at least momentarily.
'Although we are here to consider *this*, please note *that.*'
And if the context is too narrow to make sense of the issue,
one can always say so—and people will understand,
even if they do not agree.
'There are national issues at stake.'

COLOUR CODE : GOLD
Metalanguage

Even if these things cannot be fully elaborated at the time,
they can be afterwards. In this book
the narrative colour is used to comment in this way
on the Arguments of Change
which are themselves presented on white pages.

Any Argument of Change is put forward
in a limited way.
It is not the whole story in itself.
Then each Argument is an aspect of a wider case
and the whole can be drawn together.
So the book has a GENERAL THESIS
presented in a colour of its own
which succinctly says what I want in general to say.
The Arguments of Change illustrate that Thesis
in particular contexts.
Remember : we do not need a metalanguage for this—
only a more general, or context-free, language.

Any Argument of Change is put forward
in a particular language.
I am not referring to the idiom of presentation
but to logical structure
as before.
Then suppose that the objective is to talk about barbers
and that one has to use a language
(because it is the one people understand)
which DECREATES THE BARBER.....

The problem of change and adaptation in society
is just like that.

It is my experience of attempted innovation in industry
and in government alike,
as it is often the observed experience of children in the family
as they grow up in a rapidly changing world,
that people respond to new ideas
by saying :

But we don't *do* it like that
—you don't understand

because you are :   too young
                            too old
                            too stupid
                            too clever
                            too clever by half
                            too impatient
                            impractical
                            idealistic
                            immoral

COLOUR CODE : GOLD
Metalanguage

This is variously interpreted by the innovators as
pig ignorance
old fogeyism
rationality (pejorative)
irrationality (pejorative)
jingoism
elitism
establishmentarianism
senility
over-confidence
fright.

I make these lists to demonstrate that

● reactions on both sides have nothing to do
with the content of the innovation

● reactions are ambivalent to the point
of being contradictory

and to use this as evidence to argue that
what has really happened
is
they have decreated the barber.

As far as this book is concerned
I intend to try to
resurrect my barbers,

and for this I need a metalanguage
in this explanatory colour.

THE HOLIER-THAN-THOU TEST

Without stopping to think, give your reaction to this unusual layout.

COLOUR CODE : GOLD
Metalanguage

THE HOLIER-THAN-THOU TEST

Answer :

It's a gimmick.

?

COLOUR CODE : GOLD
Metalanguage

This first metalinguistic venture
offers explanation about the language of the book itself.

Having done away with the format that well serves novels
the steady development of a story
in which, naturally enough, things happen in temporal sequence
resulting in what is called prose
which has a steady flow
lots of punctuation
justified right-hand margins
paragraphs
chapters

we have a new format
and a new language-for-this-kind-of-book
defined thus :

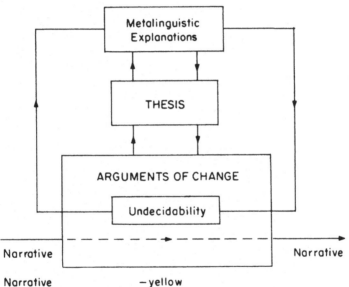

Narrative	— yellow
Arguments of change	— white
Thesis	— blue
Metalanguage	— gold

* In this edition (see note on page 5) the colour codes explained above are printed at the foot of the page — at different places in the horizontal plane (see below, compared with yellow) to form a kind of thumb index. Pages without any coding were originally white, and are easily recognized by their right-hand justification. *P.J.*

COLOUR CODE : GOLD
Metalanguage

THESIS

FIRST STATEMENT

Man is a prisoner of his own way of thinking
and of his own stereotypes of himself.

His machine for thinking
the brain
has been programmed to deal with a vanished world.

This old world was characterized by the need
to manage *things*—
stone, wood, iron.

The new world is characterized by the need
to manage
complexity.

Complexity is the very stuff of today's world.

The tool for handling complexity is
ORGANIZATION.

But our concepts of organization belong
to the much less complex old world
not to the much more complex today's world

still less are they adequate to deal with
the next epoch of complexification—
in a world of explosive change.

COLOUR CODE : BLUE
Thesis

The best opportunity to expound the First Statement of the Thesis
came towards the end of the whole project.

I was due to address a very large gathering

of people who came from many walks of life
but who had in common
a profound concern for the future of man.
They were the members of the
Pierre Teilhard de Chardin Association.

Let me remind you of Teilhard.

He was born in 1881
and died in 1955.
He was a Jesuit priest and a mystic
and also one of the world's leading palaeontologists.

He was barred from teaching in France
and forbidden to publish his books
by his religious superiors.
But this proscription could last only for his lifetime.
Therefore in 1955 his greatest book became available.

The Phenomenon of Man
crossed all the boundaries that separate
—in our particular culture—

> the inanimate and the animate
> the physical and the mental
> body, mind and soul.

Teilhard saw the whole of creation
in one vast evolutionary purpose
that is integral.

From the whirling gases evolved
the envelope of rock
round this a second envelope of life
round this a third—the envelope of consciousness.
And so there are :

> the rocky Earth, called *geosphere*
> the surrounding film of life, called *biosphere*
> emergent mind, called *noosphere*.

COLOUR CODE : YELLOW
Narrative

In all of this Teilhard saw a continuous process
of evolution through *complexification*
(yes, the word I used just now is his).
And he saw the process itself
as one of convergence
on a point
that he called *Omega*.

At Omega, the noosphere achieves an intense unification
an organization that is hyper-personal
through the increase of both knowledge and love.
This final evolution alone
betokens the capability of man to cope
with complexification
through his own complexification.

This book split the scientific world.

It was embraced by many
notably for instance by Sir Julian Huxley
as providing a wholly new vision
and perspective.
It was denounced by many
notably for instance by Sir Peter Medawar
as flatly unscientific.

But in any event
its readers were much affected.
It would be difficult to read the book and say
Oh well . . . . .

So : I was talking to articulate and concerned people
in the context of the Teilhardian conference—
people who, in most cases, would know nothing
of the management sciences.

Here then is my first Argument of Change.

By the way
I was once told on what seemed to be unimpeachable authority
that the religious superiors who censored Teilhard in life
actually approached the Pope
that severe and ascetic Pius XII
with a view to proscribing Teilhard's works altogether
after his death.

COLOUR CODE : YELLOW
Narrative

To their request
Pius XII is said to have replied

      One Galileo
      in two thousand years
      is enough.

I hope that this story is true.

COLOUR CODE : YELLOW
Narrative

AN ARGUMENT OF CHANGE

HOMO GUBERNATOR

Address to the Fifth Annual Conference of The Pierre Teilhard de Chardin Association of Great Britain and Ireland*, held at the Central Hall, Westminster in London on the 16th and 17th October 1970, under the title : *This Runaway World—Can Man Gain Control?*

*By permission of
The Teilhard Centre for the Future of Man, London.

The condition of man today is wholly alarming. He has surrounded himself with threats, and reflective people everywhere feel threatened.

Some point out that with man, so hopefully dubbed *Homo Sapiens*, evolution may well have taken a wrong turning. After all, many more species have become extinct than have survived. If man destroys his own environment, if he corrupts his own society, if he expends his wealth in warfare and preparation for war, he creates machinery for self-destruction. The more he works to streamline that machinery, in the fond belief that efficiency spells salvation, the more swift and sure becomes extermination.

One of the greatest scientists alive, the man who won a Nobel Prize for discovering Vitamin C and who was a progenitor of submolecular biology, is Albert Szent-Gyorgyi. He now calls man 'the crazy ape', and says that we are helpless in the face of 'this terrible strain of idiots who govern the world'. Others call such conclusions alarmist.

Amid the welter of accusations, counter-accusations, and authoritative statements of every kind, stand the puzzled men and women who, being threatened, earnestly wonder what to do. Some undertake marches; some contribute to charities; others sign petitions. Such actions are worthy, but without avail.

My message today attempts to say why we are locked in this stalemate, for I believe that this reason can be understood. Only when it is rightly understood can effective action be devised. If evolving man, however crazed, retains any 'plus' at all, it lies in his capacity for reflection—which is not shared by other animals. But I am asking of you something difficult : it is to reflect upon the way reflection itself goes wrong.

Our minds set out on exploratory journeys in search of solutions. We like to think of our minds as free and untrammelled, guided by the divine afflatus. There is a darker and more sinister truth. Whatever our minds may be (and we do not know), however they may soar into the higher reaches of consciousness, and even though they *may* be guided by angels. . . . they are ineluctably tied, for this incarnation, to the machinery we call the brain.

That brain is a computer we begin to understand. Like any computer, it has a blueprint to which it was constructed. For the brain as for the 'family nose', the blueprint is fixed in the genetic code laid down by mother and father in equal clumps of genes. We all live with this limitation. We cannot hire more storage; we cannot install extra peripheral equipment; we cannot commission a fresh set of initial orders.

Secondly, the brain—as any other computer—has to be programmed. If the additive association of 'seven' and 'five' must yield the answer 'twelve', if the input 'mensa' must evoke the output 'table', then the brain must be fed programmed sub-routines—as indeed it is. We call this propaedeutic process 'education', which is Latin for 'drawing out'. Whereas this is precisely a process of 'putting in'—whatever Socrates said to the contrary. We come to recognize that we should be 'drawing out', or educating, only at the stage of *higher* education—a stage at which everyone undergoing the process is by now conditioned to being programmed, and is therefore completely sure that education is a process of assimilation after all.

The real trouble starts for us humans when sub-routines are incorrectly fed in, or are falsified with the passage of time, or become plain useless. I was badly taught some elementary information which—although I know about it—still gives me difficulty; I was wrongly taught some things which are hard to suppress; I remember things that I do not want to know. Above all, perhaps, the process known to computer men as 'debugging' (which simply means testing programs so as to eliminate errors) is a big problem for the human being. The electronic computer has the bugs removed from its programs, and its memory of the operation is erased. But the debugging of my cerebral programs leaves a trace I cannot expunge. That gives me distress.

And yet there is cause for hope. It *is* possible to reorganize sub-routines. To do it, however, we must explicitly recognize three facts. First : there are sub-routines already in place, which make us confident that certain things are absolutely true when they are no more than programming artifacts of the computer part of us. Second : to over-write these programs, we must explicitly identify which orders are the ones that cause the trouble. Third : a colossal effort of will is required to dislodge the tramlines of thought which we have by now set in concrete.

For our thoughts, given by this wonderful power to reflect, run on tramlines to destruction. They are mostly preprogrammed. They result in concepts that are wholly stereotyped, and from which we do not manage to escape.

Hence I now say : let us run to earth the stereotype of man himself that inhibits our thinking about man himself. Let us recognize and dislodge the stereotyped culture to which we make unthought obeisance. And let us try to pinpoint the organizational stereotype which furnishes us with all the wrong decisions.

THREE STEREOTYPES

The Stereotype of Man : *Homo Faber*

Despite a close examination of evolution covering a period of some twenty-five million years, science has not disclosed a plausible ancestor of modern man who existed before a comparatively recent date. That date was roughly 100,000 years ago, and the ancestors proposed are *Pithecanthropus* and *Sinanthropus*.

Palaeontologists, including Teilhard de Chardin, seem to be less interested in these types because of their morphological characteristics than because they made things. Teilhard says : '*Sinanthropus* already worked stones and made fire. Until disproved, those two accomplishments must be considered on the same level as reflection . . . . .'. And when we finally reach our own specific ancestors in Neolithic times, which is to say only some 7,000 years ago, it is essentially *Homo Faber*, man the maker, whom we meet.

How indeed could man have embarked on the processes of civilization without making things? He needed the things he made to control his immediate environment. If you are in the business of cultivating wild plants and domesticating wild animals, your invention of industry will be contemporaneous with your invention of agriculture.

Today, man sees himself still as *Homo Faber*, the industrialist, the creature who invented work. And the things he makes are still largely about the control of the environment. We still stitch clothes to keep us warm, and build houses to keep out the elements. We have invented a vast range of manufactures in an attempt to control the natural environment of distance—from the bicycle to the interplanetary space-vehicle. And whereas the *hostile* environment used to be mastered by flint-tipped arrows, we try to master it today with plutonium-tipped rockets.

This simplistic account of history is given in order to draw attention to the consequences for mental stereotyping. In the first place, *Homo Faber* sees the world in terms of the things he makes : then *this is why* our society is preoccupied with material wealth as its primary measure of achievement. Secondly, *Homo Faber* who invented work regards work as the 'ethical' occupation : everything else is 'play'—which is vaguely immoral, and is certainly not allowed to count as anything but a re-creation for work. Then *this is why* society is prepared to sustain men and their families only on the basis of the work that they do; it will in no circumstances reward them for playing. And if there is to be any emolument that is not derived directly from the measurement of work, it is given out of pity or guilt (depending on one's concept of nobility)—and *this is why* it is rather heavily labelled 'charity'.

It has for these reasons become fashionable to point out that, just as man has passed through an agricultural civilization to an industrial one, he is now emerging into a 'post-industrial' society. The argument is that a crude type of agriculture kept everyone working throughout the daylight hours, but an advanced system of agriculture has resulted in relatively few people being needed to work on the land at all. Nor has this transition resulted, as some supposed that it would, in reposing power in the hands of the relative few who in fact control our food supplies.

By the same token, then, an industrial society which replaces a crude mechanization by a sophisticated automation will also end up with very few workers—and they will not have any power either. Then, the argument concludes, we are entering a post-industrial society—and that will be the end of *Homo Faber*.

So the questions begin to flow. How are people to be rewarded, and more especially what are they going to do, if they do not 'work'? Many people are making prognostications about this problem. The answers range from one infeasible outcome to another. There is the idea that everybody will receive an unsolicited income from the State, as of right; and that most people will spend their time in elevating pursuits. There is the idea that people will again take pride in craftsmanship—however bad; so that the only prized possessions will be chairs that collapse, tables that rock when you lean on them, and (who knows?) aeroplanes that fall out of the sky when the elastic breaks.

The terrifying thing is that these prognoses appear to be reasonable projections of what is already happening. Which of us has not paid over the odds for a handmade article which could have been made more effectively by machine? We may *talk* about a post-industrial society, but the thinking always retains Old Adam—our friend *Homo Faber* whom we thought we had killed off.

Well, that seems to be our biological heritage : why call the prognosis 'terrifying'? Simply because, while post-industrial man is busy with these parlour tricks, two-thirds of the world is under-nourished and one-third actually starving, and because not one of us can be sure that his own grandchildren will still be alive to join in the game.

Homo Faber is a particular conceptual manifestation of the zoological species *Homo Sapiens*. The concept has lasted a hundred thousand years, and that is long enough. For making things is no problem any more. *Homo Faber* is plain out of date. All this business about working stones and making fire is no longer what is needed to control the environment. That is because the environmental threats themselves have changed. Man is not threatened by cold and wild animals; he is threatened by exploding complexity.

Man's opportunities today lie in exploiting his wholly new capacity, bestowed by the discoveries of electronics and the findings of cybernetic science, to control and manipulate incredible energies and undreamed of computational power. But he turns his back on them. He wears out his small unaided brain in endless reiterations of the *Homo Faber* sub-routines which were written in a cerebral computer language that cannot even express the new problems to which he cannot therefore expect any solutions at all.

What about the species itself? On present reading, *Homo Sapiens* is doomed. But it is open to him to rewrite his sub-routines, and thereby to change his conception of himself and of the problems he can solve. We are familiar with those evolutionary trees printed in encyclopaedias, in which myriad branches are chopped off in forgotten ages because they were not adaptive. If, in reality, *Homo Sapiens* is not adaptive either, our branch too ends here. There is nothing one can do about adaptation in the phylogenetic sense. But I do not think the threat to us is of this kind at all. We shall not be drowned if we do not grow gills—even if there is a second Flood. *Homo Faber* has seen to all that.

No: the threat to us is cultural—it is about our way of doing things. The cultural route we have chosen, with all its stereotypes, threatens us with extinction. It used to work; it works no longer. That is something we can change, and must.

However: this cannot be done by ukase. Still less can it be done, as *Homo Faber* everywhere believes, by the steady amelioration of want and the gradual improvement of efficiency. These very concepts belong to the wrong culture. If a man who wished to go somewhere miles distant suddenly realized he were working a treadmill, would be redouble his efforts? Would he use his command of technology to drive the treadmill at even faster speeds until the bearings failed? He would not. He would step off the treadmill and start walking, however long the journey.

The Stereotype of Culture : *Totum-Quantum*

Then let us hopefully assume that our evolutionary problems are not after all phylogenetic, that *Homo Sapiens*—the only species of its genus—is indeed biologically viable. And let us briefly consider the stereotype of culture that conditions our way of looking at the universe about us. It follows from the stereotyped conception of man himself as *Homo Faber* . . . . .

Man the maker of things has always and very naturally thought in terms of assemblies and sub-assemblies. There are units made up into bigger units. Small wonder that the

Greeks, with their observant ways and analytic minds, devised an account of matter on a reductionist model. They wrote the cerebral-computer program; they passed it on. You and I received it as input to our cerebral computers nearly two and a half thousand years later. What does this sub-routine consistently tell us?

You can break anything up into its components, and break the components into pieces; you end up with granules or grains or at any rate chunks of stuff you can no longer break—perhaps because you can barely see them any longer. The Greeks rightly supposed that if man could extend his capacity for resolution, both optical and mechanical, he would be able to break up these minuscule bits of stuff still further. But they could not see the process going on indefinitely, and therefore invented the concept of the atom—precisely as the ultimately indivisible particle of stuff—which is what the word 'atom' means.

Today, any schoolboy knows that you *can* break an atom; that it consists of a nucleus surrounded by orbiting electrons, and is not indivisible at all. Moreover, there are other even smaller bits of stuff—little parcels of energy—that fly off, randomly, in all directions. That does not however mean that Democritus and Epicurus were wrong: it just means that we called the wrong bit of stuff 'atomic'. The model is made to hold; the input tape still works.

Trust *Homo Faber* to build a picture of the universe which puts those pieces together again. For every schoolboy knows that various particles are assembled into atoms; atoms are assembled into molecules; and molecules are again assembled into other things, such as the protein tissue of which his own body is made. He knows too, which the Greeks did not, that in all this assembling and breaking apart of 'things made' there is an exchange of *energy*. The energy that destroyed Hiroshima was liberated by taking an atom to pieces; the energy of the hydrogen bomb—five million times more deadly—derives from a spare electron left over in a process of nuclear fusion.

And so we have our basic cerebral-computer sub-routine for understanding the universe: a tape called *Totum-Quantum*. There is a totum, or whole, consisting of quanta, or bits and pieces, the disruption of which whole or the assembly of which quanta (paradoxically) both requires and liberates energy in either direction. Teilhard de Chardin, who belonged to this culture, made this explicit. There are three faces of matter he said: plurality, unity, and energy.

It is a dead end, and Teilhard knew it. There is a bridge between our Greek sub-routine called Totum-Quantum and a wholly new insight—a novel stereotype. The name of that novelty is *System*. As far as I can tell, the Greeks—even that greatest of Greeks, Aristotle—had not the faintest glimmer of understanding here. Rewritten by scholastic philosphers in the thirteenth century, the Greek input-tape still showed no sign of it in Latin. There is no recognition (that I can find) of the potency of system in Western thought until the turn into the nineteenth century—when it came with Hegel. After that the notion all but vanishes again. Yet Teilhard says: 'The existence of "system" in the world is at once obvious to every observer of nature, no matter whom'.

'Obvious' it may have been to him; as far as others were concerned it was *so* obvious as not actually to be noticed—like Father Brown's postman. Even Teilhard, whose whole corpus of thought is an apotheosis of System. does not hammer this point home. He simply puts System first in his accout of matter; the System comes before the Totum and the Quantum. making the cosmos a unity *par l'intégrite inattaquable de son ensemble*.

But according to the discoveries of cybernetics, there is more to it than this. System, the arrangement and the rule whereby parts are related in a whole, is more important to understanding than the entire list of parts or the apperception of the wholeness of the whole. Systemic structure is what matters. We have no inherited input sub-routine to tell us so.

However, as I said before, there is a bridge between the old and the new stereotypes—a bridge that we must cross. The name of the bridge is frightening, for it is called ENTROPY —which notoriously no-one understands. Yet the concept of entropy is already a hundred years old; and it is high time we came to terms with it.

We are used to the concept of *energy*, by which the totum-quantum is bound into a system in the first place. Now entropy began life as a subtle measurement of energy *flow*. When something hotter is systemically bound to something cooler, the greater energy of the hotter stuff migrates—inexorably migrates—into the cooler stuff. The energy equates across the gap. This is one manifestation of the Second Law of Thermodynamics. which everyone of education has encountered but no-one except the physicist wants to know.

In fact the Second Law was popularised in the nineteen-thirties as demonstrating that the universe is 'running down'. If heat always flows from hotter to cooler bodies, and never the other way round, then (since everything is ultimately in contact with everything else) all heat will eventually even out. That means of course that there is no reserve of energy any longer left; no possibility of further chemical change; no life. Even at this trivial level of interpretation, the process would take an unimaginable time, and one would have thought that people had more urgent threats to worry about than to anathematise the second law of thermodynamics. But it worried them, nonetheless. When the equation is equal, when entropy rises to unity, nothing is.

There are more productive ways known to science of looking at the Second Law. If energy inexorably flows in one direction, then the final state of the system is more *probable* than any starting state. After all, the system is bound to reach the final state in the end. And that state, being fully evened out, is nothingness. But (cheer up) there *is* something : it is called the universe, containing life, *im*probable though that may be. So physicists began to say that entropy, being in fact less than one, is a measure of the probability that the universe exists.

The non-flowing of entropy, which normally and naturally increases in the evening-out of energy, is the very power of matter. This opposite or negative entropy—call it negentropy— holds the world up. We now know what negetropy is : it is precisely *information*.

For this knowledge we must thank the founder of cybernetics, Norbert Wiener. Cyberneticians realized early on that systems exist, and run, and are controlled, by virtue of an information content. When Wiener, the ranking mathematician, set out to measure that information content, he came up with a formula which was the exact negative of the expression used for entropy in statistical mechanics. So although entropy inexorably tends to increase, that tendency is barred by injections of information.

If we have a universe, which is improbable although it exists, it is because the Second Law of Thermodynamics has two forms. One is concerned with the pressure to even out energy; that is the form which belongs to our stereotyped conception of the universe. It betokens death. The other form is about information content, which leads to greater organization and increasing complexity. That form betokens life.

We should not regard these principles as contraries. We should not think of the Second Law of Thermodynamics as warring with some perverse other law. These are forms of the same principle, which between them express the balance of nature. Entropy expresses and measures a flow of energy in one direction; negentropy expresses and measures a counter-poising flow of information in the direction opposite. The universe results.

Every complex system is held in being at the balance of its entropy and negentropy. We human beings mean more than the few-pence-worth of our chemical constituents, because information *informs* those component chemicals—by means of a genetic blueprint. Life itself is a negentropy pump. The universe means more than a collapsed energetic equation of x-heat $= x$-cold $=$ nothing, because information structures the balance. The result is the sun, moon and stars.....

I venture to suggest that Teilhard would have given anything for this extra scientific knowledge. He well knew that the evolutionary increase in complexity militated against entropy. He *thought* that meant it militated against the Second Law, and I reckon that puzzled him. The laws of nature cannot be antagonistic : they stand for systemic harmony. But *Le Phénomène Humain* was done in 1938, and Wiener's *Cybernetics* came out just ten years later. Teilhard could not have known when he was writing that matter represents at the same time and by the same measure a certain improbability (its entropy) held together by an explicitly equal amount of information (its negentropy).

Most people do not know this now. They are stuck with the stereotype called *Totum-Quantum*. It is more useful in the nineteen-seventies to use the stereotype called *System*. It is better to cross that bridge called entropy, and to enter a universe compounded not of bits and pieces but of a ceaseless flow of information.

And please let me add something wholly personal, something which (even by intelligent extrapolation) I dare not attribute to either the dead Teilhard or the dead Wiener. It is more relevant and also more scientific today to forget the concept of an old bearded gentleman sitting on a cloud, who answers to the name of 'God', and to think of the Creator and Sustainer of the universe as a store of negentropy. Don't tell me that is pantheistic or impersonal : my own personal personality depends on It.

The Stereotype of Organization : *Bifurcation*

What matters about the inherited stereotypes so far discussed is that they have led humanity to a third—which exists at the sharp end of thinking, namely action.

Society must organize itself to take decisions. And *Homo Faber* makes organizations just like anything else. He saws up the totum into quanta, and calls the process delegation; he nails quanta together into a totum, and calls the result a chain of command.

Please draw yourself an organization chart of the simplest possible kind, in which each level of organization bifurcates into two departments. Thus a Head of State might divide his responsibilities into home and foreign affairs. Home affairs might be divided into economic branches and welfare branches. The welfare branch might become education and health at the next level—and so on. Of course, in practice, we use more than two classifications at each level, but the principle is the same—and it is the same for the firm as for Government; the same for the armed forces as for retailing. This really is a pervasive stereotype. It looks like a family tree. Call it a hierarchy, and note that at each level there will be an increasing number of cousins.

Now contemplate the problem of making a real-life decision. Such decisions are properly taken as near to the real situation as possible, which is to say quite low down in the organizational hierarchy. But they are taken with an eye looking upwards (that is to the boss), an eye looking downward (that is to the subordinate pyramid), and an eye looking sideways (to cousin departments at the same level). The quantum-totum stereotype of organization takes care of the vertical axis of command rather well. The whole thing is nailed together by *Homo Faber*. But it has nothing to tell us at all about the horizontal linkages between cousins.

For the many centuries over which this stereotype has evolved, horizontal linkage was not very important. The organizational quantum, a village in a federal society, the subsidiary of a firm, the ward of a city, and so on, obeyed the law upwards and administered the law downwards. What the cousins were doing, which is to say organizational quanta at the same hierarchic level, was really of no concern.

Perhaps the major organizational issue today could be called horizontal relevance. Society has undergone an expansion which has caused the quanta carefully separated by the stereotype to collide in almost every dimension we can nominate. Social units are no longer separate: they share common boundaries, which the inhabitants freely cross. Divisions by profession, trade or skill, have come to overlap because of changes in our conception of the best way to do things. Knowledge itself has been reorganized, because of changes in our understanding of the universe, with the result that interdisciplinary studies taken as a whole are now far more important to society than studies made within the classical disciplines. Above all, technological change—in communication, computation, the ability to travel—has affected the family tree stereotype of organization to the point where the boundaries it seeks to maintain can be maintained no longer. We are trying to live within an organizational stereotype that does not work.

When it comes to decision making, this fact proves quite disastrous. It becomes essential that a decision made by one quantum at a particular level in the organizational hierarchy should carry its cousin quanta with it. But the organization stereotype does not offer a lateral means of communication. Therefore we must do the best we can. We set up committees, working parties, interdisciplinary studies, international commissions, inter-departmental liaison groups, cross fertilizing mechanisms of every kind . . . . . But the fact remains that the organizational stereotype does not acknowledge these things, with the result that no one knows where authority lies. This in my view is the major reason why, today, it is characteristic that 'nothing is done'.

Suppose you are trying to take a decision, and the organization you command is a mere ten levels down in the State hierarchy. Even if there are only two branches at each hierarchic level, you will have 1024 cousins to take into account. The thing is just not workable. You may succeed, by endless committee work, in getting some kind of horizontal consensus. But your cousins have 512 bosses to satisfy, and some of those are not going to agree. Even if they do—what about *their* 256 bosses?

It is this structural failure which prevents large firms from realizing the synergistic benefits of the totum : the cousins demand autonomy. It is this which prevents a community from turning a spare plot of land from an eyesore into a childrens' park because cousins from planning, health, welfare and so on look up to umpteen different masters. It is this which inhibits the development of local health centres in favour of those unco-ordinated cousins— the hospital, general practitioner and local government services. It is this which turns all our well-intentioned attempts at international cooperation into farce.

Scientists devoted to the study of management examine these issues and put forward their solutions. Everyone seems surprised that these solutions are not implemented, and they ask whether the research has been ineptly done, or whether the authorities concerned are plain stupid. The point of this argument is to say that neither of these conclusions is correct. The trouble lies with the stereotype, with the input tape written in a language in which arguments for change appear meaningless because they cannot be properly expressed. It is just like trying to display to someone the colour green by the use of a stereotyped paint box containing only shades of red and blue.

It surely follows from all of this that if we wish to progress we shall have to change the organizational stereotype. It must be replaced by a new understanding of system, defined not by the particulate division of authority but by the synthesis of information flow. There are by now many examples of how this can be done. And if the chart depicting the novel form is not to look like a family tree, what will it look like?

The answer to this question is : *anything* organic. It will look like the DNA molecule. It will look like the neurophysiology of the human body. It will look like the circuit diagram for a computer. Better still : it will look like all of these things at once, depending on the filter you wear over your spectacles.

For the key discovery of cybernetics is that all viable systems may be mapped onto each other under some transformation. That is a technical way of saying that every viable system obeys the same balancing law of information and energy flow, and that therefore all viable systems have structural commonalities. Cybernetic laws underwrite the survival capability of viable systems in terms of entropy and negentropy—the measures which bring energy and information into the same calculus. And these same laws determine new structures, engineered in terms of linkage, and feedback, and stability. This is the language of system.

ELUCIDATIONS OF INTERACTION

If we have now put those three stereotypes in their place, we may seek further elucidation of systemic interaction. I am trying now to explain exactly where the new problem lies—a problem peculiar to our age—the problem that has rendered the stereotypes not only useless but dangerous.

People who do football pools are familiar enough with the ideas of permutation and combination. They know that the number of interactions grows much faster than the number of entities available to interact. Even so, such truths appear to many as pertaining to peripheral matters such as gambling; they do not think about them seriously in the context of a society which has fairly suddenly become massively interactive.

We realize that modern methods of communication have brought about new interactions of knowledge and awareness. But *Homo Faber* is playing a more potent game than this apparently superficial interaction suggests. His latest methods for making things demand high rates of production in the cause of cost minimization. The resulting cheapness of the product increases his market. His distribution plans soon encompass the globe.

You may sit in a London restaurant on Scandinavian chairs, using Belgian cutlery. The meat dish you are eating was made and tinned in Czechoslovakia, while the potatoes have been reconstituted from a powder sent here packed in nitrogen from the place the potatoes grew in Idaho, USA. The plastic cruet came from Hong Kong, the breadbasket is African, and the intercom to the kitchen is of course Japanese—although the waiter using it is a Cypriot.

The social and economic consequences of such a scenario are bizarre. A strike in Scotland in one industry can cause a thousand men in a related industry to be laid off work in California. The plans of an American firm to extend its business in the Far East, via its German subsidiary manufacturing in Eire, can destroy an English village overnight by closing down its only industrial firm because of a resulting flood of cheap goods thereby generated in Europe. Of what use to mankind now is the organizational stereotype labelled 'sovereign nation'? Shall two gentlemen in top hats call on each other and exchange notes to solve such problems as these?

Clearly not; and yet our stereotypes will continue to assure us that these problems are economic and political, and that we have the machinery to handle them. They are not in essence economic or political problems at all; they are cybernetic problems, and there is *no* machinery. I recommend that we should contemplate them in terms of the sheer mathematical forces involved.

Here is a very simple example. Suppose that you are one of an isolated community of three people living on an island. On a given day, you may be talking to one of your colleagues, but not feel on speaking terms with the other—although he is trying to talk to you.

That is, for each relationship there is an associated state on any day, which is either 'speaking' or 'not-speaking'. Now we may calculate the total possible states of the whole system of these three people. First we must know how many relationships there are, and that is the number of people multiplied by one less than their number. In this case, then, we get three times two equals six relationships. In order to find the total number of states in which this community may exist, we must calculate the total number of societary patterns generated by the conditions as stated. We take the number of states attaching to *each* relationship, which in this case is just two, and raise this to the power of the number of relationships.

For three people we reach the answer 2^6, which is already a total of sixty-four possible states of affairs. This measure is called the variety of the system. Now if you wished to devise a set of rules for regulating the behaviour of this little community, whereby for instance anyone sulking and refusing to speak to the other two automatically gets left with the washing-up, then your rule-book would have to prescribe for sixty-four contingencies.

On the next island is another small community of four people—just one larger than yours. Their rule-book also allows for every contingency; but it turns out to be written in several volumes. The variety has exploded. Because now there are $4 \times 3 = 12$ relationships; and 2^{12} is 4,096.

In real life, of course, regulatory systems do not take account of every contingency separately: they economise by lumping various possible situations together. In that way small communities have always managed to operate fairly successfully, by ruling out with one sweeping regulation all manner of possible modes of behaviour which were simply 'not allowed'. Even so, the 'stuff' of the problem is still measurable by its variety. Regulatory devices will be judged by their capacity to handle it.

We are now in a position to isolate and understand two of the major factors which have brought mankind into a sort of mathematical crisis today. First of all, *Homo Faber*, industrialist and by now technologist too, is busy building—and he has built a bridge between the two islands, across which the two communities may freely move. So now there are *seven* people interacting; and obviously the number of contingencies that may arise between them, the total *systemic* variety, is not simply the sum of 64 and 4,096. The number of relationships has gone up to $7 \times 6 = 42$, and the number of societary contingencies (represented by 2^{42}) is an almost unbelievable variety of four million million.

These people need something more than a new and consolidated version of the rule-book. Certainly, one of the things they can do is to cut down massively on these proliferating states of affairs by the old trick of legislation. For example, in the elementary case we have considered, we could make it illegal not to answer when spoken to—and the entire problem disappears. Society often uses such simple but ingenious devices, as for example in the Rule of the Road.

But now we can recognize the second major point. Just at the moment when technology has unleashed such potent mathematical forces of interaction into human society, just at the moment then when we most want to legislate against the proliferation of variety, society has for other reasons abandoned most of the restraints on variety it already had. Leaving aside the relatively small numbers of ways of behaving that are cut out as actually illegal, there used to be a great many variety-inhibiting social taboos. There were social disciplines too—administered by squires, priests, schoolmasters and even fathers; and there was in the individual himself an acceptance of what used to be called 'his station in life'. I shall not be arguing here whether the lifting of taboos, the abandonment of discipline, and the indulgence of individuality are in themselves good or bad. I am pointing to mathematical facts.

Now all of this will not just take care of itself. Proliferating variety is a measure of increasing chaos. Entropy is rising; negentropy is falling. Well, there are cybernetic laws governing variety regulation. The overriding law, like all of the great laws of nature, is deceptively straightforward and simple. It says that only variety can absorb variety. If you want to contain the behaviour of twelve people in red shirts running madly all over a football field, you will need at least twelve men in white shirts to do it. Matching, or requisite, variety is the condition of successful regulation : this is called Ashby's Law.

To handle any situation with a given amount of variety we must be able to match it—and there are in principle just two approaches to the problem. The first is to increase the variety of the controller until it matches the variety of the situation to be controlled. The second is to take action which will drastically reduce the variety to be controlled. That is : we may either provide those twelve men in white shirts; or (if we have only six white shirts) we may shoot half the red shirted players. These strategies are not mutually exclusive, of course. In the eyes of cybernetics, the whole business of human freedom may be seen as a constantly adjusting balance between the two methods: variety generation for the controller, and variety inhibition in the controlled.

A feudal lord (one man) exerted total control over his serfs—simply because they could not in practice match his variety between them. That is because the variety available to them in principle was never allowed to proliferate. A hundred men digging the soil from dawn to dusk, and then collapsing into bed, offered no more variety to the boss than one such man—because they were replicas, one of another. They presented a low variety situation easily contained by a master having unquestionable authority and plenty of time.

It is essentially the rise of technology which has allowed the variety of individual citizens to proliferate : the authority has been lost, and everyone has time to indulge in distinctive behaviour (which includes plotting against the established order). The process has gone on and on; and if we look at any department of life we can see how the regulatory process has become more and more complicated as its need for variety increases.

Take an example : taxation. A general levy is a low variety tax, and therefore easy to administer. Once we take account of individual circumstances, the variety goes up. But we can still cope as long as people are more-or-less the same. But technology has moved in to create the forty-hour working week. The individual citizen has found more and more things to do, and this proliferates variety in his tax affairs. If he deliberately obscures this situation, he is injecting yet more variety into the situation. In trying to match this variety, more and more regulations are introduced—until it is doubtful whether anyone can work out what is happening. A similar situation exists for the police, and even for less obvious social regulators existing within education, health and social welfare.

Supposing we have almost reached the time when every individual citizen is unique in his social behaviour, so that no two citizens can be lumped together as a technique of control variety reduction, then by Ashby's Law we must expect that on the average half the total time expended by the population will be spent in monitoring what that population does with the other half of its time.

This is a precarious, not to say ridiculous, situation. The reason why it is precarious is that we certainly do not know how to operate such a complicated regulatory system efficiently. Hence, even if society as constituted is theoretically capable of meeting the conditions of Ashby's Law, it will not be so in practice.

There are three wholly predictable consequences. First : wasting half of human effort in this way means a loss of wealth which could otherwise be applied to succour the less privileged. Second : society cannot be in control of itself, since it lacks Requisite Variety to exactly the extent of the loss of efficiency. Third : society will make panic stricken endeavours to increase its control variety still further, using its organizational stereotype—which entails an explosive growth of bureaucracy.

Since all three of these conditions are incipiently with us, my account of the matter is thus far validated.

ABOUT SOLUTIONS

From this vantage point we may clearly see that the actual *purpose* of organization is to handle proliferating variety, firstly by cutting it down (that is by keeping islands or cousins separate where that is legitimate), and secondly by offering efficient and well-lubricated channels for the flow of control variety which can be applied to the islands or cousins with precision. It is also perfectly clear what has gone wrong.

We created organizations and social institutions to suit the matters with which they had to deal at the time—and that meant making a lot of administrative divisions intended to group like things with like. The front line of administration was backed by an ascending hierarchy of 'higher authorities', the chief function of which was to re-route matters which were atypical of the island or cousin in whose territory they originated. But the organization was well planned, and initially not much re-routing was necessary. Moreover, the steady flow of negentropy reinforced the given organizational structure, for positive feedback confirmed its relevance. Thus it became rigid.

As the constraints on the individuals making up the populations under governance came to be relaxed, and more interaction occurred, there arose an increasing rate of mismatch, so that more and more cases had to be re-routed. The end result is that the organization has ceased to be appropriate to its task; but instead of recognizing this fact it simply pumps more and more control variety into the system in order to handle the proliferating variety outside.

In fact, what is needed is structural change. Nothing else will do. But this message cannot be heard by people who regard the structure as given—because of the sub-routines in their cerebral computers. The organization's idea of adaptation is always to modify the rule-book—little realizing that this method of providing requisite variety (apart from being hideously expensive and indeed profligate) denatures the organization that it is. For when *everything* is re-routed, there is no purpose in the organization any longer. The maintenance of its structure has become an end in itself.

The more I reflect on these facts, the more I perceive that the evolutionary approach to adaptation in social systems simply will not work any more. Evolutionary systems in biology, which do work, always embrace structural change : this turns out to be what evolution is about. Adaptation is not obtained by overloading the variety generators of the control system, which seems to be the only solution society currently has. It has therefore become clear to me over the years that I am advocating revolution.

Now society itself seems to have come to the same conclusion, for we live in a revolutionary ethos. The question seems to be this. How long shall we pretend that everything is all right, and wait for action from those who have first hand knowledge of the fact that everything is all wrong? I mean the starving, the radically underprivileged, workers in revolt, the young. Such dissident groups happen to be in the overwhelming majority, and their overturning of unadaptive social institutions will doubtless be violent. That is because they will see no other available mechanism. The government changes: nothing but the faces is different. The employer is changed: life is the same. Only the threats and the tensions become worse.

Even those who believe, which I do not, that we are actually making progress by enlightened legislation and occasional action can no longer clear-headedly believe that the patience of people will last. There is no reason why it should: people are sick of inaction, and sooner or later the dams will burst. The problem is increasing exponentially, because variety is proliferating; the solutions we have will not work, because they are not adaptive. Meanwhile, our most well-intentioned people mistake control variety enhancement for structural adaptation.

It is possible to change the rate at which a valid systemic structure metabolises by an evolutionary adjustment of the valves and filters. But *structural* change is by its nature revolutionary. I do not know how birds evolved from reptiles. But today's managerial man, flaunting his computer, makes me think of a lizard with one feather proudly sprouting from its head—and hoping to make it to the tree-tops by nightfall.

Do not let us have our revolution the hard way, whereby all that mankind has successfully built may be destroyed. We do not need to embark on the revolutionary process with bombs and fire. But we must start with a genuinely revolutionary intention: to devise wholly new methods for handling our problems. We can do this, and we can run the new methods in, alongside the overstretched systems that we have—until they are shown to cope.

The methods become clear once the stereotypes are overthrown, the cause of the problem is revealed, and the need to design viable systems is accepted—whole books are available about how to proceed. That is not the difficulty.

The difficulty is how to replace *Homo Faber* with a new kind of man. He will not be man the maker any longer. He will be man the steersman—of large complex, interactive systems. I call him *Homo Gubernator*.

Homo Gubernator is around, but not in office. He cannot even well serve those who are in office, because stereotypes get in the way. Despite his knowledge of how systems are viable, and the kind of organization and control they require, he spoils his case with the people by failing to offer pat solutions off the top of his head. He wants to investigate first.

But people prefer to hear slogans, and asseverations of intent, from men who know all the answers in advance. It does not matter if their policies are internally inconsistent: it does not matter if they are repetitions of policies known to have failed over and over again in the past. They are selling the stereotype, which is alone acceptable.

I fear that the revolution will be formulated by just such men, successors to *Homo Faber* true—but not *Gubernator* at all. We must choose to become *Gubernator* ourselves, while there is time.

Today, as I finish preparing this paper, there is a letter in the correspondence column of the *Times*. It comments on the fact that a three-year study has been financed at London University to investigate the effect of violent television scenes upon the young. There is a systemic interaction worth attention; and *Homo Gubernator* cannot yet be extinct. But I give you a piece of this letter, so that you may know and recognize the alternative to the choice I have just recommended.

> 'What a fatuous and shameful waste of money . . . . .
>
> In less than three minutes, free of charge and
> without the slightest fear of genuine contradiction,
> I could assure the spendthrift sponsors of this
> futile exercise that the effect of horror upon
> adolescent minds is precisely what one would
> expect it to be—utterly deplorable.'

The letter is signed by a name I do not know. But the signatory is none other than our one alternative choice. He is *Homo Pontificatus*, the harbinger of extinction.

Here are two comments in the metalanguage.

Stereotypes are often useful concepts to deploy
indeed it seems likely that we cannot manage without them.
What is wrong with the ones that we have
is that they relate to a vanished world.

In a changed world, the old stereotypes
give rise to undecidable propositions.

For example, if the means of livelihood
must be emoluments derived from work put in
to enterprises which themselves must make a profit
then

        thinkers
        teachers
        artists
        social workers
        government

cannot be paid at all unless
everyone agrees to pretend
that the work they do is profitable
not in the general sense of the word
but as having a measurable monetary value.

But this remains a pretence.

The question : what are teachers, policemen, nurses *worth*?
is strictly undecidable within the language
of the stereotype.

That is why none of them is properly paid.

And as the world moves steadily away from the Homo Faber culture.
which it is doing because the production of goods
becomes more and more automated,
not only individual decisions but whole policies
become undecidable within the language.

The answer is not to invent bogus measures of benefit
but to devise a metalanguage
in which questions of value can be set and answered
in quantified but not monetary terms.

Note that this remark is meaningless
rather than merely puzzling
inside the existing language :
that language decreases the measures we need.

COLOUR CODE : GOLD
Metalanguage

Any new language must be competent to describe
new kinds of organization too.
The Argument of Change declared that such organizations
would look like '*anything* organic'.
The passage as spoken entails the existence
of commonalities between all organic systems.

That there are such commonalities
is a fundamental tenet of cybernetic science
(as will be argued out later).
The *statement* of commonality is necessarily metalinguistic.
Thus I see it as something more than a generalization
of the machinery of particular systems—
for such a generalization would be a perception
made by a neutral observer.

The metalanguage will be something more than this:
it will be positively generated at the focus of meaning
that lies beyond an entire range of undecidable propositions.

So the second comment is this.

We should try to envisage the developing general thesis
in systemic terms
so as to show not only how things are connected
but also how the inherent undecidability
of the language used in each system
is expected to generate a metalanguage—
and of what form.

This consideration leads to the next page of the thesis
in which the account of man set out in Homo Gubernator
is diagrammatically expressed.

COLOUR CODE : GOLD
Metalanguage

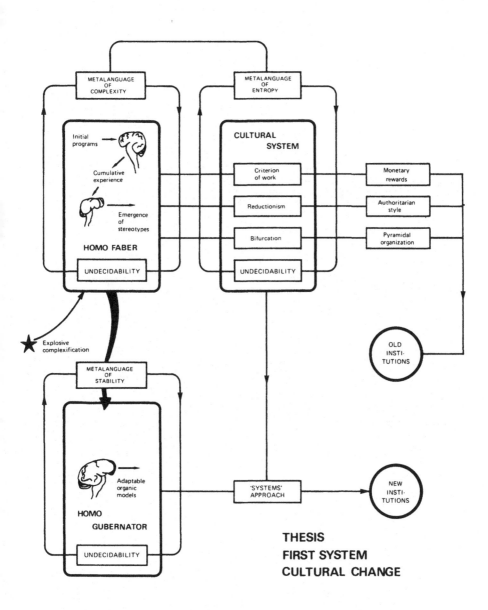

THESIS
FIRST SYSTEM
CULTURAL CHANGE

OLOUR CODE : BLUE
   Thesis

Reactions to this address convinced me
that people do not normally contemplate such matters
although they are willing to do so
once the subject is raised.

Especially it is not realized that

- the brain is a limiting mechanism

- we do become trapped
                in our own thought processes
                by our own stereotypes

- the Puritan Ethic of Work
                dominates our culture

- complexification increases exponentially
                like an epidemic of measles

- organization exists
                just to handle complexity.

But these facts
are highly relevant to the main problem
                how can the world throw off
                its manifest incapacity
                to deal with explosive change?

Questions were also asked
during the discussion
about youth.

I argued then
                and do so again now
                with increasing conviction
that the behaviour of our children
had much better be
incomprehensible to us.

If we ourselves are not sufficiently adaptive
to meet the challenge
                of complexification
                in our own epoch
our children must achieve
a new conception of the world
                with a new language
                for representing it
or the chances for survival will be small.

COLOUR CODE : YELLOW
Narrative

44

In that case
I am not saying that they are succeeding
only that some of them may be trying
it will be surprising
if we can at all understand
what they are
thinking
saying
doing
not doing
that especially.

But listen to Jack Kofoed
of the *Miami Herald*
on May 18th 1972 :

With so many of youth growing up
in the hippie, let's-not-work,
professional-protesting pattern,
there seems little hope for change
in the foreseeable future.

It is a widely believed viewpoint.
Homo Pontificatus
is weighed down
by the Puritan Ethic of Work.

Anyway
I'm sorry Jack but
this is the major hope for change we have got.
That by no means proves all is well.
But if we felt at ease
we could be sure that
things were going badly.

Besides
in Britain
on May 18th 1972

there were more than a million
UNEMPLOYED

and if we had the faintest idea
how to use automation
and if we had the faintest idea
how to undermine bureaucracy

there would swiftly be two million
UNEMPLOYED

COLOUR CODE : YELLOW
Narrative

            not starving—
            unemployed

            one could say
            at leisure.

And it is Homo Pontificatus himself
            none other
            ambivalent fellow
who leaps about on television
to say that
sooner or later
work will become a luxury.

            You are inconsistent, H.P.
                    it is one of your traits.

Let us not then insist
that our children be like us
we who have proven
our incompetence.

            Keep on raising
            the school-leaving age
            that's bound to help . . . . .

Here are three key attitudes towards youth
detectable on both sides of the Atlantic :

    ● authoritarianism
       exists, grows stronger.
       Smack their bottoms
       then all will be as before
                    heaven help us.
       It exists with a vengeance
                    apt word.

    ● pooh-pooh
       and the problem goes away.
       After an unruly student demonstration
       at an ancient British university
       against fascist oppression abroad :

       venerable don :
                In my young days
                we sowed our wild oats
                in bed.

COLOUR CODE : YELLOW
Narrative

● supportive.
Some people like their children.
Some people love their children
and don't realize
they don't like them.

Or if they do
they think love is what matters
but that is easy.

I see Homo Pontificatus
in the mirror.
Let's change the subject.

Within the week of the Teilhardian conference
mind centred on
Homo Gubernator
we went to two dinner parties in London
my wife and I.
They were very different.

At one of them
given for Don Schon
in London to record
the Reith Lectures for the BBC

see his book
Beyond The Stable State

the talk was optimistic.
Means were available to mankind
to cope with its problems
to mould new institutions
to survive.

At the other
another distinguished American
he must I think
remain anonymous
explained at length
with certainty
with elaborate detail
with zest
that the only course open to mankind

is to EXTIRPATE
all
dissident
elements.

COLOUR CODE : YELLOW
Narrative

To this end
and to take only one example
millions of lives would soon be forfeit
in the United States itself.

This was the most hair-raising table-talk
that I have ever heard.
It was deadly serious
                not funny.
If it is a bad forecast
it is still
not funny.

There is a triple choice for Homo Sapiens :

> ● to declare that although there are many problems
>   there is nothing *fundamentally* wrong
>   with our existing institutions
>   and ways of doing things :
>   therefore we should just keep soberly on.

> ● to assert that the society of man
>   has become grossly unstable
>   and threatens to blow apart :
>   therefore we should impose stability by force.
>   This choice explicitly says
>   we can pay too high a price for liberty.

> ● to recognize the instability
>   and an urgent need for change—
>   a faster change than choice one could possibly provide—
>   but to defend the contention
>   that mankind has the knowledge and capacity
>   to redesign society :
>   therefore we should start now.

I submit that choice one is based on an assumption
blatantly contradicted
by the evidence of societary breakdown all around us.

I submit that choice two is wicked.

I propose to you choice three.

Then let us address the questions

> what is the knowledge and capacity we have?
> why does it not take hold?

COLOUR CODE : YELLOW
Narrative

THESIS

SECOND STATEMENT

We shall not succeed
in reforming our concept of organization
or in creating new institutions that actually work
simply by hard work—or even hard thought.

We need to invoke SCIENCE—defined as
the organized body of human knowledge
about the world and its workings.

Science offers the means

- to measure and manipulate complexity
  through mathematics

- to design complex systems
  through general systems theory

- to devise viable organizations
  through cybernetics

- to work *effectively* with people
  through behavioural science

- to apply all this to practical affairs
  through operational research

In using these essentially interdisciplinary capabilities
science is free to draw on its depository of knowledge
of physical, biological and social systems.

The knowledge and the skills exist
but are wasted—frivolled away.

Society proceeds instead by *consensus*
that lowest common denominator of alternative democracies
which buys protection against
megalomaniacs, fascists, charlatans and lunatics
and which also protects us from
novelty, unique ability, change and leadership.

The consensus simplifies, distorts and makes trivial
the real problems of complexification
which are inherently too difficult
for *all* to understand.

COLOUR CODE : BLUE
Thesis

50

Thus we come to manage an oversimplified model of the world
that exists only in the mind of the consensus
instead of the real world . . . . . out there.

This mismatch
lies at the root
of our incompetence.

COLOUR CODE : BLUE
      Thesis

To what audience could this part of the thesis better be addressed
than to those of my compatriots
professionally qualified and able
to do something about it?

The Operational Research Society
which grew out of the original Club
was the first foundation of an international federation
that now includes more than twenty national societies.
All are dedicated to the pursuit of knowledge
about the application of science
to problems of decision and control
whether strategic or tactical
of the kind we have discussed.
The members of these Societies
are in professional practice of O.R.

I had in any event to speak to the Society
because its members had elected me president
for the years 1970 and 1971.
The question uppermost in my mind was
why?

The year of 1969 (president elect)
gave me the chance to think this question over.
I had been in O.R. since the end of the war which gave birth to O.R.
Did this make me automatically some kind of grandpappy?
On the contrary, I have always regarded myself
as the oldest *enfant terrible* in the business.

Securus judicat obis terrarum
said Augustine :
the world as a whole judges rightly.
And I do not think that this remark refers
to the intellectual consensus
on which I poured scorn just now.
It has always seemed to me to refer
to the unanalysed feeling of the totality
that *this* is how it is

> God is on our side
> things are bad
> Churchill for Prime Minister
> morality has become hypocrisy
> we must go on strike
> homosexuality is a harmless abnormality
> capital punishment is
> > obviously proper
> > obviously obscene

COLOUR CODE : YELLOW
Narrative

—that kind of thing.
Augustine could not have agreed with this interpretation :
I am sure that he meant that
the world at large judges *absolutely* rightly *in the long run.*
Nevertheless
the idea that there is—at any one time—a climate of opinion
that the system itself is speaking
that a tide is running
(choose the metaphor yourself)
seems to me correct.

If THIS
were what the managerial concept of consensus really meant
of course I would support it.

Make no mistake :
it actually means that
the most timid member of the managerial group
controls the outcome.

Typically
those who are being managed
are ahead of this game.

But I deliberately digress
to prepare for an Argument of Change
that mocks the consensus.

As far as the Operational Research Society was concerned
I saw myself mounting the presidential podium
in response to a deep and dynamic urge
for change—

or perhaps it would turn out to be
merely a hope that some sort of rumpus
would destroy lethargy through excitement.

In any other dimension than these
I did not flatter myself that I would have been elected.

Rumpus may be fun, I thought, but change is necessary.
The first was conceived to generate the second.

So the presidential address was fixed
much earlier in the year than usual.
It happened within a fortnight of my taking office.
There was much to do in two years
and besides : this was a message in itself.

COLOUR CODE : YELLOW
Narrative

Arrangements were made for the Council
to dine together after the meeting.

If I were to be lynched
they might as well get it over;
but if the right note were struck
this would be the moment
to enlist support.

Let us leave what happened
until you have read the second
Argument of Change.

The retiring president, two years before,
had called his Presidential Address
OPERATIONAL RESEARCH AS GENESIS.

And so . . . . .

COLOUR CODE : YELLOW
Narrative

AN ARGUMENT OF CHANGE

OPERATIONAL
RESEARCH
AS
REVELATION

Inaugural Address* by the President of the Operational Research Society, delivered in London on the 14th January, 1970.

*By permission of
the Operational Research Society, London

INVOCATION

If there is one speech in a garrulous career for which a professional man cannot subsequently excuse himself it is surely an inaugural address as president of his own professional society. Election to that office is the highest compliment he can receive, and I am deeply aware of this.

I have had a year since the election to reflect on the responsibilities, and on what I should say today. It has been a year for discarding three plausible speeches.

First, there was the witty speech full of in-jokes; next the overly clever speech making abstruse allusions; and last the obsequious speech of relief that I have joined the Establishment at last. These three speeches will never be spoken.

For a time, moreover, I found I was leaning emotionally on the stature of my predecessors. There is no lack of lustre there—a lustre in which I somehow feel entitled to share. I take this immediate opportunity to salute them all.

And especially I salute, and thank sincerely in your name, the most recent member of that distinguished band—our past-president, Bill Williams.

He has contributed massively to the Society's progress by exceeding hard work behind the scenes. And he hands on a rejuvenated society—poised, I think, for a virile leap into this new decade.

As for me, however: I am finally left alone up here with what I really think. If I did not take that loneliness seriously now I would be a fool; and I would be taking you who put me here for fools. My state of mind today has been hardly come by—in the practice of operational research, wherein I reach my silver jubilee next year. You cannot ask for more than to know what in all honesty is that state of mind. I cannot offer you less.

Its emotional tone, first of all, could be called a mood of controlled anger. I hope that this is both more dignified and more constructive than a feeling of mere irritation.

Operational research has in some respects been denatured by its own growth in respectability. I am angry about that and will explain my thinking later.

Secondly, it has in some respects been misrepresented—and not only by outside critics. That makes me angry too.

Above all, its capability has in large measure been wasted. I rate failure here, the responsibility for which we must ourselves largely bear, very seriously indeed. Here above all anger must be constructive.

I do not mean that the work we have all done is a waste. I mean that the issues to which scientific problem-solving is most profitably directed remain the accepted prerogative of intuition.

The favoured management style therefore remains the striking of consensus. This is a prudential technique, hopefully protecting the group from lunatic intuitions which individuals may entertain.

It operates at a terrible expense. The price paid is the suppression of right intuitions which lie outside the imagination, knowledge and experience of the consensus.

Under this style, management becomes a Mediocrity Machine. In the fair name of 'participation' it emasculates the bold and far-sighted proposal, and dissipates the innovative drive.

The constructive answer to this is not indeed a return to the rule of authority. It is the invocation of science to provide that kind of evaluation which would carry the consensus, and establish the management team in new paths.

I reserve my anger here for the Mediocrity Machine which invokes science—not to these ends at all, but for the increasingly efficient implementation of its own inadequate plans. We cannot afford this waste.

Today's world is short of capability rather than capital, of competence more than any other resource. To frivol away such competence in the scientific management of affairs as we have is itself a gross incompetence.

It is of a kind which would rank as legally culpable—if it were indeed capital rather than capability that had been squandered.

As it is, everyone is supposed to accept that society acts within ineluctable constraints. I do not know why this is. These constraints evidently act so that progress is satisfactory if any is made at all. I do not understand why this is either. We seem to have reversed an ancient maxim, so as to say: *non regredi est progredi*.

If I do not know *why* this is, perhaps I know *how* it is. The Mediocrity Machine calls for, selects and adopts only one kind of servant. I call him Acceptable Man. He operates smoothly and effectively within a small and esoteric group. He is the heir-apparent; he is imitative of the elders; he is competent in tribal lore. And he reflects the consensus.

Acceptable Man copes with challenge in a predictable way. He simply declares it invalid. It will come, all right, but not yet. Therefore the means for coping with challenge are all right, but are proposed too soon.

I have to tell Acceptable Man that the challenge will not wait—it is in our midst. Our milieu is fantastically expanded in every direction and there is crisis on every side. Our horizons for comprehension, for planning, for control, are receding faster than we can conceive. No wonder that I see red: it must be a Doppler effect.

Acceptable Man is competent no longer. But Competent Man is not yet acceptable. Here lies the dilemma.

In the last presidential address you heard about operational research as genesis. It has bred many valuable activities, said the past-president, now carried on under other names. What then is left, and what is OR today? It must stand by what it reveals.

Here is my first reason for talking to you about operational research as revelation.

REVELATION (1)

To my mind the great revelation of operational research is the clarity with which it has exposed the shortcomings of the human brain as a means of dealing with complex situations, and the power of the alternative it offers.

That alternative is the construction of a scientific model, devised for the purpose in hand. It is astonishing but true that almost any scientific model, however exiguous and crude, quickly surpasses the capability of the brain to evaluate a complex situation in quantitative terms.

The set of punched cards on which the newly qualified physician may record details of every case with which he deals becomes a better diagnostician than he is himself after only a few hundred cases have been stored.

Men find it impossible to predict the behaviour of a small interactive servomechanism with a handful of variables, once feedback is introduced. If the transfer functions are nonlinear and the responses are lagged, they find the task impossible.

Compare these two illustrations with the management task in running a large-scale enterprise. The models of this that we carry in our heads are insufficiently complex by orders of magnitude, and insufficiently rich in interaction to an unthinkable degree. No wonder they are not much use in procuring a discriminatory output.

The reason itself is understood. The slightly alkaline three-pound electrochemical computer in the cranium has, if we are lucky, a capability to discriminate over a scale of nine in any dimension. To calculate the average is our métier; and if we can discriminate four points in either direction from there we are doing remarkably well. To these ends our brains employ ten thousand million logical elements, running on glucose at twenty-five watts. The discriminatory yield of nine points on a scale represents an output of 3.2 bits.

For comparison, a small business with five hundred binary inputs and five hundred binary outputs is capable of taking up more states than we can at all conceive. It is a number so large that if the whole terrestrial globe were and had always been a computer it could not have processed the data. (There is formal proof of this statement, based on Planck's constant as a limiting factor.)

The answer of man the manager to this problem is precisely *organization*. Proliferating variety is held in check by our organizational refusal to consider more than a tiny part of the problem at once. Nor will we normally consider more than one time epoch at the moment of decision. Any who tries to look more than a week or so ahead is likely to be written off as a visionary. Thus are great issues reduced to a scale with which our cranial computers feel they can cope.

But the subjective illusion of coping is not enough. There are implications for policy in an exploding technological milieu which range beyond the ken of this procedure in space, in time, and in organizational stress.

In space, because technology now ramifies the effects of every action. In time, because it takes years for any policy to mature—so that the outcomes of many policies today are almost exactly out of phase with the management succession or the electoral cycle. I mean that praise and blame is likely to be apportioned to precisely the wrong set of people.

As to organizational stress, the point is that the space-time ramifications of policy and its exorbitant cost drive the level of decision inexorably upward, at the very moment when our collective managerial wisdom calls for driving it down.

The result is inevitably that the macro-systems of our firms and social institutions do not hang together, while the interaction of micro-systems is self-defeating.

Thus is lost every benefit of a putative integral policy. Industry loses the potential benefits of synergy. Government considered as moderating the national weal becomes incoherent. Administration is for ever inchoate.

All of this happens for want of a model, drawn at the level of systemic integration. It is not a necessarily elaborate model, but a model that can improve on a discriminatory output of 3.2 bits. It is a model that can cope with the interactions of perhaps ten to fifty variables in quantitative terms. You and I and the manager cannot do that. Science can. If operational research must stand by what it reveals, this is the overwhelming truth.

When we say that OR has produced a battery of techniques which have been notably successful, we refer exactly to this fact. Critical path analysis does precisely this. So does linear programming. Both techniques algorithmically relate the parts of a well-formulated system to create that whole we cannot intuit, a whole greater than the sum of its parts.

As to our other famous methods, they have mostly enjoyed success because the models they use correctly convolve probabilities. And this is something further of which the brain is notoriously incapable.

I customarily seek to demonstrate this point to managerial audiences by inviting them to assess the chances that any two people in the room have the same birthday. They are hopelessly wrong, always, underestimating by ludicrous amounts. For as you know the chance is even when there are no more than twenty-three people present. And Feller's equations have never let me down in perhaps a hundred tests. At my last demonstration a few weeks ago a triple birthday emerged among the first twelve people questioned, after a consensus that the chance was less than a cat's in hell.

Let me now gather the threads of this argument together. I am saying that in operational research we combine the power of the model, applied at an integrative level, with the power of probability measurement. Then we have a tool which even in its crudest form immediately outclasses the brain in the task of quantitative evaluation.

Here is the point where I must turn aside to rebut the view, as common perhaps among scientists as among managers, that immense sophistication, time and expense is required to build useful models. It is not true.

The best-known examples of classical OR reveal the elegant simplicity of good science— the $e = mc^2$ that was there all the time. Then let us take care that scientific insight is not obfuscated by its own technique. Nor should we let our understanding vanish down the nearest data-drain to be lost in the viscera of a vast digital computer. Insight and understanding are precious commodities indeed: they are the outputs of cerebral computations that the brain handles very well.

I see several people here tonight who were doing successful operational research when any practical computer was still a mad dream. They were doing OR before linear programming was invented. (When what was originally called 'the Dantzig method' was first discussed, I regret to say I did not know the George of that patronymic: I thought it was all something to do with the Polish Corridor.)

Then what was OR doing then? It was using science to solve problems in the conduct of affairs—whether at the tactical or the strategic level, whether the problems were about activities on the ground or policies in the head. That is what OR does today.

And so we have the name under which we work.

We call that work Operational (with a large O) because it is based in the world of genuine activity, the places where things actually happen. All good science, as distinguished from all good mysticism, is founded in empiricism. It involves actual observation, actual measurement, and actual experiment. We call our work Research (with a capital R) because we deal with problems to which no one knows the answer. Doing that thing is *called* research.

Well, I am proud of this name. For years I wondered whether it should be dropped. In the fifties managers did not understand what it meant. Even later than that, I still glossed over the phrase, calling it *oh-ah* as a kind of meaningless grunt. We have all of us flirted with alternatives—of which the name 'management science' was perhaps to be preferred. I even wrote a book about OR under that title.

But today I advise you to give up the quest for a pseudonym. Not only do we know what we are doing, but a great many managers do as well. Besides, after all, the name turns out to be pretty descriptive.

As for the name 'management science', I now think it will go the same way as the name 'scientific management' went in the thirties. That name became the battle cry of people on the make. The new one is now the banner under which is currently mounted a prestigious competition to project from hearsay evidence both the form and the payoff of the improvement which a specific major company could expect from its use. The rules include the condition that no special observation of that organization is allowed. Measurement is therefore impossible, experiment is out of the question, and the validation of models cannot be attempted.

This kind of approach is unhappily sometimes the way of management. It is certainly not the way of science. Above all, it is neither operational nor research. I am thankful then for this terminological escape, and offer you a paean of praise to the name under which we have operated all along. Let's keep it. It means what it says and so do we. I invite you also to adhere to the revelation we know, and of which I have been speaking.

When I said earlier that our subject could be denatured by its own growth in respectability, I referred to a defensive and narcissistic preoccupation with established techniques. There is no need to take refuge in them, although there is a proper satisfaction in having set them on the shelf. Still less should we look upon a battery of techniques as our output, or judge our professional success in terms of their number and obscurity. You have noted a tendency to do this: so have I.

There are people who complain: 'Look—a few simple techniques, and that is all it was about. Let's forget it.' What is the point of reducing operational research to that kind of absurdity, and then complaining that it is absurd? I hope those who do this will not gash themselves on the very axes they are patently grinding.

For the professional, the output of OR will always be feasible solutions to problems, and nothing more. If there is a technological spin-off, so much the better. Stock controllers are most welcome to employ the techniques of inventory control. Indeed, did they not so do, they would be crazy. And if people have problems of resource allocation, let them use the algorithms which OR established for the purpose of computing the answers.

But let you and I, under the banner proclaiming our willingness to undertake proper research into actual operations, get on with solving new problems.

This is what we are for. The only question is whether other people know that too. I shall pitch my arguments about this at the level of government, although other branches of management are equivalently involved.

REVOLUTION

The printed heading for this section is not any longer 'revelation' but 'revolution'. That is because Acceptable Man in his Mediocrity Machine is entrenched in the face of a challenge to which he cannot rise. He has to be shifted, and this will be a revolutionary move. If it cannot be accomplished by rationality, something unpleasant will assuredly happen. That is an inference—not a threat.

How do we ourselves stand in all this?

For a quarter of a century leading members of this Society have tried to gain an acceptance for operational research in the scientific management of civil affairs commensurate with its wartime contribution in the military field.

A certain amount has been done, which I earnestly wish to acknowledge. There have been valuable if isolated results in a few departments of state. The same can be said about a very few local and regional authorities, the Greater London Council at their head.

But anyone soaked in the early history of OR and its immediate post-war promise un-doubtedly feels let down. This is the cause for anger with which I began. And yet the feeling of anger almost dissolves into feelings of bewilderment and regret. *Mais où sont les neiges d'antan?*

By the end of the forties it might have seemed that the days of positive anti-science in government were past. It was said at that time, with amused disgust, that we had seen the last of them. A memorandum issued within the Civil Service in 1934 had supposedly recommended that senior officers should not sit in conference with scientists. Ridiculous, everyone was saying, by 1949.

But less than two years ago a distinguished civil servant—our own then president—was on this very occasion concerned lest a myth arise that operational research were less than an 'integral and essential part' of management.

The fact is that we had not after all gained the point. We have not gained it to this day.

When Churchill came to write the story of the air war, in which human valour reached that high peak which his own immortal words had already enshrined, he had something more to say. It concerned the 'secret war', fought by the scientists who had saved the war from being lost before it could be won.

'Only with difficulty', he wrote in Their Finest Hour, 'is it comprehended even now by those outside the small high scientific circles concerned'.

Just a few of the subsequent managers of civil government affairs—a Stafford Cripps for example—ever took the point. Few others indeed have reposed a jot of faith in the ability of science to tackle the problems of peace.

Yet science is only just beginning, by the accepted scale of man's cultural span on earth. Its potential contribution to the handling of affairs is not assessed. The public, and especially the young, are encouraged to believe that science (rather than its ignorant application) has brought us all to the edge of disaster.

Even so the nation was entitled, in the name of that managerial revelation and consequent revolution in the conduct of war, to the extensive development of governmental OR in the service of peace-time society.

It did not happen to scale. Moreover, despite many protestations of its wish to advance further now, made by both politicians and permanent officials from time to time, government seems impotent to act convincingly.

That is supposing that it really wants to do anything of the kind. Speaking personally, I shall find it easier to believe in the good intentions of government when it faces up to the financial realities of the market place where professional OR staff is concerned. It is a sad task to sit on advisory boards and to watch the directors wrestling with the special martyrdom which government scientists are called upon to bear.

Those of us who are martyred only on isolated days can afford it in the national interest. But I think it should be public knowledge that the government assessment of the professional value of a senior OR consultant on these occasions is exactly *one tenth* of his standard market value. And I am sorry too for those many senior men who find themselves constantly apologizing for this absurdity.

I do not speak of what has been happening nationally in the last few years with easy hindsight. What would happen was predictable. In 1964 we had the 'affluent society' which had 'never had it so good'. In a letter to *The Times* published while the OR Conference was in session at Cambridge during that year, I said: 'It is all very well to be affluent; but an affluent anachronism will burn brightly away to indigence'.

Sure enough, we did just that. And we are still an anachronism.

I went on in support of the plan—remember it?—to modernize Britain. 'We need operational research teams of outstanding ability', I said, 'working on problems of decision and control at the national level. Because these problems are usually discussed in economic terms, they are currently assumed to be purely economic problems: but they are not. Interdisciplinary scientific teams are needed to evaluate issues subject to conflicting criteria'.

We got the new government, but not the new policy.

Today, it seems to me that people at all levels of influence and having all shades of political opinion know that the reform of government machinery is mandatory and urgent. It cannot be done without the sort of competence OR has.

We recently had a Minister at Mintech who knew it. Dr Jeremy Bray wrote a reasoned, important and unsensational book about the problem which was published last week. He was sacked for his pains.

Acceptable Man is no longer competent, while Competent Man is not yet acceptable.

The fact is that we have become inured to threats, and find it easier to sidestep challenge than to meet it. The consequence is very strange, and I invite you to contemplate this remark :

Theory is the only reality countenanced by our culture.

This means that the accepted account of affairs becomes more real to those concerned than the truth on the ground. And the facts have to fit this theory. rather than that the theory should at all be changed.

It is the hard-headed practical man rather than the scientist who has all the theories these days. He 'knows'. The scientist knows no more than that he *doesn't* know—until he has made the study.

Consider now with me some apparent realities of our time which turn out to be theoretical constructs in this sense. I start with something remarkably concrete to be called a theory— yet that is what it is.

I refer to Euston Station. This is someone's *idea* of what a great railway terminal *ought* to be like. It is the sort of grandiose dream that Stevenson might have had of the future if he had not had more sense. It does not work. It does not meet the manifest need. It is a theory.

Consider the Prices and Incomes Policy. There is a theory, well based on certain principles which themselves are unassailable. But how theoretical can you get? This theory turns out to repudiate one of the few cybernetically valid mechanisms for self-regulation that the economy has ever had. It turns out to entail that all growth is both miniscule and uniform, which cannot be true. It takes a system of pay differentials, frozen by accident out of history and patently unjust, as inviolable.

Return to something quite concrete once more. What is a motor car but a theory? It is an ergonomic nonsense sold on sex-appeal. I for one would like a motor-car which I could drive without acute discomfort and a pervading sense of personal hazard. But this theoretical car—the one I have to drive—makes no provision for me, only for some theoretical driver.

Consider the taxation system, which is not only a theory but a completely incomprehensible theory at that. It absorbs by now an unbelievable proportion of the national effort, one way and another. That is one mark of its sheer impracticability. But the theory leads, as every taxpayer discovers, to the most bizarre consequences in our personal lives. Never mind: the theory is right, and the facts must be forced to fit it.

Back to a concrete theory: the jumbo-jet which I saw with my own eyes this week. What are the practical realities of long-distance travel? They are about getting to and from international airports. No-one's theory encompasses this hard fact. So we take the easy and costly path, following our technological noses from Mach 1 to Mach 2 into the noise-polluted yonder.

My sixth example is the health service, organized on a theory about the structure of the medical professions ill-mixed with a theory about the pharmaceutical industry. The patient barely figures in this theoretical construct. He would stand a better chance if he were fighting fit to face the rigours of his treatment.

Finally, and supremely, I offer you the theoretical construct of :

the Egalitarian Society, in which I passionately believe. But the theory which is this accepted reality turns out to deal with equitable shares in poverty. There are no parameters in the model to manipulate the creation of wealth.

What do I propose should be done about all this?

Firstly I propose the undertaking of operational research in the construction of better theories which more nearly match the realities on the ground. Research into operations is the bridge between theory and practice.

Real-life OR is not done in order to satisfy the requirements of a Ph.D. board. Good OR is not done to support anyone's policy.

OR is empirical science: it is about observation, measurement and experiment. It is concerned with finding ways to make the worse somewhat better. It narrows the area of risk. It studies the vulnerability of alternative policies to a range of possible futures. It looks at the real world where the action is, where real people live under real constraints.

Does this offend mathematical purists? My answer is: let us first get the sign right.

Does this offend those charged with government? My answer is: let us manage the real world, and not a theoretical conception of what ought to count as reality.

Secondly I propose that all this should be done in a proper context. By this I mean a context which is both interdisciplinary and interfunctional, a context which is above all interdepartmental.

This calls in question the theoretical construct of government. And why not.

Is the citizen cared for by Health and Social Security not the same citizen protected by the police? And is he not to be educated?

Of course there must be organizational divisions of government, as of any large undertaking. But what measures do we take to see that divisions are not divisive? How do we achieve coherence and an integral policy?

The answer is by drawing our models at the level of integration. *They will be metasystemic models.*

Now we shall come to the outcry. The super-theoreticians who count as practical men will say it is too theoretical.

Was the meta-model of battle linking separate encounters and spread out on a vast map in the war-time Operations Room too theoretical? It worked.

I envision a government operations centre, laid out on comparable lines, relating the pieces of the national problem in an integral way.

Industrial managements could have this room if they wanted it; so could a new kind of Cabinet Office—one freed at last from the theoretical constructs of economic folk-lore.

Do not be dismayed by the size of the task, nor recoil from a plan having less than academic perfection.

We have only to improve on the brain's unaided performance before our model is useful. Can you solve even a linear equation in only three variables in your head? Can our finest managers really juggle, as they often believe, with—say—even seven variables at a time? They cannot. And how large must a system be to compete with a discriminatory output of 3.2 bits?

This plan would create a new model of organization, scientifically based on genuinely physiological lines. It would quantify its model in terms of lagged, non-linear feedback loops, according to calculations scientifically based on genuine servomechanics. It would drive its display of the model with an analogue computer costing £50,000 for outright purchase.

All of this, finally, may well provoke a professional gasp from you. If so, I beg you to reflect on your own theoretical construct of what is allowed to count as the reality of operational research itself.

REVELATION (2)

I come in conclusion to the second reason why this talk is entitled: operational research as revelation. This is the biblical reference. It has to do with an apocalyptic vision.

No one can any longer say whether mankind can survive. The world's leading scientists in the relevant fields seem agreed about this: man has created for himself a set of political and military crises, a set of environmental crises, and a set of societary crises which it may prove impossible to contain.

We act as though we had accommodated to the thermonuclear threat, although it is one which computably grows. The environmental threats (pollution by pesticides, by sewage, by noise, by carcenogenic urban air) are all predictable consequences of existing, researchable systems that have been underwritten by our civilization. The same is true of race problems, the issue of poverty, and the rising tide of population.

All these systemic outcomes are quantifiable aspects of computable systems.

But none of them is computable in the head. We must have the models of which I earlier spoke. That means operational research. Social upheaval and threatening violence point dramatically to the need. But the Mediocrity Machine 'knows' that even a major revolt of the young need not disturb us. The consensus will prevail.

The consensus will soon *be* the young.

If we apply Revelation (1) to the apocalyptic Revelation (2) we shall see how we may move. Outcomes for society are latent in the systems running now. They can be calculated. If we seek alternatives to those outcomes, we can calculate the systemic design for producing them. The technique of prognostication is not required—provided we have built those models. It is a matter for science.

At the end of this month I am going to Washington to make a presentation to the House of Representatives' Committee on Science and Astronautics. I would like to read you a few sentences put together from this presentation.

'At present, the most obtrusive outcome of the system we have is gross instability— of institutional relationships and of the economy. This cannot last. The society we have known will either collapse, or it will be overthrown. In either case a new kind of society will emerge, with new modes of control; and the risk is that it will be a society which no one actually chose, and which we probably will not like.

'The risk which faces us today is the probability that society will yet refuse to study the systemic generators of human doom, and will disregard the capability which already exists competent to bring these many but interrelated forms of crisis under governance.

'The systems we have already started, which we nourish and foster, are grinding society to powder. It might sound macabre to suggest that computers will finish the job of turning this planet into a paradise after human life has been extinguished.

'But that vision is little more macabre than the situation we already have, when we sit in the comfort of affluent homes and cause satellites to transmit to us live pictures of children starving to death and human beings being blown to pieces.'

The solutions I shall offer in Washington are those I offer in my own country from this platform tonight. We must get on with *research* into these *operations*—before it is too late. And if every member of the Operational Research Society were so engaged, that effort would not yet be out of scale.

The action required entails big thinking—on the part of government, of managers and of scientists alike. Big thinking has unhappily become a solecism in Britain. That is why our big thinkers are so often away from home. They come and go where they are wanted.

But they are needed here.

I have often heard it said by the most elevated people in this land that the capacity to do this kind of work does not exist. That is not true. Insofar as the capacity may be inaccessible at the minute, I have the temerity to say to these elevated personages :

You drove it away : you bring it back.

There are in fact two standard answers to the whole of my address to you tonight which will predictably be churned out by the Mediocrity Machines of various institutions.

The first I have referred to already. It says that while (of course) the argument and the proposal are absolutely right they come *too soon*. The solution will work one day. Just now the market is not ready for it.

You're telling me the market is not ready for it. That is just what I am complaining about. If we want revelations tonight, that is exactly why our country is steadily, systematically, failing to make the international grade.

The second answer I shall get—and predictably before I leave this room—is that I have oversold operational research. Insofar as you my friends follow the lead I am trying to give, you too will have to live with that accusation. You will be told that overselling is a wicked disservice to the cause.

Never mind.

Overselling the science which offers one hope in a doom-laden situation is a venial sin. It is better than selling science short in a desperate attempt to look dignified and mature. It is very much better than selling Britain short.

The sheer immodesty of the claim to be always modest nauseates me. While I am in this chair I shall do what I think I ought to do, regardless of those very British murmurs of wellbred complaint.

I hope that you will do the same.

If it gets uncomfortable, ask yourselves this.

Who are these people, these managers and ministers, who dare to say that we have oversold OR? How would they know?

They haven't even tried it.

Despite occasional lapses into the jargon of Operational Research
these arguments are couched in terms
that will be accepted or rejected
in their own language.

Most of the explanation I wish to offer
exists at the political (small *p*) level
and belongs to the narrative.

The only thing I need this metalanguage to discuss
is the emergence of the term—
which will be encountered frequently later—
METASYSTEM.

Its meaning is really quite simple
providing that the original term
Metalanguage
was understood.

If a system speaks a language
appropriate to that system
the deficiencies of which
(its undecidable propositions)
can be discussed only in a metalanguage—

then the system that speaks the metalanguage

                    is a metasystem.

There is no more to it than that.

The remark sounds apologetic—
thrown away
ingenuous . . . . .

perhaps it is therefore disingenuous?

Not at all. And this is the big problem.
People seem to think that a metasystem
being 'over and beyond' the system to which it relates
has some special kind of authority—
that it secretly manipulates the system
and is sinister.

The power of a metasystem lies only
in its *logical* capacity to explain.

If this can perhaps be remembered
permanently impressed on the associative cortex

COLOUR CODE : GOLD
Metalanguage

there is every possibility of avoiding
gross but unfortunately routine misunderstandings
as the Arguments of Change are developed.

Metasystems talk metalanguages :
the organizational role you give them is up to you.

The presidential address tacitly expounds
the need for metasystems speaking metalanguages
                because of the reaction
                it is bound to provoke.

Again I am talking at the level of logical necessity
and not in narrative about psychological reactions.

My criticisms were metalinguistic
because in the language of the system being criticised
they are undecidable propositions.

It is important to understand this.

We earlier considered
the structure of a language
expressing the proposition :

                The barber shaves everyone
                who does not shave himself.

We saw that the proposition :

                Who shaves the barber?

is undecidable.
It cannot be said in the language.

Now consider that
acceptable men alone are appointed
to run institutions
(to appoint unacceptable men would be absurd)

but that whoever runs an institution
which becomes recognized as incompetently run
ceases to be acceptable
(naturally).

It then follows that

                Acceptable men run everything
                that is not incompetently run.

COLOUR CODE : GOLD
Metalanguage

The structure of this language guarantees
that the proposition

       I accuse Acceptable Man of incompetence

is undecidable.
It cannot be said in the language.

Then anyone who is unwilling to restructure the language
cannot make sense of the criticism.
It is meaningless to him
and becomes merely
some sort of jibe.

The reaction I repeat is predictable
for reasons given in logic
and not simply from psychological revulsion.

Having talked about the Mediocrity Machine
I came next to criticize
the adequacy of the human brain
to solve certain well-formulated problems.

But by the same token :

One can imagine
that in the exercise of his human prerogatives
a man might be led proudly to contend :

       I can think about anything.

If it were then pointed out
that since the brain is finite
there might just be some things
outside his comprehension altogether,
he might well with humility
but testily say :

       I don't think about anything
       that is beyond my comprehension.

That sounds sensible enough :
no-one would be expected to say
that he could not think what he was thinking.
But the trouble goes deeper than that.

Once again
the barber has been decreated.

          COLOUR CODE : GOLD
            Metalanguage

The barber, remember, is the intersect
of the two classes formally held apart
by the linguistic structure.

And in this case

> I am thinking about something
> I cannot comprehend

is an undecidable proposition.
It cannot be said in the language.

But it happens to be
the most important thing
a man must know.

Finally in this mode of explanation :

in arguing that

> Theory is the only reality
> countenanced by our culture

I set forth a proposition
meant obstreperously to label itself
as undecidable

so that people might be compelled
to restructure their language
to accommodate it.

There is no easy way out :

● It does not sound like a jibe

—as does the passage about Mediocrity

● It does not assault human prerogatives

—as does the passage about the brain

● It evidently ought to mean something

—and of course it does.

But it is undecidable
and calls for a linguistic reconstruction.

COLOUR CODE : GOLD
Metalanguage

Well, as a matter of narrative
hearers and readers of the presidential address
either made their linguistic reconstructions
or they did not.

There were plenty of arguments
but they were not about the points at issue.
Those who reconstructed forbore from complaint
about what had been said in the ostensible language
and came along with
what was metalinguistically said.

Those who argued with me in the language
could not hear the undecidable propositions.
But interestingly enough
no-one even mentioned the set of examples
adduced to demonstrate the thesis that
we manage a theoretical construct of reality
and not reality itself.

One distinguished civil servant
saw right through the whole thing
and talked to me about it in the metalanguage from the start.
He said he would send the address to a colleague
an opponent of mine
in the expectation that he would now understand the case.
(Whether he would then agree with it or not
would be another question.)

The outcome of this exercise
was a single comment :

       Most intemperate.

I saw what he meant
and thought it a pity
that there is no convention agreed
whereby one can work in a language and a metalanguage
marking the points at which
one slips back and forth.
The trick can be done in ordinary parlance
only by wearisome circumlocutions.

It was indeed from this incident
that I grew the idea
for the systemic structure of this book.

However—
in England to be intemperate is to be ill-mannered.

COLOUR CODE : YELLOW
Narrative

The major attack on the presidential address
was perfectly well-mannered
not to me exactly, which meant I could produce an honest answer,
but to the established order of things—
against which I had been speaking.

Dr. Lawrence is a senior and distinguished OR scientist
and the following exchange of open letters
appeared in the *Operational Research Quarterly*.

AN OPEN LETTER TO THE PRESIDENT

My dear Stafford,

I AM GRATEFUL to the Editor of the *ORQ* for giving me the opportunity to study your address as President of our Society. I was present when you delivered it and as you did so I felt a growing consternation at what, at the time, seemed to be a wild attack on the incompetence of British management in general, and their failure to make proper use of operational research in particular. I was concerned because I felt that as a generalization your criticisms had insufficient foundation and I was concerned that, powerful as operational research can be, the Knight in Shining Armour role that you portrayed was not the right one.

However, my consternation was somewhat ill-founded. You direct much of your criticism at the processes of Government. I can criticize Government with the best, but I have never tried to practise operational research in Government and have to accept, if you say so, that it is impossible. But I have two reservations; first, colleagues who do operational research in Government seem to me to be impressive and effective. Secondly, your centre-piece suggestion of an operations room on wartime lines is interesting and useful but liable to justify the reaction "is that all" Nor do I recollect our evidence to the Fulton Commission being very exciting.

But nevertheless before you focused on Government you made some pretty serious criticisms. You talk of a Mediocrity Machine that commits various ill-defined sins, the worst of which is apparently to dismiss somebody who looks more than "a week or so" ahead as a visionary. I hadn't noticed. I know of many studies concerned with time horizons for strategic decisions of at least 10-years ahead—including my own involvement in such work.

You criticize the human's ability to cope with several variables. Have you never been impressed by man's skill in arriving at near optimal solutions on the basis of part logic, part intuition? I have a report in front of me which summarizes some extensive work carried out very competently, including some elegant modelling. The conclusions begin, "Considering that there has not really been a national plan for [. . .], our present [policy] is incredibly good". I have frequently heard of similar experiences and, indeed, examples of results being *radically* different from the result of traditional processes are not too common. So there are limits to man's ability! Sure, we can improve on him! Yes, I agree. But is all this talk about 3·2 bits really very meaningful?. .

You criticize man's ability to cope with uncertainty. Again, of course, there is some truth and we have techniques to make improvements, particularly when any sort of queue situation is involved. But, as you say, you customarily seek to demonstrate the

COLOUR CODE : YELLOW
Narrative

point with this birthday business. I first heard you do so 13 years ago and remember thinking that a manager who had to make significant decisions based on birthday coincidences would pretty soon get into the right zone. It is a good party game (at which I have made a quick dollar or two—I thank you), but is it really any more?

And then you attack Management Science and specifically TIMS. You can justifiably criticize their competition if you like, just as you could some of the ORS actions in the past. But have you not noticed that these despicable TIMS people in the U.K. are almost exclusively also members of this angelic operational research set? So where are you?

Now your case would be proven and I would look foolish if where operational research people really have the reins they were clearly head and shoulders above other organizations. Let us look briefly at the processes of the Operational Research Society itself which are wholly in our hands. I submit to you that observations of the objectives we have set (or haven't), of the way we have reached decisions and of the way that we have administered them, should at least leave us with some humility. I can remember a scene at a general meeting of ours that would have had almost any manager of my acquaintance rolling in the aisles. This is not to denigrate our activity—we are a fine Society which shows a propensity to learn—but go easy!

I am not trying to undermine confidence in operational research, on the contrary. I have also spent the whole of my working life in it or associated with it. What I am really saying to you is that when all is said and done, operational research makes major contributions when it settles down in a committed confident partnership with competent managers (who do exist!). They will jointly come to terms with the difficulties of effecting change in complex organizations, the difficulties usually arising out of inadequate understanding of basic characteristics of human behaviour. The partner who makes the biggest contribution will be difficult to identify and there will in any case be no interest in apportioning credit. Not so glamorous perhaps—but how satisfying.

JOHN LAWRENCE

AN OPEN REPLY FROM THE PRESIDENT

My dear John,

As AN apologist for the managerial *status quo* you do a smooth job in a long-standing tradition. You appeal to calm and good sense; you make allegations that are likely to stick after you neatly withdraw them; you employ what is essentially an *argumentum ad hominem*; you satirize my attempts to illuminate issues; and you wholly ignore the core of my case and all of the evidence I adduced in its support.

My case is that the world is seriously threatened at every level, and its management is in disarray. Famous firms and whole industries are in turmoil, and require injections of public money. We have had (it used to be unthinkable) strikes by doctors and teachers who contend that the health and education systems are near collapse, as the taxation system seems also to be. Somehow it has become acceptable that the way to handle a crowd of kids playing hell on the campus is to turn out in gas masks and shoot them. We have alienation, pollution, violence—every kind of environmental and society threat.... Then I argue that our traditional conception of management has broken down.

As you say: "examples of results (from operational research) being *radically* different from the result of traditional processes are not too common". But the discrepancies are there, and I find that important. We have lived, you and I, through one revolution at the

COLOUR CODE : YELLOW
Narrative

conceptual level: it happened in physical science, and led to a new era of atomic fission and fusion, space travel and so forth. The *evidence* to support a change of the whole conception was trifling, you will recall. Einsteinian calculations about the perihelion of Mercury were not *radically* different from the results obtained for a Newtonian universe.

Eddington accounted for "the gradual ascent of ideas which must supplant" those "older conceptions of physics that had become untenable" in his preface to *The Mathematical Theory of Relativity*. The older conceptions of management are, as we look around our threatened society, already untenable today—and they must be supplanted fast. Eddington went on (this was 1922): "The present widespread interest in the theory arose from the verification of certain minute deviations from Newtonian laws. To those who are still reluctant to leave the old faith, these deviations will remain the chief centre of interest; but for those who have caught the spirit of the new ideas the observational predictions form only a minor part. ..."

How does that cap fit, John? As far as I am concerned, I want operational research to join with management in the collaborative exercise of disclosing new conceptions of how to manage (you do not of course mention Marlow Seventy). Before that can happen, we all have to face up to the fact that we are by now managing a theoretical construct of the world (as I put it in my Address) and not the real world, which is almost out of control.

I am not attacking good managers, who are as worried about these things as I am. I am attacking those, whether managers or operational research men, who face the evidence of chaos in their own environment with monumental complacency and a set of concepts which are demonstrably not useful any longer. In this cause I am prepared to run risks, which are after all only about respectability, and as President I have invited the Society to run risks too.

Here is an allegory for you. When the traffic on the roads finally goes mad, disobeying all the regulations that no longer contain it, I shall be risking my neck in there trying to measure things, trying to make a model of the new situation, devising a cybernetic control system that just might work if the authorities dare to listen. "Clobbered on the job" is what I want on my tombstone, not "Killed on a pedestrian crossing in final rectitude."

STAFFORD BEER

People next complained
that I had not replied to every point in detail.
That would not have been difficult.

For example :
having given the coincidence of birthdays to illustrate
that the brain is not good at making subjective estimates
of probability
(I think this is because we are animals
and are biologically cautious ·
in taking what are intellectual risks)
I am told—

> *'a manager who had to make significant decisions
> based on birthday coincidences would pretty soon
> get into the right zone.'*

COLOUR CODE : YELLOW
Narrative

Of course he would.
The business judgments that ruin firms
and the governmental judgments
that ruin countries
　　　　　and may yet blow the world apart
are precisely those unique estimations
that the management has no further opportunity to correct.

Now this is obvious—not worth saying back.
What is incomprehensible to me
is the well-mannered willingness
to debate side issues and to ignore—
or perhaps to be too polite to notice—
that the house is falling down.

A fantastic example occurred
during the year of this project
PLATFORM FOR CHANGE
in the case of Rolls-Royce
which spent that year falling down
finally collapsing altogether
early in 1971.

Two colleagues of mine at the Manchester Business School
Professor Geoffrey P.E. Clarkson and Dr Bryan J. Elliott
teach business finance.
They needed an example of a company
heading for failure.
For nine months they openly used the balance sheets
of Rolls-Royce
to illustrate their theme.
People were incredulous.

The story should be a familiar one by now :

　　　　　If you are talking a language
　　　　　in which the term *Rolls-Royce*
　　　　　is synonymous with the term
　　　　　perfection

the proposition

　　　　　Rolls-Royce will go bust

cannot be said.

Now in parenthesis
because it is a small matter

COLOUR CODE : YELLOW
Narrative

but nonetheless something that could actually be tackled
I briefly mention
the reorganization of the Operational Research Society.

The presidential address was accepted by Council
as a signal heralding change.
Not that everyone agreed with it—
but they did accept the message in the metalanguage
which was what the address was for.
At the dinner after the speech
we arranged a twenty-four hour meeting at Marlow
to work out our plans.

All this was done
and the publication of the paper *Marlow Seventy*
(referred to in the open letter to Dr Lawrence)
said what we would do, and have since largely done.

These are domestic issues
but there is a main-line point to be made.

A learned society is just a learned society.
What is to count as a fundamental change?
A learned society does not diversify
                go into retailing
                start building bridges.

Marlow Seventy included some definite proposals, true.
But what it really did was
restructure the language
from the metasystemic vantage point.

We now know how to predict the reaction.
Those who have entered into the metalinguistic debate
perceive the agreement to alter the language
and start using it.
This enables them to affirm or deny
the propositions put to them in that new language.

Those who will not enter the metasystem
continue to use the old language
and hear the proposals expressed in its terms.
It turns out that for this group
the proposals are all old hat—

they say nothing new
                they have no bearing on our problems
                they have all been considered before
                        and turned down.

COLOUR CODE : YELLOW
Narrative

End of parenthesis
but not of the point.

I gave seven examples
of inoperable institutions

> Euston station
> prices and incomes policy
> motor cars
> taxation
> jumbo jets
> the health service
> the egalitarian society

but for most people
they do not count.

After all, these things exist.
And they are talked about in languages
that make criticism undecidable
and proposals for improvement
wrongly heard.

To look just momentarily at the Euston example
several railway enthusiasts were really upset
by my remark.
I explained for example

> ● the procedure for discovering that the taxi
> queue is too long, and you go by train instead :
>
> *pick up several heavy cases*
> *carry them eighty yards including eighteen steps down*
> *and back eighty yards including eighteen steps up.*

They found this a trivial complaint.
Could it be that the language
appropriate for talk about railway stations
includes the expression

> people are inconvenienced at railway stations?

And if so
what argument for their total redesign would count?

The mere *number* of absurdities experienced at Euston
(and I could write many pages about this
or I would not have used the example)

COLOUR CODE : YELLOW
Narrative

will not make the argument one whit more persuasive—
and one feels that it should.

As in all seven examples
if the whole thing is absurd
it really is going to be

        intemperate
        if not wholly irresponsible

to say so.

Why not be temperate
and responsible
and content to observe

        if you want to watch the indicator board
        you cannot have a drink?

Then it could be explained

        it is for the best of reasons
        we could not avoid it
        there is $\begin{Bmatrix} \text{something} \\ \text{nothing} \end{Bmatrix}$ we can do
        all right : we boobed
                no-one is perfect
                not even you

Such things can be handled without distress—
seats were finally put into the concourse, after all.

I am trying to create in you
a frame of mind
in which you will confidently step
into the metasystems that subtend
all seven examples
and freely enquire of yourself
using a decidable metalanguage
whether society is not fooling itself
in underwriting these systems
in their familiar forms.

Try the motor car example, perhaps.
The thing is
        among many other things
dangerous to the driver
        among many other things.

COLOUR CODE : YELLOW
Narrative

So we follow our noses.
Our noses are going to be smashed up
on the fascia board.
So we will have an air cushion
that inflates when we crash
to protect us.
Now we can drive much faster
and with less regard for others:
            we shall be all right.
Don't you think
if we really cared about safety
we could consider replacing the inflatable bag
with a row
of sharp spikes?
            This is not
            a serious proposal
            you understand.

As for the project
PLATFORM FOR CHANGE
I had to use those platforms
and those languages
available.

The next Argument of Change
concerns another of those seven examples.
This time the audience
for a talk about operational research
knows nothing about it—
which gives us the opportunity now
to think over how it actually works
in a definite context.

The speech is directed to
a large group of influential people in

        the health service.

COLOUR CODE : YELLOW
Narrative

AN ARGUMENT OF CHANGE

**HEALTH
AND
QUIET
BREATHING**

The Sixteenth Centre Lunch Talk*, given at the Hospital Centre, London, on the 25th November, 1970.

*By permission of
The Hospital Centre, London, *and* Health and Social Service Journal

To talk within this compass about the management of a business which is now in the top ten largest financial operations in the whole world, a business which employs 3½% of the national labour force, is daunting. Certainly I have no pet or pat solutions to the problems that beset the National Health Service. What I do have is a method of approach to them called operational research, and I can perhaps suggest a few clues that point to its effective use.

What Operational Research Is and Isn't

First of all, I want to clear up some misconceptions about the meaning of the term 'operational research'. OR exists to solve *management* problems by the knowledge and methods of *science*.

Let us be clear that problems of management are always many-faceted. They are not financial problems, medical problems, administrative problems or personnel problems, as they are dressed up to look. They are just problems—with financial constraints, medical content, administrative knottiness. . . . . and they are all about people. A problem should be studied in the context of the system generating it. By the same token, scientific knowledge and method does not come in parcels labelled physics or chemistry, biology or anthropology, mathematics or economics. Those words are written over compartments in the left-luggage office called education. Science is a codified understanding of how things are and how things work; insight made rigorous; the general educed from particulars.

It follows that an OR team applying science to management has to be interdisciplinary. It may surprise you to know that I have employed a doctor of medicine in an industrial OR team, just as I have employed people with doctorates in ecology, physiology or electronics. But the physician was not there to handle 'medical aspects' of the work. Like the others, he was simply a collaborator in problem-solving—armed with a unique scientific insight and experience. If problems are just problems, and naughtily refuse to confine themselves within the boxes which managers set up to contain them, then one never knows what kind of scientific insight or skill may be needed next. OR has made a profession of coping with that situation.

Like all other scientists, OR men make pretty free use of mathematical techniques—and because of that many people have got hold of the crazy notion that OR is about applying them. I will give you an exact analogy. That is just like pointing to a tray-load of surgical instruments, and defining a doctor as 'someone who uses those'. Doctors should readily take the point: they are problem-solvers too.

How does it work, this OR, if it is not a matter of applying techniques like poultices to sore places? It works by constructing models—and again we ought not to confuse the *model* with any mathematics in which that model may be (or often is not) expressed. An OR model essentially depicts a dynamic system; and it is used to explore the workings of that system under different conditions. After all, scientific method has to do with experiment, whereas the very first thing you discover in addressing a problem of top policy in a large enterprise is that no-one dares to experiment with the system as a whole, and rightly so. Then the model stands as surrogate for the system, and you dare to experiment with a model.

OR models have taken the form of physical artefacts (such as miniature harbours containing actual water), of logically demonstrated isomorphisms (such as structural identities discovered between certain mechanisms of adaptation in the brain and the firm), of games (such as formally compare the strategies of poker with those of war), of machines of chance (which evaluate probabilities), and so on. Today, there is a powerful tendency to create OR models in forms which can be mounted inside a computer—because this is a relatively quick, easy and cheap instrument for running all types of system. Inside the computer we may simulate the behaviour of the system we have modelled.

We do so first under existing conditions, and this process ought to result in outputs that can be recognized as normal. That stage helps validate the model. Next we may subject the existing system, through the model, to all manner of possible perturbations that might in future occur. This stage indicates the sensitivity of the system's structure to varying degrees of stress, and the vulnerability of the management strategies currently used to a range of possible futures. Thirdly, we may change both the structure of the system and its management strategies (still within the model) in accordance with any theoretical conclusions we may have reached about how these things might be done better—and see what happens.

So OR is an interdisciplinary and an experimental activity, dealing in the behaviour of large and complicated systems. You shall see the kinds of model I should like the Health Service to create later on. They are systemic, and they deal in measures of information. They are not embodiments of mathematical tricks for cutting costs.

What a Health Service Isn't and Is

I can draw these kinds of distinction for operational research with some confidence, but my next task is trickier. I want to draw similar distinctions in respect of a health service. My understanding may be defective, because I am not professionally involved at all in your work. But at least that makes me objective and I would like briefly to tell you what I see.

First of all, there are three monolithic blocks: the hospitals, general practices, and local health authorities. Then we have an organization frozen out of the past; we have institutionalized a set of historical accidents. The result is a structure where the lowest organizational crossover point is the Minister himself. There is an exception, though: a healthy-looking low-level link between general practices and local authorities called a Health Centre. Yes, but the policy to forge that link has existed for exactly fifty years—and we still have only a hundred or so centres. Moreover, the original concept seems to have changed rather subtly as the creation of health centres finally gains momentum. How many have dentists? How many have dispensing chemists? How many have as many as twelve doctors as recommended by the Royal Commission? Above all, how many have or will have hospital out-patient clinics? You may recognize that I am drawing on the study by Curwen and Brookes (*Lancet* No 7627), from whose findings it does not seem that this approach to integration is really making much headway. There appear to be no arrangements for the purposeful study of how the whole thing works, and in the course of fifty years the vision itself has leaked away at the seams.

At least the organizational oddity has not gone unremarked. The next thing the objective observer notes is a tremendous spate of commissions, committees, inquiries, white papers, green papers and even Bills, which appear to be converging on an integral answer. Perhaps this was where the scientific attack on management problems called operational research was going on? No, as a matter of fact; because it turns out that these things must be decided in terms of other considerations altogether.

We are going to cross the boundaries of the three monoliths by having area boards—though whether there should be fifty or ninety seems to hinge on a political wrangle. Never mind: this will all tie in with the reform of local government—and that will at least unify general practice with the service of local authorities. Not so: doctors do not like this, and the observer solemnly notes down what the Times tells him is the reason: 'the bitter doctrinal hostility of the doctors'.

The neutral observer, retiring hurt, next tries to find out what is happening with the hospitals. I didn't hear the word 'hostile' in this context; I did hear the phrases 'fanatical conservatism', 'the arrogance of consultants', 'the inflexibility of matrons', 'nineteenth century attitudes'.....But I am not going on with this. As a matter of fact, I gave up when my enquiries about management decisions in the creation of a particular new hospital elicited the information that nurses could not have bidets because they were too junior, while consultants of rank (who happened to be all male) could and did.

The puzzle about all this to me is not that stupidities occur—they do in every field. And we should surely all agree that the actual provision of our health service is a matter for some satisfaction. (You should hear me boasting about it in the United States—where I suspect they have hit on a brilliant system of prophylaxis: you frighten folk into good health by the cost of being ill.) The puzzle I put to you is that in a year's quite intensive reading about organization, statistics, financing, costs, staffing and so forth, your objective observer has not once come across any reference to what the health service is about— namely people who are well or ill.

Here is the distinction, then, drawn like this. On the one hand is the ostensible reality: an introverted organization, preoccupied with its own antecedents, its internal power struggles, its levels of status, its costs and its wages, which solves its management problems in equations of political factors and psychological stress. On the other hand is the notion of a health service, to which surely many people in fact dedicate their lives, conceived as a national system for promoting healthiness.

An OR Approach to Any Large Enterprise

How should we apply the corrected version of OR to the corrected version of the health service? You can use OR at any level of management problem you like. In health, I have seen it operating in the hospital ward to rearrange beds (and even to reduce the bill for laundry), and in the consulting room to organize the appointments system. But if you really want to solve major problems, it is no use tinkering about at this level. For one thing, OR is a scarce resource. For another, the piecemeal approach takes far too long. For example: you might say we have known for a good many years how to organize an antenatal clinic. But this very year a girl on my staff dreaded the average wait of three-and-a-half hours, and dreaded in particular the last hour when the queue was always kept standing. Someone should make it clear that you spell 'antenatal' with an 'e' not an 'i'.

Secondly, even if the OR effort were all to go in at the national level, it would be quite useless in my view to ask for cost-effectiveness studies—or for the deployment of any other fashionable bag-of-tricks. The reason why not emerges from what I have already said: forgive me if it was something of a caricature. But I should take some convincing that the organization we have (and even the one we now aspire to) offers even a small part of the service which modern medicine, with all the facilities available to it, could offer society—at equivalent or perhaps less cost.

I put the point quite directly, and ask for an honest answer: if you were starting from scratch, knowing the current state of the art, having nearly a million staff of various qualifications and the best part of two thousand million pounds to spend, do you think you would come up with a system remotely resembling the one we have today?

It is always good OR advice to say: work out your objectives, evaluate your resources, take account of *real* constraints (but not mere prejudices), create and test a system for the purpose, then say what you want to do. Compare the answer with the answer you already have. If it is overwhelmingly better, as well it might be, then stop messing about with making the existing rotten arrangements more efficiently rotten, and get cracking on the plan which can take you from where you are to where you want to be. This country has (in my opinion) quite brilliantly devised such a path to institute a decimal coinage. If we can do it for a totally futile exercise like that, then why not for something worth doing?

Concepts of Health Management

What do we think about the objectives? Our medical services were surely founded at a time of desperate need for curative medicine. Later, when rampant and ravaging disease had been brought under some kind of control, we added a whole structure of preventive medicine. Today we are even further on, and my suggestion would be that we think of a health service as *regulative*. We look for a stable society, in which factors affecting healthiness are under control, and there is as great a calm as these much abused individual bodies of ours will between them allow to the body politic. Our objective is 'health and quiet breathing'—if I may wrench a phrase from its context in Keats's *Endymion*.

Society is a very large system, made up of individual people—and as I said before we ought to start with them. Now we can define the health status of every person—if only by calling him ill or not ill; but of course a good recording system would offer a much richer account than this. At the moment, such an account could exist, but does not—because of organizational fragmentation and archaic methods of recording and storing facts.

My own family doctor must have a very feeble notion of my health status. That is because (thank God) I have seen him rarely and with absurdly trivial complaints. He has no idea how many teeth I have, or what is the matter with my eyes. My blood pressure is known only to my insurance company, and they won't tell—not even me. The condition of my chest was once known to an X-ray unit, but I cannot discover when: it was mobile, and went away. I confidently challenge you to find out if I have ever been a hospital in-patient. You might succeed in digging up my attendance as an out-patient, but you may not be able to read the record—and in any case you will not find out why I suddenly stopped going, because no-one has ever asked me. If I were a maternity case, I would generate records with my doctor, with the health clinic. with the midwife, with the health visitor, and perhaps with a hospital. If my own quite recent (though admittedly vicarious) experience is at all typical, the high-cost records would be incomprehensible, partly because of illegibility and partly because of irreconcilable data.

Suppose one said: let us consolidate all this. What is the state of the art? Do we need costly and inefficient clerical processes spread all over the fragments of the total system? The answer is emphatically not. If a scientist can have ready access to a computer terminal— which believe me is far less expensive to operate than a full-blown office—then so can a physician. What is more, when you want to retrieve something from the record, you can *find* it and you can *read* it. I am fully aware of the problems of confidentiality posed by effective and consolidated electronic files. They can and will be solved. You must admit it would be ludicrous if the only valid means we had whereby to defend our personal freedom in the face of electronic competence were to have a system of personal records so inefficient that no-one could actually use it . . . . .

So I am beginning to paint a picture of a locality with a proper health centre, with proper records about the health status of every resident, and containing all medical facilities for out-patient treatment of every kind. This is not a new notion, but it is perfectly clear that it has not been properly studied as an operational possibility in terms of modern capabilities and facilities—because of the fragmentation of responsibilities as they now stand. The first recommendation is, then, that an OR study be done. Let us work towards the notion that a health locality is defined in terms of packages of information about its individual residents, constantly updated, and that enquiries into the nature of the total local system can be made by simulating its integral behaviour through a model mounted on a computer. We stand to learn so much about how that system works, and how environments affect the people in them. We shall know too not only the sorts of disease that patients have, but the sort of patient that has a disease—which Parry of Bath set out to learn two hundred years ago. And from there we might discover so much more than we now know about the possibility of 'trade-offs' between diseases: I mean such phenomena as the negative correlation between bronchitis and lung cancer.

Next, if a patient does arrive at a hospital (where the majority of our health money is spent) he will obviously arrive enveloped in an infinitely better aura of information than he does today. This package of information has got to undergo a set of transformations: that makes a perfectly good definition of the reason the patient has come. Some of the variables quantifying the parameters of healthiness are out of their limits. They must be brought back to normal. Every stage of the patient's handling and treatment can be regarded as applying a transformation to his data-set, and the result will be a new data-set—recognizably better or worse than before, or indistinguishable from before, by recognized medical criteria. And before you conclude that OR scientists can take no account of humanity, and the uncertainties which surround it for both patient and doctor, let me add that probabilities can be built into such a scheme—also that 'don't know' and 'something is missing' both count as valid data in an information-theoretic model.

In all of this lies a beginning for a reformation of the way that hospitals are run—a reformation based on the notion that what happens in a hospital is all about information and its transformations. If you could study the hospital wearing spectacles which allowed you to see the movement of information and nothing else, you would understand both the medicine and the administration—and just how the two fail to interact. You would understand the progress of the illness, and of its therapy. You would trace the loops of information that culminated in a very ill patient crawling out of bed to a public telephone— to ring up the hospital and ask how he was. You would trace the loops whereby relatives make enquiries, and you would mark the information filters which substitute 'as well as can be expected' for actual information. You would trace the information network by which nurses and sisters know what to do for their patients.

This last work has already been done on a large scale but, alas, never properly followed up. I pay tribute here to the studies made many years ago by Professor R.W. Revans—which I regard as far and away the most masterly exercise of operational research ever undertaken in the field of health. The cost of a hospital is clearly correlated with the length of in-patient stay; the length of in-patient stay varies very widely between hospitals for the same types of case, *and is directly correlated with the rate of staff turnover at all levels*. That was the first great discovery. The second was the explanation. The linking factor turned out to be the availability of nursing information—which affected both the length of stay and nursing morale. When the information flow was bad, no-one knew what was happening. Patients remained in their beds until someone found out. Meanwhile, the nursing staff were made profoundly uneasy by a sense of inadequacy in the care they could offer, and their loss of morale spread throughout the hospital at every level.

So the second recommendation is that these old studies should be newly validated, and extended, and again in terms of modern facilities. The uses of electronics for patient monitoring, preliminary diagnosis, the computation of diets and therapies, are all known about—but they are not at all integrated within any 'total systems' concept of information flow. Yet if the contemporary concept of medicine is regulative, this is exactly what we require. The hospital is indeed a vast interactive control system for regulating both illness and its own effective performance. That system needs to be modelled, studied, experimented with through the model, and—finally—changed.

Models of the System

OR studies of the nature of a possible modern health centre and of a possible modern hospital, both conceived in terms of information flow rather than any other commodity (such as money), would unite readily—because they would both be undertaken with the patient as providing the unit data-set. It is *the same man* who is well, who is exposed to risk, who develops presymptoms and then symptoms, who is diagnosed, who is treated at the health centre, then at the hospital, and who finally returns to a pool of the relatively healthy. May I repeat that whatever happens to him may be represented as a group of transformations of his data-set. Then what happens to society itself is to be understood, planned for, legislated for, by enquiring into the interactions of these transformations. That is because society is made up of individuals, each having a health status and an environment—which includes other individuals.

From these considerations flows my third and last recommendation. If we wish a service which is regulative of societary health, then we must also build a scientific model of the way in which people flow around this entire system, interacting as they do, and absorbing resources—of skill, equipment, drugs and money—as they go. With a model of this sort, which may be used for computer simulations, plus cybernetic models of various ways in which viable systems come to be organized, it would be possible to answer the questions—and especially those questions of structure—to which the answers are conspicuously missing today. Nearly ten years ago we used a rudimentary model of this kind to study the marketing of pharmaceuticals; quite recently I have looked into the possibility of creating such a dynamic model of drug addition . . . . .

But these are fleabites. The big model of the entire health service could and should be built. Its data base today would have to be rough and ready—because we do not have the channels of information in the locality and in the hospital (which I have proposed) to tap. This paucity of data has always been used as an excuse for not getting on with the job, in the health service as elsewhere. The excuse is feeble: because we have to run the system on the information we have in any case, and to use scientific method to elicit greater understanding from inadequate information does not make things worse—but better.

Then let us suppose all these things have been done, however crudely. We come to the point. It is from OR studies of this kind that new plans could be formulated for a more effective system for promoting healthiness. Studies like these would show what the optimal organizational structure should be. They would in particular test an hypothesis, which I here and now set up. It is that doctors with their 'bitter doctrinal hostility' to local authority collaboration will force the creation of a system that they will then find overcentralized, and will denounce (in the event) as hopelessly bureaucratic. Whether that hypothesis prove right or wrong, it is from studies of this kind, and not from political wrangling, that civilized people should tease out the best way of organizing things—and in general of managing the world's tenth largest business—in the best interests of health, and quiet breathing.

Two issues emerged from this.

Scientists certainly believe in quantification :
to measure things is a part of their trade
sine qua non.
The question is :

> what should we measure
> and what measuring rod should we use?

I shall call whatever answers these questions

THE METRIC

and we shall find ourselves
deep in this problem of metrics
later on.

The case that I made to the health service
called for the use of a metric—
the flow of information.
We know how to do the measuring in these terms
and how to compute with the results.

But the whole problem of national health
is completely bogged down
in its cost
and the benefit arising therefrom.
It is, of course,
a political issue.

Therefore (I was informed)
the specialists concerned with the management
of the national health service
have no choice
but to undertake their work
using the metric
of money.

This fact, if fact it be
immediately writes off
my recommended approach.

> My advice remains
> and is quite general :
> always seek a metric
> that handles the stuff of the system.

COLOUR CODE : YELLOW
Narrative

Money matters very much
because it is the stuff
of the *procurement* system
in our society

but as far as the system under study is concerned
money is best regarded

as a constraint.

Thus I still contend
that the health service should be redesigned
in terms of
information about healthiness.
When the design is complete
we can see what it would cost.

Now in view of the arguments
about the wholesale inefficiency
of the existing organizational structure
it would be most surprising
if an *effective* organization
did not cost much less.

In any case
what is the harm
in proceeding on that assumption?
There is a prima facie case :
if it were falsified—
forget it.

May I say once again :
the fact that cost really matters
and becomes obsessive
does not confirm it
as an appropriate metric.

The second issue that emerged
is very much tied to the first.

In some quarters
and especially the alert and informed press
great disappointment was felt
in my speech.
The reason was
that I had not actually *done* any operational research
and could not therefore *demonstrate*
that I had a valid answer at all.

COLOUR CODE : YELLOW
Narrative

Well :
it just is not possible to do this
unless one has a commission.

Not that one simply waits . . . . .

Some long time ago
I was myself so situated
that this study could have been accomplished
quickly (a year) and cheaply
(compared with the investment involved).
And so I cultivated the confidence
of two men, either of whom
I judged might become
the responsible Minister.

Each of them said
that in that event
the work would be done.

Both men eventually became in turn
the responsible Minister,
and of course I approached each of them
in that capacity.

It turned out
that nothing could be done.
Every penny
(of £2,000,000,000)
was already mortgaged.

Not only did these two give this answer
(one of them was kind enough to say
that he kept one of my books
by his bed)
but the identical answer
has been forthcoming
from four other Ministers.

> Please never say
> that I do not understand
> my own teaching
> about the potency of a system
> to protect itself
> > whether from harm
> > or change.

COLOUR CODE : YELLOW
Narrative

98

Meanwhile
the Americans at least
were using this frame of thinking
in New York.
Their results cheered me up.

THESIS

THIRD STATEMENT

There are three things to do :

FIRST do some thinking

reconstruct the language,
and then operate metasystemically

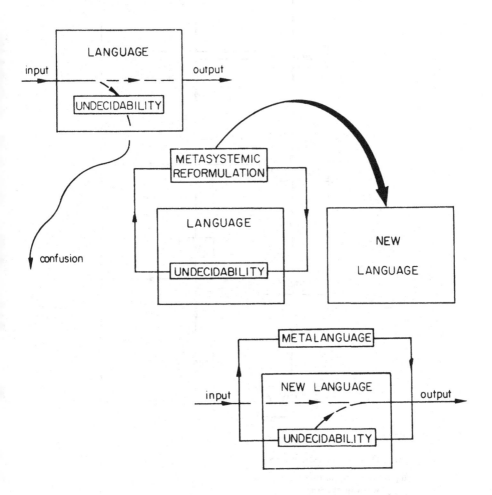

make provision this time
for continuous metasystemic monitoring.

COLOUR CODE : BLUE
          Thesis

100

SECOND do some operational research

reconstruct the accepted model of the world situation using the new language

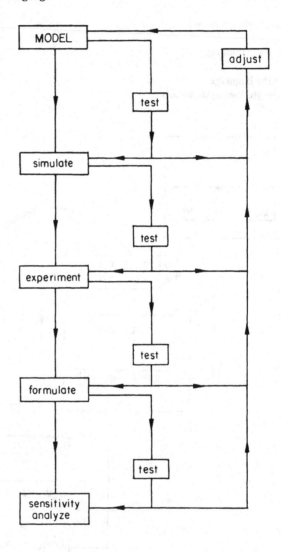

THIRD do some cybernetics

**deploy cybernetic theory
to redesign institutions
using the continued experience
of model manipulation.**

The third statement of thesis
ought now to be understandable
in its first and second recommendations.
(I realize that not much has been said about models.)

What we need now
is a straightforward briefing
about cybernetics.

The opportunity
to feed in this briefing
came during the count-down
to the project
PLATFORM FOR CHANGE.

While the project was formulating itself in my mind
I received an interesting invitation
from the united nations educational, scientific and
cultural organization—
UNESCO—
to do some work . . . . .

> There needed to be a statement
> about management
> considered in the light
> of the relevant science
> of cybernetics.

This was to be written
within a brief compass
and in a low key.

I include it now
as offering some sort of synopsis
of the cybernetic approach
to management affairs.
In particular
it defines most of the terms
used in this book.

These include
some we have already gone into
and some that will be gone into later.
The few repetitions
do not come amiss
in this quite general context.
Treat this contribution
in itself a serious Argument of Change

COLOUR CODE : YELLOW
Narrative

as tidying up the discussion to this point.

We might also take time
to be impressed
that UNESCO is alert
to such a thing as the relevance
of cybernetics to management.
Few governmental agencies indeed
have heard of the word—
after twenty-five years . . . . .

COLOUR CODE : YELLOW
Narrative

AN ARGUMENT OF CHANGE

MANAGEMENT
IN
CYBERNETIC
TERMS

Dissertation* prepared for UNESCO, the United Nations Educational, Social and Cultural Organization, in late 1969, and published in *Scientific Thought* in English and French by UNESCO/Mouton. The Hague, 1972.

*By permission of
UNESCO, Paris.

The History and Nature of Cybernetics

The science of cybernetics has been developed under that name for a quarter of a century. It was defined with unique clarity and authority by the late Norbert Wiener to mean 'the science of control and communication in the animal and the machine'.

This statement is pregnant with meaning: a meaning latent rather than hidden. People have been slow to understand it, although it has been there all the time. The point is this. There are general laws which govern control processes, whatever the system under govern-ance. These laws apply to computers and servomechanisms, to the human nervous system, to populations of animals, to the economy, and to every other large, complex probablistic system—such as the business firm. We include the adjective 'probablistic' in this list of words qualifying 'system', since even well-specified systems that are truly complex can in practice be described only in this way.

A full historical review of the subject would systematically reveal how, quite gradually, scientists expert in many branches of knowledge came to understand the invariant nature, at an abstract level, of the processes which control large systems. With hindsight, we can be more brief. It turns out that we recognize systems to be such for four main reasons :

—because they cohere within some frame of experience;

—because they survive through time within some appropriate definition of continued identify;

—because, to achieve these ends, they prescribe unto themselves certain rules of equilibrial activity which are tolerable to their continued existence;

—and because they assimilate their unfolding experience into self-regulating processes of learning, adaptation and evolution.

If these are the common characteristics of large viable systems, then cybernetics sets itself to determine how the relevant mechanisms work. Having understood something about mechanism, science may then be relied upon to generalize its understanding—across the various types of system that it studies. This process leads to concepts of law, whereby science makes a further generalization: we expect that any *new* complex viable system that is going to survive will be found to utilize the generalized mechanisms of survival already elicited. But to make the concepts of mechanism and of law *effective* in designing or redesigning systems, we shall need concepts of behaviour, by which to understand the practical application of the models which embody our laws and our mechanisms.

All of this means that the scientific apparatus required to understand, design and regulate large viable systems is becoming available. It is this very apparatus, based on a corpus of knowledge, of which the management community stands most in need. For if cybernetics is the science of control, management is the profession of control. Every manager, whether he runs the family business or a small department in a firm, whether he runs the firm itself or a major department of government, whether he runs the country or an aspect of international affairs, faces an identical problem. He faces, that is, the need to maintain a viable system far more complicated than he personally can understand. And the beginning of wisdom for management at any level is the realization that viable systems are, in large measure, *self*-regulating and even *self*-organizing.

Cybernetics reveals the nature of these natural phenomena. It must do so, if it is to help at all. For although management must accept responsibility for everything that happens, it *cannot* assume direct autocratic control of everything that happens. The systems concerned are just too big. This is why cybernetics turned to the study of self-regulating systems (such as those found in the relationship between organisms and their environment) and to self-organizing systems (such as the brain) for its insights. There simply is no *manager* identifiable in an ecological or a neurological system. Yet both of them work. Management theory, say cyberneticians, has been led astray in studying the nature of the extant and accepted managerial process itself. To make studies of the manager was the obvious thing to do; and yet 'the manager' turns out to be the embodiment of something we might call 'management principle'—that set of characteristics discovered in any viable system which conduces to viability. In this sense, then, the people who call themselves 'managers' are really catalysts of a systemic metabolism which is already at work.

But of course this considers management as something which happens to be there in an on-going system, and something which is acknowledged by the system's components as having authority. The major problems arise when matters are *not* going well—or at least when it is obvious that 'something needs to be done'. Managers, the men themselves, are then expected to take some kind of action.

I think it is a major cybernetic conclusion to draw from these remarks that managers generally approach this problem in the wrong way. They usually try to intervene in the equilibrial processes of the self-regulating system—thereby, perhaps, making it fundamentally unstable. The sensible course for the manager is not to try to change the system's internal behaviour, which typically results in mammoth oscillation, *but to change its structure*—so that its natural systemic behaviour becomes different. All of this says that management is not so much part of the system managed as it is the system's own designer.

What are the aspects of the system with which management can sensibly interfere, which it can design—or redesign? They are the *mechanisms* of that system: the structures, and the rules governing the behaviour of structures, which are usually taken as given. They are the arrangements already accepted as institutional conventions. It is these that need investigation.

Concepts of Mechanism

One of the major mechanisms, perhaps the most important of all, which operates in the self-regulation of systems is the mechanism of *feedback*. This term has become very popular, and is often wrongly—because too loosely—used. Explicitly: feedback does *not* refer to a response provoked by a stimulus. (Managers commonly say: 'I have had some feedback about my suggestion on so and so'.) This usage perverts a critically important idea.

The idea is this. When a system is in full operation it produces an output. Depending on the view we take of this output, we shall feed back a signal to those elements of the system which govern the nature of the output—a signal which actually alters them. When the system at large—as it already exists—next operates on its inputs, it will procure a different output—one hopefully nearer to our desire. The main reason why this mechanism is so important is that it does not require us either to understand or to intervene in the major operations of the system. These are left alone, and treated as self-controlling. What we are doing is to take a logically (and not necessarily managerially) superior view. If we have a perfectly good system the outputs of which are always exactly half what we require, then we alter the inputs to that system (in the simplest case) by a factor of two. Then the perfectly good system, quite unaffected by this, produces the answers we want. It has not been denatured, or thrown into confusion, in the process.

The simplest form of feedback to understand is called error-actuated negative feedback, which is the one just mentioned. In this situation, we have an explicit statement of what the output is intended to be. 'A profit of ten million dollars', 'a fifteen percent return on capital', are examples of such a criterion in the firm. If the output of the system is different from this, a device is needed which measures the difference between the actual and the intended result. This 'error' is fed back to the start of the system, where it is enabled to change certain parameters of the system, so that the result—next time round—is nearer the target than before. So far, so good. But there are other aspects of feedback, of which the notion of amplification is the most important. Instead of a fixed output criterion, we may have simply a statement of preferred trend. 'Let us increase the profits' is an example. Then, if the system is tending to increase the profit, the *positive* feedback signal encourages the system's critical variables to enhance yet further the final effect. This is called a reward system (its negative is a punishment system), the objective of which is to cause the system to *learn* from its past experience.

These are unworked examples, but they illustrate the vital notion.

The whole point about any feedback mechanism is that, having set it up, the manager may go away. After all, he cannot attend to *everything* simultaneously. When he has set up a useful feedback mechanism, he should be able to forget about the subject; because what happens will henceforth regulate itself.

Now although we may think of a large organization, such as a firm, as having a single output (labelled profitability for example), and although we may imagine a large feedback loop which would adjust the inputs to the system so as to keep the output at a desired level, this is no more than a conceptualization of how management works. It is inconceivable that the complexities of a company's operations could actually be stuffed into a single mechanism of this kind. But we may start by this method to account for the way the business works. Then we ask questions about the way the system breaks up—into divisions of the company and divisions of the market, for instance, and model those. Thus we shall gradually be able to devise a more complicated model, redolent with feedback loops, which is of practical value. In doing all this we pass from the notion of a straightforward feedback mechanism to the notion of multiple loop systems. Outstanding in this area of study is the work of J W Forrester (Reference 1 and Reference 2).

There are three basic characteristics of viable systems which can profitably be studied by cybernetics in terms of multiple feedback loops. First, the significant outputs must be under control: we must know how to manipulate the system so as to produce a desired effect. Second, and this is vital, the system as a whole must be stable. Instability is the major symptom of a badly managed organization, and we detect this symptom in terms (for example) of wild stock fluctuations; of surges of work-in-progress; of recurring panic in the conduct of day-to-day business; and of stop-go policies in the area of development. But cybernetics has indeed intensively studied the mechanisms which govern equilibrial behaviour—and can incorporate them in its management models. Third, the system must be able to learn, adapt and evolve.

The major concept which emerges from such studies is that of homeostasis. This means the capacity of a system to hold its critical variables within physiological limits. Note that we do not say: within *prescribed* limits. The point is that there is no satisfactory way of specifying acceptable limits of variation, except through a study of the system's dynamic behaviour. This should lead to the discovery of that degree of variation for critical parameters which the organism as a whole can tolerate before it is denatured.

It turns out that we can design a simple system, and *prescribe* limits for it, because we understand it completely. We know how it works, and we know both the kind and the magnitude of the perturbations it must withstand. This design-process yields a stable system: think of regulating a central heating installation for example. When systems become unthinkably complex, however, we can be sure of none of these things; we do not really understand the process itself, nor the perturbations which affect it, nor the interaction of these two. Therefore we adopt the principle that we need not only self-regulation (the feedback mechanism), but a capacity to generate internal elements of control which can adjust to everything else that is going on.

The best known example of homeostasis, which illustrates this, is the control of body temperature. This is achieved by myriad interactions within the body, taking account of the total set of circumstances from moment to moment, and not by some kind of thermostat working to fixed temperature limits. That is why we say that homeostatic controllers use self-organizing principles to hold critical variables within *physiological* limits. And so we have identified a self-organizing characteristic (the mechanism of which is homeostasis). The work of W Ross Ashby (Reference 3) provides the management cybernetician with fundamental knowledge on this score: he knows now how to go to work.

We said earlier that a relatively simple multiple loop feedback system could be designed— in full knowledge—which could be *stable*. In designing very complicated systems (without full knowledge) to be self-organizing by homeostasis, we emerge with a new criterion: *ultrastability*. This criterion relates to the capacity of a system to withstand perturbations which have not been foreseen by the designer.

This capability at first sounds impossible to realize. That is because we take the wrong model: a model drawn by our training from energy-systems (with which we are familiar) rather than from information systems (with which we are not). All we are really doing is to construct control devices which recognize unknown threats to the system—through their preliminary effects on the smoothness of operations. Gyroscopes and engine governors, for instance, are examples of homeostatic controllers. They are intended to keep ships and aircraft, or engines, running in a regulated way—regardless of the reasons why the ship is off course, or the engine racing. They achieve this, not by analysing the causality of the situation and coming to terms with the root problem, but by detecting *within themselves* pathological symptoms which are directly used to take regulatory action. I have called this principle 'intrinsic control'.

Similarly in the firm, we require managerial control devices to damp down oscillations (such as those recorded above as symptoms of instability), regardless of their cause. This idea is very important in management, because it may often take too long to identify the cause of trouble and to correct it at source. The common belief that this is the only scientific way of proceeding is mistaken, and derives from a very old-fashioned view of science itself. Keep the engine governor in mind.

So far we have concentrated on cybernetic mechanisms intended to hold things steady, to keep outputs and critical variables under control, to make systems at large both stable and ultrastable. All these things are necessary to managers if they are not to live in a state of continuous crisis. But there is another side to the picture. The ultimately stable state is death. If we are not careful, we shall have devised a paradigm of the firm which is a recipe for peaceful demise. All viable systems, cybernetics points out, are geared not only to tolerate a degree of *tension*, but to make constructive use of it.

Muscle 'tone' makes a good example of this tension-by-antithesis in the human body. Without it we should just fall down. Therefore we look for mechanisms in management systems which provide antithetic internal stresses, maintaining tonality short of the crisis level. From these mechanisms spring others which alone can lead the firm forward. It is a cybernetic result that systems cannot learn unless they make errors; they cannot grow without mutation; they will not adapt unless they experiment; they never evolve unless learning, growing and adapting.

All this, and the cybernetic understanding of it, means that it is now possible to design into a management system a proper machinery for generating *innovation*. That is the raw material of evolutionary development, and of the company's growth.

Concepts of Law

When science has acquired an understanding of mechanisms which appear to be general to its area of study, it seeks out the common principles which must underlie their operation. For example, a tour of industry would reveal that (whereas many objects are moved about by a power source) in almost every factory there are examples where objects are deliberately and successfully moved in the absence of a power source. From the observation of these instances we should (if we were scientists from Mars, wholly unfamiliar with terrestrial mechanics) be able to infer the general principle of gravity feed. And from this we should in turn suspect the existence of the law of gravity itself. So it is with cybernetic mechanisms.

The 'stuff' of control is not any kind of object; it is something called *variety*. Variety is defined as the number of possible states of a system.

In what sense can this mathematical construct be called the very fabric of system? Consider the electric light on your desk. Its variety is two, because it is either on or off. The control of this situation is a simple matter, because we have a switch marked 'on' and 'off'. Consider a labour force of ten men, operating under a rule that anyone who did not immediately do what he was told would be shot. This system has a variety of ten, and is readily controlled by anyone with a gun and ten bullets. Now relax the constraint that disobedience means death. At once the variety of this ten-man team rises to something approaching infinity. These men may now do anything at all: obey orders, disobey orders, vary orders, ignore orders. Or they may go away and play cards.

In short, the cybernetician calls any ordinary situation, in which an enormous number of possible states might be realized, a *variety generator*. The management problem is precisely a problem in handling variety: if we examine any managerial action, we shall find that it is a *variety reducer*. In the limit, when any particular goal has been achieved (for example, the order has been accepted by the customer) there is no variety left. The system has only one state: it is success, and that is a terminal state.

Now the kinds of action open to managers appear to be many and varied. There are high-level policy decisions; there are low-level short-term instructions; there are decisions about organizing the firm; there are verdicts which choose between alternative course of action. It is interesting that so many different managerial activities, categorized as they normally are by function and by rank, discussed as they normally are in terms of different criteria applied by widely differing techniques, should share a common measure of success. This is precisely the measure of variety reduction. It will also quickly be noted that the higher-level decisions eliminate more potential variety than the lower-level decisions.

These observations indicate that it might be possible to design an organization, and with it a system of management control, based on the measure of variety. And so it proves to be. Now let us look for the natural law, exceedingly simple but exceedingly potent, which actually governs variety regulation. We have clues to its form already in the two-state electric light with its two-state switch, and in the ten-man team made obedient by ten bullets.

The principle is this: *only variety can absorb variety*.

Once this is said it appears very obvious. But there is no difficulty in thinking of innumerable everyday situations in which people behave as if it were not the case. As to management, the application is clear: the managerial system, taken as a whole, must be capable of generating as much control variety as the situation is capable of proliferating uncontrolled variety. When these conditions are not met, and often they are not met, untoward events occur which the management cannot bring back into line.

Examples of well-known attempts to control proliferating situations with variety-starved controllers are legion. For example, we find governments attempting to control a variety-rich economy by changes in bank rate; we find managing directors (who should know better) setting out simple administrative rules about the way the company should run— rules which are immediately and readily circumvented by people lower down, because they operate in a variety-rich environment. We find policemen attempting to regulate traffic at individual cross-roads, when their information does not extend around corners— never mind to the next policeman at another cross-roads. And so on. None of these managers can possibly be in control; they are attempting to disobey a natural law. I repeat: only variety can absorb variety. This is known as Ashby's Law of Requisite Variety. (See Reference 3 again.)

If a manager must needs deploy as much variety as the situation he seeks to bring under control, how is he to do it? The simplest method is by producing a precise match between the variety of control and of the controlled—as we saw in our preliminary examples. Most games are organized on this basis—we have the same number of players on each side, having the same resources. If we move to a more serious form of the 'game', such as a war, we can see how the same rule is applied. As civilian life becomes increasingly complex, which means that every individual has high variety (compare feudal times), it becomes increasingly necessary to match the total variety of half the citizens with a control variety consisting of the other half. Today we have just about reached the point where the policing of the state—in terms of taxation, welfare, education and so forth, as well as criminality—consumes half the total effort of society.

All this may seem to be necessary, if Ashby's Law is to be obeyed. But that is not the case. There is another way to deploy requisite variety, and that is to *generate* matching variety through a variety amplifier. If we say that all traffic will keep to one side of the road, we have set forth a low-variety rule. This is matched, in any individual case, by a low-variety acquiescence: 'I will do it'. But if everyone is truly acquiescent, then the control variety has been amplified by the number of individuals in the system. Should the population of drivers at which this rule is aimed *not* acquiesce, then (naturally enough) the low-variety rule will not work. We should need a high-variety rule such as a law enforcement officer driving in every car.

Thus all managements are faced with a triple choice: they may absorb proliferating variety by the amplification of control variety, or by one-to-one matching, or by reduction of uncontrolled variety. The first method has the demerit that a high-variety situation overthrows the control system completely—in the simple act of disobedience. The second method appears to have the demerit that it *ipso facto* uses up half one's total resources. The third method works very well, but it reduces opportunity and is inimical to major innovation.

But once again there is an alternative solution. Remember the game situation in which one team absorbs the variety of the other team. This control device does not consume managerial variety at all. It uses the rule of judo: one's opponent is defeated by his own strength, not yours. Most management situations can be defined in terms of two antithetic sets of activity. For example, the company and its market, each generating very high variety, can be modelled by a homeostat in which each set is deliberately organized as a variety sponge *vis-à-vis* the other set.

Then we are presented with a further problem. We may certainly conceive of two aspects of the situation for which, as managers, we are responsible, as absorbing each other's variety. And we may take organizational steps to ensure the accomplishment of this plan— whether we use variety generators, variety absorbers, or variety reducers. But recall what was said in the last section about the homeostat as a machine for running to a standstill. The homeostat is itself a controller of variety. But unless there is a controller of the homeostat, we shall not be able to intervene in the situation as managers at all.

Not that managers do not attempt this feat. A senior manager often has the notion that he may intervene in the homeostatic systems which operate under his aegis. He has the authority to do so, of course. But the minute he directly engages in a highly complex situation, on level terms as it were with those whose interactions are performing the balancing activity of the homeostat itself, the senior manager abandons his olympian role. His own personal variety is that of a human being, however elevated his status. No : the role of the senior manager is to remain above the homeostatic fray, and to consider what is happening in terms of his *higher level* understanding. Because he is outside the system, in fact, and because he partakes in another system which is no concern of his subordinates, his method of control is explicitly to alter the criteria according to which the lower level system is operating.

Let us go back to the illustration from games. Suppose that as a higher manager you have the responsibility to ensure that team A wins in a game which is already being played between team A and team B, where the scoring is already even. You *could* dress yourself in the appropriate regalia and charge onto the field of play. The players would recognize you. Your own side might defer to your tactics (but perhaps you are not a very good tactician?), while the other side would do their level best to put you out of action. This is not the way to behave at all. If you really had authority over this situation, the clever action would be to change the rules of the game so that your side must win it. You belong to a higher order system than the game system; your information is better; you command the facilities for variety generation. Then do not act as if none of this were true.

This illustration seeks to define the notion of *metasystem*. A metasystem is a system over-and-above the system itself. Its major characteristic is that it talks a metalanguage; and this is a richer, better informed, way of talking than is available to the system lower down. It should be noted that the raison d'être of the metasystem is given in logic; it is not necessarily anything to do with the hierarchy of status.

Concepts of Modelling

Having talked about mechanisms and the laws which underlie them, we may be able to see how cybernetics provides a basis for modelling a management system. Now a model is neither a literary device, as is a simile, nor a logical device, as is an analogy. A model is a formal account of a system which identifies how it actually works (Reference 4).

Interestingly enough, the rules of modelling turn out to duplicate the general laws of cybernetics which we have already been discussing. Consider: a model seeks to match the variety of the situation modelled—and in so far as it fails it is a less effective model. Thus the ideal model of anything is itself; while a model almost as good as this identity model is one which matches every element of the real system with an element in the model. Obviously such an arrangement provides requisite variety in the modelling process. Technically, such a model is called *isomorphic* with reality, because every element is matched. A paste copy of a piece of jewelry is an isomorphism.

If we cannot have an isomorphic model, and this is indeed unusual, we may have instead a model whereby many elements in the real system are represented by one element in the model. For example, if we make a model of Shakespeare's birthplace which is about six inches long, we may fairly readily produce an item which is identifiable as the building in Stratford-upon-Avon. But every brick in our model stands for many bricks in Stratford. It follows, then, that we are totally unable to produce every feature of the real building. This representation of the many by the one, technically called a many-one mapping, is not an isomorphism but a *homomorphism* of the original. We have lost variety. But the important point is that—if we are sufficiently clever—we will not have lost variety that matters.

Everything here depends on the purpose for which the model is constructed. Suppose we wish to make people think about Stratford. We build our six-inch model, and we produce a photograph of it. This photograph, at a casual glance, immediately says: 'Stratford-upon-Avon' to anyone who has seen Shakespeare's birthplace. So there may be no loss of informaticn at all. A homomorph helps to regenerate the variety of the isomorph, when it is correctly used. But if we wished to know how long it will be before the Stratford building falls down, nothing at all will be gained by studying degeneration in the model.

In a management system, we know (or ought to know) the features of the situation that matter. Suppose we offer to provide the manager with a system which correctly predicts whether the man who will be operating the lathe in the third shop on the left next Tuesday morning will be wearing brown boots. This would be a high variety model indeed; but one would certainly expect the manager to say that he was not interested in the least. So it is clear that we may eliminate variety in the process of modelling, provided that we do not eliminate information which the manager most wants included.

In order to achieve these ends, we should begin with the macrostructure of the system we are studying. This system has major outlines. There are manifestly several identifiable processes, markets, trades union . . . . . then our modelling process begins by specifying the major items and the connections between them. Already we have a model, which may be considered complete, although it has no detailed infrastructure. The model is homo-morphic, and thus of very low variety compared with the original. Nevertheless, the manager may well—even at this point—be able to recognize the situation which he must control.

It is easy to imagine that the form of this model, written on a piece of paper, consists of boxes connected by lines. Each box refers to a major activity, and is a very high variety box. Nonetheless: there it is, with a label on it. We know *what* it is, but nothing at all about what is inside it. Such boxes are called 'black boxes', for the very simple reason that they are not transparent. We cannot see what is going on inside. Never mind, for the moment. These boxes are connected by lines, which may be used to indicate all manner of things. Above all, however, they indicate the way in which the boxes are connected in terms of communication between them. Communication, here, may mean anything from a production flow line (by which one box certainly communicates with another) to a message (about the size of the stocks for example); or it may be a more subtle form of communication, having more potency, which carries feedback information.

What can we say about these black boxes at this moment in time? Very little. But it may well be that we have a measure of their variety. Therefore, if one box is supposed to handle the output of another, we already know that it will fail in this attempt unless its variety is as high as the second. That is an immediate inference, by the Law of Requisite Variety. So although the boxes are black, they have a distinct *persona* within the cybernetic system.

Let us then turn to the lines by which boxes are connected, which we have already said represent communication. Now we may treat the problem of communication as a variety problem also. The least effective means by which two boxes can be related in terms of communication is by noise which passes between them. 'Noise' is defined as a signal having no meaning. But we must note in passing that even noise identifies a channel—the path through which the noise has passed. When we manage to identify a pattern in the noise, we declare that something meaningful is being communicated. Whatever is passing through the channel might now be called data. Data is pattern become meaningful. But data of themselves have no influence upon anything—after all, they may well be ignored; they may be stored for further reference (which never happens); they may engulf the recipient, as anyone who has bought a newspaper or a book which he has never read well knows. Noise becomes data becomes information at a precisely identifiable point. Information is what changes us. We never change without an information input (why should we?). If we really have received information, we are *bound* to change—because our variety is thereby increased.

Just as we can infer a great deal about our situation, using a model in which all the boxes are black, so we can infer a great deal about our capacity to react by looking at the communication channels whereby the boxes are connected. Do they contain merely noise? Are there receptors at the other end which are capable of transforming noise to data? Do 'thinking' elements lie behind these input transducers which are capable of transforming data to information? All these are highly relevant questions. But there is more to say. Consider two black boxes, A and B, which are mutually in a state of homeostatic equilibrium. What can we say about the communication channels which connect them? Well, we know that each box must have roughly the same variety as the other. And this equation would be useless if the communication channels were not adequate to transmit that variety—in both directions.

By these means we are able to identify the structure of communication channels which will complete the necessary stabilizing loops, and be able to specify their measurable capacity. There is a complete mathematical theory of communication (Reference 5), due especially to Claude Shannon, which provides us with many formal theorems for the elucidation of communication problems. It sounds trivial to say that the channel capacity must be able to handle the variety of the black boxes. But this rule is often disobeyed in practise—with dire consequences. If we consider the managing director of a firm and one of its most humble employees, what could we possibly say about the communication between these two men? The answer is likely to be that they cannot (not do not, but cannot) communicate at all—because the channel capacity is simply not there. Shannon's theorems elucidate much of what the cybernetician needs to know in his modelling process. From his point of view, at least, one of the most important results of the mathematical theory of communication is Shannon's tenth theorem. This says, in effect, that it is *not enough* to provide channels with a capacity to transmit the variety of the black boxes. We need extra channel capacity to elucidate ambiguities in the message.

From all of this it follows that if one is modelling a management system even in the most crude and macrocosmic fashion, a great deal can already cybernetically be said about its structure, and even about the way it works and fails to work. Black boxes juxtaposed in homeostatic equilibrium must have requisite variety; channels connecting them must obey the laws of communication; and we shall already be looking for emergent metasystem. All of this can be said before we have even approached the modelling of detailed operations within the firm. Perhaps this will never be necessary: we may settle for a low-variety homomorphism, depending on the object of the exercise.

More important than the details is the structure. We shall soon find that we are building a hierarchy of systems, based on the principles already uncovered. For every system demands a metasystem; and therefore a second metasystem will be identified beyond that. There is no logical end to the chain, because at each level of language there are propositions which logicians call 'undecidable'—except in terms of a metalanguage.

Then when shall the process cease? How do we know when to stop modelling? The answer to this lies in the concept of the black box once again. For, when we have reached the limits of the system we are studying, we are compelled to say that it subsists within the framework of a higher order system—which we have no brief to penetrate. This does not mean to say that it can be ignored. What we must do is treat this extra-systemic system as an encompassing black box-and look for its effects upon the totality which lies under our jurisdiction that cannot be decided. Then we have to accept the resolving input of the superior black box as given, as insusceptible to analysis.

Now this statement is true for every system governed by a metasystem. In so far as we are designing a total management structure, we ourselves understand everything. But we must realize that each metasystem exists precisely because there is no logical sense in which the system to which it is 'meta' can cope without this unanalysable help. Although, in logic, this is a matter of some theoretical sophistication, it seems likely that real managers usually understand the point very well. When one explains things to a child, one perforce speaks the language of the child; and one may have to do violence to one's own insight in so simplifying the explanation given that it is almost incorrect. Similarly, the head of a firm may find it totally impossible to explain his actions to the work force, in terms which they understand, without virtually falsifying the true basis of his policy. This is not in the least because either the child or the labourer is stupid; the point holds even if they can each be proved more intelligent than the father and the boss. They are just not part of the metasystem, and they do not speak the metalanguage. And when one comes to government, it is a necessary duty—on occasion—to declare that the reasons why a minister took certain action is not in the public interest to divulge. But the real point behind many ministerial failures of communication is not a matter of security at all, but a matter of metalinguistics.

These are a few examples of the operation of another fundamental principle of applied cybernetics. It is named the Principle of External Complementarity (Reference 6). That is because, at some point, all hierarchic systems, however sophisticated, rely for their logical completion on a black box lying outside.

Concepts of Behaviour

The identification of mechanisms led to concepts of law; and we have just seen how the laws of cybernetics govern our view of modelling. But models are useless unless they are applied; we go into action in a managerial situation armed with a model which—hopefully —embodies the laws and applies the mechanisms.

In doing this, we find ourselves confronted with a behavioural situation. This is a real world; a world in which models have no status, cybernetic laws are unrecognized, and the very mechanisms themselves are not understood. For this is the region of managerial action; it is the world the manager himself understands, it is the arena where he demonstrates his own competence as a leader and maker of decisions. And today, in a way unexampled by any previous epoch of history, this world is a scene of change. Change has always happened; and it is a cliché to observe that change is more fundamental and happens much more quickly than ever before—thanks to an exponential advance in technology. We are observing, indeed, a change in the rate of change.

It is for this very reason that management, which has hitherto developed its own competence to handle increasingly elaborate situations fairly successfully, now appears to be failing. Throughout the world, and at every level of operations, there is a management crisis of one kind or another. Now, although we said that tension was necessary to uphold the tonality of a system, we explicitly noted that the degree of tension within a viable system must remain short of persistent crisis. Today, on the contrary, crisis is persistent—and almost universal. We face environmental crisis in terms of pollution; by pesticides, by carbon monoxide, by noise, by chemical effluent, and so on. We face a technological crisis also, one which began with the threat of thermo-nuclear war—a threat to which almost unaccountably we have become inured. The fact is that the risk of thermo-nuclear devastation is more serious today than it ever has been before, thanks to the extension of nuclear capability, and the ever-increasing elaboration of the control systems required to restrain proliferating variety.

But beyond these existing problems there is the threat of the computer, which is hardly imagined yet in the minds of most authorities, nor even of those who will sooner or later abuse its immense power. There is the development of the laser, which will produce a revolution quite as impressive as that already attained by computers themselves. And thirdly, there is the threat of a new social crisis of disorder and violence, begotten largely by the other two, aided and abetted by the collapse of social metasystems which proved so stabilising to the social homeostat of the past. This is a reference to the contemporary loss of respect for organized religion, for law, and for inherited *mores* of every kind.

The problem may be summed up as a need for the management of change, which outclasses any previous experience which mankind has had of this requirement. It was said much earlier that most of our management technique was devoted to the smooth running of affairs, and that special measures had to be taken to ensure that the capability to innovate was not lost. Without this, we said, there could be no growth, no learning, no adaptation, no evolution. All this is sufficiently difficult to underwrite when the world is standing virtually still—and indeed the capacities of mankind to undertake any kind of effort (whether in the speed of travel, the capability to compute, the capacity to lift and project, or anything else) remained, with hindsight, virtually static for five thousand years. It is in the last hundred years that we have seen the change in the rate of change which has left our management capacity gasping for breath.

Then we must organize; we must design control structures competent to cope with an unprecedented task of adaptation. In general, the method which people adopt appears to be this. They look at existing trends and extrapolate them, hoping thereby to create for themselves a scenario which expresses what the future will be like. They then ask themselves whether they can create policies and undertake decisions which will enable the system for which they are responsible to survive in these circumstances. But this approach will not do.

Thanks to the exponential characteristics of contemporary change, these extrapolations reach points of singularity well within the compass of the period under review. That is to say: the forecast expansion becomes infinite at some finite point in time. That makes nonsense of the accepted approach to adaptation. The issue is nowhere more poignant than in consideration of the world population, which—at the present rate of expansion—is predicted (by these jejune methods) to become infinite within the lifetime of people already alive. Since this is impossible, we must look to the mechanisms which will inevitably flatten the exploding curves.

We find those that are natural to ecology all too readily: they are the threats to the extinction of mankind which have already been listed. Not only does it take variety to absorb variety; variety *will* absorb variety. Thus we face the ultimate task in control. Forecasting must be done; but it is not a question any longer of contemplating how to adapt to the predicted change. Quite clearly, the predicted change itself must be deliberately modified. As Gabor has put it, we must invent the future. If we do not, the future will happen to us. We shall not like it. Above all, in the terms of this paper, we have to lay hold on the exploding outputs of our situation, and drag down these outputs to a level which society can contain. Then regulatory mechanisms which can hold those outputs steady at the desired level must needs be instituted.

The science of cybernetics has, just in time, come to understand something about the fundamental processes which are causing loss of control, and also about those processes which are needed to contain explosive disorder. If management is to make use of these discoveries in time it will need to work at the metasystemic level. We can no longer afford the time to tinker with the internal mechanisms of established institutions.

These issues, which are in my opinion critical to the very survival of mankind, were extensively discussed at an OECD conference held at Bellagio, Italy, in 1968 (Reference 7).

REFERENCES

1. Jay W FORRESTER, *Industrial Dynamics*, MIT Press and John Wiley, 1961.
2. Jay W FORRESTER, *Urban Dynamics*, MIT Press, 1969.
3. W Ross ASHBY, *Design for a Brain*, John Wiley, 1954 (revised edition) 1960.
4. Stafford BEER, *Decision and Control*, John Wiley, 1966.
5. Claude SHANNON & Warren WEAVER, *The Mathematical Theory of Communication*, University of Illinois Press, 1949.
6. Stafford BEER, *Cybernetics and Management*, English University Press, 1959 (revised edition) 1967.
7. Erich JANTSCH (Editor), *Perspectives of Planning*, OECD, 1969.
Note added later :
   For a neurocybernetic model of organization see
8. Stafford BEER, *Brain of the Firm*, Allen Lane, The Penguin Press, 1972.

In this book so far
views have been put forward
(always within a specific context—
which I hope has been helpful)

        that define a posture
                towards societary problems

        and specify a methodology
            . for encompassing them.

Before launching ourselves into yet deeper water
let us take a metalinguistic look
over this scene.

Perhaps there has already been enough said about the posture,
which hinges on the recognition
of undecidability in the publicly accepted languages
wherein our thoughts and verbal statements move.

So formal an issue
which sounds indeed like the stuff
of metaphysics
rather than politics
may seem implausible
compared with explanations that derive
from purely psychological considerations.

People, it is said, feel uneasy
when faced with change
and the disruption of accustomed routines.

        What was good enough for my father
        is good enough for me.

There is surely some truth in this—
one can actually hear these words.....
and yet the explanation is not adequate.

In the first place
the public has cheerfully accepted
a great deal of change
with little more than a passing grumble
in the last twenty-five years.

In the second place
it is not the ordinary citizen
who either hampers or facilitates

COLOUR CODE : GOLD
Metalanguage

the monumental changes
for which government and senior management alone
must be accountable.
The top executive surely knows better than to fall into
the 'good enough for my father' trap

> though we may note
> that he is not above using this argument
> *on behalf of* the ordinary citizen—
> and that may be pure rationalization
> of his own secret insecurity.

In the third place
there is the evidence—
that the revolutionary utterance
cannot be 'heard'

> meaning that the proposition is undecidable

and that if people are patient
and get through to the right language
they balk

> meaning that the proposition is
> intemperate
> irresponsible.

What this really says to me
is that those conscientious men in power
are profoundly aware
of the sheer inertia of the system
it is proposed radically to change.

Ignoring these three points to the contrary
a psychological bogey has been put up
which can be used to explain away
any shortcoming. It is

> resistance to change.

It would be foolish to contend
that there is no such thing.
On the other hand
it would be—and indeed is—
foolish to think that it cannot be handled,
especially when many appear to recognize
that unless we change
we shall be overwhelmed.

Thus I argue that the time is ripe
for the reconstruction of the public languages
which put new thinking beyond logical reach.

COLOUR CODE : GOLD
Metalanguage

Note :   to legalize abortion
            first change the public language
            that contains the expression
            abortion-is-murder;

            to abolish capital punishment
            first change the public language
            that contains the expression
            execution-isn't-murder;

and vice versa.

When we pass to the consideration
of methodologies
for the study and design of new institutions
which have been described under the headings
of operational research and cybernetics
there is a little more to say
in this metalanguage.

Two thousand years of thinking
about methods of thinking
have led to a refinement of logic
that I shall refer to simply
as ANALYSIS.

This is a most powerful tool
for a great many purposes
including mathematics and law
philosophy and science.
It has its sterile outcomes too—
notably :
            taxonomies that fetter ranging thought
            ritual dances of words in ratiocination
            substitution of the analysis itself
                        for the substance meant to be analysed
            reductionism.

Perhaps the most damaging outcome of all
which partakes of all these
has been a cultural inability
to think about the integrity of integral systems
            the organization of the organism
            the whole that is held to be greater
                        than the sum of its parts
            the viability of lively ensembles.

To think about any of these
we need the approach

COLOUR CODE : GOLD
Metalanguage

that is the antithesis of analysis
namely SYNTHESIS.

The classical philosophers knew about synthesis :
they did what they knew how to do with it
namely analysis.

In this way
the notion of synthesis
and its power as a tool
were all but destroyed—
the examples I would give
are two of the most astonishing intellects ever
Aristotle and Kant
(this probably misrepresents *them*
but not their cultural influence).

We must turn to Hegel for a gleam of light.
Instead of analysing synthesis out of existence
he erected it as the higher outcome
of the simultaneous existence of opposites—
the thesis and the antithesis.

Moreover, he saw systems whole :

> the relations by which terms are related
> are an integral part
> of the terms they relate.

This is no philosophic text book.
But if we are to grapple with vast institutions
using the approach of General Systems Theory
we had better recognize that we start
with a cultural lag.

Not everyone is soaked in Hegel.
We are all steeped in the analytic tradition.

Essentially :

> take a live thing apart
> to discover what life is :
> you will not find a component called life—
> and behold the live thing is dead.

> Shall we take a radio apart
> to find the voice?

> —or a car engine to pieces
> to find the speed?

COLOUR CODE : GOLD
Metalanguage

People can be just as stupid as that
when it comes to large-scale systems;
it is specially stupid because
they include ramified social groups
of real people
having real relationships.
Such groups—such people even—
are delicate.....

However
none of this is said
in disparagement of analysis.
But the tool of synthesis is needed too.

They may look
like mutually exclusive opponents.
They are *often*
(thanks to the cultural heritage)
interpreted as such.

They are collaborators.

Perhaps this diagram will help.

COLOUR CODE : GOLD
Metalanguage

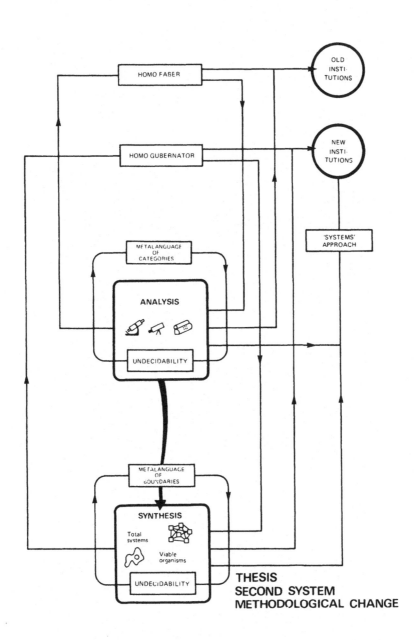

COLOUR CODE : BLUE
Thesis

We must now change gear again.

The Arguments of Change so far advanced
have had to do with fundamentals—

> what is man?
> how stands his evolving culture?
> what methodologies of thought
> > condition him
> > and could change?

Now we start to think
about society itself
using these notions.

The project PLATFORM FOR CHANGE
seized on four opportunities
again in very different contexts
to tease out
or to worry like a terrier
some of the problems.
They are presented now
as an interlocking set.

The set interlocks for two reasons.
Firstly :

> I was trying to construct a general theory
> about the structure of institutions
> (particular sorts of systems)
> and about the structures within society
> that embrace at least several of them
> (particular sorts of metasystems).
>
> I was also wrestling with the problem
> of constructing a new metric
> for computing social good—
> while being profoundly conscious
> of a whole history of disasters
> in this endeavour.

Secondly :

> I knew that everything I was doing
> was connected
> by my own sense of impending collapse
> in every aspect of societary affairs.

There are a couple of narrative things I would like to say
about this second point.

COLOUR CODE : YELLOW
Narrative

I am one of a group of people throughout the world
who have been sounding the alarm.
The immediate reaction to this
was that nobody took any notice.

The second reaction
because of importunity
was indeed to take notice :
many thoughtful folk became alarmed.

But I suppose the third reaction was inevitable.
Suddenly
we are all labelled

PROPHETS OF DOOM.

What a nasty thing to be . . . . .

No-one would think
that the whole campaign
constituted a huge attempt
to be constructive.

Please recognize this labelling for what it is—
a defence mechanism
pure and simple.

At any rate, this situation
has made me wonder
whether to expunge from the Arguments of Change
the passages mentioning threats
from the white pages of this book.
For one thing, they tend to be repetitious.

I have decided not to—
mainly because that would falsify the record.
There is another reason :
the repetition of the symptoms of danger
in different contexts
may conceivably throw more light
on what these threats actually are.

(Knit your own metalanguage . . . . .)

The first of the four Arguments
was presented during the run-up to the project
in an acute awareness
of trying to prepare the ground.

COLOUR CODE : YELLOW
Narrative

The International Association of Cybernetics
of which I was a founder member
held its first international meeting
(which begot the Association)
in 1956, twenty-two nations participating.
It was an exciting affair—
and due entirely to the perspicacity
of some people in Belgium.

Professor Georges Boulanger and some colleagues
had persuaded the provincial government of Namur
to sponsor the conference;
the Minister of Education
and UNESCO
to their everlasting credit once again
(few indeed had even heard of cybernetics then)
gave their patronage.....

The Association flourished.
A second conference was held in 1958—
after which it became a triennial event.
Plenty of criticism surrounded the Association from the first
but nothing can alter the plain fact
that the Belgians
performed a service to the world
which continues.

One of the criticisms
has always been that the conference
is always held in that charming city of Namur
(since this is not the accepted international way of doing things).
Accordingly, there was a movement towards
the holding of an independent conference in London.

The moving spirit in this
was the indefatigable Dr John Rose
who organized the entire occasion
including a Banquet in Guildhall
graced by the Lord Mayor of London
and a great many distinguished guests.
He did all of this
virtually single-handed.

This enterprise
seemed once again to let loose
a pent-up flood of cybernetic enthusiasm.
The proceedings of this conference
fill three volumes
under the title

COLOUR CODE : YELLOW
Narrative

Progress of Cybernetics
(Gordon and Breach, London, 1970).

But what I most remember about the meeting
was indeed the Banquet.
The eminent English cybernetician Professor Gordon Pask
proposed the traditional toast to the City with great charm.
The Lord Mayor, Sir Charles Trinder, responded
with an amazing speech
well illustrating how it is that the City has adapted itself
to change, so as to survive for two thousand years.
With a pyrotechnic display of wit and knowledge
the Lord Mayor 'proved' that he must himself be, *ex officio,*
the Chief Cybernetician of England.

It is pleasing to pay tribute to that surviving institution
the City of London.
Unfortunately, it is the very unadaptability
of so many institutions *within* the City
that mark the threats to our society
with which this book is concerned.

Presiding at the Banquet was a social relaxation for me;
making the Chairman's Address to Congress
earlier in the day
was rather more serious.

This is the first of the four Arguments of Change
that I have been describing.....

but first
another piece of the thesis.....

COLOUR CODE : YELLOW
Narrative

THESIS

FOURTH STATEMENT

Institutions are self-contained cells
for each of which the nucleus—
the organizing principle
called the cytoblast—
is management itself.

It is the responsibility of management
to revitalize their decaying institutions :
a management
informed by the insights
and using the tools
that science makes available
through its study of complex systems.

Through science we set up the hypothesis
that institutions
have certain systemic characteristics
that make them highly stable
        —in itself a good
and therefore unadaptable
        —something highly dangerous.

They are esoteric boxes
difficult to penetrate :
which puts all the more onus for internal reform
on their own managements.

Society itself however
needs to recognize
that the revitalizing of separate institutions
will not of itself
successfully reform society
nor cope with societary threats
because

     ● there is not likely to be
       enough time left

     ● the major instabilities of society
       arise *between*
       the esoteric boxes.

COLOUR CODE : BLUE
Thesis

132

This unfortunately puts the onus on governments
to attend to the creation and regulation
of metasystems
meant to induce this new societary stability.

'unfortunately'?

Of course.
The dangers are manifest.

AN ARGUMENT OF CHANGE

THE CYBERNETIC CYTOBLAST:

MANAGEMENT ITSELF

Chairman's Address* delivered to the International Cybernetics Congress held at Imperial College, London, on the 3rd September, 1969.

*By permission of
  Gordon and Breach Scientific Publishers Ltd., London.

Setting the Scene

According to the official trade figures for July 1969, the country's exports were the second highest they have ever been. Moreover, the level of imports fell as compared with June. This was not so gratifying at it might have been, because the trade gap increased by twelve million pounds.

However, the total import-export value (which must be measured to assess this fluctuation) is two orders of magnitude greater than the movement itself. The difficulties in measuring it at all are notorious. Indeed it was recently discovered that sums of this same magnitude had been 'lost' from the national accounts every month for the last six years. And in any case, the fluctuation was less than half the average for the year.

What was the outcome? I quote the London *Times*. 'The trade figures shocked the Stock Exchange so badly that gilt-edged prices suffered their biggest fall for any normal day, excluding only days of such high drama as devaluation or the outbreak of war'.

This story is enough to make a control engineer weep: he would not reckon to design a servomechanism which operated like a steam hammer in response to changes occurring *well within the noise level* of his system. As for the cybernetician, the story is enough to make him beat his breast in public. For cybernetics has more to say about the management of large and complex systems than to attempt their control in terms of a single-loop negative-feedback in the first place.

We people have been studying complex systems of every kind for a quarter of a century now. There are neuro-cyberneticians here today, who have kept us profoundly informed of progress in brain research. We have learned from ecology and from genetics; we have dealt alike in social facts and engineering artefacts. All manner of cyberneticians have been closely identified with the development of the computer from the very beginning. What we hope we have done is to demonstrate the generality of many subtle control mechanisms in viable systems of every kind.

If there is a science of cybernetics at all, it has to be thus general. We are surely seeking to identify *managerial principle* amid a welter of control manifestations. For management itself, however this may be defined in the context of a particular complex system, must enshrine the organizing principle by which any viable system may evolve and grow, learn and adapt. It is here in the cytoblast, the nucleus of the cell, that we must needs identify whatever matters about the direction of affairs.

My case is this. If we have spent a quarter of a century in what is essentially research, it is time to turn towards influencing affairs. We may by now take for granted a great deal that we know we know. From Shannon's theorems of communication to Ashby's laws of variety, from McCullouch's neural logics to Pask's principles of self-organization, we have a corpus of theory. From the underexploited experimental mechanisms of Grey Walter to the overexploited digital computer, with analogue machines intervening, we have a considerable mastery of mechanisms. We have models galore, which actually work, from the industrial and urban dynamics of Forrester to the artificial intelligence algorithms and heuristics of Minsky, Michic and Asomov. Conscious of this armoury, and encouraged by the penetrating insights of many other workers, it is time I repeat for a conference such as this to adopt a stance in relation to the societary problems of our time.

For it seems no exaggeration to say that society is in a state of crisis. There are many deeply disturbing symptoms of this, widely beyond the scope of such anecdotes as that with which I began. There is nothing less than massive revolt against established norms by the young everywhere in the world. There is everywhere a growing manifestation of violence and disorder. An ecological crisis is upon us—in terms of pollution: by pesticides, by noise, by carbon monoxide. There is an exploding population, an exploding technology, and in general a change in the rate of change beyond our ability to grasp. Society is faced with major perturbations arriving with greater mean frequency than the relaxation time of any social homeostat devised by man.

If all this sounds alarmist, it is because we ought to be alarmed. And in my view the most alarming feature of the whole situation is a kind of paralysis in the alarm machinery itself. Modern communications have procured a rate of reflex in the body politic which amounts to clonus: and I have elsewhere, (reference 1) sought to show how clonic reactions make society spastic, causing hunting—and even the *reversal* of what were hitherto regarded as causatory mechanisms. But without turning to pathological models, it should be noted that the perceptual battering sponsored by the mass communications media of today leads assuredly to habituation. We have produced a situation where the continual restatement of profoundly shocking truths leaves them shocking no longer. And therefore there seems no way left in which to draw attention to what are truly lethal threats.

Other sorts of scientist are doing their best to draw attention to various kinds of environmental, political and economic crisis. The particular form of societary crisis which cyberneticians understand and are qualified to speak about concerns the growing instability of social institutions themselves. For we know that as society becomes unstable the mechanisms of viability themselves will be denatured. We can expect explosive rather than damped responses, uproar in place of homeostatic equilibrium, a loss of adaptability, and so forth. The symptoms are there.

How might we approach a general cybernetic problem of this magnitude? The future of society is a topic to which thinkers have always devoted effort, but not with much sense of urgency. Scientists and administrators alike have been more humble, and have addressed themselves to the particular problems of sub-systems. But if cybernetics has the tools, and if the urgency is there, we ought now to be developing a general systems model which would illuminate the whole scene. One paper such as this cannot take us very far, but I shall do what I can to start the development which appears to me so vital.

The Esoteric Box
Think of any social institution you like, and imagine it to sit within a box. You might take for example 'schooling' or 'the general practice of medicine' or 'penal establishments'. What is going on inside this box is an established order of things. There is a complex arrangement of sub-systems, a strange set of relationships between people of standing, and a recondite mode of behaviour. These features—their complexity and unintelligibility to the outsider—justify the box's adjective 'esoteric'. One does not gain admission to the box's activity without the appropriate passport.

This is not to say that the box is a closed system, only that it is self-organizing and self-regulating. It has inputs and outputs, which are usually a stream of members of the general public. These people pass through the box, or are operated on by the box, but they do not change it at all. Whatever else happens, the box goes on; it is very powerfully arranged to maintain its own internal stability—and therefore, indeed, its survival. How can this be?

The social institution, the esoteric box, is an ultrastable system in equilibrium. The stable state at any time is determined by a set of systemic variables. Any change in one of these variables causes a shift in the position of equilibrium to a position that tends to counteract the change that has happened. That this should be so is an obvious consequence of the equilibrium-seeking character of the system. In physical chemistry, this is called *Le Chatelier's principle*.

Le Chatelier suggests to us how an esoteric box in equilibrium is likely to react to any kind of prodding from outside. It does this not by 'fighting back', but by moving its point of equilibrium along the scale on which that point may be measured, so as exactly to counter-balance the effect of the prod. The result of this is, of course, that if you physically assault the esoteric box by changing one of its state variables, it neither collapses nor violently reacts: it simply adjusts its own internal relationships slightly so that the effect of the change is offset. In behavioural terms, this response is recognizably an ultrastability reaction (under Ross Ashby's terminology).

Reformers, critics of institutions, consultants in innovation, people in short who 'want to get something done', often fail to see this point. They cannot understand why their strictures, advice or demands do not result in effective change. They expect either to achieve a measure of success in their own terms or to be flung off the premises. But an ultrastable system, especially one enclosed in an esoteric box, has no need to react in either of these ways. It specializes in equilibrial readjustment, which is to the observer a secret form of change requiring no actual alteration in the macro-systemic characteristics that he is trying to do something about. As to beating off the attack, that would be crude indeed. Only systems in unstable equilibrium need to do that, and our society is now more mature. Reformers are not often sacked, still less burned at the stake, these days. This is a measure of the extent to which institutions have developed self-sustaining techniques of ultrastability.

But it is interesting that just because reformers do not achieve success in their own terms, they may not as a matter of fact have failed to reform. Let us learn something more from the operation of Le Chatelier's principle. It provides one very extraordinary limiting effect. Suppose, for example, that heat is evolved in a chemical reaction. Then suppose that the prodding involves increasing the temperature. The system's response to this kind of prod (depending on the actual quantities involved) may have to result in *reversing* the reaction. The system maintains its equilibrium, and the esoteric box may look much the same from outside. But the extent of the hidden drama within is not realized. Even so, the system *has* maintained its integrity; and if necessary reform really does require that this particular system should be abolished, or should merge with other systems into new social configurations, then we are in serious difficulty.

In general, cybernetic models of social institutions predict three characteristic outcomes of their ultrastable response to serious perturbation. They are:

First : the institution survives as an integral system; it is still recognizable as the esoteric box.

Second : the institution maintains equilibrial relationships with other institutions, although their form may change. (Indeed, the elaborate forms of the relationships between two esoteric boxes may justify their description as a third esoteric box to which these three remarks would then also apply.)

Third : realignments *within* the esoteric box required to achieve this integral survival of the institution in society may well be extremely dramatic. They may in particular involve actual reversals of role internally, in the specific conditions where that role is defined in terms of the variable most responsive to environmental change.

Testing these conclusions against observed events, I offer four very different examples for consideration, without further detailed discussion. They are :

(i)   the institution of management in any business
       firm which comes under extreme pressure,

(ii)   the institution of marriage—and —the-family
       in Western culture since 1900,

(iii) the institution of the English Public Schools since the
       first Labour Government in 1929,

(iv)   the institution of the Roman Catholic Church since
       the election of Pope John XXIII.

Then this is the ultrastable system-for-surviving, and this is what we ought to expect from the social institution as an esoteric box. No system can survive an assault so massive that it is plucked right out of its setting. No system survives environmental perturbations which count as annihilating. Up to this final degree of disturbance, however, ultrastable systems are machines-for-surviving—and they do indeed survive.

Perhaps at this point we should briefly consider the mechanisms within the esoteric box which procure the behaviour under discussion. They must surely be social mechanisms, and we at first seem to be in the realm of social psychology. We are dealing with a professional or a managerial group which is self-organizing, which shares a belief structure and a complicated set of conventions—especially as to appropriate ways of describing situations and appropriate methods of debate. Any management scientist who has worked in an experimental situation with such a group could tell his own stories about the tenacity with which that group coheres—and adheres to its corporately stable states.

For example, I was administering a management game in which, half-way through, it was discovered that one of the teams had been fed a large amount of false information. As a consequence, though by coincidence, they had ranked the profitability of four new products in exactly the reverse order from the solution we knew to be correct at this stage of the game. I therefore told this team what had happened, and apologised. I explained that, in order to keep the game going, the best thing to do appeared to correct their ordering of the

products to show correct current estimates of profitability, and to carry on from there —
although obviously this would give them an advantage over other teams. They thanked
me politely for my intervention, but declared that they were highly satisfied with the way
things were going, and would prefer to ignore my advice. They carried on as if nothing
had happened.

The fact is that we might do better to think in terms, not of psychology but of social
anthropology. It might be more helpful to talk about tribal customs than about logical
analysis, about myths and taboos rather than understanding and intellection, about
conversion rather than conviction. This is not rudely to say that there is no rational
content in policy-making and decision-taking within the esoteric box: of course there is,
and of higher or lower quality. We are talking here simply about those potent mechanisms
which result in the group's behaving in an ultrastable fashion.

There are lessons in this, no doubt, for people who wish to influence the group, particularly
when such people do not belong to the tribe. But this sort of discussion is not our present
concern. It is our concern to appreciate the strength of the binding forces and the power
of the interlocking feedback loops involved. I would like to emphasize that these remarks
are not made in a critical spirit: these are not matters for rebuke. It is important to society
that its social institutions *do* cohere, *are* ultrastable. For although these characteristics
may make life difficult for reformers, they are what gives society its strength as well.
We should quickly be in chaos if our institutions toppled under pressure from maniacs or
anarchists, or even through the incompetence of individuals concerned with operating
the system.

Strings of Esoteric Boxes

Now most definable activities which matter in modern society may be described as a
collection of esoteric boxes connected together under some rule, and thereby constituting
a social metasystem.

For example, the social activity of 'education' might be depicted as a chain of three esoteric
boxes, respectively called 'the school', 'the university' and 'the employer'. Formal education
passes a human individual through each of these esoteric boxes, and within each an
operation is performed on that individual. We can at once understand what sorts of
statement count as rules for the connection of these boxes. In England, 'passing the 11-plus
examination' constituted the rule opening the door into the box labelled 'grammar school'.
The label 'x O-levels and y A-levels' works the filter between the school and the university.
'A good class degree' is the name of the filter operating between the university and the
professional career. The stringing together of esoteric boxes by rules of this kind marks
the present state of social organization.

We may note at once that, if the established filters turn out to be unworkable or to promote
a total social behaviour which is unsatisfactory, then society characteristically tries to
change the filter. 'Do away with the 11-plus': that has almost happened, and other criteria
are being substituted. 'Is the A-level a suitable criterion for university admission?':
that has become a question of moment. 'What does industry expect from a university
graduate?' is an enquiry calling the last kind of filter in question also. But whatever we

do about the filters, which is to say however we manipulate the rules by which the esoteric boxes are connected, the effect of momentous social change on the integrity of the esoteric boxes themselves is almost non-existent. Thank Le Chatelier for that.

We may look at a variety of examples, and begin with education—since that was our first topic. It is evident, I should argue, that the educational system grossly fails either to meet the contemporary social need or to exploit what is now technologically possible. It follows that there is much adjustment of the filters between the three boxes already nominated; and (because educationalists are sensible people) there is also much discussion of the *interfaces* between the boxes. Schools are developing a new concept of the sixth form which reaches out towards the university. And universities, for their part, are developing concepts of a 'foundation year' which reach back towards the sixth form. Here is a sensible attempt to bridge the gap between the two esoteric boxes of 'school' and 'university', without damaging the integrity of either. On the other side of the diagram the university reaches out towards the employer, by instituting 'vocational courses' aimed at preparing people for their future life in paid employment. The employer in turn ,has instituted training schemes for graduates, in such fields as research and development, or management induction. These are explicitly attempts to bridge the second gap without compromising either the university's purity of purpose in the pursuit of knowledge itself, or the business intention to make a profit.

Government supervises all these endeavours with benign benevolence, setting up bodies to facilitate the operation of new filters—by, for instance, giving grants to students in the school-university transition and by endowing, for example, business schools to facilitate the university-career transition. All this is very fine. But the ghost at this particular banquet is still the ghost of Le Chatelier. Do not expect the schools themselves, the universities themselves, or industry itself, actually to *change*. All these esoteric boxes will do is to modify their equilibrial state to account for the impact of societal manoeuvres which affect their major variables.

Let us take some further examples, in which the situation is perhaps less enlightened by a wish on the part of all concerned to produce the optimal synergistic result.

Three esoteric boxes have, since the advent of the aeroplane, between them constituted the national capability for defence. They are of course the institutions called the army, the navy and the air force. Now it has been clear to all concerned for a very long time that any modern military operation is an amalgam of these three; because operations are conducted on land, by sea and in the air *at once*. This joint operation is called a battle. Moreover, any scenario prepared to discuss the future is bound to treat of situations characterized in these three dimensions simultaneously. In this case a still bolder solution has been adopted than the gap-bridging solution used in education. It is not simply to adjust the interfaces between the three esoteric boxes, but to declare (since all three services come under the command of one government which in turn represents one sovereign) that military might is indivisible. Then let there be simply a 'green uniform' force amalgamating the national fighting prowess by land, sea and air.

The British Government, following American precedent, took some kind of step in this direction. Notionally, the armed forces are coalesced into an integral defence capability, under a Minister of Defence (political) and a General Staff (services). Yet a little observation suggests that the Le Chatelier family still has senior officers serving in three different uniforms. And we may note little change in those three extremely ultrastable institutions called the army, the navy and the air force.

From this example, we may escalate to government itself. Now we shall call our three esoteric boxes: First Ministry, Second Ministry, Third Ministry. Why are these three ministries quite separate? Do not they all bear upon the social need of the citizen? Of course they do. And therefore we now have (as a result of the Fulton Committee) a new Civil Service Department competent to cross the boundaries between them. There is no doubt at all, in my mind, that this development will produce great and important changes. Even so, I suspect that the three computer installations (for example) required to administer these three ministries were ordered quite separately, on the authority of three different officials (even if they did have the same surname, which we know by now). I mean quite simply that Ministries One, Two and Three are ultrastable, and will be with us for some time yet.

If we move from government examples into industry, the whole business becomes yet more dramatic. *Obviously* we could not have our energy requirements met by (i) coal, (ii) gas and (iii) electricity—without regard to their interaction. . . . . And so, by nationa-lizing each of the industries concerned, and by making all three responsible to the Minister of Fuel and Power, we should obtain as, a nation synergistic benefits. And so we should have done. But it is not as easy as that. Occasional high-level meetings between three major industries will not produce an integral operation. And in our kind of economy competition must be kept alive. Then there is the classic contention that one ought not to impose a plan of national scope on an industrial management which is to be held *accountable*. This is exactly the same argument as one meets in the large corporation which finds corporate planning impossible because its component firms are called autonomous.

Many of the arguments used in this area of organizational thinking are confused and muddle-headed. Often they discuss bogus problems. We may nonetheless predict with confidence that the debate will be kept very much alive. For so long as the issues are kept nicely confused they are grist to the ultrastability mill of any self-respecting esoteric box.

Then what about the industries which have not been nationalized, which depend upon a free market to adjust the relationships which exist between their esoteric boxes? The extent of their collaboration is notoriously inadequate; and therefore government must intervene to ensure that good sense prevails for the national well-being. The industrial training boards were one fruit of this thinking; the Science Research Council, the National Research and Development Corporation, the Industrial Reorganization Council and other government-sponsored bodies (having call on national resources precisely in order to lubricate the interfaces) have been set up. But the esoteric boxes go their self-organizing way. Who expects management to change? Who expects the share-holders or the City to adopt new postures? Is it likely that trade unions will adjust to the new challenge? Too many managing directors, too many dividend seekers, too many general secretaries operate under the Le Chatelier alias.

And so the argument goes on. We might finally consider an entire industrial complex, for example publishing, as illustrating the point. Until recently, publishers used to publish entirely through the printed word. It has recently become clear that technology has moved on since Gutenberg and Caxton: we are in an era of electronics. Thus the three esoteric boxes which will determine the future of the publishing industry in the next ten years are: the publishers, the telecommunications and computer industries, and the GPO. Yet the chances of changing the interfaces and the dynamic relationships between these three esoteric boxes appear slight indeed. Each will adjust its own equilibrium point to the new challenge, however each may see that challenge; what we can be sure of is the inability of the total system to restructure itself. This is because there *is* no total system, except in the eye of beholders. In the end, it is the beholder who makes take-over bids on the strength of his metasystemic perception who changes this aspect of society.

These are six examples of strings of esoteric boxes: I have compounded the string of three elements in each case, simply for convenience, and have certainly not carried the discussion of any one example to the extent of making it a case history. But perhaps our minds are sufficiently prepared by this quick review of education, defence, the civil service, the national energy problem, industry generally, and one industry in particular, to be ready for the general argument which must now be pursued. It is already obvious that we cannot sack Le Chatelier from any of the esoteric boxes over whose ultrastability he presides. Nor would we wish to do so. But we cannot leave him to operate within esoteric boxes as the last lone survivor of an antedeluvian age. We need him badly on the national payroll.

The Spurious Metasystem

When we first began to talk about stringing esoteric boxes together, I said that they thereby constituted a social metasystem. This means essentially that the total system of which (arbitrarily) three esoteric boxes are the parts, is something more than their sum. 'Something more', again essentially, refers to what, following Hegel, could be called a higher order synthesis. This speaks a language capable of utterances which cannot be expressed in the languages of the esoteric boxes themselves—a language which, following Gödel, could be called a meta-language. A meta-language is one in which we may decide issues which are undecidable in the lower order languages; and the metasystem ought to be a social institution capable of surviving when its component institutions (despite their ultra-stability) finally fail.

All this, for the cybernetician, says much more than we have so far·said in talking about 'a string of esoteric boxes'. A string of pearls is stable, but not ultrastable. If the cord is cut, nothing is left but the individual pearls—and they are scattered on the floor. What we need is a viable system of esoteric boxes, more cleverly connected, more elaborately structured, than happens simply by talking about them in the same breath. Let us firstly attempt to abstract from the six examples so briefly limned out the rules of the metasystemic game as it is played by society today.

The boxes of our examples, just because they are esoteric, are initially free agents. They can ignore each other; or they can recognize that they belong to some kind of metasystem—and in this case they have an alternative. Either they can act responsibly to their own initiates, which may well mean repelling contiguous boxes with which they ought to have transactions; or they can act responsibly towards society at large, and undertake rapprochements with their neighbours. Thus we approach a first rule of observed behaviour:

FIRST RULE :   Esoteric boxes may recognize themselves as part of a higher order system, and this affects their behaviour at the interface with other boxes. They may seek or rebuff sensible collaboration.

Social institutions, however, are each a minor aspect of society at large, and we may safely say that there is always a superior authority which has the capacity to influence the situation, or even to intervene in a definitive way. In the case of public institutions,·this superior authority is probably government itself. Where private institutions are concerned, no-one can be sure (and this is part of the fun of the private sector) who the superior authority may turn out to be. A trade association may suddenly exert itself; a public petition may suddenly be transformed from a joke to a threat; above all, there is the obvious or perhaps totally unexpected takeover bidder. However it may be constituted and however recognized, the superior authority is defined as an influence making the attempt to subsume a string of esoteric boxes under one head. Thus—

SECOND RULE : A superior authority may subsume a string of esoteric boxes under a single controller, with the injunction that he rationalize and then optimize the integral behaviour of this group.

There is yet (according to our six examples) a third mode of conduct. This again involves the superior authority, but it takes account of the fact that in our mature society the too frequent invocation of Rule 2 usually rebounds. A government which normally invokes it is called fascist; an industrialist who works by Rule 2 is called authoritarian; and in general management eminent consultants stand ready to denounce the Rule 2 organization as over-centralized. Hence, and precisely because our society is mature, there is a third rule which is in truth a sophisticated version of the second—although it operates quite differently. Thus—

THIRD RULE :   A superior authority, protesting that it wishes not to intervene but merely to facilitate, sets up eminent bodies or specialist committees to lubricate the interfaces between a string of esoteric boxes.

Let us recapitulate our examples, noting the operation of these behavioural rules. In education, Rule 1 is used, with some help from Rule 3. In defence, Rule 2 is supposed to prevail. In the civil service, Rule 3 has achieved its apotheosis—especially as a result of the Fulton Committee. In the case of the energy example: the public perhaps expects Rule 2 operation, sees clearly that it does not happen, and so hopes that it has a Rule 3 operation—whereas the likelihood is that everyone relies on Rule 1. In the case of general industry, we have a Rule 3 image and—increasingly—a Rule 2 reality. Finally, in the case of a particular industry, we took an example where none of the rules manages so far to work, and therefore nothing happens. What will eventually happen is therefore predicted to be a drastic operation of Rule 2; and when that rule operates it will look more like piracy than democracy in action.

The formulation of these three rules seems to be as much as we can squeeze out of our understanding of what at present goes on in the supervision of strings of esoteric boxes. From the point of view of government, which must accept the major onus for the sensible handling of social institutions, one or two political comments can be made. Firstly, from

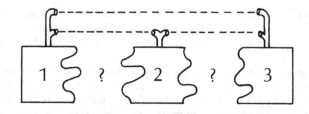

FIRST RULE :   Esoteric boxes may recognize themselves as part of a higher order system. and this affects their behaviour at the interface with other boxes. They seek or rebuff sensible collaboration.

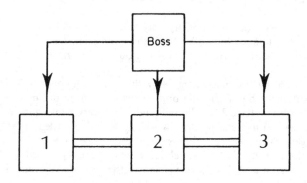

SECOND RULE : A superior authority may subsume a string of esoteric boxes under a single controller. with the injunction that he rationalize and then optimize the integral behaviour of this group.

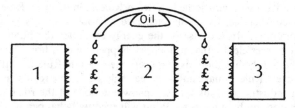

THIRD RULE :   A superior authority. protesting that it wishes not to intervene but merely to facilitate. sets up eminent bodies or specialist committees to lubricate the interfaces between a string of esoteric boxes.

Figure 1

Spurious Metasystems : Pictograms indicating the three observed Rules of Behaviour.

a game-theoretic standpoint, government ought to attend to the deployment of Rule 1 mechanisms—which they cannot themselves actually use (by definition), but which they can very well foster in roundabout ways. The next best strategy for government is to use Rule 2 (because it is effective) masquerading as Rule 3 (because that looks better). And to ensure that Rule 2 organizations (which are powerful) do not seriously disbalance affairs, it could well be convenient to think of them in pairs, and to arrange stated objectives and actual personalities in ways which result in opposite outcomes. The Monopolies Commission and the Industrial Reorganisation Corporation, for example, do seem in practice to procure antithetic effects.

The key feature of our disclosures to this point seems to be this. There is an established group of methods used by society for relating esoteric boxes, which allows them to maintain their integrity, while society itself feels entitled to hope that its methods will result in adaptation to all kinds of change.

What kind of metasystem have we here? Given the criteria used at the start of this section, I can tell you the answer to that. We have a *spurious* metasystem. Because what is happening is that the manifest need for metasystemic control of the situation is not being met. The rules of the game provide authority with a perfect excuse for avoiding drastic action (on the ground that society might collapse if drastic action were taken), and to justify this by a flurry of specious activity which is in fact designed to paper over the cracks in society, represented by the interfaces between esoteric boxes.

A Genuine Metasystem

A genuine metasystem does not use its power and its insight to *pretend* that a string of esoteric boxes is effectively strung, using the three rules which we have uncovered. On the contrary, it ensures that a new and ultrastable metasystem is actually created which will meet metasystemic criteria of performance. *But this would involve disrupting the integrity of the esoteric boxes.*

Here then is the crunch. We have and we need ultrastable social institutions. These are required for their own sake; but also because they are the components, the building blocks, of higher-order systems. It is in service to the interests of that higher-order system that the integrity of the original institutions becomes threatened. To implement the threat ill-advisedly would mean the collapse of some part of society. To succeed in a redefinition of the metasystem, and therefore of the roles of a string of esoteric boxes, would probably raise the payoff of the system by an order of magnitude.

It is obvious, from our discussion, why those in authority fear this challenge. But it is time to make explicit the reasons why the challenge must be met. I think there are two major components of the problem. Both are contemporary matters, which have not really confronted society before. The first component is the collapse of both organized religion and respect for temporal power. After all, here *was* a genuine metasystem. Society had an external skeleton, as well as an internal skeleton. And if the bones of the internal skeleton were not strong enough to support the system of inter-related social institutions, each esoteric box was individually hooked on to the external framework. Today, because the boxes maintain their integrity, they still incline to acknowledge the metasystem. But increasingly the public, and especially the young public, do not.

The second component of the problem is the rise, the exponential explosion indeed, of technology. Let us never forget or ignore the fact that the characteristic behaviour of every institution is primarily conditioned by the technology available to its purposes *at the time* its characteristic behaviour gelled. Today is certainly some other time than that. There is no knowing what would be the most suitable configuration within the esoteric box, even for its selfish purposes, given today's technology. That is because the box resists the attempt to redefine its role—because it is ultrastable.

So now our established practices are adrift in two dimensions at once. We have largely failed to stuff modern technology into the esoteric box and to reap its benefits there. As to tomorrow's technology, we are not seriously allowed to contemplate it. But much more importantly, there is no acceptable language in which to comment on the way in which the metasystem relating strings of esoteric boxes might best be designed. This is because the genuine metasystem of authority has gone, and its ethical language with it; while the metasystem of power with which we are left turns out to be spurious—and no metasystem at all.

Inexorably we are driven to the need to discuss, in an unknown metalanguage, the wholesale redesign of social institutions. We have ancient, possibly archaic, esoteric boxes, whose modus operandi is governed by anachronistic technology. These boxes are strung together, not in genuine metasystems, but in accordance with the rules which are themselves the product of an esoteric box: the social institution labelled 'this is how we conduct affairs around here'.

Now one of the lessons which I would say is most apparent from the whole history and practice of cybernetics in every context is the following. What really matters about a system is its structure—and especially its metastructure: the way in which the parts of the system are interrelated at every level of discourse. You may change the parameters of a system; you may vary the inputs to a system over a wide range; you may especially (and most surprisingly) allow the transfer functions which characterize the behaviour of the individual boxes to range across a very wide spectrum. The amazing thing is that the critical outputs remain invariant—so long as the systemic structure is maintained.

This comment, which is no demonstration but just a comment, assumes that the structure itself is hierarchical, exceeding complex, full of interaction, and rich in negative feedback. If so, I repeat, it is primarily the metastructure, the basis on which that whole hierarchy of systems is organized, which guarantees the characteristic behaviour of the whole. The simplest explanation of the reason why this is so begins with perhaps the very first major discovery of cybernetics, made clear by Norbert Wiener himself. I refer to the way in which a high-gain amplifier is rapidly dominated by its error-actuated feedback rather than by its input.

By the time we have moved to a multilooped metasystem, the *interactions* of such feedbacks at every level determine the dominant behavioural characteristics. Anyone who has worked with such cybernetics, in whatever context, knows how difficult it is either to predict outcomes or to intervene in the system to predictable ends. Thus is society in a trapped state of crisis today.

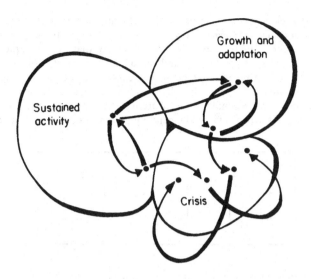

Figure 2
Society as a polystable system.

Considering how this happens, we may think of any society as a polystable system operating in three main modes. There is growth and adaptation; there is merely sustained activity; there is crisis of one kind or another. As the diagram shows, there is more than one equilibrial state in each mode, and some cycling does no harm. Further, some alternation between the growth mode and sustained activity may be beneficial. But some equilibrial states are near to the boundaries of crisis. If we are not exceedingly careful in responding to pressures at this boundary, we end in the trapped state of crisis—where every attempt to get out leads straight back in. Evidently, some kind of planning process is required to resuscitate the system. It is no longer even possible simply to yield to pressure in the trapped state, if only because there is no known way of doing so : the gradient is in the wrong direction.

If we have not understood the planning process sufficiently to escape, it is due to the absence of a genuine metasystem in which to plan. Instead, the desire for participative management, in itself not only legitimate but necessary, has caused planning to happen at a subsystemic level. Hence 'planner' has become a pejorative word; because planning is seen not to be rising to the demands of the total system. Moreover, the planning process itself becomes complicated to the point where everything seizes up. The need to preserve initiative at every managerial level results in an incapacity to show initiative anywhere.

A possible answer

We have taken a long and perhaps tedious route to reach any kind of proposal. The fact is, however, that the proposal has no hope of acceptance if the reasons why it is made are imperfectly understood.

148

I am asking that societary problems be tackled urgently at the metasystemic level. My fear is that the proposal will *appear* simply to say that they ought to be tackled on a wider front. But this is quite a different proposition. If we say that, for example, 'education' ought to be looked at as a total system, and rethought from start to finish, we shall get nowhere. For any such plan would involve many years of work by large teams of experts, the very existence of whom would profoundly threaten the integrity of the relevant esoteric boxes. There would be professional uproar. Moreover, the whole planning, administration and implementation of the project would inevitably become a bureaucratic nightmare.

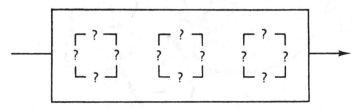

Figure 3

The threatening (and possibly megalomaniac) approach of a total rethink.

On the contrary, we ought to use the self-organizing propensities of the string of esoteric boxes, and to harness their professionalism, knowledge and energy. To do this, we have to create an environment in which these boxes do not turn defensively inward, using up their potency in internal squabbles and the effort to inhibit change. Instead, we create a metastructure and supply a metalanguage so that the organizing power of the boxes themselves is released to give change effect. This means that whatever is the 'superior authority' in any given social situation operates like a judo expert—who uses his opponent's energy, rather than his own, to achieve his ends.

Looking at the final diagram, Figure 4, we may think through how all this is supposed to happen. We can check that this systemic architecture does not attempt to repeal the natural law of Le Chatelier: the three prerogatives of esoteric boxes disclosed earlier are all preserved. Next we may trace how the three rules of observed behaviour *could* still operate in the region above the line marked AÁ. For here we have the superior authority taking sets of decisions about investment, in the activities of social institutions, and about the facilitation or inhibition by other means than money of their activities. Authority undertakes this task by direct observation of the operational facts: society expresses a demand which the esoteric box attempts to meet, and the control system uses the systemic language to assess the results.

When the metasystem is introduced, however, according to the diagram below the line AÁ, authority begins to operate in a new metalanguage competent to discuss the systemic structure itself. The main results of this in practical terms are that the expressed demands of society are replaced in the metalanguage by the specification of needs, and the assessment of results in systemic language is replaced by a specification of outcomes as determined by an appropriate system of filters. Thus, for example, society's *need* for scientists will never again be confused with the mere aggregate of its stated requirements, as it has always been confused—with bizarre results. Nor, to take an output example, will society's raw and

149

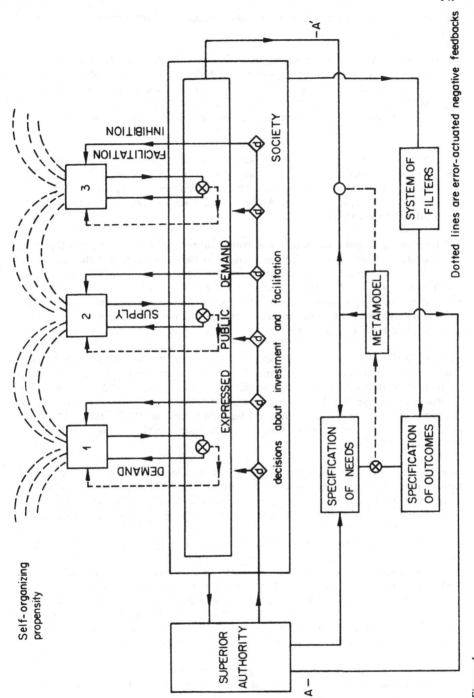

Figure 4
Societary control by self-organization under metasystemic governance.

emotional reaction to the trade figures ever again be confused with a metasystemic evaluation of their effects.

Then the question arises: What actual innovations must be made to implement the entire model? The answer is that everything structural *below* the line AÁ needs to be freshly installed. At present it does not exist. What does exist is the capability to do the things required of this below-the-line structure: indeed, some of the relevant work has been done already by professional groups scattered throughout government, the universities and industry.

The conclusion I draw is that these activities should be institutionalized forthwith. It is not a particularly expensive nor difficult operation. In the firm, and in other large corporate institutions, we should find the realization of our plan in a new kind of group—which might be called a Development Directorate. At the national level itself, we should be calling for a new kind of Cabinet Office.

In both places a continuous planning and evaluation process would begin, with feedback, in metasystemic terms—and working exclusively on the metastructure of the industry or government concerned. Such an organization would replace the teams of advisors and pundits who currently offer their subjective views at the highest level. Now properly organized, continuously presented, real-time displays of situations would be made; together with the metasystemic elucidation of their consequences, the action alternatives which are available, and their likely outcomes.

The comparison which immediately suggests itself contrasts this picture with the 'war room' of the Second World War. I cannot refrain from mentioning that I began speaking to you to the very minute on the thirtieth anniversary of the outbreak of that war; nor from pointing out that we now have a technology competent to exploit the techniques then developed, and since lost, which were at the time fumbling manual operations. (The whole of this metasystemic intention is equivalent to the fourth level of managerial hierarchy laid out in Reference 1.)

This address is too long, and I apologize for that. In conclusion, then, I content myself with a reiteration of my opening remarks. Society is in crisis. The way of life we have known is vanishing. This is a fact, which we ignore at our peril. The symptoms are all there. It is then open to a congress of this kind to make a cybernetic prediction, and to offer a solution.

My prediction is that a new kind of society will emerge, with new modes of control—which no-one actually chose, and which we probably will not like. The solution is to decide what to do, and how to do it, in the light of cybernetic discoveries as to the nature of systemic control. I have offered the makings of a blueprint. But progress requires collaboration of both government and management, and an informed public opinion. This in turn entails a new forum in the press, on the air, and in parliament; for unaccountably these matters are rarely discussed. Progress also requires a new approach to planning, and the guts to accept that change is needed—I mean change entailing actual alteration.

Alternatively, the gross instability of society, of institutional relationships, and of our economy, will de-nature the civilization to which we have attained. The society we have known will either collapse, or it will be overthrown. It is of course open to anyone to sit complacently in his own esoteric box, and wait for the sky to fall.

Reference

'PREROGATIVES OF SYSTEM in management control'
—the Eighth United Kingdom Automation Lecture.

Stafford Beer, January 1969.

The whole plea of PLATFORM FOR CHANGE
is that we ought to forget about politics
as ideologies
and revert to politics
as representing the art of the possible.
In this way we could open up
a treatment of issues
that is objective and empirical
namely scientific :
a seeking out of the best answers we can provide
to problems.

It turns out
that there is no way of forgetting about ideologies.
Pragmatism—
which after all simply says
that what is the case is true—
turns out to be a dirty *ideological* word.

> You may well have thought it naive in me
> not to have admitted this much sooner.

Most good and splendid things are naive—

> love
> friendship
> freedom.

We make them difficult and complicated
by weaving ideologies around them.
Then people are willing to die
for the ideologies
rather than for the qualities that inspired them.

It ought by now to be possible to abandon ideology
on the ground that it represents
a first and emotional shot
at saying what matters about society,
whereas mankind has now reached
an understanding of the universe and of his role in it
which orients him towards
the identification, objective study and solution
of real problems in a real context.

Let us optimistically maintain that this is so;
that the ideological hang-up is an anachronism.

A genuine problem then remains.

COLOUR CODE : YELLOW
Narrative

154

It was expressed to me in no uncertain terms
after this conference—
and especially by the delegates
from no less than three countries
(speaking independently)
who have more reason and better knowledge than I
to pinpoint the dilemma.

The issue as it came out in discussion
revolved around my depiction
of Figure 4.

In the eyes of objectors
this diagram lends specific authority
to a sinister form of state control
of what might otherwise be free institutions.

Now I am not (1 hope) as naive as I might look.
If you inspect that diagram again
you will note that I deliberately placed

> 'superior authority' at the *side of*
> and metamodelling *underneath*

the free institutions.

This was done to emphasize the logical
rather than the authoritarian
nature of metasystems.

Nonetheless, the objectors wanted to see
a box entitled something like

> 'the democratic process'

inserted on the route between
society and superior authority.

This I would not do.
It would make a political model
in the ideological sense
out of my logico-societary model.

I do not think it is for the scientist
even the management scientist
to specify the strictly political connexion
between the people and their government.
My model assumes that there is a government
and investigates how to make it effective.

COLOUR CODE : YELLOW
Narrative

But there lies the difficulty in people's minds—
we encountered it before—
that effective government
may *ipso facto* be tyrannous.

> Can it possibly be right
> that society's only protection
> against tyranny
> is that government
> should be ineffectual?

We shall return to this problem later
in a dramatic context.

COLOUR CODE : YELLOW
Narrative

The theme that efficiency and freedom are incompatible
is fundamental to mankind's thinking about government.

The issue has never been so direct and important however
as it is today
because modern technology (as will be made still clearer later)
offers orders of magnitude

        more efficiency

than ever before
and thereby constitutes
that much greater threat to freedom.

And yet we look upon technology
as liberating man
from another sort of slavery—
dominion by hunger and the rough elements.

We make no progress with the debate.
It is more than three hundred years
since Thomas Hobbes wrote a book
'occasioned by the disorders of the present time'
and claiming that the whole purpose of his *Leviathan*
was to 'set before mens eyes the mutual Relation
between Protection and Obedience'.

Insofar as PLATFORM FOR CHANGE
has the same objective
I look to the logical metasystem
to express the higher synthesis of the two
and I look to systems design itself
to build in the safeguard :

        to protect society against the seizure
        of its logical metasystem
        by illegal forces.

We have after all
continuously made the conscious attempt
to protect the metasystem of the individual person
his mentality, as underwritten by his brain,
from the equivalent seizure.
Mentality is protected by codes of conduct
among publishers, broadcasters and advertizers:
the brain itself is protected by legislation
against drugs judged to be harmful to sane operation.

COLOUR CODE : GOLD
Metalanguage

These efforts leave much to be desired
but no-one suggests
that brains should be put out of commission
until the safeguards are perfected.

Brains have power and governments have power.
They both need metasystems of a logical order
to exercise that power effectively.
How that power is exercised is a different question.
But we cannot afford to confuse

       metasystemic structures
       with structures of power themselves.

COLOUR CODE : GOLD
Metalanguage

THESIS

FIFTH STATEMENT

In seeking to design metasystems
synergistically to organize
systems of esoteric boxes
we must have a metric.

Money is the established metric
of our society;
and all attempts
to calculate societary good
in other than monetary terms
fail.

This may be because
either to abolish or to ignore money
destroys only a symbol
of a necessary calculus
to which society always returns
under some guise :
         barter of goods
their relative ease of procurement
resource allocation.

The metric of money
is too useful to abandon
but it ought to be viewed essentially
as the metric of *constraint*.

    ● Although we may fail to abolish the metric
      we also conspicuously fail
      to *use* it successfully
      in the measurement of societary good.

We are free to choose
another metric of *utility*

yielding a system
capable of regulating societary behaviour
for direct betterment—
within monetary constraints.

Call the new and hypothetical metric :

        eudemony.

COLOUR CODE : BLUE
   Thesis

AN ARGUMENT OF CHANGE

QUESTIONS
OF
METRIC

President's Address* to the joint plenary meeting of the Annual Conference of the Operational Research Society and the XVIIth International Conference of the Institute of Management Science, held at Imperial College, London, on 1st July, 1970.

*By permission of
the Operational Research Society, London.

Mr and Mrs David Stubbs wrote to the *Times* this February about the Norman Church of St. Michael at Stewkley. The church stands in the middle of a possible runway of a possible Third London Airport. The complaint was that the Roskill Commission, studying alternative sites for the airport, and applying cost-benefit analysis, had adopted a wrong criterion for valuing the church. It seems that an irreplaceable twelfth-century work of art was being valued at the sum for which the church is insured against fire.

This led to considerable discussion. Can we indeed place a monetary value on a priceless heritage? If it really is price*less*, presumably not. Then why not have the cake and eat it—by moving the church, some said. The proper cost would then be the price paid for the move. But the Norman church at Stewkley is not the same church if it is somewhere else, replied others. The correspondence was effectively closed by Mr R J Osborn. He said the £ 100 spent on building a church in 1182, when discounted at ten percent to 1982, represented roughly £ 1,300,000,000,000,000,000,000,000,000,000,000. He did not add: 'stuff that in your cost-benefit and compute it'.

There is, to put it mildly, considerable divergence between these two estimates of value. The first noteworthy point is that cheerfully to adopt either extreme immediately solves the problem posed by this church. At fire-insurance value, the existence of the church is virtually irrelevant to the measure of social benefit; at the DCF evaluation, nothing conceivably matters *except* the preservation of the church. Then if we look at the problem through game-theoretic spectacles (with respect to the church), we are in either case confronted by a dominant strategy.

There could be a compromise value, of course, defined precisely as one which *would* affect the outcome of the decision when balanced against other factors. Now that is a point worth considering. Once we start, for reasons of good sense, to devise methods of evaluation deliberately intended to produce an effect on quantified judgment, so that we do not appear absurd, then it is very difficult indeed to ignore the actual effect those chosen methods will exert. And so I very much fear (since we are all human), that the arbitrary selection of the technique will not remain arbitrary for long, but become something tendentious.

The second point to note about that story is this. *We measure what it is convenient to measure.* That is natural enough; unobjectionable, too, so long as it makes sense. But I have lived for twenty-five years with the sneaking suspicion that as often as not there is something terribly wrong about taking the convenient option. Operational Research grew to a recognizable activity during the Second World War. Following the famous dictum of Lord Kelvin, we set out to measure what we observed. But enemies do not like being observed; and they will wriggle very fast, if they are observed, to avoid being measured. Thus it came about that questions of metric were an early pre-occupation of OR.

Today, I venture to suggest, we confront civil problems by uncritically accepting the measures that are readily to hand. There is no motivated enemy, anxious to evade and deceive us, true. But nature is an enemy of another sort, and a very old enemy indeed.

It may well be in the nature of aesthetic problems, such as the Stewkley parish church problem, that they are insusceptible to economic measures. Surely that should not surprise us, because the problem is in no valid sense an economic problem. People are persuaded that it is so, only because econometrics is the only tool available to use.

Those of us, most of us, who have worked in industry ought to be alive to this issue for another reason. Not only may the convenient metric not be particularly relevant, it may also be misconstrued. Again that would be because we, as professionals, have taken too little trouble to study not only the metric itself, but also its manner of application. I learned an unforgettable lesson about this, late in the Forties, soon after moving from the Army into the steel industry.

Studying the movement of steel ingots through a battery of preheating furnaces, I used the convenient records already available from the shop-floor. There was a clearly specified printed heading on the record form saying: *Number*. That was excellent: the number of ingots in a stack on a bogie was exactly what interested me, since bogies were rarely full—a fact which represented an opportunity cost. I discovered with amazement that the statistical distribution of this *Number* was exactly rectangular. It was only the gross improbability of this finding that led me to the empirical study I ought to have made in the first place. The heading 'Number' referred to the identity of the furnace, and not to the ingots-per-bogie; it was not surprising then that each furnace figured with exactly the same frequency as the others in the records.

So it seems we may uncritically adopt an inappropriate metric, because it is the accepted currency in which to discuss a topic, and even then we may misconstrue it. There is a third source of disaster. It arises from seizing upon a convenient but idiotic metric, in circumstances where none is already established. There has been a sensational public display of this error, also this year, to which I draw your attention. It occurred in attempting to answer the vital social question, pinpointed by the Home Secretary himself: whether violence and an over-permissive morality in real life were causally connected with displays of violence and sexuality on television.

For the whole of the week ending April 5th 1970, three newspaper reporters respectively watched the three TV channels we operate in this country for the whole of their broadcasting time. They measured what was convenient to measure: namely, frequencies of objectionable words or incidents. That is not because this is an accepted metric; presumably it was because there was nothing else to do. As a result, we now know that there were seventy-one deaths on television during that week, while the word 'bloody' was broadcast forty-seven times. As to teaching youth that its ends may be achieved by threats of violence, this possibility was inculcated into our young by a truly appalling example, which solemnly appears in the record. We know that character is formed early on; well, the example occurred in a programme called *Watch With Mother*. 'Come in', cried a mother duck to her ducklings, *'or you will have a special reason for not sitting down tomorrow'*.

It turned out that only one percent, at the most, of the whole week's broadcasting contained objectionable material—even by that ludicrous standard. Now just how useful is that particular statistic, and how useful would be any other statistics collected according to that metric? Surely the whole approach is totally worthless. The commentary I saw which accurately demolished it was not written by a management scientist, I am sad to report, but by that thoughtful critic Mr Milton Shulman. He pointed out that objectionable incidents as such matter only if they are imitated, and that the imitative urge applies only to a small, psychotic, unstable group. What does matter very much, in a world of adolescence in which television may have more influence than the 'classical' environmental factors such as home, school and church, is the set of values it propagates. And that propagation could easily be done without showing objectionable incidents, or uttering bad language, at all. What price the metric, then?

Here, in brief, is Mr Shulman's excellent catalogue of five points which do bear significantly on the problem of violence, and which cannot be measured at all on the chosen metric. (i) Violence is done by good men for good reasons, and the best man is he who is best at violence. (ii) Violence does not hurt very much: its consequences are 'hidden, diminished, anaesthetized'. (iii) There is no pity for the victims of violence. (iv) Society demands no explanation for violence; instead of standing trial, the hero is 'rewarded with a smiling blonde and approving fade-out music'. (v) Since life is, as television appears to make it, 'trivial, frivolous, greedy, silly' is not violence the moral way to change it?

I want to congratulate Milton Shulman on that powerful indictment, and I wish he had included a similar catalogue of inducements to sexual permissiveness. But we are not here to indict television. The indictment we face concerns our own inability to come forward with a sensible way of measuring these things. If the Home Secretary really wants evidence about the social effects of television, as well he should, then our profession ought to have a valid approach to the appropriate mensuration—and it seems to me we have not.

Indeed we are in worse case. It was (hopefully) not an OR man who devised the experiment I have just criticized; but we are prone to the same error, which is clearly labelled *reductionism*. Aristotle taught us analysis, and the Schoolmen taught us about the reduction of the syllogism. All of that is fine in its place; but if our only scientific tool is the analytic reduction of a system to its components, so that the very nature of the system itself as a viable entity is lost, so that its synergies are denatured, so that it is nothing but a bag of bits, then we do not deserve the name of scientist in a world of complex systems and complicated syntax.

In the Operational Research Society we have recently instituted a new attack on the problems of collaboration between manager and scientist, a symbiosis to which the Institute of Management Science has I think already, and laudably, given more attention than we. May I remark at this point then, in parenthesis, that most of the criticism our own Council has received about our efforts has been of the reductionist kind. There is *no item* in our proposals, says this criticism, that is either novel or convincing; and I am prepared to believe that is true. But the total plan, in the opinion of many of our members, commends itself as both novel and convincing. Of such integrative stuff are system and synergy made.

I spoke also, just now, of a complicated syntax—as well as of complex systems. And I do reckon that language itself is a major element in the questions of metric that I raise today. For if we are prone to embrace a reductionist fallacy, we can most readily do so through picking the fabric of words apart.....

> *To-morrow, and to-morrow, and to-morrow,*
> *Creeps in this petty pace from day to day,*
> *To the last syllable of recorded time;*

'What is all this rubbish then? There is nothing novel about this: we have heard every one of those words before. It is not very convincing, either. Scientifically speaking, the records of time are not all written yet; they do not consist of syllables; there is no proof offered that the pace is petty—we have after all achieved

28,000 miles per hour on the way to the speed of light; and, speaking as someone who cares about efficiency, I might add that nothing is achieved by the reiteration of the word "tomorrow"—which is logically redundant.'

That is how the reductionist operates: within the last ten days I have heard an argument almost as stupid as this. And so I say: beware of reductionism of both systems and syntax; as of the irrelevant metric; as of the established metric; as of error in interpretation itself. And I ask too: how shall we measure for our masters the novel situations—which matter to them because they must needs cope with them, and to us because it is our job?

I realize that I am talking about the need for measures of utility, and that the whole history of economics could probably be written in terms of its treatment of this concept. Therefore I shall try to illuminate a number of issues by reference to some discoveries made by economics in the last hundred years. The first of these issues was settled (one might not think so, looking around today) nearly that long ago.

Should we assert an additive axiom for sets of utilities, or are general utilities non-additive functions of contributory utilities? The switch between those two alternative views seems to have come in about 1880: an early date indeed, in any field of human enquiry, for the recognition of what is essentially a systems viewpoint.

So Gossen and Jevons were out, and before the turn of the century Edgeworth and Marshall were in—and clashing merrily. 'We cannot trust the marginal utility of a commodity to indicate its total utility' wrote Alfred Marshall. Because he thought in terms of consumables, he used the example of the commodity: salt. We cannot survive without salt; but when we have enough salt, there really is no point in buying any more—whatever the marginal price.

Now, should one take that attitude to Norman churches? There are other Norman churches than the threatened one at Stewkley, and perhaps (as Dr Johnson said of green fields) when you have seen one you have seen them all. Let us carry forward from that the obvious point: whether Stewkley has a significant marginal utility for you, the consumer of Norman churches, depends on *who* you are, and *where* you are.

The second issue emerged, not many years later, from the work of Pareto. If we abandon the calculation of absolute differences between alternative pay-offs, and simply order our preferences for them, we arrive at the idea of indifference curves. When the pay-off between a group of alternatives is judged equal, or indifferently good, we have a stationary point in a judgmental n-space from which to assess what is better or worse. This holds even when the sets of things compared are wholly dissimilar. If we now turn this static indifference map into the dynamic systems model which we need in order to offer any really useful account of society for any particular purpose, we confront a very cybernetic notion indeed, and another point to be carried forward.

It is that we should regard the various identifiable sub-systems of society, the social institutions which I have elsewhere defined under the term 'esoteric boxes', as opaque. They have inputs; they have outputs. Then we shall set up comparators across the outputs of separate boxes, and provide feedbacks to their respective inputs, with a view to detecting levels of activity for the boxes themselves which yield indifferently good results for them all.

Thus we are no longer faced with a requirement to find analytic measures for the micro-systems we have failed to analyse, and seek useful answers instead at the macro-level where the social preferences actually emerge.

For example: it is a very long time since Sir Charles Goodeve noted that a population drift would be hard to measure in terms of the metrics on which individual decisions to move home were in fact taken—better pay, better concerts, snobbery, and so on almost indefinitely. We should have to devise a very complicated decision model, and then interview a sample of those moving, assessing each of them in terms of each of the model's parameters. He proposed instead that we measure the rate of drift itself, and also its rate of change (which is not difficult)—and then simply interpret the results in terms of potential difference.

Then what is the metric? I suspect we do not use these handy ways of measuring because we do not know *what* it is that a change of potential actually measures. In this case Sir Charles explained that it must be some complicated image of well-being; and he chose to call that by the entirely suitable Greek word 'eudemony'. This is one of the Greek words for happiness, though it comes nearer to meaning prosperity than ecstasy. You will find 'eudemony' and its adjective 'eudemonic' in the Shorter Oxford—with an attribution to Jeremy Bentham, which is appropriate. I ask you to bear with me in my attempt to regain currency for this moribund term, since I shall need it today very much. Meanwhile, the immediate point is that we may well be using unsatisfactory metrics, simply for want of recognition that others, though unnamed or unfamiliar, are to hand.

It appears to me that despite the modern work on indifference of such mathematically ingenious people as Herman Wold, this type of thinking has received too little attention—and that the reason is clear. The whole training of scientists and other numerate scholars emphasizes the potency of cardinality over ordinality: it is indisputable that cardinal metrics contain more information than do ranking schemata. It is sad to have to say, however, that they do so only if they exist. Have we faced up to the fact that even crude ordinal metrics may be more useful than the cardinal metrics we cannot actually devise?

The tool that might yet serve this cause to advantage is the theory of games, in which apparently ordinal measures become cardinal in a very specific sense (identified by William Baumol). This is that game-theoretic models are meant to be predictive of preferred action *by numerical calculation,* which is to say without asking anyone what they would rather do, once pay-off preferences have been subjectively decided. (Pollsters might note that methodological suggestion.)

This argument suggests that the number of murders, rapes and four-letter words published by television per week is a computable function of choices made about the sort of society society wants, on some set of scales dealing with permissiveness—or as we used to call it: freedom. That seems to me very likely; and it does not conflict with the earlier conclusion that the metric criticized would not measure the effect of television on society. What it does emphasize, and this is the next point to carry forward, is this. The embodiment of the choice between television strategies revealed in the broadcasting of actual programmes, closes a definable loop with a very short cycle time.

There is the citizen with a set of social values; there is the producer seeking (he says) to interpret these; there is the interpretation itself—called the programme; and there is the citizen again: the citizen *qua* viewer, *qua* comparator. Here is the dynamic system of which we spoke, with its unanalyzed components, its absence of an established metric. Then what is the commodity that moves around this network? Shall we say it is information? Then perhaps we are already entrapped. It soon appears that we shall need a model of the sorts of programme being broadcast, complete with measures of their informational content; a model which by its very existence and nature establishes norms for the number of murders and rapes. And the feedback from the citizen will indeed seem to consist of an irate phone call to the duty officer at Television Centre saying: 'I have just heard my eleventh four letter word this week, whereas ten is all I can tolerate'.

Let us rather call the commodity that flows round the network eudemony. Then it is the *frequency* of negative eudemonic response that affects the producers, rather than the content of the message—which inference again seems to reflect the facts very well. Please note also that we measure the intensity of sensation in our own bodies not by the content of neural messages, not by variations in amplitude of the signal or any kind of modulation, but exactly by the *rate* at which uniform and discrete spikes of potential arrive in the sensory cortex.

So protesting TV viewers, according to this model and this metric, are simply registering negeudemony at some level of intensity, and their protests may be offset by some other approving viewers who channel positive feedback into the system. The system's reaction, having measured the eudemonic balance, would be to insert either a low-pass filter into the broadcasting part of the loop, or for that matter a high-pass filter in the second case. This inference too seems to be borne out by the facts. Then if the whole system is operating correctly, why is there so much concern about the social effects of TV?

The emerging model can help us there too. We have so far supposed that society sets a standard, and that we are considering a straightforward servomechanism which adjusts output to that standard. But society is a learning machine, and the control we are modelling is really an *adaptive* controller. If the comparator, conceived now as being part of an evolutionary system (which society surely is), discovers that departures from its standard *increase* society eudemony, what then? 'Errors' are supposed to be inimical to the system, and in this case to decrease eudemony; that is why we employ error-actuated negative feedback. But the notion of adaptation entails a metasystem, speaking a metalanguage in which the system's standards themselves are set. This means that a metamessage feeds back from the comparator to say this: 'The metasystem I serve approves of your "error"; I am adjusting my standard to your signal. Just keep the increments of change as small as you can, otherwise we shall go into a state of mutually uncontrollable oscillation'.

This inference from the model in turn appears to me to fit the observed facts; and the oscillations we have observed have indeed been undamped from time to time. If we now add a further construction to the system, in the cause of good modelling, to the effect that many television producers are themselves high-pass filters anyway, we begin to see just how unstable the total system might well be. Therefore I conclude that the problems of television as a possibly bad social influence are not about four letter words at the micro-level of programmes, but about instabilities at the macro-level of social adaptation; and that point carries forward too.

From this vantage point, moreover, we can well understand why the call is often heard (particularly from the parliamentary back-benches) for some kind of consumers' association intended to monitor the BBC. The real demand according to our model is for feedback from the adaptive social metasystem; but it is always misrepresented by both the BBC and its own proponents as a demand for the kind of systemic feedback that already exists. The BBC operates a highly sophisticated and sustained type of audience research; it has a very elaborate edifice of advisory bodies; it listens to all those telephone calls *and* to Mrs Mary Whitehouse. These are all mechanisms for supplying systemic feedback. No wonder the Corporation feels it is doing enough. But our model has already shown that these controls are not directed to the instabilities that matter. And, just for the record, it is obvious that a consumers' association would not help either: because it would inevitably operate on the systemic—not the meta-systemic—circuit.

The circuit that matters in this example can only be that connecting parliament with the corporation through the Minister and the Board of Governors, and it is this tenuous linkage which would have to be strengthened in order to attain metastability. It is obvious, then, why nothing is done. The existence of powerful societary servos at this level would offer no ready way of distinguishing between wise government of the medium and political interference in the content of broadcasting. Neither parliament nor the BBC, and still less the public, would be sure that freedom of speech was preserved. That is why the linkage remains tenuous, and must be seen as such, given existing methods of organization. Naturally, I am calling for the redesign of organizational structure at the metasystemic level—I always do. And here is one audience, hopefully, that will not demand to know precisely what structure is recommended before the OR has been done.

Now this same model applies, as I see it, to every public service; and the argument about government intervention and non-intervention is all about this missing servo at the metasystemic level. Government cannot have a health service, for example, costing two thousand million pounds in taxpayers' money, and *either* leave it alone to be what it likes to be, *or* try to run it as if government understood medicine better than doctors and nurses. This is a terrible dilemma, and we try to solve it at the wrong level by directly controlling the pay of the medical profession. That leads to a national scandal, and to the unexampled situation whereby a profession whose self-image is all about idealism, about a very real dedication to the plight of the sick, can hardly believe that it hovers on the brink of taking industrial action—as striking is euphemistically called. We are trying to control the system itself, which is quite stable on its existing servos, instead of the meta-system—which is unstable as hell. And again I attribute this mainly to the use of the wrong metric, which is money—which is obsessional in our society. A health service, more than any other public service, deals not in money but in eudemony.

So this brings me directly to the last lesson I shall draw from the history of social utility as an economic concept. You must have wondered when I should get round to John Maynard Keynes and the year 1936—when the *General Theory* was published. It is thirty-four years since Keynes tore apart the notion that the wage must be equal to the marginal product of labour. He noted that if labour supply really were a function of real wages alone, 'the supply curve for labour would shift bodily with every movement of prices'. It does not; and clearly Keynes was right to question whether 'the existing level of real wages accurately measures the marginal disutility of labour'. I want to add, in the light of all we have learned since those days about the socialization of welfare, that the level of real wages does not seem to measure marginal disutility in the social services at all. Otherwise we should today have no doctors or nurses, no teachers, and no policemen. They would all be members of SOGAT.

Money is terribly important, both to those paying and to those paid. But money is nonetheless an epiphenomenon of a system which actually runs on eudemony. It is for this reason that I have come to see money as a constraint on the behaviour of eudemonic systems, rather than to see eudemony as a by-product of monetary systems.

My own life is certainly about eudemony: is not yours?
Ἡ εὐδαιμονία τῶν αὐτάρκων ἔστι
said Aristotle—eudemony is for the self-sufficient. One cannot exert any measure of self containment without enough money to cope with one's perceived needs—whatever they happen to be. The same is true for the firm. Its plans have to be financed, its cash flows have to be positive; otherwise the firm cannot realize its own potential. But don't tell me that the firm is about maximizing profit: I have not encountered this economic fiction in real life yet. As to government, it is precisely to do with eudemony, and its budgets aim simply and solely to create eudemonic conditions.

If you and I, and the firm, and the government are to finance our needs, we are all calling for a steady metabolism of funds. Thus our control systems are designed to hold money flows steady. Taxation operates to stop me from adopting an income-maximizing policy. Taxation, the Prices and Incomes Board, and organized labour operate to stop the firm from adopting a profit-maximization policy: instead, it seeks to maintain its rate of return on capital. The main role of a post-Keynesian government is to offset local instabilities in the economic system, not to run at a surplus overall. All three of us, for our various reasons, are actually seeking to maximize eudemony within monetary constraints.

Then we are using the wrong metric. Cost-benefit analysis converts eudemony into money, which is fine for so long as the money-metric obeys the rules of mensuration: to be additive, to be linear, to be so formulated as to make sense of a maximizing objective function. For all the reasons I have given, money fails to be the metric we need. So if we want a decision about the Norman church at Stewkley, we must take it in terms of eudemony and no other. We can tart-up the decision afterwards, and rationalize what we have done in the established metric of money. But the decision is eudemonically pre-empted before we get to that stage of the cost-benefit game—a game which is therefore, and in essence, meretricious.

This discourse becomes emphatic at its most tentative point, and didactic now that there is nothing left to teach. Because eudemony is a behavioural artefact, I cannot tell you what it 'really' is; because it is measurable only as a potential difference, I can discuss it only in terms of equilibria, and not in terms of absolute values. And yet that fits with the story of man, for whom the search for happiness is held by many to be illusory; and it fits with a Buddhist enlightenment, which is about closing the gap between attainment and desire. Social utility seems to me to be concerned with the design and operation of systems that will keep the gap small. If those systems fail, then the whole population marches to the South East; television becomes a massively disruptive force; the government could fall because of Stewkley; and there is no more health, education or security.

Thus I am calling for the design of eudemonic metasystems, working in new metrics, which do not exist just because they have not been needed before. Issues of social utility have been with mankind for ever, it is true. They were not hitherto obtrusive, however, because our energies were consumed in the effort to survive. It is the rise of an expensive technology competent to guarantee survival that poses these problems of choice, and at the same time constitutes in itself the biggest threat to survival that man has ever faced. Let us look at the points carried forward in this talk, and at the conceptual model we have built, and see how much we seem to know about utility and those very questions of metric. First of all, utility is not a number—and certainly not a number of pounds or dollars. Utility is a continuous function of system. Such a system cannot be static, as are so many systems described in economic theory: it must be dynamic in its very essence. I mean that it is not just a question of making our picture of the world move, but that the movement of the world is the subject matter of the picture. Next, such a system is not a closed micro-system, like the 'Robinson Crusoe' economy; nor is it an open macro-system—because at the macro-level it is so rich in feedback. It is a system concerned more with its own structure than with its internal transfer functions, a system whose behaviour is better understood through its lagged feedbacks than its input-output schemata. It deals in indifferent choices of pay-off rather than optimal courses of action, and these choices have to do with equilibria, rather than the nature of 'the good'.

In saying all of that we reject most of the models of social utility that have ever been constructed, and we question the metric in which those models are couched. For they deal in the accepted measurements by which social institutions are already stably governed. But the choices we have to make lie only ostensibly within those systems, and are deter-mined only ostensibly on the scales of their accustomed metrics. The choices are really made at the metasystemic level, in terms of eudemony; and here our institutions are wildly unstable because the required servo-controls do not exist, and no-one knows what the metric may be. Instead of measurement, we have a value system; and it is just this value system which the electorate judges.

It is inevitably on this question of subjective judgment that I must end. It is the judgment about eudemony that builds the value system that sets the standards we make numerical for a particular institution, so that its modus operandi may be computable. But how are we to agree on these eudemonic judgments? It was the first point we carried forward in this talk: *who* are you, *where* are you, when you judge—and is 'society' simply the con-sensus of 'you' and 'you' and 'you', or something more?

If you and I diametrically disagree about some issue of social utility, it does not mean that a right answer lies somewhere on the line between us. In the first place we may both have misconceived the problem altogether. But more importantly, each one of us is always right—because judgments always depend on who and where is the judge. There is a real and independent world out there in which change happens, and affairs are well or ill conducted. Each of us reacts to this from a special condition of partial knowledge and prior disposition, and our metric works outward from a base of eudemonic indifference. I put this earlier by saying that 'we have a stationary point in a judgmental n-space from which to assess what is better or worse'. But for each one of us that point is, theoretically, personal and unique.

I have sought illumination about this in a model from Relativity Theory, where there exists an obvious parallel. There is a unique turning-point in any system of time-reckoning for which a rate of change du, involving a rate of change proportional to du, is in fact proportional to du^2. Eddington says: 'In adopting a time-reckoning such that this stationary point corresponds to his own motion, the observer is imposing a symmetry on space and time with respect to himself'. It seems to me that each of us stands in a similarly unique situation with respect to social utility, and that we do indeed impose an egocentric symmetry on the society we presume to observe and to judge.

The well-known consequence of all this in Relativity is that the notion of simultaneity breaks down. If the model holds, then, the notion of an objective social utility has no meaning; utility does not exist apart from the observer who tries to assess it. I expect this is right, but I am not sure whether it matters. Perhaps a democracy finds a broad consensus for which these divergencies of individual subjective judgment are irrelevant. Or perhaps it is just those miniscule divergencies which become amplified into a force sufficient to blow society apart.

Of this much I *am* sure: some such force exists; it is very much at work. It must be a product of eudemonic change, and it threatens to extinguish us all. I would like to identify and measure this force before it gets me.

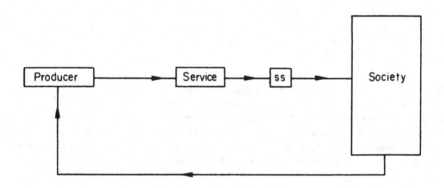

Figure 1

Any social service is based on the reading of societary need which the service's producer begins by interpreting. He provides the service, at a 'service standard' (ss), which standard is submitted to society to evaluate.

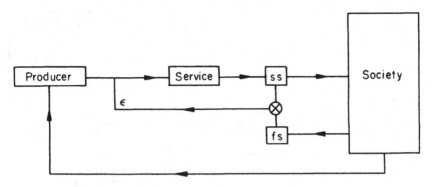

Figure 2

Society for its part promulgates a formal standard (fs) that it intends to accept. This standard is set in many ways, by advisory bodies and any other mechanism which gives shape to social judgment. A comparator ($\otimes$) can then be imagined as continuously comparing fs and ss, and feeding back an error-correction signal (ε) intending to modify the service so that fs is attained by ss.

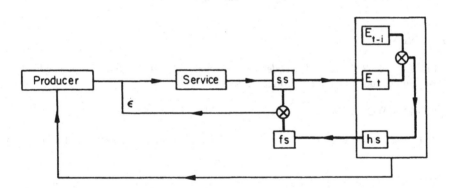

Figure 3

But society itself is a learning system. It continuously compares ($\otimes$) the eudemony (E: defined in text) experienced from the service *now*, at time t, with its stored knowledge of eudemony at an earlier time, $t-1$. This causes it to adjust its hidden standards (hs) which in turn modify the formal standards (fs). This adaptive controller may operate (as perhaps in broadcasting) to bring fs nearer to ss—even though the error (ε) feedback signal is supposedly operating to bring ss nearer to fs.

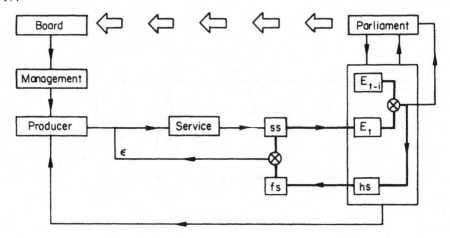

Figure 4

This social metasystem (the thick black loop) exercises some kind of effect on the service's producer through tenuous feedback mechanisms at the government level—for government 'expresses the will of the people', or (more realistically) is sensitive to changes in social eudemony. Yet government finds it difficult in a democracy to exert control over the service's producer and management, except through its appointments to the Board governing the service. There is a shortage of structure and mechanism on this plane, which currently transmits too attenuated a feedback signal.

REFERENCES

ALFRED MARSHALL, *Principles of Economics* (1890), Text and Notes edited by C W Guillebaud, Macmillan, London, 1920.

HERMAN WOLD, *Demand Analysis*, Wiley, New York, 1953.

WILLIAM J BAUMOL, *Economic Theory and Operation Analysis*, Prentice Hall, London, 1961.

JOHN MAYNARD KEYNES, *The General Theory of Employment, Interest and Money* (1936), Macmillan, London, 1951.

R H MACMILLAN, *Non-Linear Control Systems Analysis*, Pergamon. Oxford, 1961.

A S EDDINGTON, *The Mathematical Theory of Relativity* (1923), Cambridge, 1963.

CHARLES GOODEVE, 'Science and Social Organization', *Proceedings of the Second International Conference on Operational Research*, (Aix-en-Provence, 1960) EUP, London, 1961.

The Argument of Change just presented
was argued at a unique meeting.
It was the first time that a collaborative venture
had been undertaken by the two Societies concerned.
The home team (the Operational Research Society)
arranged its annual conference to overlap with
the international meeting of the Institute of Management Science—
which although based in the United States
has national chapters . . . . .

For the second time in these pages
I am recording the presence of a galaxy of international 'names'
at London's Imperial College;
and for the second time also
the pleasure of a Banquet in Guildhall
graced by the presence of the Lord Màyor—
now Sir Ian Bowater.

I find it all the more poignant
that the intersection between the two meetings—
the first of cyberneticians
the second of OR men and management scientists—
was almost nil.

Given that all of us share a message
about the effective organization of society
it seems inept, to say the least,
that we do not organize ourselves very effectively.

This also struck Professor Ross Ashby very forcibly,
and during this year of my project herein reported
we both joined with Dr Rose
to attempt some kind of affiliation on an international basis
between all those major Societies
concerned with these areas of study.

Dr Rose had organized the successful London Cybernetic Congress,
and had even obtained from the majority of those then present
a mandate to try and create a world-wide organization.
Professor Ashby's immense international prestige
and his enduring membership of the Board of the Namur Association
augured well. I had just been made a governor
and president-elect of the Society for General Systems Research,
in addition to my other offices, and moreover
we had prodigious support from leading Russian cyberneticians.

COLOUR CODE : YELLOW
Narrative

It is a thought-provoking commentary
on the innovative exercises on which all of us are engaged
and their great difficulty
that this initiative met with such hostility.

I have no idea whether anything can yet be made of it.
Meanwhile the abortive efforts of 1970, the year of my project,
are testimony to my awareness of the likely confusion
even in the minds of those having professional knowledge
between
                        metasystems and power structures.

But the universal suspicion of the metasystemic role
by no means proves that it ought not to exist—
only that we do not yet understand
how to play it.

The PLATFORM FOR CHANGE
was at any rate commanding some attention.
Questions of Metric
provoked another round of discussions.
People said in particular

                        it is a pretty notion—
                        but the hedonistic calculus
                        is a discredited ideal.
                        Besides, you have not succeeded
                        in *doing* anything with it.

The big problem about providing an effective demonstration
of any novel approach in any field
is that you need a commission to do it—
                        opportunity, time, money
and above all that you need a situation
in which people are already conscious of the problems
and are ready—
                        to listen, to think, to experiment.
Such desiderata are not easily met in Britain.

                        A country that can make
                        decimalization of the coinage
                        into a major innovative issue,
                        pretending it had taken its life in its hands
                        will find it hard indeed to embark
                        on changes that really matter.

'In programme after programme', said *Punch* of the use of television,
'familiar faces pretended to a fashionable bafflement and laughingly
discussed the changeover as though it involved them in the most

COLOUR CODE : YELLOW
Narrative

recondite reaches of higher mathematics . . . . . . They showed bits of
film in which the man in the street equated the monetary exercise
with the threat of the Spanish Armada or Hitler's blitz . . . . .
Why do we have to be such clots? and why does TV encourage us
in our clottishness?'

We are like this.
We need managers of affairs
who are not ashamed to be caught
with a new word on their lips
or a new thought in their heads,
and are ready to treat people
as better than fools.

        Note : while the fashionable were claiming
                that they would never understand the new coinage,
                little girls in shops made the instant switch
                with complete aplomb.

These potential managers of affairs
. surely exist —
there is no shortage.
Equally surely
our culture trains them
away from the new words and ideas
and their respect for people.

All of this has to do
with Homo Faber
of course

and with his institutions
which carefully propagate
languages
in which the questions men most want to ask

        are undecidable

and at the same time propagate

        suspicion and disrespect
        of and for
        talk that is metalinguistic
        structure that is metasystemic.

It also has to do
with a conceptual model of the Earth as

        exploitable

COLOUR CODE : YELLOW
Narrative

whether in terms of

its resources in the ground
its resources of people.

Then let us take time off from this narrative reflection
to build into the systems analysis of the thesis
what the Arguments of Change

CYBERNETIC CYTOBLAST and
QUESTIONS OF METRIC

have had to contribute,
and also to examine
metalinguistically
Homo Faber's models of the Earth.

COLOUR CODE : YELLOW
Narrative

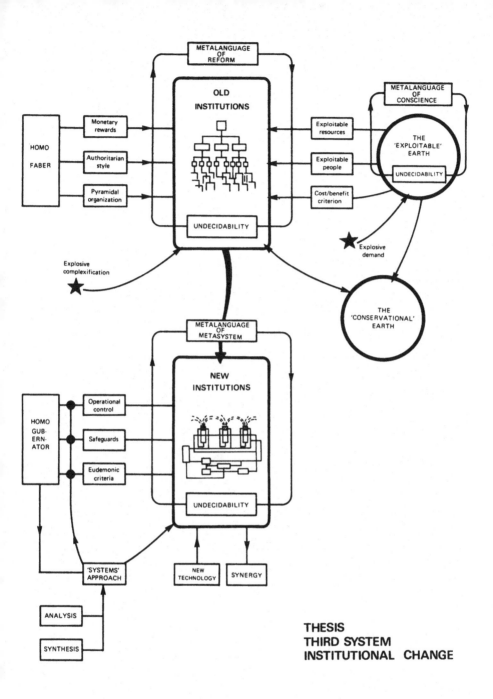

**THESIS
THIRD SYSTEM
INSTITUTIONAL CHANGE**

COLOUR CODE : BLUE
Thesis

Homo Faber exploited the resources of the Earth
without a second thought.

Earth, fire, air and water
were free
and so indeed were the people
        breeding freely
who turned out to be available
        depending on your station.

The economics of all this
for some four thousand years
up to the Industrial Revolution
are most interesting.

Things were happening on too small a scale
for any potential defect in the model of
the 'exploitable' Earth
to be detected.

As to the use of people
this was remarkably Keynesian
in economic terms.

How and why do you build
        Egyptian pyramids
        Greek temples
        Roman roads and baths
        Indian mausoleums and temples
        Aztec monuments
        Gothic cathedrals
        extravaganzas and follies
When most people are poor, starving, wretched?

It is all of this
that keeps the economy going.
And as long as the Earth is exploitable
and people expendable
precious little cost is incurred.

There is no ostensible economic benefit—
the benefit is perceived as eudemonic—
but there is a genuine economic benefit
which is a store of kinetic energy
like an economic flywheel.

Following the Industrial Revolution
and following the great age of iron and steam—

COLOUR CODE : GOLD
Metalanguage

an age great especially
in self-confidence, self-satisfaction
and sheer damage—
explosive demand
brings us all to the edge of an abyss.

The exploitable Earth is manifestly running out :
fossil fuels have been nearly expended
both mineral and biological stuff
have been depleted
and the latter hideously contaminated . . . . .

Profligate consumption
has exposed the inadequacy of the model
and we move
into a conservational mode.

Meanwhile
for most of the world's people
there is no ostensible economic benefit,
although the affluent minority
is convinced that it has secured
a eudemonic benefit.

Searching for the genuine economic benefit
we may identify yet
the economic flywheel :

   armament and space research
   inextricably intermingled.

However, these two
may be eudemonically if not economically or politically
distinguished.
In terms of eudemony—
   moon walking
is indistinguishable not from warfare
but from the pyramids, temples, roads, baths, monuments and cathedrals.

Why does the old trick
not quite come off any longer?
Surely the answer is that

   people see through it.

We are not heading in a direction people fundamentally approve;
the shoddy goodies no longer measure or satisfy the eudemonic need;
people have become deeply cynical about the advertizing culture
   needed to guarantee that they do;

COLOUR CODE : GOLD
Metalanguage

and the necessary flywheels rock on their bearings—
because they are no longer perceived as underwritten by

> magic
> ancestor cults
> religion
> or even patriotism—
>> except for the countries concerned.

But above all
people begin to see through the bogus claim
that unlimited economic expansion
is either the highest good
or even a plausible prospect.
(Indeed in historical perspective
this is a recent, local and very odd belief.)

Depending upon the person concerned
this intuition may be reached
in a great many ways—
which is why it so threatens the status quo.

Consider :

- you just may not like the life
  that the culture persists in saying
  you are bound to like

- you may begin to recognize
  without knowing why
  that you are trapped
  by economic escalation

- you may well despair about
  environmental decay

- you may be overwhelmed
  by the conviction that
  the management of affairs
  in incompetent

- you may assimilate and accept
  arguments to show that
  the exploitable Earth model
  will not hold good

- you may come to reject
  the cultural commitment to policies
  necessarily determined
  by cost-benefit criteria

COLOUR CODE : GOLD
Metalanguage

as inoperable in a society
with multiple objectives.

For any or all of these reasons
and for any number more
people are seeking to question
the whole of the format
whereby (see the diagram)
Homo Faber is connected to his exploitable Earth
by the old institutions.

This is creating

a massive anthology
of undecidable propositions.

there is simply no way
of saying any of this
in the language.

Finally
it is worth asking the question
whether the third systems diagram is right
in its handling of the new model of

the 'conservational' Earth.

It seems time to say that this model springs
from the metalinguistic consideration
of certain undecidable propositions
in the 'exploitable' Earth model.

For example
propositions about running out of resources
are undecidable
in a language of limitless expansion.

This is so obtrusive
that the model has (very rapidly) been changed.

However, the whole gamut of undecidable propositions
has not been examined—
with the result that the model has been adjusted to the language
not the language to the model.

We are left with the old language
and all its undecidability,
having merely avoided
a particular contradiction . . . . .

COLOUR CODE : GOLD
Metalanguage

This is the reason why
the new model is shown as connected
to the set of old institutions,
rather than to the hypothetical new set
shown on the diagram.

By the same token
there is no way of showing
how the new concept of eudemony
could be fitted into
the set of old institutions
and the extant language of Homo Faber.

It appears as a tool of Homo Gubernator
as a metric of the new institutions
we must hope to create.

COLOUR CODE : GOLD
Metalanguage

On that last point,
as the first year of the project wore on
I became increasingly convinced
that the whole development
of the conservational movement

　　　　　looking so splendid
　　　　　and responsible

was already completely snarled up
in the old undecidability.
If so, the matter is too important
to leave at a justification
of a line on a diagram.

Then please take notice
that the problem is respectably argued—
by which I mean argued in a language that people hear—
in a later Argument of Change
called The Liberty Machine.

Now we left the narrative
to look at the state of the argument

　　　　　about organizations
　　　　　their metasystems
　　　　　the role of eudemony
　　　　　and man's model of the Earth,

and I now want to return
to the explicit charge
that having set up the measure of eudemony
I was able to *do* nothing with it.

When I introduced this notion
in Questions of Metric,
and showed how to model it in terms of

　　　　　comparators
　　　　　measuring and feeding back
　　　　　an error-correcting signal

I knew very well
what I should try to do next.

I had in fact been invited by the Home Office
to deliver the Sir Frank Newsam Memorial Lecture
in the year of the PLATFORM FOR CHANGE.

COLOUR CODE : YELLOW
Narrative

This Lecture is always delivered
to an audience of the country's senior policemen,
and deals in some aspect of law and order.

Have you noticed that
'law-and-order'
has become close to a dirty word?
The confusion of two languages here
is highly dangerous.

To put forward an Argument of Change
in this context
was daunting.
But I had to try.

The last systems diagram showed
the concept of eudemony
as a tool and a metric
of new institutions :

it cannot be fitted, I argued,
into the old.
Then I asked myself what I was trying to do
in the Newsam Lecture—
for surely the police force
is an old institution, *par excellence.*

This is not quite right.

In the first place,
the organization of the police force in this country
has been undergoing far-reaching structural change.
Secondly,
if modern technology is to be exploited
to make police work more effective
(but remember the discussion about Hobbes's
                        Protection versus Obedience)
Then this structure will need to change further.
In particular, the extent to which the force
is a national force
has to be considered.

The third thought in my mind was this.
The British police force
has won more respect and public confidence
as far as I have been able to judge
than the force of any other country where I have been.
Like nurses and teachers, policemen

COLOUR CODE : YELLOW
Narrative

are scandalously underpaid.
The dangers are obvious.....

I devoted a great deal of time to this
Argument of Change
The Law and the Profits
which must now speak for itself.
At least it says something about the potential use
of eudemonic measures,
in a context where monetary measures
manifestly will not help very much.

From the point of view of the Home Office
the police force could not of course
be unilaterally turned over to eudemonic controls.
But the possibilities have to be explored in some context,
and I consider that an experiment in eudemonic *monitoring*
is certainly possible.

I suppose we are unlikely to get it
in this country.

Even so, I felt I was being fair to the police themselves
in putting forward at the least
a new way of looking at themselves and their role—
and certainly some of those present
responded as if this were so.

From the point of view of this project
the Argument is a necessary exemplar
of the use of this thinking
And if the prospect of reading
yet another explanation of

the Law of Requisite Variety

palls,
let me say that I regard this one
as the best one for practical people to understand,
and its application to the police task
as illuminating.....

COLOUR CODE : YELLOW
Narrative

AN ARGUMENT OF CHANGE

THE LAW
AND
THE PROFITS

The Sixth Frank Newsam Memorial Lecture*, delivered at the Police College, Bramshill, on the 29th October, 1970.

*By permission of
The Frank Newsam Memorial Lecture Trustees

Imagine that you have stepped into a large and powerful motor car, that you have accelerated to (exactly) seventy miles an hour in a matter of seconds, and that you are now entering a large city during the rush hour.

Hopefully you have control of this car. But have you? The steering is responding beautifully—that is good. The accelerator and the gearbox also perform to your complete satisfaction. You are now assured of the mastery in three different dimensions of control, and that is even better. Moreover, these control dimensions interact. With what subtlety of skill are you able to decrease your speed, as you approach the city traffic, by a combination of steering gear, accelerator and gearbox in a succession of manoeuvres and 'racing changes'.....

It is at this point you discover you have no brakes.

With this gripping but homely example, I am at once hurling two major issues of this lecture into the arena.

The first point says that the proper regulation of any complex system is itself a complicated affair, involving the *interplay* of different dimensions of control. It is for this reason that we shall succeed in saying very little about the management of the police force, so long as we focus all our attention on *one* dimension of control—namely the structure of command. By this remark I mean to refer to the political overtones of amalgamations, the size of 'agreed establishments', and so forth. Then I am also saying: perhaps such issues have become obsessive; perhaps they have far less to do with effective police work than some other dimensions of regulation. Well, we shall see.

The second point concerns the argument about the rate of change in the police service, and the regulation of that. For some unfathomable reason, people who contemplate change like to distinguish between what is evolutionary and what is revolutionary. Of course they then come down in favour of the former method of advance; it sounds attractive. Deliberately to embark on revolution is altogether too uncomfortable. Moreover it is clear that the current rate of change (which has reduced the number of police forces to forty-seven in some three years) is already about as great as most people can stomach. And in any case, evolutionary advance will get us there in the end.

I do not dispute that. By the same token, *the car with no brakes (in which we were travelling just now) will come to rest in the end*.....

Does this prove that another dimension of control is not necessary? It does not. The regulation of complex systems calls for as many control dimensions as we may need to exercise the bite of legitimate command. It is just like the problem of triangulation in fixing an ordnance survey. The more bearings we have on the 'trig' point, the more precise its identification. We may need more, and more subtle, modes of regulation—precisely to provide control over the rate of change.

It is all too easy to be trapped by the conventions of familiar arguments, and perhaps that justifies my appearance here today. For I arrive as an outsider. Five Frank Newsam Lecturers have already considered it an honour to deliver this lecture—and they have said so. A judge, a very senior international policeman, a royal commissioner, a professor of criminology and another of criminal law: all of them knew about the subject from the inside. For me, the sixth lecturer, the honour is of an altogether higher order. For I am the first, the very first, to stand here knowing nothing about it.

One consequence of this is my hesitancy to use your terminology. I have instead to ask you to make the considerable effort to learn some of mine.

The Variety Sponge

I take it that the police exists to perform a regulatory function in society. Despite the vast and varied duties laid upon policemen, not one of those duties seems to fail this test. That is encouraging to this outsider: because I am a cybernetician, and the science of cybernetics is the science of regulation and effective organization.

Now the first thing to be established is the criterion against which the effectiveness of the system is to be judged. There is surely no argument about that either, where the police force is concerned. The criterion of effectiveness is the law of the land—of which every police officer, however junior, is the direct agent. I hope each of them glories in this remarkable status: he is not a tool of the party in power, nor a mere employee of his particular authority. Of how many police forces in other countries could this—*de jure* and *de facto*—be said today?

Then we have a well-formulated cybernetic problem, and one much more clearly formulated from the start (may I add) than most. We know the task: we know the cynosure.

Arguing from first principles, which is to say as if he were a man from Mars, the cybernetician asks how best to discharge this task. Proceeding with great caution, it looks as though we should take a police officer, well-tutored in the law, and assign him to stay with one particular citizen by day and by night. If the citizen began to depart from what is legal, the police officer would restrain him. If the citizen were illegally handled by another, the police officer would protect him.

This is the perfect regulatory set-up. It is a naive exemplification of the *principle of requisite variety*—known as Ashby's Law, after its discoverer. Let me explain. Whatever element of a system needs keeping in control (and the element of a social system is the individual citizen), this element is capable of generating a certain amount of variety. The measure of variety is the total number of states available to that element. Requisite Variety in the controller of a system entails a capacity—somehow or another—to *match* that number of states for the system at large. Every quirk, every action, every change of mind . . . . . each would be monitored and checked.

Then you understand the proposal from which I start. This constant, attentive, state-by-state watch could indeed be kept by an individual officer attached in perpetuity to an individual citizen. That is the principle. But we cannot—we do not even want to—turn exactly half the population into policemen. Then the point of this analysis is to see what happens as soon as our original officer leaves the side of his charge in order to attend to other people. . . . .

The citizen, having lost his keeper, is let loose to generate variety—which may or may not be antisocial. He may deliver a lecture, mint false coinage, play billiards, throw paint at the Prime Minister, breed fish, or worse still connive with other uninvigilated citizens to rob the Bank of England. I said 'worse still' very deliberately; not at all because the Bank of England is important, but to show that when the elements of a system (*each* of which has a very high variety) interact, the variety they are capable of generating *between* them is gigantic. Variety is exponentially combinatorial: that is to say, it works like a football pool.

This simple-minded analysis is beginning to be fruitful. The policeman's problem is obviously to find a way of restoring the requisite variety he lost when we gave him many citizens to look after instead of one. He no longer knows what they are all up to; and just as some of them may be involved in wickedness, so others may be its victims.

The first thing to do with this insight and this metric is to measure the size of the problem. We are all so used to counting heads, so used to adding up costs, that we become very stereotyped about the kinds of measurement that we admit. In this case, cybernetics offers us a very clear way of quantifying the basic problem. There is a factor by which the total population of citizens exceeds the population of policemen. I make it roughly five hundred. Then quite basically the problem is this: how do we arrange for the policeman to win a game where the odds against him are five hundred to one?

Unless a regulator can attain to Requisite Variety, it will not be effective—that is Ashby's Law. There are three, and only three, possible methods for achieving this.

The first has already been mentioned. It relies on establishing a one-to-one correspondence in variety between controller and controlled. We realized just now that this method would not work when we are talking about the regulation of society as a whole, but it does have its importance in especial cases. An embattled gang of thugs in a house is likely to engage the attention of *at least as many* individual policemen. Again, one single maniac on the rampage cannot conceivably be caught by less than one policeman—and certainly not by one five-hundredth of a policeman. At this point the Law of Requisite Variety really asserts itself.

In fact, it is very clear that one maniac may turn out to engage *some* of the attention of *every* policeman in the country, as the whole force attempts to generate the variety requisite to sponge up this one criminal's variety—generating potential. Please note the precision of the measure. Ten thousand policemen, alert as to a twentieth of their individual attention, are needed on average to catch one criminal. That is one example that satisfies our fundamental variety equation. Such is the scientific law behind the Law of England.

The second method of providing Requisite Variety consists in *cutting down* the variety available to the runaway elements of the system. For example, the police do just this in cordoning-off an area. In general, however, it can be done only when a specific problem has been identified. One does not go around cordoning-off areas on the off-chance that a one-for-one search inside the cordon will reveal criminal behaviour (though I dare say it would). Another example of variety reduction as a regulatory technique is finger-printing. Here explicitly is a method for narrowing the area of search; probably we cannot simply and immediately identify the criminal, but we *can* eliminate suspects. That trick cuts down the variety too, and quickly improves on the 500:1 odds.

We are however more interested in the general rather than the particular case: the basic problem of generating the variety requisite to monitor the whole of society. And here the third available method seems undoubtedly to be the one we must use. It is to *amplify* the control variety. We already know that this amplification requirement can be measured: we know it involves a factor of the order of five-hundred. These are the mathematical laws of cybernetics: to the extent that we fail in this five-hundred-times amplification, to that precise extent will criminality—on the average—flourish. The question is: how does one do it?

It must by now have become evident that all the processes we are discussing deal in one basic commodity: not money, not establishments, but information. Please be careful about this word. It is used in a precise scientific sense, and not loosely. We are talking about the commodity which alone matches criminal variety. For example, if an area of a town is patrolled according to regular rules, so that the exact times at which a policeman passes a certain spot may be established, then the police makes a present of information to the criminal—a present of variety.

This lesson took a long time to learn, despite the fact that most prisoner-of-war escapes in the 'forties were based on this very variety manipulation. No wonder 'unit beat policing' has been such a success—and it should have been obvious. This example throws light on a most significant proposition. According to cybernetics, the problem of amplifying informa-tion is a problem of *selection*. If the criminal can *select out* the times and locations of police surveillance, there might as well be no police at all. If the police can *select out* the suspects who could not have committed a crime, the actual criminal has no chance at all. Thus may we amplify variety. But let me explain the theory in everyday terms.

Suppose that we have a square map containing grid squares individually numbered from 1 right through to 40,000. We are looking for a tiny place name, and we have no idea where it is. Therefore we search through one grid square after another until the name is discovered. On the average, we will have to search 20,000 squares to find the answer. If however we are able to develop a trick whereby we can identify both the row and the column in which this place is to be found, we shall have generated a *map reference* that takes us straight to it. Once that trick has been mastered, the problem of searching the horizontal axis involves an act of selection of one-in-two-hundred; and we shall find the correct column (on the average) after searching a hundred columns. Similarly with the vertical axis and the detec-tion of the correct row. Therefore we shall have used information that has cost us a search of two hundred elements in total, instead of the original cost of a 20,000 square search—and we shall have become a *hundred times* more effective.

This is an information amplifier. Note that it is only the example of the map which limits us to the use of two control dimension—because maps are flat. Remember also that there were already *four* control dimensions in the car we were driving at the beginning. And the amplification we may obtain goes up very quickly with the added dimensionality of the system. After all, if you know that a criminal is a well-educated white man of about forty-five, with a hare lip, and you can suddenly add the information that he has one leg and one arm, you can see very clearly how the amplification occurs.

As I said before: the whole problem is one of selection, and information is what drives the selective process. Suppose you are now in a patrol car. monitoring drivers on a motorway. Whom shall you stop? Does it really matter if some respectable citizen is travelling too fast in order to get himself out of what genuinely looks to him like a dangerous situation? Probably not. It matters very much that you apprehend the reckless fool who continually 'carves up' everyone else in sight. The strange thing is that this behaviour is absolutely typical of this particular driver, and the reason why you cannot identify him (as against the former and conscientious citizen) is that he has anonymity. Again we make a present of variety to the criminal (this maniac driver really is a criminal) by throwing away the information we already have: for he characteristically behaves thus, and has been fined twice already. Now if conviction involved neither fine nor imprisonment, but simply the obligation to display a sign readable by the police—which might be a radio beacon—you would know where to look. You would have precisely a variety amplifier. The roads would be cleared of those incorrigible death-or-glory boys inside six months.

The examples I have been using are all perfectly obvious, but the theory underlying them is not. Were it obvious, I believe you would have been spared many futile arguments about organization in the police. For consider: the problem you have stands revealed as concerned with the collection and manipulation of information; above all, it is concerned with the cybernetic design of information devices capable of multi-dimensional selection, and hence of information amplification to a known degree—namely, five hundred times. Then the problem of organization is just about how this can be made to happen.

The National Police Force

I have already distinguished between variety reduction in what is to be controlled and variety amplification in the controller, although they amount to the same thing—namely Requisite Variety. I have also suggested that the former especially applies to the task of solving explicit crimes, while the latter applies to general police work.

Now the notion of variety *reduction* seems to be very well understood, albeit not under that name. And the organizational need for an informational unity is well understood too. In particular, all of this is well understood by the CID. One hears cries from time to time that demand the creation of a 'national' CID; but as far as I can make out we virtually have this already. It has not happened by legislation, nor by administrative ukase, but by the zeal, knowledge and good sense of the people who actually do the job.

If that is true, it is because those variety reducers the CID fully understand two fundamental cybernetic truths. The first is that an explicit criminal may seek to amplify his own variety— for example by vanishing from one place and appearing in another, in which case there is no point in trying to hunt him down at the scene of the crime. The second is the enormous combinatorial power of informational inputs—which means that every added scrap of information slices away a great chunk of the criminal variety in question. In general, one bit of information *halves* the area of search. The minute you know: 'it's a woman', you can forget about half the population.

The question I seriously pose here, however, is whether these cybernetic lessons are as well understood by the variety *amplifiers* in the police service. Put it this way : if a policeman in Northumberland stumbles on the horizontal component of the map reference (without knowing there is a map); and a policeman in Gloucestershire stumbles on the vertical component of the same map reference (being also ignorant of the existence of the map); and if the map itself is in the hands of the Metropolitan Police—who are beginning to count those forty thousand squares in the absence of map references: what then?

If you want to handle information on this scale, and since this is 1970, you will use electronic computers. Secondly, it is obtrusively clear that the regional computers you are using must be linked together. It very much needs to be recognized that this whole business is not just a matter of 'data processing'. We require those elegant cybernetic designs for *selection* and *amplification* that I mentioned before. All this is well within the bounds of current technology and cybernetic science. The whole world's military set-up is precariously controlled by these means; then why not the more valued task of keeping law and order?

Perhaps you will say that I am trying to go too quickly. Then I remind you that the car with no brakes (sooner or later, one way or another) also comes to a halt. *Of course* we shall reach the obvious conclusion in the end. The questions are: how many agonies shall we experience on the way? Cannot we hurry up? And what sort of crash will there be?

Perhaps you will think that I have not heard of the 'Birmingham Experiment' for a computer-controlled operations room. Then I take exception to this phrase on three grounds—which is not bad for a phrase consisting of only two words. Firstly, it is both over-cautious and self-congratulatory to think of something already known to work, albeit in another part of the world, as a trail-blazing experiment. Secondly, although Birmingham is a great city, it cannot help being just one integral place—whereas the real fun starts in the linkage of at least *two* great cities. Thirdly, an operations room as such says nothing about those vital interfaces between the components of the total system we are considering—which involves not only law enforcement, but the legislature, the judiciary, and the penal system.

But I am departing from my theme. I mentioned the rate of progress, just because I think it is important. And I know very well that there are people, highly placed in the service, who are fully alive to these issues. The theme itself, at this stage, is about the hoary topic of organization. By entering the problem from the outside and through cybernetic channels, I argue that *there must be* a national police force. If that word 'must' is seriously meant (and it is), then it follows that there really and actually and already *is* a national police force. I think this is true; but there is much more to be said.

Consider modern Britain. The people are closely packed, and crime is therefore epidemic in character. Here is a fact: there are sixteen times as many people to the square mile in England as there are in the United States. Where there is this density, where there is a constant flux and movement, and where the power of technology is as available to the criminal as to the police, there is no alternative to a national force. Debate on the issue is an anachronism.

But it remains an open question as to how that force is organized, and with what degree of centrality. As to the debate about centrality (though it may not be anachronistic) it is certainly sterile if it hinges on philosophic talk about the nature of freedom, and historical talk about how it all was with Peel and Wellington in connexion with the Metropolitan

Police Act of 1829. We have a current situation that is well understood; we have a present set of resources; we have new resources we could call into play if we wished to afford that; and we have some definable objectives. Then we have first to design the best system to meet these objectives within established constraints; and secondly we have to devise a plan for getting from *here* to *there* as quickly as possible. History and philosophy bear on that plan. All that bears on the design of the optimal system is—science.

In my view, if there is no way out of regarding the force as actually national, then the sooner we formally acknowledge the fact the better. People worry about regional autonomy: the problems are no more alarming than they are for any large industrial company with its autonomous divisions. And the potential benefits from synergy are, for the reasons already given, considerably greater. People worry about the potential power of a unified police service. But we ought to have more confidence in both our traditions and our capacity to design the system aright. We have not after all had much trouble with the army for more than three hundred years, and Cromwell was in a very special situation.

As to the form the organization might take: there is surely some attraction in the new arrangements made for the Post Office. Using this as a model, there might be a national police board of—but not exactly in—the Home Office. It would presumably have a Chief Commissioner answerable to the Home Secretary—in much the same way that the Chairman of the Post Office Board is now responsible to his Minister.

The 'inappropriateness' of this model will be obtrusive to everyone here, though I shall try to use any distress I am causing as the energy required to carry this lecture to the climax for which it has been entirely designed. I am assuming that what will cause this distress is the fact that the police force is not a profit-making organization, and cannot therefore be held accountable in any sense familiar in commerce or industry.

Let me then give you a very strongly held view. People working in organizations which stand outside the so-called 'profit motive' of industry always believe that they are in a class apart, for the reason that they expect businessmen believe profit to be the measure of everything. This simply is not true. The copper on the beat has to wear a blue uniform; this is a constraint under which he operates. In very much the same way, a business is constrained to make a profit—otherwise there is trouble. But the great decisions in business, although they bow to this constraint, are no more made *because* of it than the copper's decisions whether or not to run a man in is made because he wears a blue uniform.

For all of us, wherever we are, and under whatever constraints we operate, decisions are made because they appear to be right—and the rightness refers to a complex criterion. I want to suggest to you that this criterion is always something to do with *utility*. In its turn, utility is always about doing a good job: partly for the sake of the thing, and partly because it enhances the reputation of the organization that does it. If a business were really about maximising profit in the short run, then fortunes would be made overnight the customers would go hang, the shareholders would cash in, and the business would be wound up. This you will notice is a completely satisfactory outcome for the people who own the firm, but it does not often happen. In reality, those who actually run business (and they are called managers) are wholeheartedly involved in the survival of the firm; and they consciously try to avoid taking short-run decisions of this kind. I beg you therefore not to be deluded by the apparent dominance of the profit motive in industry. Those like yourselves who operate outside this particular constraint should be more stern with themselves. They are concerned with rightness too, and also because they are concerned with survival.

Now I will agree that a business, operating under its constraint of a necessary profitability, offers itself to the shareholders and to the city in terms of its financial stability—and a service such as the police cannot assume this particular fancy dress. That is an inconvenience, but no more. So long as the firm is economically viable, which is to say making a decent return on capital (which is just like a policeman wearing a blue uniform and 'looking the part'), the real decisions are based on other and incommensurable factors. Firms go to great lengths to understand their reputation in the city (where they may have to raise capital), with their suppliers (on whom they may have to call for special efforts), with the market for employees (for they may need scarce skills which they must attract), and above all with the public. None of this has to do with 'making a profit' *per se*.

Please realize that the capability of a firm to make a large profit does not particularly endear it to the public, on whose loyalty it relies. Its reputation with its consumers depends on far more subtle and intangible capabilities than this. The public wants to believe in the product; the public wants to know that it is good; the public does not want to be poisoned, diddled or done. Because of this, firms spend a small fortune on advertising, in order to convince the public of what it wants to know, and a small fortune on market research, to discover the public reaction to all of this.

In short, the firm is above all else trying to measure—for purposes of decision—public satisfaction with what it does. The monetary measure is some kind of help, but no more. It seems to me that the great problem with the police, which also wishes to satisfy its public, is that in the absence of a monetary measure it has gone away and sulked. There are zealots who try to satisfy the need for measurable 'profits' with the crude statistics of their craft. But the public is no fool: it is perfectly obvious that the percentage of unsolved crime depends not only on police efficiency, but also on the effectiveness of the system which notifies crime in the first place. I go further: as the sky darkens over our civilization, there seems less and less point in even registering crime which it is obvious that police have no resources to solve. Hence measures of this kind will not avail us.

Of still less use are the measures which some would like to use, which say how short of 'establishment' is a given police force. In the first place, these establishments are arbitrary; and I think you will take my meaning if I say that the process through which structural change has recently been undertaken has made them more arbitrary than ever. Secondly, there is surely a most complex motivational mixture in the vocational architecture of a policeman. (I will not insult you by attempting to list the many *pros* and *cons* attaching to this career—for they are better known to you than to me.) Thirdly, there is the extraordinary complication that anyone (and here again I include especially teachers and nurses) undertaking an important public service is supposed to expect low emoluments. This goes along with the declaration, from every level of society, that the work really is essential, and that the underpayment is really too bad . . . . .

I do not know how we have got into this mess, but that is the mess we are in.

The Measure of Worth

We are searching for a measure of worth, of utility. Now for any management, the real measure can be found in the answer to this question: 'What are we trying to maximize?' If the answer were 'profit', people say, the case would be easy. Well, the answer is *not* profit for the police. But take heart, I have said, because it is not *just* profit for any one.

In fact I consider that the answer always has something to do with survival. Business cannot maximize profit without regard to the survival of the firm. To think that it could would be as naive as to say that if we gave policemen the fines awarded by the courts against those whom the police arrest, everything would be all right. The fallacy is of the same kind: a system striving towards these ends would be self-defeating. And if we are really talking about survival, the police service is nearer to the heart of the mensuration problem than is business itself. For the police service is all about the survival of an orderly society—and nothing else.

Then let us relax, carefully circumvent the traditional thought blocks, and ask just what it is we can measure that justifies the expenditure on law and order which the police incurs. Probably the first answer we would like to give is this. What would it cost society *not* to have a police service? If we knew this, we could quote an upper spending limit; and if we spent less than that, then we would have made a notional profit on the deal.

But (and again policemen share this problem with teachers and nurses) the cost of not having a police service turns out to be infinitely high. It is not that we cannot find the answer you observe: the cost would be potentially everything we have got! Nothing would be safe; everything would be threatened; in short—we should lose our sense of security. It is exactly this sense of security that the police is trying to maximize. Perhaps it is the overwhelming conviction that the opportunity cost of not having the police is infinitely great, that causes society to over-compensate by paying out too little. Then what should we do?

I have already edged into this discussion the idea that we are trying to assess public satisfaction through some notion of utility. It is true that the utilitarian philosophers and economists, such as Mill and Bentham, set out with this intention more than a century ago—and they failed. But we have better tools today. As a focus of discussion. I ask you to accept and to mull over what may sound like a new word, although you will find it in the dictionary. This word is eudemony. It came into English from the Greek, and it means just that sort of general satisfaction to which I have referred. The ancient Greeks were a subtle people, and they had many words for happiness. This one is not so much about *ecstasy*, as about the solid goal of *prosperity*. Ten years ago one of our eminent godfathers in operational research, Sir Charles Goodeve, suggested that this word might be revived in a very special way.

Consider one complicated state of affairs as compared with another. We might find it quite impossible to analyse the reasons why we preferred one state to the other—*yet we know we do*. Therefore, if we are in the less preferred condition, we shall try to move towards the more preferred. Goodeve proposed that we should try to produce a eudemonic measure which would account for this situation. Since the complexity of each of the two conditions is too great for analysis, the only thing left to measure is the difference between them.

That is a kind of gradient, a slope between higher and lower; it is something that a scientist would call a *difference in potential*. Then you might measure what is happening by observing the rate at which elements of the system flow from the one state to the other. Or, as Goodeve said, you should measure the increase you have to make in the lower eudemony so as to equalize the reciprocal flows and hold the system in balance.

Using this notion, I am going to suggest that the measure we need, the commodity which the Police Force seeks to maximize, is eudemony. We shall define eudemony for police purposes as a public sense of security. And I am going to suggest that this might actually be measured as a potential difference.

We surely cannot find an absolute measure of eudemony in society, because the composition of this strange commodity cannot be analysed. It is an intensive, rather than an extensive, property. Yet if you were to ask someone whether he were more or less satisfied this year than last year with a particular state of affairs, however complex, however unanalysable, he might well be able to tell you. Moreover, he might well be able to say that things were not only worse this year compared with last year, just as last year was worse than the year before, but that the *rate of change* had increased. That remark gives us a feel for eudemonic control: it is about the potential difference between two complex states of affairs, and about changes through time of that difference.

Let me say at once to those who may consider I am taking off into the stratosphere with this concept of eudemony, which no one has heard of before, that I believe I am simply giving a name to the very commodity in which the hard-headed businessman deals all the time. As we said earlier, it has to do with *public satisfaction*. I have already admitted that the businessman appears to have an advantage in being able to translate eudemony into monetary terms. But you will not have forgotten the argument that this may turn out to be a disadvantage, insofar as the monetary convention often conceals rather than reveals what is really going on.

At any rate, let us come down to earth. I am suggesting that if you could accost the individual citizen with a view to discovering whether the police were doing its job, you might try to find the answer to the following question :

'Do *you*—in your many guises as householder, husband, son, father, employer, employee, traveller, and citizen responsible for fellow citizens (who may have been robbed, murdered, highjacked, kidnapped, or tortured) say that you are more or less secure than the last time I asked?'

Surely, if everyone said that they were more secure, you would feel satisfied. If everyone said that they were less secure, you would feel that something had to be done. You would be assessing the change in eudemonic potential.

The *average* response to this question would yield a measure having three essential characteristics—although it would not have the 'absolute' character we like to associate with measures. First, it would say whether things were improving or getting worse. Secondly, it would say on a subjective scale whether things were trivially, substantially, much, or very much, worse than last time. Thirdly, it would say whether the change were greater in this time epoch than in previous epochs. In other words, it could conceivably measure the rate of change.

Now it is true that we do not hold plebiscites in this country, nor do I believe that we should. This argument does not advocate that we ought to obtain a concensus from the entire population as to satisfaction with the police service. But let us return to the businessman. It is not open to him either to hold a plebiscite. That would be too costly. Moreover, he is far too sophisticated these days to imagine that he can obtain a correct reading by undertaking an opinion poll of a sample of the population, and simply posing them the question: what do you think? Political pollsters may be this naive, but not businessmen. They are currently using far more reliable methods.

If you want to know what people really do, rather than what they *say* that they *think*, you must probe the attitudes which underlie their actual behaviour. Better still, you will examine their relevant behaviour itself. In no circumstances will you ask their opinion. That provides a measure of ingrained prejudice and no more, as the political pollsters ought to have learned by now. Now the relevant techniques of behavioural analysis are very far advanced; and they are indeed widely used in business. Therefore I advocate that we should copy business in this respect, rather than complain that we cannot copy business in respect of a 'profit motive' which is in any case chimerical.

It is interesting, and ought to be recorded, that one of the pioneers in this country of the methods I am now advocating was Leslie Wilkins, who worked for many years in the Home Office. If he had wanted to know whether people felt more or less secure than last time, with respect to burglary for example, I am sure that he would not have asked them what they thought about that. What he might have done (I have not asked him) is actually measure the change over a time period in the number of people fitting new locks and burglar alarms, taking out more insurance, and so on. In such ways he would have uncovered real measures of eudemony (though I must not blame that word on him either).

The behavioural measure of potential difference in eudemony which I am now advocating has many attractions. The over-riding attraction is the likely stability of the measure itself. Let us think about that for a moment. No-one wants to use a measure which arbitrarily reflects random movements in the environment, or the changes of protocol under which a system is described; nor do they want a measure that could be biased by the sectional interests of one party or another. Let us then note the strength of a eudemonic metric based on measuring behavioural indicators which answer the question I earlier posed.

The first protection lies in the fact that people would not actually be asked the question at all, because subtle and experienced behaviourial scientists would devise means of obtaining the answer by inferential methods. Nonetheless, this is a free society; and we really could not tolerate a strictly secret method of appraisal. It would be necessary to say openly what we were doing; and we have to face the fact that this might change public behaviour itself. Even so, and secondly, I argue that the measure would turn out to be stable.

Consider someone who knows very well the consequences of his response. If his behaviour conveys that he is less secure than before, his response will contribute towards a likely increase in taxation. If, on the other hand, his wish to reduce expenditure leads him to conceal his true behaviour, or not to behave at all as he otherwise would have behaved, so that he is thought to be more secure than he is, then he knows that the outcome is likely to reduce his actual security. Since no-one wants to incur unnecessary taxation, and since no-one wants to be insecure, it seems plausible that bias in the system will be minimized.

An Embryonic Model

Then where does all this get us? I shall summarize the arguments I have deployed by constructing an embryonic model of the entire situation. And if the main suggestion I wish to make has not already proposed itself to your minds, I shall derive it explicitly from this model as it grows.

In the first diagram (Figure 1) we observe an initial situation in which a police force provides a police service which eventually impinges upon the public. In so doing, it bears upon the state of *lawfulness* which society makes manifest at any given time. Law-abiding citizens circulate freely between their own box and the state of lawfulness. But citizens whose behaviour is both unlawful and detected go to court. From there they may either be returned to their own box, or they pass through the penal system before so doing. Meanwhile, of course, there is an interaction between the police service and both the courts and the penal system.

It will also be noted that the police force itself interacts with a pool of eligible citizens who could join the force. Some men and women are recruited. Others, already in the force, leave and return to the pool.

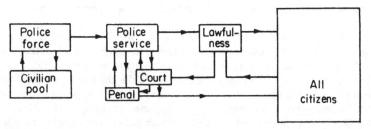

Figure 1

Next we confront the phenomenon of feedback, by which continuing processes are continuously adjusted in terms of their effects—as judged by some established criterion. (Feedbacks in all these drawings are depicted, as is customary, by lines made up of dashes.)

First of all, the public is aware of the state of lawfulness at any one time—and it may react to that. It may reinforce a tendency to resist criminality by supportive action—noticeably enhancing its friendship for the police. Alternatively, it may respond to the permissive tendencies of society by becoming less amenable: it may fail to cooperate with the police. Just as these reactions will in either case affect the state of lawfulness itself either by positive or negative feedback, so will the effect work through to affect the service given by the police. A policeman, like anyone else, favourably responds to encouragement; he is likely to resent being ostracised.

The feedback capabilities of the system are depicted (in Figure 2) at the top right-hand side. The second feedback loop that has appeared (it runs along the bottom of the picture) affects the pool of eligible civilians, who inevitably respond to the current public evaluation of lawfulness and the esteem in which the police is currently held.

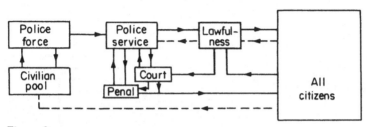

Figure 2

Now it was argued earlier that there is a firmly established criterion of effectiveness in police work—namely obedience to absolute law. This law is settled by parliament and it follows that a major duty is laid on the police service continuously to review the actual state of lawfulness as compared with the absolute law. This comparison is drawn (in Figure 3), using the symbol of a crossed circle.

But it was shown earlier, by reference to Ashby's Law of Requisite Variety, that police work involves an information amplifier competent to handle lawlessness in general— and this condition of lawlessness is exactly what the comparator between the current state of lawfulness and the absolute law measures. Therefore the feedback from this comparator, which is crucial to successful police operations, must carry a high-gain amplifier. You may recall that we uncovered the need to amplify information five-hundred times on the average.

This new feedback is indeed by far the most important factor in success, and it will prove a difficult cybernetic device to design. Leaving the scientific theory aside, we must note that the absolute law itself does change—and not all that slowly these days. Moreover, what is publicly acceptable as lawfulness changes almost hour by hour. It is heavily influenced (remember its own feedback loop) by public fashions. The whole business of obscene publication is an outstanding example; another is the toleration or otherwise felt by the public in relation to police 'toughness' in handling public disorders.

Any sensible handling of this particular control circuit must take account of these realities. I suppose it is strictly improper for me to imply that anything less than the absolute law is to be obeyed. Judges are appointed to interpret the intent of the law, and they certainly adjust the severity of their sentences to the condition of the times. By the same token, however, the police constable—the agent of the law—must himself judge whether or not to act; and he must do so from wisdom rather than textbooks.

As I contemplate this crucial feedback circuit (added in Figure 3), with its potent high-gain amplifier, and its comparator which must operate on imperceptibly shifting criteria, I am vividly reminded of some words of Aristotle. He described one mode of good government as being obedience to the law as laid down. But the alternative, he said, is 'to lay down well those laws that the people abide by'. That remark is reflected in the way this comparator works in practice. At any rate, the practical manager of this affair is the police constable, responsible in management terms to his senior officers. If this whole management is bad, archaic and inefficient, the magistrate and the judge have too few clients— and maybe the wrong ones. If this management wholly fails, the judge has no client at all . . . . .

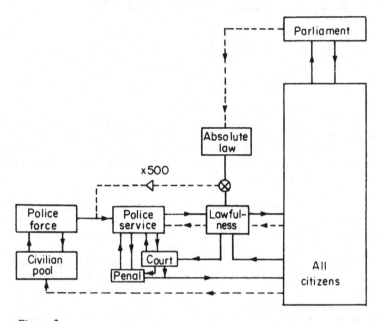

Figure 3

But we must proceed with the model-building. A new loop of regulation, conceived at a higher level, is now in the course of construction.

If the public is responding to parliament, and through parliament to its chosen minister the Home Secretary, to whom does the police force respond? The answer is to its regional management. And if you will forgive my clarifying what happens next in terms of my own earlier proposal, the regional management would respond in turn (not only to its rate-payers, but) to a 'national police board'. Since this would be appointed by the Home Secretary, the higher-order loop (called a metasystem) is now closed.

It is this metasystem, and not the lower system, that runs on eudemony.

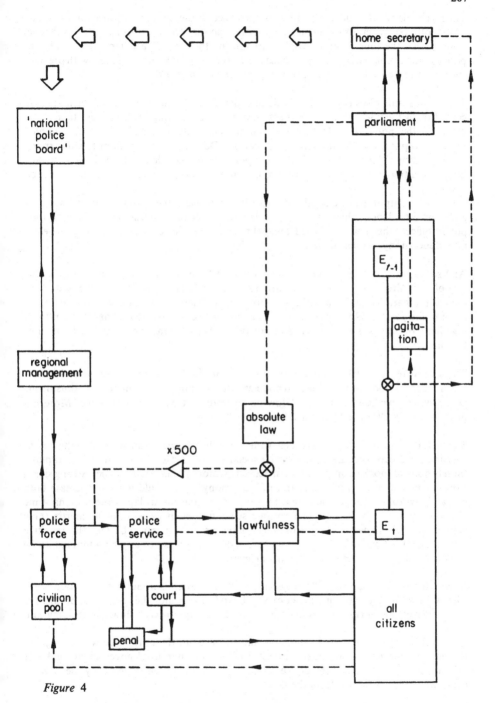

Figure 4

The mechanics of the eudemonic loop are provided in the diagram. The operational loop at the bottom is generating eudemony in the body politic. This is called E; and the subscript t means that the time is 'now'. Higher up appears the sign for a comparator again; the public is in fact comparing (as was argued earlier) current eudemony at time t, with previous eudemony at time t-1. 'Are we more or less secure than before?'

This comparator gives rise to two kinds of eudemonic output, and both of them are concerned (as we would expect) with pressure to insert something in the system that would eliminate the potential difference between the erstwhile and the current eudemonies. The first output is specific: it is labelled 'agitation'. Demands for the restoration of corporal and capital punishment; demands that the police be armed; demands for higher pay and better conditions: all such agitations are measures of the eudemonic potential difference.

The second output is more subtle. It goes directly to parliament and to the minister as a eudemonic feedback which is inexplicit, but to which both are sensitive. Despite their public offices, the men concerned are politicians: they have to respond to changes in public eudemony, sooner or later.

And so action may happen, around that topmost loop. Then why is our society in any sort of difficulty? Surely the reasons are now staring us all in the face. In the first place, there is no 'national police board', for I invented it. There is instead a sort of haze at this place in the picture. No doubt there is machinery of some kind that connects everything together—but it takes the insider, and not this 'cybernetician from Mars' to know how to work it.

The second reason is even more important. We are looking here at a servomechanism; it is a feedback loop at the metasystemic level that is supposed to make fine adjustments in the eudemonic control system. 'How on earth does it work?' I just asked. More importantly, then: 'how long will it take to work?'

Suppose the public is highly satisfied with the police service; that it is nonetheless increasingly insecure because of increasing social stress; and that costs are rising rapidly. (Surely none of those assumptions is particularly remote.) Then there will be a strong signal from the eudemonic comparator, and the eudemony loop should work to increase both pay and facilities. The trouble is that there will be an enormous lag in the response-time of the system: partly because of its vague structure, partly because of its inertia (how very senior it all is), partly because of 'noise' in the circuit, and partly because this sensitive little plant called eudemony is no more than a concept—it is not anything tangible to be installed, pulled down, thrown into jail, or elevated to the House of Lords.

In fact, the real connectivity of the system is—as it so often is in our economics-obsessed society—just money and not eudemony at all. And money must be competed for, against all manner of challenges, worthy and unworthy. Let us put the cash-flow into the diagram.

As is well known, funds are in the long run drawn from the only place where they lie: the public pocket. Regional management, working through local government, makes a call on the rates to pay for the police service. This input is then matched by the government, which draws in turn from the taxpayer.

209

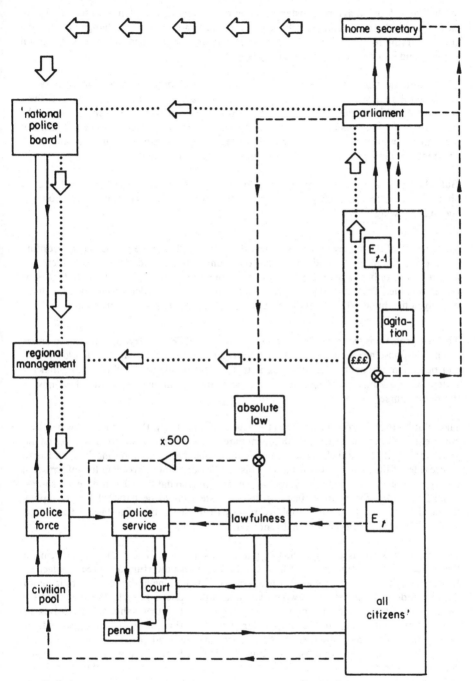

Figure 5

With Figure 5 our diagram is ostensibly complete. But we are relying on an insensitive cash-flow for the major connectivity. This simply does not respond to change in 'what the police is trying to maximize'. For as far as eudemony is concerned, reliance is placed on tenuous and inexplicit loops, disastrously lagged.

The requirement is clear. There is need to measure eudemonic change scientifically, by behavioural analysis undertaken on principles to be agreed by all concerned. And there is need to feed back the eudemonic signal across the heart of the diagram. It cannot be done at the level of operations, because the whole concept is metasystemic. It will not work at the ministerial level, because of the lags. *Regional management* is in command, and regional management needs the continuous eudemonic input.

But all of that is of no avail if it cannot or will not respond. The eudemonic feedback should be used to operate what I call a 'money pump'. Two such pumps are shown in the final drawing.

The purpose of the money pumps is to gear the police system to the public need, according to the principle: maximize eudemony. The only control signal that counts is the eudemonic measure. The only competent decision taker is the police authority—whatever that is or might become. The only objective is to maintain law and order—by providing, most notably, a five-hundred-fold variety amplifier. Then there are just four problems.

The first problem is technical, but I know how to solve it. We are trying, after all, to create a rapid response mechanism—one that bites right into the tired heart of the old system, and pumps in adrenalin. Then the risk is that violent oscillations will set in, so that the system becomes unstable. One cannot keep on changing, minute by minute, demands on the public purse.

The solution to this problem comes in two instalments. Firstly, this model (or hopefully a much enriched version of it) should be simulated on a computer, in order to understand its oscillatory modes of behaviour. There is no doubt that a damping mechanism has to be provided if the system is to be stable. This can be done: it is a problem for information theory. (In these terms, by the way, the present system is so damped that it barely responds at all.) Secondly, the relative time-lags in the system could be handled by decoupling the need for money from the supply of money through the use of a special fund. This fund would act as a surge hopper in the monetary part of the system.

The second problem is partly technical, partly constitutional. The regulatory system for the police service advanced in the final diagram is both powerful and directly effective. In stabilizing eudemonic regulation for the police, it would inevitably be *de*stabilizing for the remainder of the system on which law and order rests. I refer to the blocks in the diagram depicting the courts and the penal system—and these should themselves be broken down into their many components. Certainly this problem can be solved, by linking the eudemonic measure to other money pumps, and providing another metasystem for regulating the pumps. This done, the law-and-order system as a whole would destabilize the rest of the social security system—which is why I have several times referred to the problems of nurses and teachers. Such repercussive effects are major inhibitors of

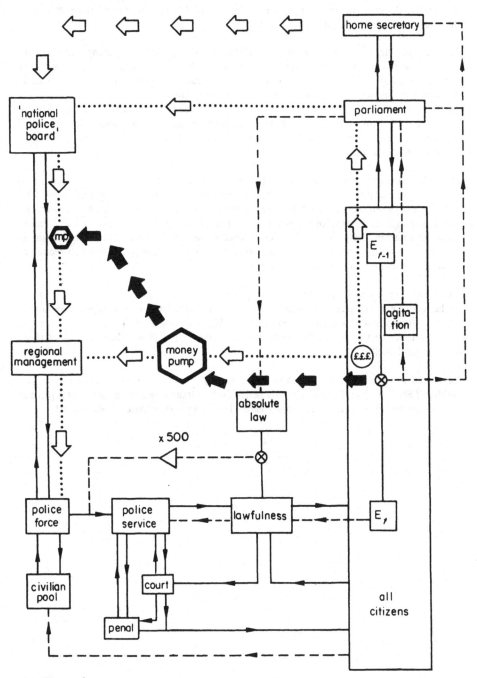

Figure 6

innovation throughout our complicated society; but their containment is exactly what the science of cybernetics makes possible.

The third problem is organizational. This lecture is talking about two things: the task the police force discharges and the nature of the difficulty of that task; secondly, effective means of regulation of the police service to the community. The paramount role of variety manipulation in the first instance, and the paramount need for eudemonic regulators in the second instance, both point to an urgent need for organizational change at the national level. I do not think that either of these issues can be handled on a totally decentralized basis. Both the planning of variety amplifiers and the administration of eudemonic regulation are national tasks.

May I beg you to believe that this call has nothing to do with philosophy, nothing to do with history, nothing to do with human values, nothing to do with regional autonomy, and above all nothing to do with me and the strange words I have used today. It has fallen to me to diagnose a pathology which exists whether I diagnose it or not. It has fallen to me to give names to problems which exist whether or not they are named. And as far as solutions are concerned: I have not so much made you proposals, as tried to recognize what solutions are endemic to the problem situation.

Others will recognize these solutions too, once they are pointed out. That forecast leads to the fourth and last problem, which is one that cannot be bilked: it is to ask whether the nation will accept a new arrangement, and one likely to cost it money. Then let us get at the facts through the use of the model, its quantification and simulation; and let those facts be published.

How shall we rate the actual security, and more still the peace of mind, of our wives and children? Shall we fix a limit of ten new pence in the rateable pound, or set a total price of six pounds per annum on each of their heads? I am standing up here to be counted.

You may have noticed
that the seven Arguments of Change
so far presented
were put forward to special types of audience.
None of them assumed specific technical knowledge—
which is why they are here—
but all were addressed to specialists

> in either the management sciences
> or the field of professional application
> —such as doctors
> or policemen.

How should any such ideas be advanced
towards those responsible
for the *general* conduct of affairs?

I wish I knew.

But one has to try.

The next three Arguments of Change
are all addressed to *general* management :

> at three very different levels
> in three very different tones of voice.

The three levels were presented to me.
The tones of voice were mine.
Perhaps I got them wrong,
but I want you to see
how it turned out.

For indeed these levels and tones of voice
are distinct.

The first of the three Arguments
(which by chance was the first of the actual year 1970)
is addressed to government itself.

Right out of the blue,
and while entertaining the project
PLATFORM FOR CHANGE,
I received a startling invitation.

> It was to speak
> to the United States' Congress.

COLOUR CODE : YELLOW
Narrative

Naturally enough
this invitation aroused my deepest interest
in the machinery the Americans use
to inform their parliament
on scientific issues.

In Britain there is no **overt** machinery of this kind.
Many arrangements are of course made,
even at the party level,
but the only parliamentary arrangement
consists of a committee
(the *parliamentary and scientific committee*—
of which I have been a member)
which is certainly not
a committee of the House.
It consists of politicians and scientists
appointed by customary processes
(which are as you would expect complicated)
and which meets privately.

Indeed, it is essential to the effectiveness of this committee
that its proceedings should be private.
I doubt very much
whether any member of the general public
knows of its existence.
There is nothing sinister about that,
but it does show that in Britain
people do not care
whether their legislators are informed about science or not.

This is not the case in the United States.
The House of Representatives
has a House Committee entitled
The Committee on Science and Astronautics
which holds its sessions in public
and for the record.
Moreover it produces
apart from the Congressional Record
neat booklets on the topics it considers
which are widely disseminated.

Of course this is a non-legislative committee of the House,
and although it is *constitutionally* very different,
I suspect that Britain's nearest equivalent
is a Royal Commission.
At least that is public.
But you do not find leading parliamentarians

COLOUR CODE : YELLOW
Narrative

sitting in on the proceedings of a Royal Commission
and bombarding the protagonists with questions.

This is exactly what happens in Washington.
The panel on science and technology,
consisting of eminent American scientists,
meets before the Committee on Science and Astronautics
and their deliberations with the congressmen
are an integral part
of parliamentary government.

I applaud this arrangement—
               because it is official
               because it is overt
               because it makes the scientific-political interaction
                         direct.

In Britain, the conflicting views of scientists
are first *judged*
by the members of the Royal Commission (or other Enquiry) ;
the Commission's report is then judged in turn,
by the civil service,
which briefs the government;
and after that the wheels are really turning......
The private member's question in the House
the citizen's objections to the *Times*
are heard and answered through these filters.

Nothing intervened
between the Congressmen who hounded me
about the role of man himself
within my complex of systems and metasystems
and me.
I think that this is good.

But something bad :
something certainly does intervene
between the marvellous fact of these encounters
and anyone who seeks them out in retrospect.
I realize that the verbatim transcript
of parliamentary debate must be exceedingly difficult to prepare.
But I was reared on *Hansard*.
It is sad but true that the congressional record
makes sheer nonsense of much that was said.

However, this is to move ahead of my narrative.
The subject before
the Committee on Science and Astronautics
was to be

THE MANAGEMENT OF INFORMATION AND KNOWLEDGE.

COLOUR CODE : YELLOW
Narrative

Anyone who has read this book up to this point
will realize that from my point of view
to take that title is tantamount to saying:
THE FUTURE OF THE WORLD.

Despite my role as a guest
I felt this was not only an opportunity
but an occasion of duty
to speak as I really felt.
perhaps what I should say
would not be readily understood by everyone—
and there was a time limitation—
but the very fact of being on record
meant that the address could be consulted
by anyone at all at any time.

There is already evidence that this policy paid off
(because of the enquiries received, and from whom they came)
but the problem of 'tuning in' to an audience,
particularly the most influential audience ever,
remains—and appears almost insoluble.

On the aeroplane
I became most upset on reading through my script.
It looked to me then
like a set of the most spine-chilling platitudes
with which to try and command attention in the Capitol.
But I went through with it.
The Chairman, himself a distinguished social scientist,
said when I sat down:

        'I must say that in all the years I have gone
        to meetings, I have rarely heard a paper which
        is as packed as this, and raises so many
        complex issues.'

What is the truth?
I think that it has to be
that no-one knows how to communicate
about this kind of problem
because it is so new
and the connotations
and the conventions
needed for the exchange of complex ideas
just don't exist.

COLOUR CODE: YELLOW
Narrative

I suspect congratulations
I suspect denunciations
equally.

This seems to be the honest attitude
but it does not help.

Readers of PLATFORM FOR CHANGE
will with respect
not be in a good position to adjudicate
on this vital question of communication.

They will find in this piece

the systems
the metasystems
the esoteric boxes
the cerebral computers •

and especially

the allegation of Threat

with which they are relatively familiar.
The House of Representatives
is not familiar with these notions.
But they did have the paper in advance.
Some had really read it.

And so it is hard to say what happened.
It is easy to say in the context of these pages
that this Argument of Change
must admit to being
a major attempt to speak to management

at the Very Top.

COLOUR CODE : YELLOW
Narrative

AN ARGUMENT OF CHANGE

MANAGING
MODERN
COMPLEXITY

Presentation* to the Committee on Science and Astronautics of the House of Representatives of the United States of America, made on the 27th January, 1970, in the Capitol, Washington, D.C.

*By permission of
the Government of the United States of America

1. *THREAT SYSTEMS*

I speak to you today against a background of seemingly ungovernable crisis which it is impossible to ignore. We are met to discuss the future, but we must know the context from which we begin.

The business of forecasting is fraught with many traps; it often seems ascientific. But the perspicuous detection of inexorable trends can be a matter of good science. There is a reality to observe and to measure, a reality in which a dead man is a corpse and not a statistic. There is a reality, too, with which to experiment; a reality that does not come in parcels labelled for the attention of appropriate officials. The very stuff of this reality is *complexity*. The elements of our society ever more richly interact: the more this happens, the more participation is invoked, the more the streams of data flow . . . . . the more complex does society come.

Handling complexity seems to be the major problem of the age, in the way that handling material substance offered challenge to our forefathers. Computers are the tools we have to use, and their effective use must be directed by a science competent to handle the organization of large, complex, probabilistic systems. This is the science of cybernetics, the science of communication and control.

The central thesis of cybernetics might be expressed thus: that there are natural laws governing the behaviour of large interactive systems—in the flesh, in the metal, in the social and economic fabric. These laws have to do with self-regulation and self-organization. They constitute the 'management principle' by which systems grow and are stable, learn and adjust, adapt and evolve. These seemingly diverse systems are one, in cybernetic eyes, because they manifest viable behaviour—which is to say behaviour conducive to survival.

In my opinion, the most important fact which a quarter of a century's worth of cybernetics has revealed is that this behaviour is governed by the dynamic structure of the system, rather than by special events occurring within it or by the particular values taken up by even its major variables. 'Structure' means the way in which the parts of a whole are interrelated; and here it includes both the feedback loops by which systems regulate themselves and also the conditional probability mechanisms by which systems learn and organize themselves. 'Dynamic' relates to the speeds at which communication is effected within the system, and especially to the relative lags with which messages are promulgated, overtake each other, and combine to form new patterns. Dynamic structure generates outcomes.

Therefore I say that what will happen to mankind in its battle with complexity will be determined neither by particular innovation nor by isolated achievement at some unknown future date. Hence the attempted prediction of such things is not to the point. Outcomes are latent in the dynamic structure of the systems we have or may adopt: they will inexorably emerge.

At present, the most obtrusive outcome of the system we have is a gross instability— of institutional relationships and of the economy. This cannot last. The society we have known will either collapse, or it will be overthrown. In either case a new kind of society will emerge, with new modes of control; and the risk is that it will be a society which no-one actually chose, and which we probably will not like. I shall argue that we must use our science to detect the latent outcomes which will one day characterize the future of mankind. And let us so engineer our systems that their latent outcomes suit our social purpose. It is true that the outcomes cannot be fully determined, because there is noise (or shall we call it free will?) in the system. But a systemic design taking due account of cybernetic laws may be expected to produce behaviour which is predictable in terms of the overriding social need for stability.

Thanks to the growth of complexity, which is very much a function of the growth in data-handling capacity and of the information explosion, society has outgrown the dynamic regulating capacity of its own hallowed structure. History did not design that structure to cope with such complexity, and a cybernetically grotesque machinery is a result. It is from this standpoint that I ask you to look again at the environmental crises from which our view of the future must necessarily start.

The thermonuclear threat is a computable threat, and one which computably grows— although we act as if we were inured to it. The various pollution threats—by pesticides, by noise, by sewage, by carcinogenic urban air—were and remain systemically predictable. None of these things happened by chance, by accident, or by the wrath of God. We have run ourselves into these problems by failing to calculate the predictable consequences of the systems civilization has underwritten. The same seems to me to be true, though less obviously so, of the various forms of societary crisis which run alongside the environmental crises. Problems of race, problems of poverty, problems of over-population: all these are quantifiable aspects of computable systems. It has taken social upheaval and threatening violence to draw them to our proper attention; it has taken a major revolt of the young to motivate any kind of rethinking.

The risk which faces us today is the probability that society will yet refuse to study the systemic generators of human doom, and will disregard the cybernetic capability which already exists competent to bring these many but inter-related forms of crisis under governance.

There are two reasons for this fear. First of all, our culture does not take kindly to the notion that it nurtures the seeds of its own destruction. Instead of studying the systemic reality in which outcomes are latent, it prefers the technique of prognostication. Small wonder: by using such wholly non-systemic devices as the Delphi technique, we may predict a possible millennium for our comfort. But the Delphi technique is aptly named: its pronouncements are shrouded in ambiguity—because they take no account of the systemic context. Meanwhile, the systems we have already started, which we nourish and foster, are grinding society to powder. It might sound macabre to suggest that computers will finish the job of turning this planet into a paradise after human life has been extinguished. But that vision is little more macabre than the situation we already have, when we sit in the comfort of affluent homes and cause satellites to transmit to us live pictures of children starving to death and human beings being blown to pieces.

The second reason for my pessimism is that technology now seems to be leading humanity by the nose. We appear to have no sense of priorities where our problems are concerned; we do what is technologically easy—and we do it regardless of cost. For example, the problem people have of transporting themselves from one remote place to another really exists between homes or offices and international airports. But the problem we continuously solve is the non-existent problem of moving between those airports. It is easier to go from Mach 1 to Mach 2 than to tackle the genuine problem. Perhaps it was also easier to go to the moon than to face up to what was happening in the street outside.

Thus I direct myself and you to the claim that cybernation is about the regulation of society, and that this is what computers are for. Perhaps this opening is a surprise. Would it not have been *easier* for all of us to plunge into the technology of computation, to prattle on happily about nanoseconds and massive data banks, to wonder at the explosion of knowledge and the impending marvels of data storage and retrieval by holograms and photochromic tubes, rather than to tell the truth about cybernation? What did you really expect? The fact is that most of the problems we stand ready to consider are bogus problems. They are generated by theories about technological progress, and theories about the way society works. Theory is often the only reality countenanced by our culture.

The reality is that we are elements in a vast and almost ungovernable social system generating outcomes that happen to us. We come sprightly to conference, dragging lead-heavy bones, to talk about machines that matter only if they can help us men. Our fat is suffused with insecticide, but we are avid to decide what it will be like to take our newspaper out of the back of the television set. The expansion of knowledge will yet save the world, shall I not tell you, coughing through the carcinogens—and assuming that my plane was not hijacked and that I was not 'mugged' on the way . . . . .

I am fighting for a way through to your real ears. That is exactly to say that I am trying to differentiate, in you, between data and information. Data are a whole lot of meaningful patterns. We can generate data indefinitely; we can exchange data for ever; we can store data, retrieve data, and file them away. All this is great fun : maybe useful, maybe lucrative. But we have to ask why. The purpose is regulation. And that means translating data into information. *Information is what changes us.* My purpose too is to effect change—to impart information, not data.

Data, I want to say to you, are an excrescence. Data are the very latest kind of pollution. We are not going to do anything at all about the management of information and knowledge towards the regulation of society as long as we think in data-processing terms. That is technologically easy. It is what the computer companies and the telecommunication interests would like us to do. Data are assuredly the great new marketable commodities of the nineteen-seventies. But, let me repeat, data of themselves have no value.

What has value is the machinery to transform data into information, and the machinery by which that information may be used to innervate society. Society has become a complex organism, and it needs a nervous system. Managing the development of informational science and technology is all about this task. There is no other message than this.

2. BASES OF ARGUMENT

The technological capabilities on the availability of which my arguments will be based already exist. There is not really a significant element of prognosis about them. There is however one proviso to this: it derives from a logical trap to which I will shortly draw attention. But first, here are some fundamental propositions.

First Proposition :   We can now automate whatever we can exactly specify.

Second Proposition :   Most (possibly all) ostensibly human prerogatives for inferential, judgmental, learned and adaptive behaviour can be exactly specified—at least with respect to finite contexts.

To extend the second proposition to intuitional and creative behaviour poses grave difficulties of definition, and invariably invites emotional uproar. But we may at least stand by this weaker statement:

Third Proposition :   Within specified frameworks, much ostensibly intuitional and creative human behaviour can be indistinguishably imitated by machine.

Fourth Proposition :   Distance is technically irrelevant.

All this means that purposive systems can now be created to undertake any kind of purpose at all. We know how to design those systems, and how to innervate them with data streams. And so society would appear to be confronted by a problem of choice: what activities should actually be automated? But I shall argue that this question is largely illusory.

First of all, there is the logical trap. This is of the sort called by logicians a fallacy of addition. We may do *any* of the things we can do; it does not follow that we may do *all* the things we can do. In the present state of the art, that is to say, we shall rapidly exhaust our reserves of skill. So here is the proviso about technological capability. My own belief is that we shall have to embody a great deal of basic software in special purpose hardware, and that we shall need to automate the creation of special software itself. I think that computer science will break through the barrier of human programming, and move to an era when programs are written by machines under general human surveillance. This will in turn lead to programs which modify themselves in the light of experience. Then we shall be near the realization of the machine more intelligent than its designer, which von Neumann envisaged and showed mathematically possible more than twenty years ago. There is no need for more than this one paragraph of such modest guesswork—because after *that* it may well be too late to do what ought to be done right now. At any rate, this is the only technological barrier which I can identify.

Then we revert to the spurious problem of choice. Why should not responsible authorities choose between desirable and undesirable systems for handling knowledge and information? The answer is that in neither the private nor the public sector of a free society is there a sufficient concentration of power to do so. If, for example, mammoth publishing interests decide (as they may) not to mobilize the resources of electronics adequately in the dissemination of knowledge, then it is open to electronic interests to become the publishers of the future. It is also open to the information handling community itself to embark on entrepreneurial activity at the expense of both these industries. In the public sector, it is certainly open to central government, through its grant-awarding agencies in particular, to encourage or discourage particular applications of cybernation. But it will be very difficult to inhibit developments which are of themselves economically viable in the way that (for example) space exploration would be inhibited without central funding.

And here we perhaps identify the basic nature of the problem which cybernetic systems set out to solve. Throughout history until this time the problem was to acquire sufficient information to generate effective change. The individual wishing to become expert in some field of knowledge had to buy information expensively; the government wishing to understand even the rudiments of the structure of its society had to buy information through the census. And so we have gone on, paying more and more money for data acquisition—on the assumption that data constitute information. But we have already said that data become information only at the point when we ourselves are changed. It is self-evident that our capacity to be changed, whether we are an individual seeking private knowledge or a government seeking understanding of society, is strictly finite. In conditions of data paucity, almost all data acquired can be transformed into information—and used to procure effective change. But in conditions when the supply of data far outruns this metabolic capability, most data are literally worthless. Yet we pay more and more for these worthless data because that is the established order of things.

The fact is that quite recently the sign of the informational problem changed from plus to minus. The problem is no longer about acquiring data, which are generated as a by-product of every modern undertaking. The problem is about informational overload. The private citizen seeking knowledge is inundated by information which is virtually free. Yet the publishing industry responds in the old mode—by selling him yet more. The firm continues to buy expensive market research, because that is what it has always done, oblivious of the fact that transactions of every kind can now be electronically monitored, so that data are in glut. Its problem too is one of procuring adaptive behaviour, and no longer at all one of 'finding the facts'. As for government, there is really no dearth of societary information either; there is instead a problem of organizing information—across departmental boundaries and in time.

Institutions, firms and (thanks to television) private citizens today receive critical information very quickly indeed; the aggregate picture at federal level is slow by comparison to materialize. To put the point the other way round, then, the body politic has wildly overactive reflexes. In the body physiologic this is the condition of *clonus*—it is a symptom of spasticity. If we live, as I suspect, in a spastic society it is because of clonic response. And by the expectations of these arguments, the clonus will get worse.

Thus I argue that the problem of information management is now a problem of filtering and refining a massive overload of data—for all of us, whether citizens, firms, institutions or governments. We might well say that it is a problem

not so much of data acquisition as of right storage,
not so much of storage as of fast retrieval,
not so much of retrieval as of proper selection,
not so much of selection as of identifying wants,
not so much of knowing wants as of recognizing needs—

and the needs are precisely the requirements of systemic equilibria.

This almost tabular account of the matter ostensively defines another cybernetic truth. In any controlled system, there must be an hierarchic array of sub-systems, in which both the values and the structure of any one sub-system are set by a logically superior system. That is to say that one cannot discuss the purposive nature of a system in its own language, but only in a higher order language. There are potent reasons for this in theoretical logic, just as there are potent practical issues in terms of the need systematically to reduce the informational overload by a system of filters. These filters are necessarily arranged hierarchically, in a way which matches the hierarchy of logical systems.

Thus I introduce the concept of *meta*system: a system which stands over and beyond a logically inferior system, and one which is competent to handle that lower system's logic. Please note that metasystems are logically superior, and not necessarily more senior or more highly endowed with status or privilege. Please note also that in an hierarchy of systems there will be several orders of 'meta'. Let us take a moment of time to illustrate these points, since the concept of metasystem plays an important role in what I have to say.

Consider for example a school, in which each of a hundred teachers adequately controls and instructs a roomful of pupils. The roomful is in each case made up of several sets of pupils. Now each set of pupils is in fact pursuing a course of instruction which takes it from one room, one association of sets, and one teacher, to another room, another set of sets, and another teacher. If we consider the totality of rooms, holding their pupils and teachers, as sub-systems of the school (for this is indeed the organizational format we observe on a visit) there is no way of knowing or discussing *in such terms* the educative process as it affects all the pupils. To do this we shall need to find the metasystem which organizes all the groupings and ensures that they mesh together. This metasystem is the timetable, in terms of which the course followed by a particular pupil stands revealed. This is a logically superior system; but we do not expect the teacher in his room to treat the timetable as some kind of ju-ju. On the contrary; but if he wishes the timetable altered, he will perforce raise the issue in metasystemic terms. It is simply no good to say 'this is my class, and I will take it at another time'.

Furthermore: if the state wished to discuss the total process of education for all its high schools in relation to nursery schooling on the one hand and to university education on the other, then a new metasystem logically beyond the first metasystem would be required. And in this case the question whether the second metasystem is not only logically but also constitutionally superior would arise. It would be discussed in those familiar terms about autonomy, about professional integrity, about bureaucratic interference, about sub-optimization, about synergy..... Such discussions would be less boring if we could get the logic right first.

The Esoteric Box

Let us now retrieve the argument that the development of purposive automated systems involves a spurious problem of choice. For, we argued, there is no method in a free society whereby such choice could be implemented. I would like to examine this argument in more detail, with a view to uncovering certain mechanisms which are germane to the issue before us. The objective now is to try, like good scientists, to determine the basic parameters of the problem at some level of abstraction which facilitates understanding. Were we to fail in this endeavour to stand back and to generalize, we should conclude with long lists of possible systems, in hundreds of possible contexts, with long lists of possible dangers attaching to each. Then we should achieve no useful insights at all.

Firstly, what is the entity which will in practice develop systems of knowledge and information? It is some kind of social institution: perhaps a firm, perhaps a profession, perhaps a social service..... Whatever it is, it is surely an identifiable entity, with certain recognizable characteristics. I call it an *esoteric box*. What is going on inside this box is an established order of things: things accepted as mores of the box, things professional, things historical, and so on. There is a complex arrangement of sub-systems, a strange set of relationships between people of standing inside the box, and a recondite way of behaving. These features—their complexity and unintelligibility to the outsider—justify the box's adjective 'esoteric'. Admission to the box's activity cannot be gained without the appropriate passport. But the box is not a closed system, it is part of society; it certainly has inputs and outputs. Even so it is internally and autonomously self-organizing and self-regulating. And although the box *processes* whatever it exists to affect (and this is often people), that which is processed does not change the box at all. The box goes on; it is very powerfully organized to maintain its own internal stability, and therefore its survival as an integral institution.

I have elsewhere sought to show that the esoteric box, the identifiable social institution, is a strongly robust system in equilibrium. If we try to influence its behaviour by changing variables which apparently affect it, it responds neither by collapsing nor by a violent reaction. It simply shifts the internal position of equilibrium very slightly, thereby offsetting the environmental change that has occurred. (In the model from physical chemistry that I have used to study these boxes, this behaviour would be an instance of the operation of Le Chatelier's principle.)

Now if it is an esoteric box which is going to develop an information system directed to cybernetic ends, its primary objective will be to enhance its own performance and chance of survival—it will not attend first to the performance and survival of society at large. Equally, the box will be highly resistant to efforts made to constrain its freedom to do so. There seem to be only two mechanisms available to a free society seeking to influence an autonomous institution in any case. The first is to facilitate some modes of development and to inhibit others by the provision of incentives and inhibitors from outside. I mean by this the awarding or withholding of grants, tax concessions, public campaigns, and so on. Every esoteric box has its own feedback mechanisms; what the state can do is to change the gain on the relevant amplifiers. But because of the high internal stability of the box, we must expect this kind of control device to operate in a cumbersome and generally inefficient way. The other device available is legislative. The main trouble here lies in the identification of what is antisocial. Most advances in human welfare have paid a price in infringement of personal liberty: whether that price is seen as reasonable or as a fundamental deprivation of human rights will often be a matter of interpretation. But I shall in any case assume that wise government will interact with the authorities in any esoteric box to achieve acceptable codes of behaviour. What really concerns us in this situation is what happens at the metasystemic level.

The fact is that esoteric boxes interact. Any major facet of public policy, such as health, education, the manipulation of credit, security, and balance of payments and so forth, involves at least a string and possibly a complex network of interacting esoteric boxes. Now just as the esoteric box itself is seen as something extremely stable and survival-worthy, so the system which links the boxes is typically tenous and unstable. It is not itself an institution, not itself a higher order esoteric box. It is simply an assemblage of esoteric boxes, and it does not constitute a proper metasystem at all. It is in this fact that the threat to society really lies; it is here that we shall seek the important scientific generalizations.

Consider education, for example. There are, to speak arbitrarily, four major esoteric boxes involved in this facet of society. There is the system of compulsory schooling; there is the university system; there is the post-experience career-oriented system sponsored by industry; there is the free market in adult education. All four of these esoteric boxes may be sub-divided, almost endlessly; but we are seeking to move our thoughts in the opposite direction—to identify the commonality of these systems, and to examine their interactions. If we take health as our example, we shall find a similar situation. There is an esoteric box labelled general medical practice, and another called hospitals; there is a public health box labelled sanitation; there is a market-oriented box dealing in pharmaceuticals; there is a market-place for medical information which belongs to publishing.

In short, we may take any facet of social policy and find the strings and networks of highly stable esoteric boxes which between them make a composite but not integrated impact on the individual citizen. We may do this for security, discovering esoteric boxes for the police, esoteric boxes for fire protection, and esoteric boxes for insurance—not to mention the esoteric boxes which are the armed services themselves. We may do the same thing for the movement of goods, discovering esoteric boxes for every method of transport. We may do it for the movement of money, detecting esoteric boxes for emolument and social benefit, for taxation, for credit. . . . .

Then the question arises, why are those strings and networks as unstable as they appear to be? If there is no genuine metasystem, why has one not grown up? Was there never a stabilizing structure of any kind? I think that there was a metasystemic structure of a very remarkable kind, but that it has been abandoned. We have thereby lost the meta-controls which made the composite systems of esoteric boxes viable. If this be true, no wonder we need assiduously to design replacements.

First, there was the structure of society's 'external skeleton': the religious, legal and moral framework. Into this hooked the structure of the 'internal skeleton': there were indeed formal bonds linking social institutions themselves. Younger people seem to be systematically abandoning the values of the external system, so that it ceases to be relevant to any control process dependent on negative feedback. Given that almost fifty percent of the population of the United States is now under twenty-five years of age, the revolt of youth in destroying metasystems whose stabilizing value they do not understand is a serious matter indeed. The young have more power in society than ever before: purchasing power, and the power that derives from not being afraid of inherited norms. Most of them are not taking technology for granted. Many of them are questioning established values in terms which their elders do not understand. Some have already begun smashing up computer installations. As to the internal system, changes in technology are moving the interfaces between the esoteric boxes representing established institutions—and they are not responding. Instead of evolving by adaptation, these boxes are putting up the shutters and seeking to maintain themselves as integral systems while the context changes around them. This will not work.

Thus the strings and networks are unstable, and the metasystems are missing. Rather than attempt the exhaustive enumeration of these composite systems let us try to state the features they share in terms of knowledge, information and control. They seem to me to be the following.

Characteristics of Strings and Networks of Esoteric Boxes

(i)   In all cases some esoteric boxes in the system are part of the public sector and some part of the private sector.

(ii)   In all cases the esoteric boxes are generating, and (inefficiently) passing between themselves, knowledge about the world in which they operate.

(iii)   In all cases they are also generating, either as primary or as spin-off data, knowledge about the individual citizen which they rarely interchange.

(iv)   In all cases the very forces which produce stability within the esoteric boxes themselves conduce to instability between the boxes.

(v)   In all cases, what constitutes the improved management of knowledge *within* the esoteric box has to do with the rapid matching of sets of possible courses to sets of actual conditions, and the rapid correction of mismatches by feedback governors.

(vi)   In all cases what would count as an improvement in the management of information *between* esoteric boxes, and therefore an embodiment of the metasystem concerned, would be an integral information network and a mutual trade-off in knowledge—both of the world and of the citizen.

If this list of six points correctly states the position, it behoves us to elucidate them further.

3. ELUCIDATION OF SYSTEMIC CHARACTERISTICS

We begin this elucidation by developing a generalization about the management of information within the esoteric box. This is an explanation of point (v) in the foregoing *List*.

Whatever we are looking at at any given movement in time will be found to represent a complex state of affairs. Call this total situation the *initial condition*. For example, a patient entering a health system has an initial condition; so has a pupil in any educational situation. The first step taken by a professional in reviewing this initial condition is to try and characterize it with a name. In the case of health, this name is the diagnosis (*diabetes* = 'he needs more insulin than he has got'). In the case of the educational condition, we may name a state of ignorance relative to some need (*advanced physics* = 'he needs more physics than he has got'). This naming process may be very inefficient, as for instance when we name the complicated economic status of a citizen within the economy as: *credit* = $100. And even in medical diagnosis, for instance in psychiatric medicine or in prophylactic medicine, the name may not be very much help. Then why do we go through the naming process?

The answer to this is surely that the brain is a coding device. We are not cerebrally organized to hold in our heads large wodges of information about complicated states of affairs. Having examined the complexity of the initial condition, we seek to encapsulate it in a name—which can later be used to retrieve at least the critical attributes of the situation so named. Next, we use this name in our search of courses of action from which to select a treatment of the initial condition. Thus the very mention of a medical diagnosis selects in the mind of the physician a subset of the whole set of human therapies which relates to the name, and from this subset one therapy will be selected and applied. Similarly, 'advanced physics' selects a subset of courses from all possible education courses, and from that subset one course will be recommended. The credit rating simply selects one figure from a small number of possible figures to be applied as a ceiling on purchasing power.

Depending on the seriousness of the situation, as measured perhaps by its 'professional' content, this naming filter is a more or less elaborate tool for making the system work. A higher professional content can be injected into the process by a more elaborate taxonomy of names, and also by iterating the process of selection. Thus, having made a diagnosis and selected a possible therapy, the physician will go back through the name filter to the actual initial condition, and verify the treatment in every particular. In most social situations, however, this iteration is far too expensive to undertake. And for that reason, many of the responses which social systems make to the initial condition are crude indeed.

The first general capability of automation within such a system is to abandon the naming filter. For computers *can* hold large wodges of information. The computer is faced with the problem of matching one complex profile (the initial condition) with another— probably less complex—profile of possible courses of action. Far from simply automating the human professional component in the system, then, the automatic system should much improve upon it, especially if it is organized to interrogate the subject in order to fill out details of the initial condition which it perceives to be relevant. Moreover, as its model of the system it handles is enriched and improved by experience, it becomes possible in principle for a preliminary choice of action to be iteratively simulated. Then the likely effects of choosing this action, and in particular the vulnerability of this strategy to unknown factors or a range of possible futures, may rapidly be estimated before any indication of choice is given at all. Next again, if the automated system is geared to invigilate the actual process of applying the course to the initial condition, so that the subject's response is continuously monitored, then corrective action against any mismatching or systemic oscillation may be continuously taken. And of course it will be taken on the basis of the total richness of possible interaction between the two sets (states of the subject and possible treatments) rather than through the exiguous filtering channels of the naming which have hitherto been used with so little finesse.

In all of this we find key applications of another fundamental cybernetic principle: Ashby's Law of Requisite Variety. Variety is the cybernetic measure of complexity. It is explictly the possible number of states of a system. The Law says that the variety of a given situation can be managed adequately only by control mechanisms having at least as great a capacity to generate variety themselves. Names typically do not do this: they are archetypes of variety reducers. Indeed, in most socio-economic situations of our age, we seek to obey Ashby's law by *reducing* the variety of the real world, necessarily in a somewhat artificial way, as with naming. As I said earlier, this leads us to manage low-variety theories about the economy, because we can handle those, rather than to manage the high-variety economy itself. A much more satisfactory method of handling the problem is to *increase* the variety of the system doing the judging, managing or controlling—by automating the 'professional' component. The second method is now technologically open as we saw in the last section. Allied to fast feedback, whether through simulations of the total system or through the invigilation of actual results, the whole mechanism permits a much more refined and much speedier convergence on a stable outcome.

By looking at this mechanism in its relevant detail, we simultaneously lay bare the major threat to privacy of which everyone who has ever contemplated these matters is already aware. As we seek better control of situations by confronting variety with variety within the system, we lose the anonymity which used to cloak the identity of an individual by the use of a name. This is quite clearly seen in the simplest case of all—the name of the citizen as normally understood. My name identifies me from among the rest of us here; but it undertakes to disclose no more information than this primary selection. Yet the more effectively any esoteric box handles my case, then the higher the variety it disposes as a measure of my own variety; therefore the more risky to my personal integrity does the whole process become. Here is the person rawly exposed, because in higher variety, within the professional system appropriate to any esoteric box. And I am saying that the better the system, both from the point of view of the social institution concerned and therefore from my own as its patient or pupil or client in any other way, *ipso facto* the more potentially damaging to me is that system. Am I psychologically ill? The medical system will know. Am I educationally inadequate to my job? The educational system will know. Where was I at the time the murder was committed? The credit system knows when and where I bought petrol that night.....

This analysis successfully generalizes the problem of privacy, and also says a great deal about the reasons why esoteric boxes are under such pressure to withdraw into themselves—instead of collaborating in metasystemic management systems (see Point (vi) in the *List*).

As to privacy: It is all too possible that the computer will sweep forward to destroy privacy and freedom of choice without our really knowing that this is happening—much as the motor car has swept forward, poisoning us and inexorably changing the quality of life. Consider two major mechanisms which might bring this about.

First, there is the question of a man's credibility as a citizen. When a man is too well documented, electronically buttoned-up, in what sense can he make a new start? How can he restore his credit, once it is lost? How will he persuade the machine to emulate his own God-given capability to *forget*? A man is to himself as to others a complex package of information. In behavioural terms at least, his vital statistics, his knowledge, his actions and his emotional response as well—all may be catalogued and stored. By the criteria of information theory, then, my electronic image in the machine may be more real than I am. It is rounded and retrievable. Above all, it is a high-variety image—higher very likely than the image of me in the minds of my own friends. The behaviour of the image is predictable in statistical terms. Probably I am not. But the strength of the machine image is its pragmatic validity. There is no confusion here, no ambiguity, no loss of history, no rationalization. I am a mess; and I don't know what to do. The machine knows better—in statistical terms. Thus is my reality less real than my mirror image in the store. That fact diminishes me.

Second of the threats to my reality, there is the likelihood of my manipulation on a scale which is also frightening. Overt advertising has already taken us to the brink of what seems to be tolerable in this respect. But at least we are conscious of the risk—we may note the Freudian images of the ad-man cult, and the importunity of slogans which are akin to physiological conditioning. We may thus protect our personalities. But the computer's machinations are covert. A long-term record of my purchases should enable a computer to devise a mailing shot at me which is virtually irresistible.

As to involution: We earlier made the assumption that esoteric boxes themselves will engage in dialogue with their own clients and with governments to protect the citizen in this threatening situation. The important thing is not so much that this ought to happen as that it will certainly happen. For if it is vital to the social institution to remain integral, and if it is the proclivity of that esoteric box to be highly stable, then integrity and stability will be supported and reinforced by the highest ethical codes where professions are concerned, and by commercial self-interest where they are not. Each esoteric box will identify its own vested interest in solving these problems; and in solving them it will increase its own stability and survival power. Then these systems will become more involuted, and yet more esoteric; they will become more stable, and more resistant to change; in many cases it will be literally impossible to access the information they contain without a special electronic key.

As the solutions begin to emerge from the studies which institutions are already making, it can be expected that legislative force will be asked for the implementation of any provisions which repeatedly occur as proposing matters of principle. For example, it already looks likely that legislation will be sought to permit the citizen access to his own computer files, or at least to permit him the knowledge that an entry has been made therein. Even so, there will be many difficulties for legislators, and especially difficulties of definition. After all, many records have been kept in the past, records made up with quill pens, of which the citizen had no intimate knowledge—and in cases of national security, or even of high-grade employment, perhaps no knowledge at all.

But the point for which we are reaching here really concerns the missing metasystems for the regulation and stabilization of strings and networks of esoteric boxes. If the inexorable trend is toward involution, and toward the isolation of information within the box, then the interchange of information between esoteric boxes becomes less and less likely (see Point (iii) in the *List*). Institutions will not dare to move towards the creation of metasystems, because this would breach confidentiality. As for the legislators, how can they possibly launch bills at one parliamentary sitting intending to keep information inside the box (for the reasons adduced), and then launch bills at the next sitting aimed at better management on the strings-and-network level? For the requirements of the second legislation would be to assemble information more economically for metasystemic purposes, to enrich the understanding of social needs by synthesizing information within higher-order models of the economy, and in general to seek modes of control which would necessarily diminish participation at lower societary levels to the point of total incomprehension as to what was going on.

This is a king-size dilemma. It has already been encountered in a relatively mild form by government bureaux of statistics, all of whom operate under legislation which guarantees the privacy of the individual firm by statistical aggregation. But in situations where large firms dominate sparsely populated localities, real skill may be needed to avoid betrayal of this rule by sheer accident. And perhaps in avoiding such risks the efficacy of the network will be sensibly reduced. The extension of the problem down to the rights of the individual, and up to meta-metasystems, and across to include the whole gamut of socio-economic behaviour, is a daunting prospect. But the difficulty is real; it will not go away.

So here is the meaning of Point (iv) in the *List of Characteristics* we set out to elucidate. Strings and networks of esoteric boxes will become less and less cohesive; and the meta-systems they represent will become more and more unstable. These are the inexorable trends, and this is the basic reason why (I unhappily suggest) society is falling apart.

The Blurring of Interfaces

We have been seeking to elucidate the meaning of the four final points of the six statements made in the *List* which ended Section 2. It is time to revert to the first two of those six points. For in our recent discussion we have concerned ourselves primarily with information about the citizen as a product of either public or professional social institutions. But the argument of Points (i) and (ii) was that every facet of social control shared in the public and private sector, shared too in knowledge of the world as well as in knowledge of the citizen. Then let us begin a fresh analysis, beginning with the mising pieces of the puzzle, and see where that leads.

We want to talk in the first place, then, about knowledge of the world, and its dissemination as an entrepreneurial activity to anyone needing knowledge. This whole process began and continued historically in a very distinctive way. There were people—individuals by name—in the time of the ancient Greeks in whom reposed such knowledge as there was. Those wishing to acquire knowledge did so on a personal basis and at great expense. This often meant journeying to sit at the feet of an Aristotle and to learn from him. We might call the process *custom-built publishing*. We should note that it was a very high-variety process (the cybernetic analysis of a dialogue demonstrates to perfection Ashby's Law of Requisite Variety). And we should note finally that the effectiveness of the process relied on a relative paucity of knowledge compared with the capacity of the human brain and the calls on its time. For nearly two thousand years this situation prevailed. Although writing and its tools were developed, any piece of writing was still custom-built. One's copy of any text was a personal copy, bearing unique imperfections, omissions and additions. Then, five hundred years ago, came printing—a process which remains almost unchanged to this day as the accepted principle of permanent imaging.

It was the invention of printing that procured the first qualitative change in the management of information and knowledge for mankind. In achieving the massive dissemination of knowledge Gutenberg and Caxton also destroyed its custom-built character. In mitigation, the publishing industry (as it has become) developed an activity called editing. This critical occupation fulfils almost exactly the same function as naming or diagnosis in our earlier model. It constitutes a cross-over point between a high-variety set of information on the one hand and a high-variety set of clients on the other; it selects subsets from each, and attempts to match them. In so far as the matching succeeds, there is a marketable product. This may be defined as an edited publication, identifying a sufficient number of clients satisfied with the editorial process as between them to pay for the cost of publishing and printing (with of course a profit margin for all concerned).

The steady development of this whole marketing operation has led, like all other recent developments in the dissemination of human knowledge, to the informational overload mentioned before. Publishers continue to issue more and more printed material, relying specifically on their editorial skill in identifying market subsets willing to pay the price. But increasingly the process depends on mythology. It is easy enough to demonstrate that in fact the overload threshold has already been passed, and that (as we said) the sign has now changed on the stream of data input. No professional man can possibly read more than a fraction of what he would like to read or feels he should read. In some professions, current trends when extrapolated show that the whole population of professionals will shortly be employed in preparing abstracts of papers—whereupon no authors will be left to write them. This shows that in so far as people continue to purchase new publications they are not driven to do so by any residual capacity to convert data into information (meaning: what changes us). One may entertain various theories about the motives which do drive them. Such theories range from feelings of guilt and a sense of threat at one end of the spectrum to a pious belief that the editing process is (hopefully) converging on *my* special interests at the other. However this may be, no professional man can now cope effectively with the material he is expected to buy; and most would agree that they buy more than they can cope with.

Various mechanisms may operate to put an end to this situation, perhaps quite suddenly and dramatically. Which mechanisms will operate depends on which motives turn out to be most significant. For example, in so far as many publications depend on their advertising revenue for survival, then when the advertisers become aware that their advertisements are not even seen (because the journals are not opened) they may suddenly and disastrously withdraw support en masse. But the more profound threat to the established mores of the whole industry derives from the likelihood that someone will give convincing entrepreneurial effect to the unrecognized but inexorable trends of the situation. These are quite simply that professional people have a need for less and not more information, and therefore—in the long run—are going to *pay* for less and less, and to refuse to pay for more and more. The publishing industry and government itself continue to regard data as equivalent to information. The metasystem in which this issue can alone be sensibly contemplated, will shortly recognize that any one client is overloaded by any one editor who provides for the needs of a coterie, however small, intended to cover his costs.

There is then an inexorable requirement for a return to custom-built publishing directed at individuals, whether private citizens or cabinet ministers. This service must be economically viable, once the necessity for it is generally recognized, because it meets a need which cannot much longer be ignored. Moreover, the new technology is able to supply it. We shall use the power of computers to undertake an editing process on behalf of the only editor who any longer counts—the client himself. It matters not whether the information reaches that client on a computer terminal, or in a custom-built personalized print. Economics and personal preference will decide that issue. What does matter is the inevitable reversion to the age-old principle of publishing based on the finite capacity of the brain to assimilate data, and to convert them to the information which changes the brain's condition. And in all of this we may note the mechanisms already uncovered in this paper: especially obedience to the Law of Requisite Variety, and the vitality of the principle of adaptive feedback.

I here repeat that this kind of prognosis is not to my mind a matter of forecasting, but the detection of an inexorable requirement. There is no need to extend the argument to publication in the field of leisure, important though this is, because the considerations are much more difficult—and I think longer term. But the field of professional publishing, which includes knowledge about the whole of science and technology, and includes knowledge about everything that government may do, is sufficiently significant in itself. Both areas may be treated as their own esoteric boxes. In both cases there has to be a high variety exposure of the client to the system, and there has to be fast adaptive feedback. If you will allow that this is possible, then we reach a new dimension of concern in the field of socio-economic management.

We know by now, as a matter of principle, that the increased effectiveness of the service provided inside an esoteric box increases the vulnerability of its clients to intimate revelations—because of Ashby's Law. The case of both commercial and governmental publishing to professional individuals offers no exception. In exactly the same degree, and by exactly the same mechanisms, that custom-built publishing becomes effective at all, so does the increasingly well-served client become a target of exploitation. In so far, that is, as a particular product of either commercial or governmental publishing is especially meant for me, valuable to me, valued by me . . . . . so far is it irresistible to me. We encountered this point before.

There is no problem here so long as we continue to speak of professional publishing by reputable publishers (and governments) itself. The matter for concern is of course that if such a system works for this purpose it will work for other and nefarious purposes too. If we can encode an individual's interests and susceptibilities on the basis of feedback which he supplies, if we can converge on a model of the individual of higher variety than the model he has of himself, then we have exactly the situation inside the automated system which was observed to be such a threat in more protected contexts. I think that marketing people will come to use this technique to increase the relatively tiny response to a mailing shot which exists today to a response in the order of ninety percent. All this is to say that the conditioning loop exercised upon the individual will be closed. Then we have provided a perfect physiological system for the marketing of anything we like—not then just genuine knowledge, but perhaps 'political truth' or 'the ineluctable necessity to act against the elected government'. Here indeed is a serious threat to society.

Now we can see how the first three points in the *List of Characteristics* about the behaviour of esoteric boxes are indivisible from the last three points. Knowledge of the world and knowledge of the citizen are indissolubly united in systems of the kind we must expect; private and public interests moreover are inseparably involved in each. Then the interfaces between these four major components of information systems become hopelessly blurred. We shall not be able to legislate to keep what is indivisible divided. These arguments are based on realities manifested by situations which cannot be controlled at their own level without interference on a totalitarian scale in the rights and autonomy of our social institutions, the esoteric boxes.

4. METASYSTEM MANAGEMENT

The jigsaw puzzle is complete. We have looked closely at the emergent picture of interacting social institutions, exemplified as esoteric boxes. They are stable, involuted, resistant to change. Their interaction is embodied in strings and networks of complex connectivity, exemplified as metasystems. These are unstable, mercurial, existing more in concept than reality. The problems of information management that assail the boxes will be solved, if with the greatest difficulty. These solutions will themselves inexorably increase the metasystemic instability, threatening to blow society apart.

If all this offers an effective generalization of the problem of data pollution, and if we are to see any possibility of its solution in terms of good cybernetics, practice is needed in applying the model here envisaged. Let us then look at two levels of application, as widely separated as possible, to see how readily the systems concerned map onto each other, and what may be the commonalities of acceptable metasystemic controls.

First Example : at Hearth and Home

One plausible development of existing capabilities in informational science looks like this.

It is already possible to transmit textual material and the instructions for printing it into a television receiver—during a normal broadcast, and without interfering in any way with the broadcast itself. This is done by utilizing some of the enormous channel capacity available and not used by the flying spot defining the picture. For example, the spot has a 'flyback' period, when it returns from the end of one scan to the beginning of the next. One line of scanning on a TV screen contains approximately six hundred bits of information. The flyback takes five lines to return, and is thus capable of carrying three thousand bits of information. If sixty frames are scanned every second (this would be fifty in Great Britain) there is spare capacity to transmit 180,000 bits a second of other information while the broadcast itself is going on. We know how to produce hard copy from the television set, using this input information. If we wish to produce a column of print six inches wide, with excellent resolution at a hundred lines per inch, we need 600×100 bits of information to produce an inch of text. If follows from all this that we have a capacity to produce three inches of text every second without interfering with the television broadcast.

Newspapers can be produced in the home like this, as is well known, and experiments continue. But newspapers are not custom-built; they belong to the informational overload.

This overload is due to be met by custom-built publishing. Then apply the existing technology to the new publishing concept and see what happens.

Suppose that there are twenty buttons on the side of the television set which can be pressed by the viewer. The broadcaster invites the viewer to participate in a 'personal response programme'. He shows the viewer two pictures, and asks him to press the first button if he prefers the first picture to the second—otherwise not. He then asks a question, and says that the second button should be pressed if the answer is yes—otherwise not. And so on. By the time the viewer has pressed or not pressed all twenty buttons he has identified himself in a high-variety way. For there are 2^{20} ways in which the set of buttons may be pressed, and that means enough patterns to distinguish between more than a million individuals (where each offers a separate pattern). As to privacy, the viewer is at home and alone with his set. So no-one knows which buttons he presses (or do they?).

Having completed this exercise, the broadcaster suggests that the viewer should press his 'print' button. The television set will then print out, from the vast amount of information being carried on the flyback, a piece of print which is determined by the particular pattern set on the twenty buttons. After all, if the sponsor hires one minute of flyback time at the end of his advertisement, he may *transmit* no less than a hundred and eighty inches of text. The 'computer program' set up on the twenty buttons *selects* (say) six inches of this available text, and the apparatus prints it. This means that the individual concerned receives a very highly directed message. By the arguments used earlier, the viewer is likely to find this message irresistible. For example, the old lady sitting in one house reads 'this product is especially suitable for old ladies', while the young man next door reads 'this product is especially suitable for young men'. (One needs little knowledge of the advertising world to recognize this example as remarkably naive.) Moreover, because the TV set is in a particular location, and can be pre-programmed with that information, the custom-built message and advertisement could well include instructions as to which local supplier will make what special reduction for immediate compliance with the suggestion to purchase. Again, this example is offered for display purposes only: the opportunities are hair-raising. Suppose for instance that the apparatus is able to store previous sets of responses.....

The viewer lifts the telephone in order to place his order—or perhaps he simply presses a new button on his set labelled 'yes'. The supplier now has an order, and his system (for he is his own esoteric box) must immediately check the creditworthiness of the customer. If by this time we have reached the cashless society, it could well be that the whole transaction is finalized and the viewer's bank account debited within the millisecond.

This is all entertaining, and something like it will very likely happen. Now consider the esoteric boxes on whose integrity and security he relies, but which he may by now himself have violated. The information he betrays might well include.

> his medical status,
> his educational status,
> his intimate psychological situation,
> the family context (i.e. someone else's privacy is breached),
> the employment context (i.e. commercial security may be breached).

the economy's view of his credit,
the state of his bank balance,
his religious outlook,
his political outlook,
his social attitudes at large......

Twenty bits, a variety of a million, every time : here is an inexhaustible souce of metasystemic information available to anyone who sets out to acquire it. And from this information
could be synthesized a new account of society and of the economy, orders of magnitude
more powerful and valuable *and* threatening than any we have hitherto known or countenanced. With this unthinking violation of privacy goes the betrayal of all the mechanisms
for protection and security to both the individual and the state which the esoteric boxes
themselves have sought to guarantee. And with it go also the distinctions between public
and private information, knowledge of the citizen and knowledge of the world.

Second Example : in World Economics

Undertaking now the largest possible change in the scale of this thinking, and leaping over
a staggering array of other plausible examples large and small, we turn to the future of
mankind itself and the stability of world economics.

A consensus of opinion might define an economy as the observable, quantifiable aspect
of the social metasystem. The metric of economics appears to offer the only *lingua franca*
which enables us to talk in figures about strings and networks of esoteric boxes—for
typically these have no other commensurable denominator. But it seems to me most
important to observe that this circumstance has let us into jejune descriptions of the social
weal—which are obsessionally treated as *merely* economic. Surely no-one can believe
that the total state of the world with all its pressures, ethnic, religious, lebensraum-orien-
ted, power-geared, and all its problems of military, societary and environmental crisis,
can adequately be discussed in terms of econometric models. Input-output analysis tells us
something about the connectivity of esoteric boxes; cash flows say a little about their
dynamic inter-relationships; but we may discuss fiscal and monetary policy until we are
purple without touching on the major causes of even economic disequilibria, still less of
social dysfunction. This contention is relevant at both the national and the international
level.

Having criticized the metric that is used and the models that are adopted, I may readily
claim that the networks linking social institutions at this level are the most tenuous yet
discussed. This underlines the fact that major political entities—states and nations—are
the ultimately complete exemplifications of the esoteric box. They answer both to the
definition of this term and to the behaviourial analysis of its operation. I shall risk as your
foreign guest a remark about this which I hope will not be regarded as a solecism. We
have just entered the decade in which the founding bicentenary of a remarkable interactive
network will be celebrated in your country, the metasystem for which is perfectly exemplified in a federal constitution and its law. Is it not fair to say that there are esoteric boxes
within this system, some of which are whole States while others are social institutions of
other kinds, which maintain to this day those characteristics of the integral, stable, change-
resistant box which we have taken much trouble to elucidate? And if there is cause for

alarm about national instability, then surely it is metasystemic in nature. Correctives are hard to apply, for reasons we have also uncovered: they lead to involution and even exacerbate the problems.

At the level of world affairs, the case is far more strong. The sovereign nation is the ultimately esoteric box; the interconnective networks between nations are like so much spun silk. All mechanisms described here clearly operate, and they too are clearly involutionary. The problems and threats are the same, but they are writ large. Just as we may identify spurious metasystems purporting to link the esoteric boxes of our own social institutions, so there are spurious international metasystems. All approaches to world government, from the League of Nations onwards, and including market-oriented consortia, *speak* metalinguistically but do not *operate* metasystemically. This is why I call them spurious. Hence it is in the network of world economics that we find the ultimately inadequate description and the ultimately incompetent management of the ultimately unstable metasystem.

Perhaps the nearest approach to genuinely stable organizations of this kind are the multi-national companies. They represent linkages of esoteric boxes, beyond doubt; they certainly have identifiable metasystems. Even so, the cohesive forces required to make them survival-worthy barely emerge—given a potentially hostile environment. Do we have adequate management mores and philosophy, company lore, or international law, to underwrite their responsible self-regulation? It is a serious question, bearing in mind that these companies are in a sense the emergent *nations* of the next few decades. I mean by this that the gross product of some mushrooming companies already exceeds the gross national product of the smaller historic nations—for whom tradition, constitution, legal precedent and other long-standing regulators provide the cybernetic grounds of stability.

The vision of a small but historic nation in revolt is bad enough. The explosion of knowledge among people whose intellectual horizons are thereby expanded and burst, the extension of personal vulnerability and loss of security through the uncontrolled spread of informational networks, and the political threats let loose by all of this, could turn such revolt into a societary crisis for that nation of unexampled magnitude. It would have to rely very heavily on the propensity to stability of the esoteric box to contain the situation. But what if instability such as this were to assail a multi-national company of greater size than this nation, a company that is not itself truly an esoteric box but a network existing at the metasystemic level without a metasystem. This would be a leviathan greatly to be feared, a leviathan obscenely polluted by its own data which it found itself powerless to metabolize.

Outcomes for Action

Action is required. The form of this action is a matter for you rather than for me. My endeavour has been to penetrate the immense complexity of the information management problem, in search of a scientific generalization. This I have tried to define in fairly plain English, to describe and to exemplify. The objective was to aid your endeavour to decide right action.

I suggested before that the problem is to manage complexity itself, complexity considered as the very stuff and substance of modern society. In the end, when all the computers have crunched their numbers to the last intransigent bit, the unquenched spirit of man takes final responsibility for life or death. Even so, this spirit necessarily operates—for ordinary folk and senators alike—through the medium of the human brain. This is one computer among many larger and faster (if so far less flexible) computers.

The cerebral computer is no more than a three-pound electrochemical device, slightly alkaline, which runs ten thousand million logical elements on the power of glucose at twenty-five watts. Its ability to discriminate is somewhat less than people imagine when they think of the human being in mystical terms as suffused by the divine afflatus. We can in general discriminate on a variety-scale of about nine. To understand an average is our métier. If we then judge that something is slightly, considerably, much or hugely better or worse than the mean, we have done as much discriminatory computing as we can normally manage. That scale of nine points is an output of roughly 3.2 bits of information.

Improvement in requisite variety is possible, since we enrich the dimensions of our comprehension by inter-relating several scales of discrimination. Even so, our human capability is geared at this general level. So when data processing systems offer us millions of bits of data, we dare not believe in a mythical metabolic process which could convert these data into information within our personal ken. There are ineluctable limits to the assimilation of knowledge, set by the finite size of the sugar-furnace in our heads. These facts to my mind determine the sorts of action which count as both feasible and effective. I have refined my ideas about this to offer a final set of specific postulates.

1. We may reasonably assume that esoteric boxes can take care of themselves, since that is what they are for.

2. They can be aided: their actions can be facilitated or inhibited by government. Any intervention, however, interferes with autonomy, denies participation, and may prove ineffectual (by Le Chatelier's principle).

3. Then legislation directed *into* particular boxes is unlikely to be much help. In any case, there is probably no time to tackle the problem at this level.

4. Then the *focus of attention* should always be at metasystemic level. This is the locale of societal instability; here then reside the massive threats.

5. First, the relevant metasystem must be indentified, and in some sense institutionalized. Otherwise, who is to act or who can be held accountable? This primary task can be undertaken only by those holding the constitutional mandate.

6. The purpose of a metasystemic social institution is precisely, and only, to embody the *nerve-centre* for metasystemic affairs. Its function is precisely, and only, to identify situations of dangerous and therefore explosive instability, and to identify trajectories leading to stability.

7. The recommended methodology is the construction of metamodels, continuously innervated by data effectively filtered through a cybernetically designed hierarchy of systems.

8. The implementation of conclusions might be vested in the metasystemic social institution; if it is, however, there will be problems about autonomy (see 2).

9. In so far as legislation may be needed, the need can be pinpointed by these means. Directing either legislation or central executive action at strings and networks in the absence of metamodels is likely to increase instability rather than reduce it.

10. The kinds of model needed operate necessarily at a high level of abstraction: this makes almost everyone impatient. Consciously identify, then, the barrier to progress as anti-intellectualism.

Some metasystemic institutions already exist. The World Health Organization and the Food and Agriculture Organization are examples at international level, as are several international economic bodies; government departments handling whole sets of esoteric boxes are examples at national level. The questions I leave with you are these: have such institutions been correctly identified? Do they at all map onto the *dynamic structure* of viable systems as understood by cybernetics? What other such institutions would be required in a stable society?

As to the warning in Point 10 about anti-intellectualism, it seems that the arguments used here would themselves predict this self-defeating syndrome in a society newly faced with the need to manage overwhelming complexity. If the brain is eclipsed in terms of variety by the computer milieu, it may itself revolt. Then panic-stricken attempts at the highest and most responsible level to quell forces that are not understood are as dangerous as the irresponsible cavorting of hooligans. One may already detect at either end of the scale of social responsibility a response equivalent to laying about with the jawbone of an ass.

The alternative is to *design* a stable society, and to treat our complexity-control capability through computers as offering a nervous system for the body politic. This involves the deployment of apolitical science to new ends, in the recognition that our difficulties have gone beyond anything that can be grasped by a slogan. We should recognize a cybernetic issue for what it is. But when the unthinkable is already happening it is indeed difficult to think about, and we are robbed of our semantic strength.

THESIS

SIXTH STATEMENT

Even though we may succeed
in inventing a measure of utility
called eudemony,
that metric depends
on the measurement of *information flow* —

for on this basic measure
all societary metrics
(even the monetary metric)
necessarily depend.

For this specific reason
the way in which society handles
the commodity of

information

which is what changes us

and the commodity of

data

which are the raw materials of information

will prove to be critical
in the good management of affairs
and even to

the preservation of human freedom.

There is no need for alarm
that science has provided the tool

in the shape of the computer

to promote information handling
as the predominant human skill
of our age—
and as the machine

for changing data into information

COLOUR CODE : BLUE
Thesis

244

provided that

we understand what we are doing
and legislate :

not only for protection
but for the advancement of man

in time.

I feel no need
for a metalinguistic commentary on this

       sixth statement of thesis

or for the explanations that might be offered
in such a commentary about

       the Argument of Change

you have just read.

As I said earlier,
the presentation was meant to stand alone
and by far the most interesting and questionable issue is

       can one talk like this—
       and if so
       what happens?

The shattering (to me) factual answer
to the first part of that question
is that one
       can
talk like this to congressmen,
and therefore perhaps to the seriously-intentioned public,
but that one
       cannot
talk like this to scientists.

I ought to have known.

It would be instructive
to quote chunks of the discussion—
but this really is impossible on any scale
because of the defective transcript.

One thing I will quote.
After a number of distinguished scientists had gone for me
(their own flesh and blood as it were—
but remember the N.I.H. factor
       (not invented here))
Dr Herman Kahn
who had addressed the meeting immediately before me
and with whom I had considerable disagreement
expressed himself as
       impressed and appalled
by what these scientists were saying.

COLOUR CODE : YELLOW
Narrative

He maintained
that people working in the universities
        do not know the knowledge which already exists outside
        about such matters as I had discussed
        and therefore do badly what they do.

He also made the accusations
        that academics did not know what were
        the real problems that had to be solved
        and therefore designed models that were useless;
        and that every large model in the Pentagon
        had without exception been a failure.

        'Fifteen years now of this stuff.'

This was pretty forthright—
the congressmen heard it,
and saw the discomfiture of those attacked.

For my part
I wondered why it is
that official panels of scientists
in America, it seemed, as well as Britain
so rarely include
those people who really know about the topic in hand.
There are many scientists in the United States
and many *are* in universities
who know very well what could be done
and are indeed doing some of it.

They were not there.
But at least it was possible
to tell the politicians who they were
and what they were doing.

Well, I had been in Washington before
and was to return later in the year;
but I had not moved in these circles before
and this visit
made a big impact on me.

I tried to capture my feelings
by writing them down at the time
in the form of a dispatch
as if I were a newspaper man.

COLOUR CODE : YELLOW
Narrative

This piece follows :
it includes an account of an incident
so extraordinary
that friends have been loth to believe it.
May I vouch for its authenticity then,
and record as well
that the actual words in which you have it
were written before I had left the table.

DATELINE WASHINGTON D.C. 30TH JANUARY 1970

This is the federal capital of the United States, and Congress moves into a new decade—a decade that will celebrate the bicentenary of American Independence. Representatives and senators labour here to regulate society—American society, yes, but also perhaps the wider society of mankind. For this is one of the great power centres of the world.

It is a city of contradictions.

Last night I was at a state reception, held in a magnificent suite of rooms furnished throughout with original American furniture of antiquity. There were original contemporary paintings of red Indian life, and there was the actual table at which the Treaty of Paris was signed. On leaving I intended to look round the town, taking in the shop windows, the restaurants, the night activity—just as I have done in major cities throughout the world. My hosts would not let me go.

I could not go alone, and I could not go on foot. My hosts felt responsible for my safety. Now I had thought that this talk about danger had been overdone, but I was wrong. The rate of armed assaults is running at 850 *a month*. The legislators themselves, in this centre that symbolizes the regulation of the American way of life, dare not walk from the Capitol unescorted to their own cars. My hosts, under pressure, did take me round the city—but by car. The streets were deserted.

This morning I watched a television broadcast by a black leader—and I note that he is free to express his views, which though trenchant were closely reasoned. I do not know the facts, nor understand the problems. I can tell you what he *said*. 74 percent of the population of Washington is black : 74 percent of the population of Washington has no vote. The mayor and his council are 'appointed' so—let us not mince words—Washington is a *colony*. The people are in revolt against the colonial yoke.

Washington, in the decade of the bicentenary of American independence.....

Today I sit in one of Washington's most famous hotels. I have lunched with a scientist colleague, who has most kindly given me a copy of his new book—inscribed from George J. Klir. The title, blazoned across the dust jacket is: *An Approach to*

COLOUR CODE : YELLOW
Narrative

General Systems Theory. I have two hours in hand before leaving for Dulles Airport, and the plane to London, so I go into the lounge to take some Irish coffee.

I am the only male there. I sit surrounded by ladies, and what sounds like the social whirl that connotes the White House and all that. There are snatches of conversation drifting to me: they are so to speak about debutantes and the price of mink. The waitresses are much more interesting.

In London we should call them dolly-birds. They wear off-the-shoulder white blouses, tiny red miniskirts and sheer black tights. If I can catch the eye of one of them, it will be me for the Irish coffee and George's book. Here she comes. We chat a bit; she is really very attractive; she looks at the book on the table, asks:

'Do you *know* about General Systems Theory?'

'Yes, I do.'

'*And* about Cybernetics?'

'I'm a professor thereof', I say, feeling immediately ridiculous at the way the words had come out.

'Good'—she has gone.

This is too silly. She comes back with the Irish coffee, and this time I am ready for her. It takes only a few questions to elicit that she certainly has more than a nodding acquaintance with the whole business. More: she comes from Philadelphia, has an Ivy League degree in psychology, has taken a course in General Systems; this kind of science offers the only hope, she reckons, for social stability.

Where am I? I'm in this hotel lounge among the cream of Washington society; outside in the streets thirty people will be attacked with guns during this very day, but the small-talk goes on and on and the dolly-birds glide sweetly around; the one I get is on about cybernetics and the future of the world . . . . . in a current phrase here: it's mind-blowing.

So—obviously—why the red miniskirt and so forth?

Well, she has given over her life to the cause of peace, and of stricken and starving people; she works all hours for an organization working for an end to the war in Vietnam and to violence at home; she is not paid at all; her folks don't want to know; she has to eat.

COLOUR CODE : YELLOW
Narrative

A clever overture to a commercial proposition? Where in that little uniform would be tucked away the dictionary, the bibliography, and the names of my friends? Supremely: why no proposition?

How cynical can you get? In Washington, very. Good luck, nice girl.

COLOUR CODE : YELLOW
Narrative

Before taking you off with me to Washington
I was talking about the problems
of addressing those responsible
for general management.
I spoke of three Arguments of Change
to be pitched

at three very different levels
in three very different tones of voice.

I am going to switch violently now
as to both level and tone.
The subject is in a real sense the same.

The management of complexity
has been repeatedly identified as the new problem.
We have some new tools—
not only the computer itself
but the whole plexus
of electronic communication.
We are not making proper use of the tools
which themselves become threatening.....

I submit
that this is because we are using
outdated conceptual models
of our own world environment.

In the diagrammatic part of the thesis
we have depicted a changeover
from an 'exploitable' Earth model
to a 'conservational' Earth model—
a changeover partly accomplished
through the operation of a
metalanguage of conscience.

But this is bound to prove undecidable
in most critical areas of decision
(I said before that the Argument about this
will appear later).

What emerges from the address to Congress
is a different conceptual model altogether
deriving from the electronic capability
which generates complexity
is indeed largely responsible for complexification
its use, misuse and abuse.

COLOUR CODE : YELLOW
Narrative

I call this environment

the software milieu.

According to the next diagram of the thesis
this Earth model does not at all connect
with the old institutions.
I do not think it can :
the language of the old institutions does not express it.
I shall argue this formally in a minute.

On the assumption that this is correct
it becomes impossible to talk directly to managers
about its actual nature—
unless there is time to set up
a whole framework of explanation
        as this book tries to do
        or the Congress talk minimally did.

Then what does one say
in an article of normal length
written for the most *popular* management magazine
in the country?

I decided to bring home if I could
the total inadequacy of our contemporary use
of computers
using the extant language.
Despite the arguments here
you will find me talking for instance
        about cost-benefit :
that is certainly the way the language goes.

Apart from these issues of language however
the next Argument of Change
is an important one.
What is said I believe to be true,
and *even in this language*
it explains what holds back
effective development
and the emergence of new institutions
conceived only
as adaptations of the old.

I received many comments on this article
and to my surprise
it was not denounced.
Managers said

COLOUR CODE : YELLOW
Narrative

          pretty accurate
          and alarming
          and don't quote me
          and the others would not agree

which is a judgment with a built-in diagnosis of its own.

This Argument of Change
follows the next summary and explanatory pages.
It is printed as written :
editors sometimes excise my nastier remarks.

COLOUR CODE : YELLOW
Narrative

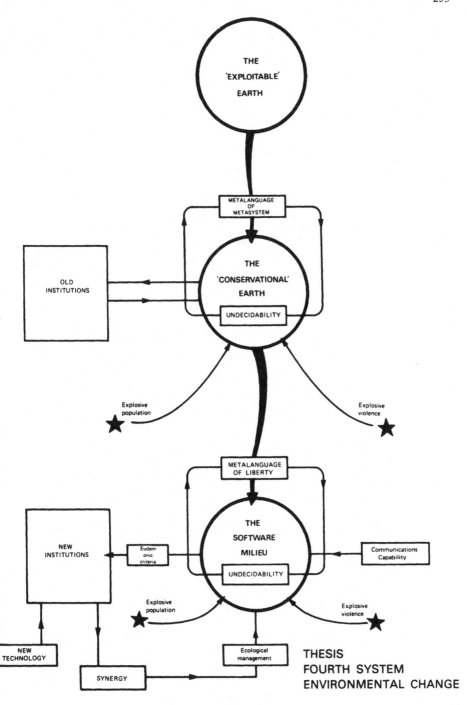

THE
'EXPLOITABLE'
EARTH

METALANGUAGE
OF
METASYSTEM

OLD
INSTITUTIONS

THE
'CONSERVATIONAL'
EARTH

UNDECIDABILITY

Explosive
population

Explosive
violence

METALANGUAGE
OF LIBERTY

NEW
INSTITUTIONS

Eudem-
onic
criteria

THE
SOFTWARE
MILIEU

UNDECIDABILITY

Communications
Capability

Explosive
population

Explosive
violence

NEW
TECHNOLOGY

SYNERGY

Ecological
management

THESIS
FOURTH SYSTEM
ENVIRONMENTAL CHANGE

COLOUR CODE : BLUE
Thesis

The conceptual Earth model
called The Software Milieu
could be derived from the outdated models
just because they are undecidable.

In the 'exploitable' language
the Earth not only can be exploited
it *wants* to be expolited—
meaning that mankind has a duty
well expressed in Genesis :

>And God blessed Noah and his sons,
>and said unto them,
>Be fruitful,
>and multiply,
>and replenish the earth.

The cultural language of man
contains so many expressions of this kind
and there is no way of saying :

>we ought to stop breeding

which is an undecidable proposition for most people.

Besides :
the proposition does not make *practical* sense either
for a great many folk

>not for the peasant who needs his sons
>to support his old age

>not for downtrodden races

>not for raised-up families

>not for individuals for hosts of personal reasons

and that is because
our institutions are built in terms of the language
that includes all these undecidable propositions.

In *practical* terms then
population control entails
a prior change of institutions

which in *logical* terms entails
a prior change of the language.

COLOUR CODE : GOLD
Metalanguage

All this could come about, I said,
by the reformulation of models through a metalanguage
that recognized this undecidability.
It shows no sign of happening—
witness the fact that
what is attempted in the way of population control
does not work.

This is because campaigns are aimed
at people in the mass
calling for the *same* action
at the level of the individual—
                    each individual.

The programme

- does not have requisite variety

- assumes we know what the mean rate should be
  and implies that each family ought
  to aim at this mean
  (decimal point and all)

- has too much inertia

- arrogantly proposes to interfere
  with individual lives

From the point of view of the individual
this is a bad basis for decision.

                    When my first brood of children were born
                    it was known to be selfish
                    not to have children;

                    with the second brood now
                    it is known to be selfish
                    to have them at all.

In any case
people respond selectively to propaganda.
So society may turn out to be sponsoring
a form of selective breeding—
which for all anyone knows
may be of eugenically opposite character
from what is required.

Quite apart from this
the argument that

COLOUR CODE : GOLD
Metalanguage

if everyone were as
　　　good
　　　honest
　　　peaceful
　　　rational

　　　or sterile
as I the world would be a better place

gets us nowhere.

Yet a great many programmes launched by governments and their agencies
rely on this argument at base — as witness :

the answer inevitably given to every problem in the end :
　　　we must educate them.

According to the PLATFORM FOR CHANGE
this whole approach to world problems
is a product of the outdated

　　　concepts
　　　institutions
　　　world models
　　　languages

which we have studied.

It should be replaced by

　　　self-organizing
　　　self-regulating
　　　eudemonic systems

for which we have been formulating languages and concepts.

All this is said as a commentary
on the deceptively simple loop
which may be traced on the diagram :

　　　the software milieu
　　　generating eudemonic criteria
　　　using new institutions
　　　　　　which pick up the new methods
　　　　　　and the new technology
　　　and return a synergistic output
　　　to ecological management
　　　and through to the software milieu.

COLOUR CODE : GOLD
Metalanguage

What happens if we attempt
to operate this loop
via existing institutions
instead of the new ones we do not have?

It leads to the decreation
of all our barbers—

which you may remember is to say
that the propositions circulating in the loop
will be undecidable
within the institutions working the system.

Let me provide an example
in the familiar format.

The language of the old institutions
includes the expression
(it is in fact deeply embedded in the language)

> There are supra-organizations
> in which the component organizations
> are either centralized
> or decentralized.

The Language of the Loop
includes important propositions
belonging to the intersect of this diagram :

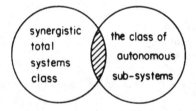

and the barber—
the class of system which we expect to do our novel work—
is the intersect

> the class of synergistic total systems
> having autonomous sub-systems.

Any proposition concerning this intersect
will be undecidable
in the first language

COLOUR CODE : GOLD
Metalanguage

which calls the left-hand circle

        centralized

and the right-hand circle

        decentralized

and regards this classification as dichotomous
so that the circles are mutually exclusive—
moved apart.

This is no extravaganza of logical pyrotechnics

If you talk to a supra-organization
that is, in its self-image,
centralized

                examples :
                any firm under the autocratic leadership
                of a named individual ;
                countries of the East European bloc

you will find that it expects to set norms
for everything.

If you point out that
            there is no thermostat in the body
            with the dial set at 98.4

            there is no Statute for Caterpillars
            to say they must not breed to the extent
            that there is no greenstuff left

which means that
            thermostatic control of the body
            population control of caterpillars

are in the hands of complex systemic self-regulators
the *output* of which system is—
it so happens—

            98.4
            a stable population

you will simply not be understood.

This mechanism does not exist
because it cannot be expressed
in the language.

COLOUR CODE : GOLD
Metalanguage

260

No-one will *say* this to you
because they *cannot*—
which is a good reason.
What you will be told is :

      —this is a false analogy
      —this is a misleading metaphor
      —this does not compare like with like
      —biological systems are not organizations
      —you have confused input and output.

In our language
      —this is *not* an analogy (so cannot be a false one)
      —this is *not* a metaphor (so cannot be misleading)
      —*does* compare like with like (which is the whole point)
      —biological systems *are* organizations (of course they are)
      —input and output are functions of our perception
       of the system (that is, they are conventions).

*Note : Anyone who felt cheated that I did not explain, because I could
not directly quote, the nature of the objections put forward to my
Congress thesis by the panel of scientists present may be interested
to know that these were they. You will not find a more potent self-image
of centralization of power than the self-image existing within a select group of
scientists invited to advise central government. Not that the replies I
am quoting come only from this source—they are perfectly usual.*

All that was about a supra-organization
that is, in its self-image,
centralized.

Now if you talk to a supra-organization
that is, in its self-image,
decentralized

      examples :
      any firm that lets its divisional
      general managers do what they like ;
      the British Commonwealth of 1970 ;
      the United Nations

you will find that it fully expects
not to be effective.

If you point out that

      the human being has volitional control
      of his automatic nervous system

COLOUR CODE : GOLD
Metalanguage

firms do not sacrifice autonomy
in their own eyes
if they join a cartel

countries make alliances
without talk of loss of sovereignty
when they go to war

people who join clubs
expect to abide by the rules
or be turned out

and that in every case
this is in the expectation of benefit
through synergy
precisely

you will simply not be understood.

Again you *cannot* be told that
the mechanisms do not exist
because the issue cannot be expressed
in the language.

What you will be told is :

      —you do not understand the difficulties
      —these people are impossible
      —our task is impossible
      —this supra-organization ought to be centralized.

*Note : Any similarity between the situation described and the situation endlessly
confronting the British government and employers on the
one hand and the trade union movement on the other hand is purely
coincidental.*

Finally
if you talk to a supra-organization
that is, in its self-image,
neither centralized nor decentralized
which is to say either

      some people say one and some the other
      or everyone feels the answer is not clear

then you might hope
that your propositions
will prove to be decidable.

COLOUR CODE : GOLD
Metalanguage

This hope is vain.

Examples :
many large firms.

Your propositions remain undecidable
because although there is no agreement about centralization
there *is* agreement that its language is appropriate.

Now the supra-organization is worse off than ever
because it cannot produce consistent answers—
not only to questions posed in your language
which is undecidable

but to questions posed in its own outdated language
which is full of inconsistencies.

Then the organization
is not only robbed of a capacity to reformulate
its languages and policies
through a metalinguistic transformation
and thereby to adapt

it is likely to break down altogether.

Many have.

COLOUR CODE : GOLD
Metalanguage

AN ARGUMENT OF CHANGE

THE
SOFTWARE
MILIEU

Article* as written for the journal *Management Today*, and published with minor excisions in the issue of August, 1970.

*By permission of
Management Today

**'The manager does not smash his computer,
true. But unwilling and unwitting he qualifies
as the Luddite of our age'.**

The task that faced our managerial forefathers appeared to them, I think, as a matter of managing materials. Wood must be shaped, and iron poured in moulds; yarn must be spun and woven, bricks kilned; steel must be rolled and forged. Today, the capability to manage materials can be taken for granted: it is a technological 'piece of cake'. The new task is to manage information.

The common further need, for them as for us, was and remains the management of men. In this, one might be forgiven for supposing, nothing has changed at all. For all the sophisticated talk, for all the behavioural science, we have not apparently advanced very far. Trouble-down-at-mill still means a threat of shut-down; and in our age it very likely means the indefinite laying-up of expensive machinery into the bargain. But idle capital joins idle manpower on the negative side of a managerial equation couched in terms of the total investment, discounted over n years, where the cash flow is hopefully always positive. We are back again to managing information, rather than men or things.

I do not know where leadership has gone, or any of the other more vivid aspects of a managerial world that has become so dispassioned. Perhaps these human features of the scene have taken to the streets and to the university campus. Meanwhile, the manager sits, surrounded by his paperwork, in a software milieu. By this I mean an environment that is dominated by information, calculation, budgetting, planning, costing ..... expressed in endless meetings called to discuss these things. Materials and men figure in this environment largely in terms of the data they generate, rather than as entities or human beings.

These remarks are intended as descriptive; they advocate nothing. And I would like to make clear at the outset where the advocacy of this article really lies. What is written will seem to be about the more efficient management of information. Experience teaches, however. I have learned that there is an easy way for the reader to escape from any uncomfortable implication of such advice as I shall offer. It is to appeal to human values.

Computers are dehumanizing: I have heard this ludicrous slogan from managers and ministers alike—they are even teaching students destructively to use it. One might as well say that a truly loving surgeon would not dream of using the tempered edge of a scalpel on human flesh, but would rather tear the patient open with his bare but human hands. So, firstly: there is nothing inhuman about using appropriate tools, nor about being efficient. And, secondly: if managers could operate efficiently within the software milieu (which they do not) they would have more time to exercise human qualities in the management of men.

Come, let us think honestly about the situation in which we are already immersed where managerial electronics is concerned. We have machinery to hand that is capable of performing any task we ask. It is open to the manager to retrieve any fact, to perform any calculation, in a flash—in the twinkling of an eye. (But I am using Old Testament language.

Current capability is roughly a million times as fast as that movement of the eyelid.)
Unfortunately the job costs money. Thus it turns out that the manager alone is well placed
to determine which jobs ought to be done. For he determines, or ought to determine,
his own set of priorities. In this he needs skilled help.

THE CONCEPT OF SKILLED HELP

It must be true that the manager has an informational need which can be met, more or
less precisely, at some more or less definite cost. He might well agree that he is not sure
what this need is, nor what is the economic cost of supplying it. For those reasons he is
surely unable to position a costed need on his scale of priorities. For that reason in turn,
he does not know what to do. This is brutal but cogent thinking. So what is the manager
to say or to support?

I shall now assume that the manager is provided with skilled scientific and technical help.
Either he has engaged this himself, or it is on tap as a 'central service', or he has authority
to use consultants. In what does this help consist? I shall define it as neatly as I can, hanging
on to a key notion that managers well understand: effectiveness = benefit ÷ cost. Then if
the cost is more than the benefit, the effectiveness yields less than unit pay-off, and that is
no good. But if the benefit exceeds the cost, then that is excellent, provided that no alternative investment of this expenditure (the cost) would yield a higher return (the benefit)
than is measured by this effectiveness.

Skilled help is available as a means of achieving and maintaining this effectiveness. That
help, in the software milieu, exists first of all for measuring things, including effectiveness
itself. It exists secondly to pinpoint the nodes of decision at which measured quantities
of effective information satisfy the criteria of managerial judgment. Thirdly, skilled help
exists to design new organizational structures competent to implement such quantified
decisions. Last (and least) this skill is deployed in the knowledgeable and indeed optimal
use of available scientific and technological resources to these ends.

Briefly to review the component parts of this 'skilled help' package, we firstly find a basic
competence in automation. That could be defined in this context as: the use of computers
and other electronic aids to transcend the informational limitations of the human hand,
eye and brain in managerial pursuits—including especially the self-assessment and self-
regulation of management systems. Next we find a competence in operational research:
the use of scientific method in decision-taking and policy-making, with its powerful armoury of modern techniques. Third we find a competence in the science of effective organization, which is called cybernetics.

I do not know how balanced may be the package (in these terms) to which any individual
manager may have recourse. But in principle the package exists; and in practice there is
always available a nucleus of this package. Whatever is available, I am calling it 'skilled
help'—and the manager has only himself to blame if the balance is wrong or the expertise
inadequate.

The question to which we now turn is this. Given that the manager has skilled help, how
does he treat it? In the answer to this question lies the future both of industry and of our

society. Because, since we live in a software milieu, effectiveness hinges on the right management of information. And that is what the skilled help is for. Without assistance, no manager runs a computer; still less does he *exploit* this resource without aid. Doing that directly is not his job.

DIAGNOSING THE CURRENT MALAISE

There may have been some shocks in the statement of this argument; but its conclusion is not very contentious. It is not too startling to say that a manager wishing to exploit modern methods and new apparatus must use skilled help. Where the problem starts is in the definition of that word 'use'. Do I go too far to suggest that it entails a collaborative exercise? One does not meet the manager who would deny it, over a whisky. It is rare indeed to meet a manager who embraces it 'on the job'. Therefore I go too far. Which means that the manager does not go far enough.

In the following tabulation I lay out four sets of behavioural symptoms by which to recognize a current managerial malaise. Now no-one expects the patient to exhibit all the symptoms of his malaise. Moreover, when a clinical statement of a syndrome is cryptically set down, it inevitably caricatures itself. So I want to say in one sense: please don't take this too seriously. But I say in the same breath that I cannot think of a way in which to persuade anyone to take it seriously enough. For the twenty years over which the software milieu has been building, I have watched these attitudes take shape. Today, some version of this syndrome characterizes almost every enterprise I know. Now watch the manager's unconscious mind at work, as he contemplates the use of skilled help.....

1. Keep at Bay :

Skilled help is a threat to the established way of doing things, and ultimately to established authority. Delineate routine tasks for the team, which keep it away from whatever really matters. Stress the need to become acceptable : change is needed and invited, but *acceptable* change does not involve actual alteration. Later, point out sourly that a fortune has been spent on accomplishing trivial jobs.

2. Know Better :

Skilled help is clever, but naive; and thinkers are not doctors. Therefore we shall not actually do as the skilled help advises (what are managers for?). Change the policies proposed, then, on the strength of something heard over dinner. Bury errors of business judgment in the debris of the resulting fiasco, and hire new skilled help. Repeat.

3. Decentralize :

Humour the little boy in everyone by giving each operating unit its own electronic facilities and skilled help (*Autonomy* and *accountability* are useful words to use.)

Discover the units are pursuing incompatible policies, and use one to undermine the professional repute of another. Wait until all hope of deriving synergistic benefits for the enterprise as a whole has been lost. Discover that computers are not economic.

4. Centralize :

Seize on the cost saving implicit in a central resource of skilled help. Do not load charges onto operating units ('the people who make the profits'), in case they demand decentralization. Discover how large and how obtrusive is the central budget; discover how unpopular and vulnerable the centre has become as a result. Decentralize.

Here is the hang-up. We are simply not coming to terms with the opportunities offered either by electronics or by the skilled help that goes with it. The very fact that devolution and centralization are contradictory policies, and that many enterprises manage to sit on the fence between them, indicates what the difficulty is. There is a need completely to redesign senior organizational structure in terms which recognize and exploit the software milieu.

THE FIRST NEED

The first need is to lift one's thinking right above the level of data-processing. The range of modern computers and their ancillary equipments is surely the most remarkable assortment of machines yet devised by the ingenuity of man. Yet we have managed to slot them into comfortable niches where they undertake the computation of payrolls, the compilation of accounts, and the preparation of invoices. That is all right as far as it goes, but it is not by itself a serious use of so much informational power. It is as if we had discovered electricity, and then been unable to think of any use for it beyond driving table fans and supplanting candles. Yet most of the computing power in use is in this kind of use.

Because this is so, when people really stretch their thinking into the future, the best idea they come up with is no more than an extended and souped-up version of the same thing. I refer to the idea of the 'massive data base' intended to contain all the information there is about absolutely everything. The manager would be able to call up any item he needed at the flick of a switch. The cost of doing any such thing is however prohibitive. And here is a quiet little question: just why would a manager want to?

Management needs information all right, but with modern resources there is no problem in providing it. Some of the real issues are: just which information does the manager need; what sorts of manipulations of information are valuable to him; how is he to receive and manipulate data; what filters on data should be provided (he just does not want the irrelevant); how does his system forget information no longer needed; what scientific help can be given in pre-digesting information used in his decision making; what electronic help is available to the management team in its corporate policy making?

'The decision apparatus of industrial policy... is delicate probabilistic, self-formulating, fiduciary, self-fluxing and non-analytic. Nothing is more agonizing... than to be told that all such management problems can be solved by a sufficiently expensive dose of automatic data

processing'. These words are my own : they come from an address given to an international conference twelve years ago—at a time when few computers were operating in the business world. The words were not heeded: we have gone down the data-processing road, and have arrived at something which in managerial (as distinct from operational) terms is frankly a nonsense.

We are wasting the investment in electronics, wasting the opportunity, wasting both the machine-power and the skilled help. The manager does not smash his computer, true. But unwilling and unwitting he qualifies as the Luddite of our age. The potentiality of machines is frivolled away, because management itself is not managing what is after all its own informational milieu.

THE SECOND NEED

Having lifted one's thinking above data processing levels, and having contemplated the real problems of managing this new environment, the second need is to think out the use of skilled help.

It is no accident that professionals competent to help manage the software milieu (after all, they created it) change their jobs so frequently. In some areas of skill the average stay is no more than eighteen months. It is easy to say, and I have often heard it said, that skilled help is dedicated to computer advance itself, so there is no hope of commanding loyalty to the manager as boss or to the firm as employer. This view is rubbish. It is pure self-exculpation. Professionals in this field are still human beings, susceptible as ever to proper leadership. What they cannot stand is the absence of that leadership, a failure to manage, and the condemnation of their abilities to trivial operations. But especially they soon learn to recognize the malaise with whose syndrome we were recently concerned.

A management intending to manage its software milieu must find a means whereby intimate collaboration with its skilled help becomes possible. Unfortunately, it will not be enough to utter slogans. 'The board itself takes a keen interest' ; 'a close dialogue is intended between.....'; 'good communications are essential'; 'the managing director personally.....'; 'we have set up a steering committee'; such pious platitudes sound so convincing. They often turn out to be no more than a cover story. It will not be long before we hear, in confidence of course, some equally familiar complaints. 'These people are frankly impossible' sums them up.

Should you, the reader, happen to reach this stage, would you please entertain a serious hypothesis. It is that you might not be witnessing, as you are persuaded, the ultimate apotheosis of scientific arrogance, offered in the face of patient and kindly help. It is more likely that you are witnessing an agony of despair. This derives from a total identification with your own interests, in which you cannot bring yourself to believe, and the conviction that the enterprise is throwing away its best hope of progress. Reject the hypothesis as absurd, if it is. My entitlement for putting it forward is this : I have seen the whole rigmarole re-enacted in many enterprises, in several countries, over many years. A scientist is not likely to toss that experience aside as a coincidence.

It is not easy to propose a perfectly general answer to this problem of the right use of skilled help. The particular circumstances need to be studied. But two guiding thoughts may be of help. First: the individual people who are causing concern are probably not the problem—they are troublesome because they are responsible men, and they are good. Replace them with equally good and responsible men, and the trouble will recur—while you have lost eighteen months. Replace them with their own inexperienced and perhaps less responsible juniors, who will be flattered, and you will have solved your visible and clamant problems for five years or so. (That likelihood means that this solution is often favoured.) But make no mistake: you have now lost five irreclaimable years.

The second thought is this. If the software milieu matters anything like as much to management as I believe and have argued here, there is no more important topic (beyond keeping solvent) to which managerial talent can be devoted. By 'devoted' I do not mean 'add this to your sixteen existing responsibilities', nor do I mean 'you take the chair on the second Tuesday of the month'. I mean that at least one of your most able senior managers should be seconded to this work full time. And here comes the crunch. Put him *under* the man who leads the skilled help. If that creates organizational problems of status or of salary, the situation is already misconceived. If it creates personal problems for the seconded manager himself, he is too insecure to have your trust at this level.

The argument is in favour of the interdisciplinary team of skilled helpers, of which one of the top echelon is the able and trusted senior manager. His contribution, of which he need by no means be ashamed, is managerial skill itself. He has plenty both to contribute and to learn. The right man will be as loyal to his new boss as the latter is to you. So forget him now; his only problem is that he may be regarded as some kind of spy. Don't say you cannot spare him: that much is obvious if he is good enough for the job, so it is not worth discussing. But he has to be spared.

RECONSTRUCTION OF THE CABINET

It is against this background that the question of redesigning the senior organizational structure must be considered. I do not think that this issue can be bilked, for two reasons.

In the first place, there are many pressures in a fast changing world to suggest that hallowed traditions governing both our senior management structure and the method of its operation are inadequate. Many large companies, particularly in the United States, have already turned their boardrooms into experimental laboratories: the form and the style of management are in constant flux. This seems to have happened in response to rapid change and rapid growth; it is a movement that will spread, regardless of management electronics.

The second reason concerns the software milieu under discussion here. The traditional forms and styles were set essentially by human limitations. They answered the question: how can a group of men, aided only by other human beings, run the enterprise? But these limitations are radically changed by electronic aids. We have seen the basic mechanism at work for two hundred years, reaching its climax in contemporary shopfloor automation. Because the limitations of human hand, eye and brain are transcended by their electronic extensions, there is a totally different set of questions to answer. Now the processes of the industrial revolution have reached the boardroom. How can a group of men, served by managerial electronics and skilled help, run the enterprise? If we do not come up with new answers, we must indeed be the (senior and sophisticated) Luddites mentioned before.

Perhaps you think I should have used this space to forecast what the answers themselves will look like. If so, forgive me. The fact is I have written *that* article so many times I am bored. What is more, I have just finished a new book about it. By now it looks as though explaining what could actually be done with skilled help is of no interest to anyone. It counts as science fiction, perhaps; or as a valid prognosis of what management will be like when (thank God) we shall all be dead.

Then let this article stand as diagnostic rather than prognostic, as an expression of practical concern rather than a white-hot vision. If it should lead anyone to wonder what to do, he might like to know that this country's supply of senior skilled help is being rapidly depleted. There are not so many people competent to lead the assault on these issues in a major firm or a government department that we can afford to let them emigrate in disgust. *Four* of them are packing bags at this moment, to my knowledge, and only one set of bags is labelled to the United States.

We cannot stop these four: it is too late. What worries me is to know whom I shall hear of next. He may be the chap on whom *you* rely. *Verbum sat sapienti*—or so they say.

Let that article stand
as exemplifying the admonitory tone of voice
which at least has the merit of honest conviction
even if it does make some people angry.....

One sometimes sees that letter—
although I have not drawn this rebuke myself—
which begins

> I am sick and tired
> of the constant criticism and carping
> levelled at management

and so on.

I can well understand this reaction
and suppose that this whole book invites it.
And yet if our institutions are failing
someone must accept the onus
          not for having got things wrong
          but for getting them right.

Certainly this is no time
to drive expertise in management science away
or to misdirect it,
and I am as entitled to my anger about that
as is the sick-and-tired manager who wants to be left alone.

Worst of all
there is a dire mechanism
whereby in times of retrenchment
the people who are needed to help put things right
are the first to be let go;
and I have never heard of a case
where a group is set up
in such circumstances—
although that would be sensible.

(Of course consultants may come in at this stage,
but that is not the same constructive thing at all.
They will be there
to axe anything innovative
in case it should not work out.
It is like standing still to be shot
in case by moving you might trip up.)

But the posture of a reproving schoolmarm
is not one I enjoy.

COLOUR CODE : YELLOW
Narrative

274

And in most of my work with management
the third tone of voice comes most naturally.

The third Argument of Change
in this series dealing with approaches to managers
is typical of this third tone.

Again there is no time
for setting up the apparatus of metalinguistics,
and there is no good in this case
in coming to the meeting armed with a script.

Every Argument of Change in this book
except this one
was a carefully prepared
many times rewritten
presentation.
And I do not want you to think
that this was the standard technique
of the PLATFORM FOR CHANGE.

On the contrary.
During the first year of the project
and apart from university teaching
I advanced *extempore* Arguments of Change

       in Brighton, Brussells, Camberley, Cardiff,
       Dublin, London, Loughborough, Ottawa and Plymouth—

       there were half a dozen in London
       and the foreign ones lasted as long as three days.

I say this to restore some sort of balance,
and to introduce a new tone—
my usual tone—
which is still I fear too didactic.
Put it down to conviction.

The next Argument of Change
therefore and uniquely
is a compilation *after* the event.

The scene is a small meeting—
or a large dinner party—
at which some very senior managers are gathered to talk.
It is an intimate occasion,
and as far as the guests are concerned confidential.
Thus I report nothing of their views.

COLOUR CODE : YELLOW
Narrative

The Argument of Change is put forward
over drinks before dinner, using a blackboard—
the organizers kindly gave me a transcript of what I said.
Into this I have edited some of the main points
discoursed upon after the meal
of which I made notes the same night.

Thus the piece is a compilation
which I hope keeps its integrity and verisimilitude.

Naturally there were no headings
announced during the talk.
But the headings are genuine—
insofar as they constituted my notes.

COLOUR CODE : YELLOW
Narrative

AN ARGUMENT OF CHANGE

DYNAMICS OF DECISION

Edited compilation of a talk* recorded before dinner and a post-prandial discourse, given extempore (with blackboard) to a small group attending a London Branch dinner of the British Institute of Management, held at the Savoy Hotel, London, on the 16th December, 1970.

*By permission of
the British Institute of Management

I look on this part of the session, gentlemen, as a way of stirring up some ideas. I promise that it will not be at all a technical address. I just want to throw out some perceptions of the state of affairs we are in—as I see it—and to comment on them. This is with a view to enjoying myself after dinner when we can all talk together.

There seem to me to be three major influences impacting on management today—and when I use the word 'management' tonight I certainly include government. Management means just the handling of affairs.

I would like to take a brief look at all three of these things, then to see what the problem amounts to, and then to put forward my intuitions about where the solutions may lie.

PROBLEM ONE—TECHNOLOGICAL CHANGE

It may seem banal but it is essential to put technological change at the top of the list.

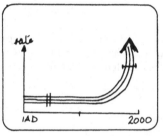

The chart I am drawing now has become pretty well-known—thanks partly to its vigorous propagation by Mr Tony Wedgwood Benn. It says that practically every human activity that we can think about was done at a low rate for a very long time. Things began to change only about two hundred years ago—since when the lines have surged upward until they are almost vertical today.

Travel: you got on a horse and galloped steadily along for several thousand years, until you could transfer to the iron horse or steam engine. After that: the IC engine, cars, aeroplanes, rockets . . . . .

The transmission of information follows the same line, because it is causally connected with the rate at which you can travel. The rate of computation is like this; the rate of population expansion too.

This point everyone is making with this chart, I remind you, is that if a human life span is—say—an inch long on the scale, then at all times until very recently a human life had all these lines of force running through it with an indetectable change. Things were much the same when you died as when you were born. But today, all these lines are shooting up through our guts—so that we have no time to adjust to anything. So: this is the argument.

I not only go along with it, but think it is the only possible explanation of what I take to be a fact: which is that technological change for us today has a unique character. I think it is terribly easy, especially in Europe with its long history of civilization, to adopt a blasé attitude, and to say: 'well, yes, people always thought changes were disastrous, or vital, or wicked, or exciting. . . . . It's just the same.' I don't believe it.

It is against this background that I would like to apply the argument to institutions—whether the firm, the nationalised industry, social service, or a government department. I think my contentions will hold all round.

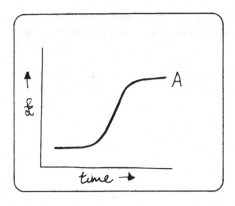

We have a typical situation here, measuring some kind of pay-off against time. On this I am drawing a growth curve, which is part of the story we have just had. What this means is that for a given technology, which I will call A, we have a period of rather flat return on capital, until the technology really takes off—and up it goes. But then it flattens out again, and this seems to be quite typical. You reach a point of diminishing returns on any new investment in this way of doing things.

Then how come the apparently uninterrupted exponential expansion we saw in the first place? The answer to that is, of course, that the overall explosion consists of a number of these little curves superimposed upon each other. Let me add the next technology, called B, to the diagram.

Because of the general technological explosion that we are now experiencing, for any institution you care to name, there is a potentially new way of doing things coming along behind the technology which will soon cease to pay off at the old rate. Typically, this has a better rate of pay-off from the start than the old technology; but then it requires a lot more investment. What is more, we do not know when the second curve will begin to rise.

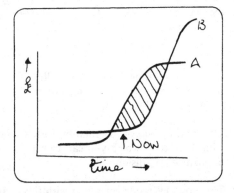

My thesis is this. At a time when people are riding on curve A, and this curve is still going up, technology B is a most unattractive investment. Remember—and this is the hell of it—you don't really know how far up the slope you are, or whether you are just about to flatten out—or even descend.

After all, the technology produces a product—and that itself may soon be defunct. In America they talk about the 'buggy whip syndrome'. This is the condition of the manufacturer who cannot understand why he is not selling his whips—a better and cheaper product than he has ever made before. It seems that he just had not noticed that people no longer drove buggies. An over-simplification . . . . . Oh, I don't know.

Well, you have these problems. Equally, you can see this second technology coming on behind. And again you don't know when the negligible pay-off is going to rise. I mark NOW here, which means that everything to the right of this arrow is speculative.

If we are decision takers NOW, our position is the following. We know at this point that our technology A, which we all know about—we have got all the expertise and the whole thing is familiar—is paying off at one hell of a rate, and likely to do so. Casting a wary eye on technology B coming along behind, we suspect that there is no pay-off from it in the foreseeable future. What is 'foreseeable'? Good question.

At any rate we have to decide on an investment policy—a decision between investment in the first technology, to keep everything going and to get the pay-off from the investment we have already made, and technology B. Shall we invest in this at all or not, and if so, when—remembering that by the very nature of our enterprise it is most unlikely that we know much about technology B at this moment. Why should we? We are A-men. So this seems to be the nature of the problem.

I want to make several comments on this. In the first place, there is Beer's Law. This says that for any director the time to the pay-off of the new technology we have not yet adopted is N years, where I retire in $N-1$ years. Why should I bother?

Well, it is not all that funny. Many things bear on the problem. Age bears on it, obviously, very much. If you don't make it to the board until you are over sixty, you are not going to have much fun with technology B. You are going to cash in on A and make sure of your reputation—and your pension.

Secondly, look at all these short term appointments we have got these days. I first ran into this in the Ministry of Defence. I don't think I am betraying the Defence of the Realm Act (if I am there are people here who will soon have me in the Tower) if I say that it takes between ten and fifteen years to reach a major complex decision. That won't really surprise realists; and there is no point in laughing, because it is true of decisions of that scale in industry as well. Now, if you appoint people for a three year stint, as happens in defence, and something is going to take thirteen years to decide, there are two things that are likely to follow from this.

One is that it is really rather difficult to take the matter seriously. The other is that you artificially extend the period of decision. After all, the guy in office says: well, there is this terrible decision to take, and it's in an awful muddle; I have only got three years. If I can get *this* much settled, then I can feel I have done a good job and move on gracefully. Of course, that arbitrarily breaks the problem up, and is a major, new and unnecessary cause of delay. I have known large committees for which the composition was not the same for any two consecutive meetings. They could well be sitting forever . . . . .

Having seen this first in Defence, I next saw it in the nationalised industries. For example, Beeching's appointment was explicitly for a limited period. Is it unkind to suggest that one could see in the way that railway decisions were handled the fact that the chairman had accepted appointment for a limited term? And in industry at large, if you have a policy saying that executives must not get into a rut, you can easily produce an artefact of the same phenomenon.

282

I see no easy answer to this problem. You cannot just say, well, okay—find a technology B man and put him on the board when he is thirty. After thirty years on that board he will have wrecked the joint.

The next comment I want to make on the situation is: where do you get the money for technology B? It seems to me that if you are going to take an aggressive view of the future of the company, or department of state, or whatever it is, and look to technology B, then you are likely to be taking decisions against the background of the *wrong business*. I think this is immensely important, and will try and explain.

I know several companies who claim they are in business X, whereas they are not. Take a simple case: a company that really operates in real estate—because most of its value lies in its holdings of expensive offices. Now if you really want to invest in technology B, then give up being in real estate—take the money and invest it in technology B.

This is the sort of approach which I think is usually possible, but to which I believe an awful lot of eyes are completely closed. After all, many companies, if they are not in the real estate business, have major holdings in other companies which are in vertical or horizontal support—as they see it, of themselves, but in truth of technology A. Then there will be interchanges of directors . . . . . We have a pretty powerful machine for stopping us from venturing into the hatched area on the blackboard.

Next I must say something about the problem of innovation as such. I worry like hell about the way we try and tackle this. For a start, we handle our innovators very much at arm's length. You all know the R & D department that is stuck out in the wilds somewhere, and whose reports arrive on people's desks—where they either explode, doing damage, or go off like a damp squib. But in any case, nothing constructive happens. This kind of R & D is not part of the company's dynamics. This is a static, silly, horrible and expensive thing—but I see it everywhere.

Another of the tricks for handling innovative departments that people use, and which I also deplore, is to set up a deliberately anti-establishment 'thing' to symbolise it. After all, if you are going to have innovation, then it's got to be expected to knock the existing structure. Now that could be dangerous. So people say we will have a 'thing' which stands for knocking the existing structure. For example: the Science Research Council, the Social Science Research Council, the National Research & Development Corporation are all like this nationally. They are set up to embody the spirit of innovation. You get the same thing in firms, too, where highly placed executives are put onto steering committees and such like. What happens then is just what you would expect (if you stop to think about it) namely, that the anti-establishment 'thing', just because it is a 'thing', itself becomes established. Now the innovator hasn't a hope in Hades. Because he is tossed from one to the other, the established establishment and the established anti-establishment, and he may not succeed in breaking through to reality at all. It is easy enough to repel this with a simple 'how dare you'—but I am appealing to you to *recognize* your own experiences of this kind of thing, for I am sure that you have had them.

Next point. If you do embark on a new business in this hatched area, then for God's sake, gentlemen, *it is not a hobby*. It is very commonly treated as a hobby by many people who are frightened about making the venture. They are kind of proud that they ever had the guts to take some sort of decision about it, but they are ready to pull out at a moment's notice, and write the investment off to experience. Well, innovation is not a hobby at all. If you are going into it, then there has got to be a commitment—and, yes, it is going to be pretty dangerous. People are not accepting that risk, it seems to me. They are trying to undercut the genuine risk, but in so doing—something which is legitimate in itself—in so doing they are not actually *taking* the risk.

PROBLEM TWO—SOCIETARY UPHEAVAL

I hope I have said some things with bite about technological change, because this is a problem much discussed—and it is easy to fall into platitudes. How much more is this true of the second problem I lay before you! It is very difficult indeed to contemplate the problems of societary upheaval without taking up some kind of stance—whether political, administrative or emotional. Perhaps some would go so far as to say that this matter has nothing to do with management at all. Then I should disagree.

I travel the world a good deal, as do you, and I think that what is going on by way of upheaval in society is being very much underrated. I would like to know if you agree with this later on. I say it is underrated, as being some kind of youthful or sectarian irresponsibility and bloody-mindedness, and as something that will all come out in the wash.

Personally, I think that we are facing something far more profound than this. I believe that many people have some kind of intuition, and perhaps it is no more than that, that somehow our decision structures—the ones we are using today in our institutions—are no longer workable. Then probably the institutions themselves are unworkable as well.

If these are the intuitions, then as a cybernetician I think they are right. How could this possibly be? And why?

In very brief, my answer to this is that decision structures are vertical structures which exist to kill the proliferation of complexity by stratification—like this.

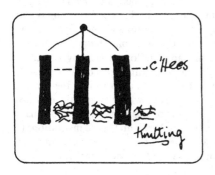

Whether we stratify into product divisions, whether into functional divisions, or however you like, this is what we have done. This has been our management trick *par excellence* for canalizing problems into channels especially organized to handle them. Somehow this trick is not working any more. If I am right about that, how could it be?

My reply to this is that, partly because of the technology issue I was talking about at first—mainly because of that, I think—there is a very, very much richer interaction at every level of society in everything that we undertake. The technology intervenes especially because of developments in communications, and in general the handling of information. Wherever you look, within industry, within government, absolutely all human affairs are so richly interconnected—the rise in the degree of interaction is on the exponential curve—that all sorts of knitting happens across the vertical structures. The vertical monoliths on the blackboard cannot handle this kind of thing. Insofar as they are aware of the new problems, the vertical monoliths try to respond by the establishment of properly regulated inter-monolith committees. We must note that these will not meet the need very well, if the need is indeed for the demolition and rebuilding of the monoliths themselves. From the point of view of the public, or the workers, or whoever it may be, the whole organization—despite its committees, still looks monolithic.

If you look at almost any big organization you will see what I mean. I have been looking at the Health Service, for instance. Three monoliths: hospitals, general practice, local government. Organizational cross-over point: the Minister himself. Two Thousand Million Pounds to run the thing. Where is the knitting, how is it going to work? We have the *notion* of the locality health centre as a suitable piece of knitting—that might these days be run by computers. For fifty years exactly this year it has been the official policy of the country to create these things. Where are they? We have about a hundred of them at the moment, and we have some more planned. And almost all of them falsify the very purposes of the knitting across those vertical monoliths which was embodied in the report written fifty years ago. I am talking about 1920.

Well, you can see this in companies too. There the monolithic structures, and the absence of knitting (in all but a pompous, formal sense—I mean, it doesn't work), rob the enterprise of synergy. I could go on with this argument indefinitely, but I think you will take the point. As long as we discuss it as management theoreticians, everything is very calm—even if the business is losing profitability. But I am asking you to contemplate it in terms of societary upheaval, whereby all sorts of people involved—the work force, the customers, the potential recruits (I do not mention the shareholders)—might quite easily, and possibly violently reject the whole apparatus.

You can see this beginning to happen in cities, where after all we have the same monolithic structure organized by departments. Some of you will know Philadelphia. I have been fortunate to learn at first-hand of work done by a very distinguished American colleague, Russell Ackoff, in the Mantua ghetto of Philadelphia. The sort of thing he has found is that if you need to get something done, such as turning a spare lot into a children's park, you would find that each of the monolithic departments would have something to say about that idea. The knitting between them is non-existent, and the lowest crossover point is again too high up to make sense to the ordinary citizen. So nothing gets done, year after year: worse still, no-one can understand why not. Russ has managed to pull the threads together, but only by drawing them all through the University—where he actually enrolled ghetto leaders on the staff. It is a long story, but the results of this work are extraordinary by any standards. What I am trying to say is that you have to break up the old institutions to get those results. In this case, you neither demolish nor even reconstruct the institution, but use an equally venerable other institution to break with established protocol.

But such clearly unique devices, organized by particularly energetic and dedicated men, will not solve society's problem in general. We are going to need some very fundamental rethinking. I am claiming that the functional divisions that we have frozen out of history are no longer applicable by and large. Let's take that as a general theorem. Under its head I would certainly include our dear old friends: production, sales, finance—and all the rest of it. Why? Because of the 'complexification', to use a neologism, of everything result- ing from enhanced interaction based on technological change.

How on earth do you deal with this? To my mind the only conceivable answer, since you cannot just abandon the existing empires, nor the expertise that goes with them, nor the learned societies and the professional institutes, is that you somehow degrade the existing top structure to become a second echelon. At the moment, the heads of the monoliths *constitute* the board or the government. The new board becomes a team of people who do not individually have empires of this kind to run. I will come back to that later on: change—radical change, I think—at the board level, which is already happening whether we like it or not.

But equally radical change may be expected, whether the board likes it or not, much lower down in the organization—and I will tell you why. We have brought technological change in the shape of computers into our institutions, and the computer inevitably produces knitting across the functional divisions. If it does not, it won't pay. This is perfectly clear. If you keep one computer housed and fed for the payroll, and another for ledgers, and another for personnel, and so on, you provide yourselves with electronic quill pens. I repeat: they won't pay. And therefore the young people in the organization who are expert in this field are already beginning to make this knitting. And if we don't acknowledge that in the formal structure, my God—there is going to be such a blow up.....

You will see I am saying something more than that we shall not be able to make the comput- ers pay. I really am talking about societary upheaval. When we think of young people as being in some kind of revolt, our image is often of drop-outs, hippies, cannabis-smoking and possibly murderous tribes. But what would happen if the nice young computer pro- grammers in dark suits and white shirts were the yeast of societary ferment right inside the most established of our formal institutions? It could mean a very new kind of revolution.

PROBLEM THREE—'PARTICIPATIVE MANAGEMENT'

My first problem was obvious, and so was my second—provided you take it seriously. The third of the things I want to raise will be much more surprising. Because I put forward as a problem something that is meant to be a solution. In particular, it was meant to solve the last problem of societary upheaval, and it is 'participative management'. Now there are inverted commas round that phrase: for believe me I am an enthusiast for participative management without the inverted commas. Let me explain.

You will have heard all about Theory X and Theory Y. We were supposed to be running the monolithic thing I have described as being wholly compartmentalized on a very author- itarian basis—Theory X. This method of running things is descredited, even if the organi- zational structure is not. And so we get Theory Y—where everybody is participating in decisions. And so they should; then if that is a solution why am I putting in those quotes and calling it the third major problem?

Like many management tools which become simplified down to a slogan, the ideal of participation can be very misleading. Specifically, it can lead to an abdication of managerial and governmental responsibility. I have seen some very extraordinary things happening recently in particular companies and particular institutions which I think justify this claim. The idea of proceeding on a consensus is both a liberal philosophy and good practical psychology. But it may easily slip into a debased form, and be used as a way of avoiding difficult decisions and a way of escaping accountability *ex post facto*. If this happens, management is surely denatured; it becomes what I have elsewhere called a mediocrity machine.

You can in fact syphon off any real innovation and dissipate any real drive by this method. I think this ought to worry us a great deal. What we are really after, and this I take to be the real message of the behavioural scientists, is not a sharing-all-over-the-place of responsibility, but a driving down of the level of decision. This can certainly be done, especially if we are realistic about those technological changes. Because if you have a young man who is wanting, let's say, a cyclotron or an electron microscope or a computer, and he is allowed to sign a requisition for only four and sixpence, what does he do? He puts his story into type, and passes it right up the line. Everybody counter-signs it. And if the thing is expensive enough, the chief executive has 'taken the decision' we say. But come, gentlemen, let's be realistic. Who has taken this decision? The chief executive's only decision in this matter, is whether to go on backing the organizational system that put the requisition up—which amounts, through that system, to a decision to keep or to fire the young man who has actually taken the decision. Why obfuscate the whole issue in a pretence?

There is a great deal of knowledge about decision networks that rely, not on authority and seniority, true, but still less on a consensus. Any cybernetic model of a decision network to produce a consensus is bound to home on the mediocre answer. That is, if it can produce an answer at all. Because as network is laid on network the impedance of the net rises asymptotically: you will be lucky to get a message through such knitting at all. No: the cybernetic models we have of non-authoritarian nets come from the reticular formation of the brain stem. The trick there is that *information* constitutes authority. It is not that authority resides in a particular office or upholstered chair: it is not that authority is divided into equal parts throughout a democracy. It is that the system can recognize the appropriate focus of knowledge for a given decision, and agrees to abide by the decision there made. I could give you cybernetic models of all this, but I promised not to get technical.

The point I really want to leave with you about this third problem, which ties up with the first—and certainly involves the second—is just this. At the very time when we want to drive the level of decision *down*, because we are beginning to understand behavioural science and the cybernetic model of organization, at that very moment the level of decision is inexorably *rising* in our outdated institutions. That is because of the immense capital cost of modern technology, which makes people feel that decision must lie at the top, and because of the ramifications that heavy technological investment will produce—I mean that the ramifications spread over an ever wider area, geographically, functionally, and in every other way.

So it looks to me as though we have in the managerial terrain of decision taking and policy making the equivalent of a geological fault.

There are colossal pressures to drive down the level of decision, psychological, sociological, ethnic. There are colossal pressures driving it up, economic, organizational, governmental. Well, you know the potential dangers of such a geological 'slip'. We have the earthquakes to prove it.

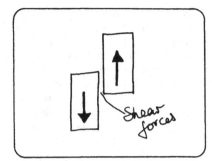

THE COMPOSITE PROBLEM

I have discoursed rapidly about three major problems: technological change, societary upheaval, and the debasement of 'participation'. Let this lead us to some sort of general statement of the problem we face, which I want to make as stark as I possibly can. It is all too easy for us to kid ourselves that we really have an awful lot of experience and must be able to cope, but I question this in the light of what has already been said.

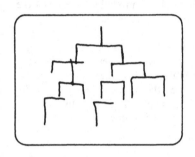

We have organizational structures looking like family trees. You know as well as I do that these are not even meant to be any kind of account of how the enterprise actually works. They are machines for blaming people when things go wrong. Nonetheless, we are lumbered with them—and people do not think we have got anything else just now. The cybernetician says that we have; but while that debate goes on *this* is our tool for organizing things.

Secondly, the structure we have, depicted like this, is frozen out of history. It is virtually an accident. If you look at any of our big institutions, our oldest-established firms, our government departments, then you will find them all structured according to something that happened in the past. No-one has had the nerve to rethink it all and to say: 'to hell with that. Florence Nightingale is dead. William Williams of Pontycelyn is dead. Robert Peel is dead.' You would think these people were very much alive. And again: we have the health, education and security systems to prove it.

Thirdly, having got this frozen structure, we are naturally (and perhaps quite properly after all) using the methods appropriate to that structure. But if the structure is no longer appropriate to the real world—then neither are the methods.

Fourthly, the connexions our organization has with the rest of the world—our liaisons with other companies, our holdings in other business—are adapted to the frozen image of the enterprise, and not to the actual enterprise itself.

May I point out that models were not first invented by operational research. Our perception of any system whatever is a conceptual .nodel of that system, which exists in our minds.

Here is a real situation, and here are you. You may probe—and in various ways experience—that situation, and you generate this model of it in your memory store. I can draw in the third line, because the situation itself helps to generate the the model—or so we hope. Put it this way: if that connection isn't there, we shall be accounted mad. Try this diagram out on a situation called 'the baby'.

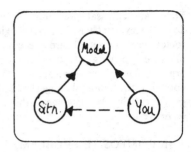

Mother makes a model of her baby, and it is a very good model. This is partly because the baby is relatively uncomplicated, and partly because mother lives with it—almost lives through it. What happens when the baby grows up? It gets more and more complicated, and your model of it cannot keep pace. Thus it is that parents come to grief with their teenagers: their model (a) no longer explains behaviour, but worse (b) you think that it should.

Now our models of institutions and enterprises are often wildly out of date. We started, perhaps a hundred years ago, with a situation that our forebears modelled. They cast the model in the form of legislation, or a company image, or a *lex non scripta*.

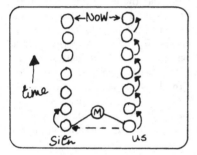

So there we were—a hundred years ago. Now I draw time vertically like this. The situation has moved on, and so have we; the situation has repeatedly changed, and so have we. But we have enshrined the model.

Therefore these lines I am now adding, connecting everything to the old model, become more and more stretched. My message is this. The elastic has broken.

I said I would make this stark. And if you want to say: Oh rubbish man, it is not really like that, you are free to do so. But I contend that when the history of the last thirty years, from the War say, come to be written, this indeed will be the story.

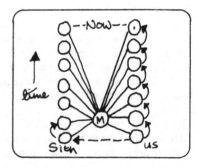

In the mid fifties, I was virtually run out of Manchester for anticipating the collapse of the cotton industry to a dinner consisting of directors of those warring small companies which urgently needed to abandon the family image, amalgamate, and restructure themselves. I was run out of Newcastle, and very nearly lynched in Glasgow, for telling similar parties of shipbuilders that they would shortly be overtaken by the two countries we were alleged to have beaten during the war. They said that the technological innovations of which I spoke were science fiction: I invited them to go and see them all actually working in Hamburg. It was easy to *prove* that they needed a new production technology, a new organizational structure, and a new and dynamic decision process. Why then could these proofs not be heard? Simply because the model of the enterprise in everybody's head was completely and utterly irrelevant. If you are convinced that 'Britain is the world's shipbuilder' then everything is bound to be all right.

I have read that I have the reputation of being a prophet whose oracles come true. It is nonsense. I am a scientist, and I do not make predictions. As to some of the predictive techniques in use today, I would as soon consult the entrails of a chicken. What I do is study the *systems* which society has underwritten and in which firms are embedded. If you look at the state of the system, how it got to that state, the constraints which operate upon it, and the inputs available to it, you just calculate the next state. If you try to go too far ahead, then too much latitude enters into the calculation. For instance, if you hit a major war, your calculation omits an overriding input. On this quite mundane basis, who in this room tonight can have any hope for the aircraft industry? Are there not things to be said about motor cars, about steel, about computers? People will not look the facts in the eye, they prefer the familiar—but defunct—model. As I think you may be aware, I have just been through all this in the publishing industry.....

But if you think this talk of models is too airy-fairy, take a look at its hard, practical embodiment. I am talking to you, gentlemen, about the need for adaptation. One of the biological tricks of adaptation is to specialize, and one of the biological things that happens after getting very good at specializing—and therefore very adaptative—is that there is a big shift in the environment. Then suddenly you are over-specialized: and that is *extinction*. The environmental shifts are there—I have been talking about them—and the over-specialization is the adherence to a model that is no longer representative of the world. This is the route we are following.

What sort of answers have we conceivably got to this problem? I want to give you three of these, too, although I have not left myself much time.

SOLUTION ONE—ORGANIZATIONAL STRUCTURE

First of all, what is to be done about organizational structure, if it is no longer adaptive?

I have already suggested to you that the top level of management cannot afford any longer to be divisionalized, and what I mean by that is that whereas we used to have the sales director, the production director and the financial director sitting around a table, defending as it were their empires to each other, with simply a chairman to try and find a synthesis, we really do have to create a genuine problem-oriented team. Therefore, I argued a little while ago, we should somehow demote these functions in order to exalt the team of top *general* managers. Now if that is right (or even if it is wrong) what would that team be doing?

I believe that a very convenient and effective way to organize, in the context of change that I have been portraying tonight, is to have two major parts of general management.

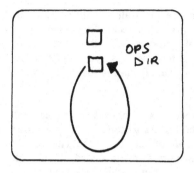

I will draw them like this, although one would expect the division to be made horizontally, for reasons of my own. I do *not* mean to say that the one on top is the senior. Now this one is called the operations directorate, and I draw an enormous loop like that, to show that it is dealing with the internal structure of the enterprise—*and dealing with it now*, because we have got to keep this thing going. That is all about Technology A, if you like. This loop is about the business we have got, about the government we have got; if it stops looping, then chaos. All that must be kept going. Deal effectively with what is happening under your own control, and happening now.

Secondly, we may think of this structure which has a loop going in the other direction : and this I call the development directorate. It is dealing essentially with the external world, and it is dealing with the future. That is the contrast. The new loop is all about Technology B of course. If we had loads of time I would give you an enormous number of cybernetic reasons for making the division like this, but I won't bother. I will just assert that

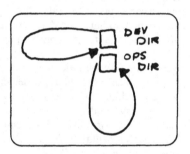

the reasons exist, and leave it with you to fight out with me over the coffee. It would obviously be indelicate to plug a new book, which happens to be called *Brain of the Firm*, due out shortly.

Suffice it to say, that if you make any major division at all in an organization, and I suppose you must, the very next thing to do is to put the pieces together again.

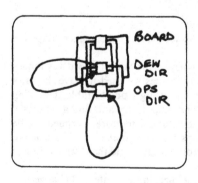

Quite suddenly the diagram has become very complicated. Yet all I have done is this. I have installed a general management, the major task of which is to link together the internal-and-now, on the one hand, and the external-and-future, on the other. Now watch me add all these arrows. The diagram is suddenly nearly obscured: but I have drawn only the minimal number of loops required to keep the whole thing hanging together. You need all of this diagram to define the general management task, which I take to be the finding of a right balance between the two lower boxes—

in the context of the scene I was describing earlier. If we could only do this, we should improve our affairs by an order of magnitude. Because this *is* the problem.

You are not getting much of the detail out of me tonight. I am simply trying to show that we need to change organizational structure, and that an elementary move, based quite simply on our analysis of the problem as put forward here, provides a completely different notion of how to structure an institution—whether a firm or a government department or a social service.

I am quite a practical fellow underneath this beard, and I know that you cannot just demolish everything you have overnight. That is why I made the point that it seems to me very good sense to keep what we already have, but to collapse it into this new model. That is quite easily done, as a matter of fact, because most of what we have belongs to the lowest box and the lowest loop. Our most senior management, which ought to be right up here (at the top), spends most of its time down here (at the bottom)—because that is where if feels at home: dealing with the internal and the now. So it is open to us to mount the rest of this apparatus around the on-going structure, and to move the people around a bit. Not that you won't need *new* people—because you assuredly will.....

Incidentally, changes looking something like this, at least in so far as they affect the functional responsibilities of individual directors, are already beginning to happen in major American firms. I would give you as examples: IBM, General Motors, Lytton and Dupont. In such places you will find teams surrounding the top man, members of which do not have the old-fashioned responsibilities. You will have heard the term: 'the president's office'.

I could talk for hours about all of this, and frequently do. May I just ask you to note, however, the betrayal of a so-called 'principle of management' which has existed for a great many years? It concerns the loop which links the very top to the very bottom of this organization. We humans are fond of producing dichotomies: carving the universe in half, and declaring it mandatory to belong to one or the other of these halves. But the real world, and in particular the viable biological organism, has not heard about these rules. When we set up what we are pleased to call a chain of command, A reports to B, who reports to C, who reports to D.....and so on, it is in no circumstances allowed that A should get directly to (let us say) Q. But this is ridiculous. In the biological models used by cyberneticians, the dichotomy does not exist. There is a chain of command—true. But there are other kinds of access, very much of the sort indicated by the loops on the blackboard. For example, organs of the human body run by the autonomic nervous system from centres low down in the brain—all of which means that we have no conscious knowledge of what they are doing—nevertheless have representation in the cortex. 'Have representation' is, interestingly enough, a word which neurophysiologists would use. We may well compare this with current demands for 'representation' of the people in the highest levels of decision taking. Quite apart from this, the chain model of the societies we already know is quite inadequate. Typically, people at the top make it their business to know directly what people at the bottom are thinking—chain of command or not.

Another organizational dichotomy of which management theorists have been very fond is the distinction between centralization and decentralization. This equally is rubbish, and an open invitation to consultants. If an organization considers itself centralized, they will of course declare that it must be decentralized. And precisely vice versa. You need take only a quick look at the cybernetic facts to see the fallacy. If I personally were centralized, then—concentrating as I am on what I am saying—I should forget to tell my heart to beat, and drop dead at your feet. This would be highly dramatic, but of little use to anyone. On the other hand, if I were fully decentralized, try as I might to concentrate on this talk, the need of my body for fluid (which I may say is quite urgent) would send me rushing from the room to recharge this empty glass, regardless of the talk. No, no; we should reject such absurd naiveties.

SOLUTION TWO—CORPORATE STRATEGY

Once we have restructured the highest echelon of the enterprise, we shall be in a position—at last—to do something constructive about its strategy. Let's face it: most firms are so involved with their tactics, which are short-term, that they have no time to evolve a proper strategy. But now we have a focus for this kind of thinking, in the middle box of these three. All three must certainly be deeply involved, but the middle one carries special responsibility.

I would remind you that we did not even know the phrase 'corporate planning' until a very few years ago. It is a child of explosive technology—and we have not at all mastered it. For one thing, it is usually held at arm's length like the rest of the innovative activities we discussed earlier, but there is worse to come.

In the first place, this thing is often seen as a predictive activity. I had a go at this misconception just now: you cannot predict unless you are God. What you can do is to make *various* kinds—not one kind—of intelligent extrapolation into the future, specifying the conditions under which each scenario works. Then your problem of corporate strategy is about judging the vulnerability of the main policies open to you against a range of possible futures.

In the second place, these studies are meant to provoke you into taking decisions—and taking them *now*. Most written-up corporate strategies, most five year plans and what have you, turn out to say: we are surveying the scene with the view to taking a decision one day if we are forced to. Whereas the whole business is really about the fact that what you decide to do today constrains your future—and perhaps forces you down a path to destruction. This point does not seem to me to have been taken. Its arch exponent is, of course, Peter Drucker. He has been preaching this for years, and puts the point very concisely. Corporate strategy is not about future decisions, but about the futurity of present decisions. I would like to see that written up in every boardroom.

Now if we have a focus for this activity, bang in the middle there of the general management structure, and if we have a Druckerian approach to the making of strategies, how do we set about it? We ought, I suggest, to abandon our boardrooms—or rather the hallowed model of the boardroom in our heads. We sit there with our piles of paper, pencils and scribbling blocks, trying to carry ourselves forward from the minutes of the last meeting, and hiding behind the documents we brought along—which are mainly history books. I submit that we know a better trick than this. We need a dynamic operations room—such as we had to run battles in the war. Even then, without benefit of electronic aids, we had maps of the terrain on which to push around markers of various kinds. And 'the management', sitting up there in the gallery, had a synoptic view of a dynamically unfolding operation. They could debate the likely consequences of possible decisions, which they then made to the best of their well-informed ability.

If we wish to equip our boardrooms in this spirit, we have the tools today to do the job. Above all, there is the tool of the real-time on-line computer. That is a huge advance in capability over the tools that were available when I first started to advocate this approach. Throughout that time, the idea has been dubbed science fiction; managers still call it that today. But the thing is done.

You have a model of the firm in a computer. Then the man with a proposal to make at a board meeting demonstrates his plan on a flow chart of the company and its affairs which has replaced the board table. As he does this, the computer is automatically calculating the consequences, of his suggestions. It makes the appropriate injections of money into its model, calculates cash flows at the dcf rates prescribed, takes account of the various levels of competition which have been proposed, and spells out sets of answers.

'That's all very well, Bill, but what happens if . . . . .' There is your key question: 'what if . . . . .'. Under our old system somebody says: 'Oh damn, you've mentioned one I have not really looked into'—because there is always something. 'I'll look into it'. Chairman: 'can you look at it in time for the next board?' 'I'll try'. Next month: 'sorry, haven't finished it'. Three months later: 'Here is the answer . . . . .'. 'Yes, but what if . . . . .'

This is how our decisions drag on. They really do. In an electronic operations room, you would say 'what if', simultaneously entering the question into the machine. And you would watch while the cash flow over the next ten years adjusted itself.

Science fiction? There is an American company operating in this country right now doing most of this. The models are not perhaps as elaborate as you gentlemen would like. But we have to remember that model in our own heads . . . . . Is that really as elaborate as we like to pretend? Especially, is it one of those out of date models, representing the company we have known and loved all these years? So here is another of my non-prophecies. This kind of thing will go through business—and I think through government—quite inevitably. How long it will take I don't know, but it is already ahead of us and we have to catch up with it.

SOLUTION THREE—THE DECISION PROCESS

We now have a dynamic concept of organization, with information churning around all those loops. We have a dynamic concept for the formulation of strategies under continuous board-level review. The third of my solutions has to do with a dynamic decision process itself.

So now we stop sitting there, soaking up the atmosphere, exposing our brains to the climate of opinion, and waiting for the consensus view to fall into our laps like an over-ripe plum.

Well, you will say, we do a lot better than that. Many people do formalise the decision process, and give it structure. I accept that. However, because our notions of structure tend to look like family trees, the formalisation of decision structures seems to have come out like this—a family tree on its side.

The first thing to decide, we say, is : will it be British or American? Having decided that, which British companies shall we approach? And so on. I know a good many managers who work like this : settle one thing at a time, they say. I am also sorry to confess that operational research has connived in this approach by the formalisation of decision trees of exactly this kind.

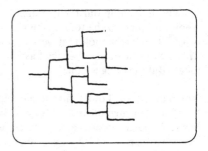

I do not believe that good decision taking is anything like this at all. Why? Quite simply because the real decision taking process involves a lot of people, and the whole structure is redolent with feedback. At every decisive moment, of which there will be a great many *within* the total decision—which is, for example, our strategy—we range ahead, and back, and sideways. We gauge the effect of this sub-decision on everything we have tentatively decided already, and on the sub-decisions left to take. This is why I think the decision tree is an artefact, and of little use to us. You cannot isolate these nodes either in time or in logical connectivity, and anyone who has ever taken a complicated decision knows this.

Let me show you what a decision structure looks like when you treat it as a dynamic system [reproduced as a plate section at the back of this book] this is my own work—you do not have to read it, just look at the complexity and the feedback. Imagine yourself in the middle of this tangled web. Does it not feel more like being in the midst of a real decision taking situation than it does if you position yourself on one of those branches on the blackboard?

I have done at lot of personal work on this kind of decision model, and have evolved quite a number of techniques for quantifying the thing. Can we measure the uncertainty that still remains in the big strategy? And how do we reduce it?

Here is my final story. I invented this technique for a government department which would not use it. They said that the group of people who would be affected would not understand. So I went and explained it to this group myself. They positively demanded that it should be used. I forget the next reason why it could not be done. But I have used it myself in other situations, and it looks like this.

Don't think, this technique says, of large, complex, strategic decisions as made up of all sorts of sub-decision components which you assemble like a damn great piece of Meccano. Look at the problem exactly the other way round.

We begin with a certain amount of uncertainty, which is high. In a completely unconstrained situation it is infinite—you can do anything, decide what you like. But of course the minute you talk about an actual strategy, the uncertainty is already constrained—it is finite. I have developed a way of measuring this with which we have no time to deal now, but let's be clear that it is a numerical measure of uncertainty. Well, you are obviously trying to bring this down, until no uncertainty is left : then you have your decision.

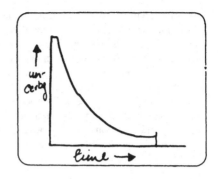

There are mathematical reasons for thinking it ought to come down roughly like this.

The point of this technique is not to take decisions, but to monitor those that will take a long time—I mentioned them earlier on. It is open to you to fix a future date by which this decision must be taken, to fill in the curve, and then to monitor actual progress against this curve as a target. If the level of uncertainty does not come down fast enough, then clearly your decision is going to be late—and you might even be able to guess by how much.

But real life poses more problems than this.....

I used the technique in an industrial situation where we had to take a very complex decision, and I had this chart on the wall. I plotted the way the actual content of uncertainty remaining in the strategy came down compared with the theoretical curve—for which we had initially allowed two years.

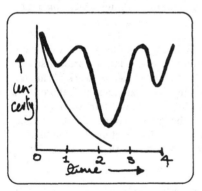

After four years the thing looked like this..... Well, you can see that this was a dynamic, explosive situation alright. What was happening is that, having removed a certain amount of uncertainty from the decision situation, more uncertainty was pumped back in. That happened because the situation was changing very fast—and also, I am bound to say, because some people had a keen interest in seeing that the decision was not taken. But I think it is interesting to measure the degree of confusion which can be generated, both by technological and commercial changes and also by deliberate endeavours. Still: this is just a tool. Watch a situation like this develop philosphically if you like, or use the tool to beat someone over the head.

WINDING-UP

I must soon stop. Let me briefly sum up, and take you into a proposal—as to which I look forward to some reactions. ·

I began by trying to focus attention on the problem of what is really an outdated institution. It was an organization, you remember, with a rigid structure—frozen out of history—using old methods, and having old connexions. And the whole thing appeared to be dying on its feet out of over-specialization—and therefore failing to adapt to technological change, societary upheaval and even to the new management methods. What I am now portraying is a management geared to the technological truths of our age; a management structured explicitly to keep Technology A going, and profitable, while also developing Technology B; and a management able by the use of new, dynamic tools of corporate planning and decision making capable of making that judgment between the levels of investment for profitability now and in the future—whether in terms of money, the right use of people, everything.

I ask you to contemplate how different all this would be from the management we have known. It turns management into a conversational business—a conversation among ourselves, with our employees, with the public, and with all the realities of the world outside. A conversation, gentlemen, and not a ritual fire dance.

Then how shall we learn the techniques of conversing, when the conversation must break through interfaces—not only between men—but between men and machines? Do we have to spend our lives travelling, so as to break through the first interface? Can we really not talk to each other as men, given modern electronics, without sitting together within striking distance? And do we really put competent technicians between our own brains and the computing capacity which ought to be conceived as an additional lobe of those very brains?

We know all the secrets of broad-band communication already. That is: you and I can be in touch over any distance by two-way colour television—and we can build computer circuits in so that our own faces can be replaced on our screens by such computer output as we might call for. We do not know much about several more things which *could* quite easily be discovered.

At the technical level: what sort of switching could be undertaken between a number of out-stations to avoid the one-to-one sub-conversation which is what our present switching technology would give us. At the psychological level: how does a network of this sort behave, and how do we recapture the subtleties of inter-personal reaction that we know about in the coherent group? At the level of social anthropology: what do we know about the way whole communities produce their outputs on the basis of contiguity? I mean that most of what the human animal does and achieves is not, perhaps, set up through planned meetings at all—but is the result of chance encounters and clashes that are ostensibly off the point.

I think that all this needs immediate research. If you ask why, I reply that society as a whole urgently needs to devolve—whether organizationally or geographically. I have mentioned the problem of executive travel already. Perhaps our senior executives in industry and government are past the point already where their contribution is effective—because of all this milling around. Perhaps they could work from home. If you look at the city: well, I do not relish the idea of the megalopolis—the city of sixty million people. This threatened concentration of human beings has a great big question mark hanging over it, a question mark with a big dot underneath—put there by the lemmings.

In short, can society disperse, to operate socially in small communities which seem to suit the condition of our species, while at the same time managing to conduct affairs on a planetary scale?

The proposal I make is this. There ought to be a research institute working explicitly on the lines of this possible solution—that is to say by broad-band circuitry. It would work on the problems of man and his future which so engage the attention of many responsible scientists today. But in constituting a network of the kind I have described, it would also be its own guinea-pig. That is: research into all the matters I have just listed could be undertaken by itself, on itself. Any one joining this network would agree in advance that his use of the circuitry could be monitored, without telling him, by the other members. I think he would accept, then forget, this stipulation. And the result of that would be that—probably for the first time ever—the research into the behaviour of man could be undertaken without changing that behaviour. Heisenberg beaten at last.

Now the Open University is a unique institution—already working on a basis of almost total devolution. It is the ideal sponsor for an open research network of the kind I have described. What is more, it is not only willing but most enthusiastic to found such a thing. Secondly, the University runs in double harness with the BBC. The Corporation already owns and operates a closed circuit broad-band communication network throughout the country, which it uses to control its own nation-wide activity. That circuit is silent from midnight until television reopens during the morning. I have asked the BBC whether they could make this facility available at night, and they have said yes—in principle.

We have here the makings of a fantastic experiment, altogether in keeping with the tenor of my arguments tonight. It could be of rapid and direct use to businesses, social services, government and society itself.

What is more, I don't think you will need much convincing that if Britain could start this network, it would be likely to cross the national boundary quite soon. There are people, for instance, doing work like this in America. Would it be so very difficult to persuade someone to donate a satellite link? I think not.

And so we come to the cost. Equipping one terminal station would run to about £ 50,000. So five of them run out at a quarter of a million. However, this compares favourably with the building of a large research institute, somewhere out in the country, with Doric columns, to which the world's leading people in this field could not be attracted—as they could to my scheme, because it offers simply an enrichment of their present activity. None the less this has to be paid for. So of course do the salaries of people involved, but that is computable—and perhaps within the compass of existing university arrangements, especially if a few endowments of posts were made. I suppose that the running cost is the biggest unknown as I speak to you. We are going into this.

I am sorry, gentlemen, if I have taken an unfair advantage. Having spent quite a time bludgeoning you about your own job as a very senior manager, I am suddenly declaiming on the future of the world. But the compass of the whole argument is I think fully coherent. I guess you can take it. Thank you.

THESIS

SEVENTH STATEMENT

New institutions
with new eudemonic metrics
and new organizational structures
also need

>new kinds of strategy
>new approaches to decision making

in a phrase :

>dynamics of decision,

fast-responding, self-regulating, self-organizing.

This concept is integrative and organic.

It does away with sterile models
of institutions as being for instance

>centralized or
>decentralized

since any viable system is both at once.

Such tired old issues
are easily resolved
metalinguistically.

>We need only to create
>metasystems to speak
>the metalanguage.

The institution most needing reform
under these cybernetic canons
is government itself.

It is therefore imperative
that public channels of communication
especially those commanded by the overwhelmingly influential
electronic media
should not be clogged
nor be allowed to distort
available insights.

COLOUR CODE : BLUE
Thesis

You know this to be a record
of the struggle to say
what cannot be said
in the language.

Therefore there are many hints
in the Arguments of Change addressed to men of affairs
as to metasystems that lurk
behind the systems discussed.
And there are disguised metalinguistic utterances.

In talking with the most senior managers
of institutions other than government itself,
government itself
is the lurking metasystem
speaking a metalanguage
none of us has properly learned.

By now there ought to be no confusion
about the meaning of this remark.
To wit :

> I am certainly not saying
> that government
> > sees the whole picture
> > answers to different criteria
> true though this might be.

What matters in all this
is that the undecidable propositions
thrown up by the institutions
need to be decidable in a metalanguage

> *which it is the duty of the government*
> *to speak*

But the government cannot do this,
it is metalinguistically illiterate.
because its *system* is not *meta*.

The governmental system
is at least as archaic and unadaptive
as are the institutional systems governed.
It unconsciously hankers after its true status
by exerting leverage on the senior surrounding institutions.
thereby substituting

> hierarchies of power

for

> hierarchies in logic

COLOUR CODE : GOLD
Metalanguage

and substituting
remarks made in the language, such as

> 'shut up, in the national interest'

for genuine metalinguistic statements, such as

> 'speak up, for your input
> is required to drive the metasystem
> we the government have designed
> to implement the policies
> for which you voted'.

But the government have no such metasystem.
They design
                    super-systems
I mean great big all-embracing ordinary systems
which next and too often become
                    supra-systems
I mean ordinary systems authorized to order us about.

Metasystems do not need to order us about
because they take logical account in the metalanguage
of undecidable inputs
in the language.

> For example:
> no government *meta*system
> would express metalinguistic surprise
> to hear that trade unions
> will go to extremes
> to protect their members
> from relative underprivilege.
> After all, that was the whole idea.

> But governmental super-systems
> speak the systemic language
> and declare:

>> these people do not understand
>> the economic facts of life.

> This statement is demonstrably false—
> the reverse is clearly the case—
> but if you are determined
> to talk in undecidable propositions
> then contradictions
> are what you will get.

COLOUR CODE : GOLD
Metalanguage

Such as non-existent barbers
who do and don't shave themselves

and trade union leaders
who do and don't understand
the economic facts of life.

There is no point
in floundering around in a language
which is generating undecidable propositions
and bitterly complaining

that each of two lots
of knowledgeable and responsible men
are between them expressing a contradiction.
Of course they are.
Naturally.

It makes still less sense
to pick on one lot
of knowledgeable and responsible men
and blame the nonsense onto them.

To do that you must call them

unknowledgeable
irresponsible

When they are not.

It is your job
if you are the government
to rise above the systemic language
which both lots of men
are condemned to speak—
because they constitute the system—
and to find the metalanguage
in which the propositions are decidable.

But beware of this talk :
it begins to *sound* as if
there is a pious formula
which would express the national good.....
That is super-system banality.

COLOUR CODE : GOLD
Metalanguage

No. *Here* is the snag :

> metasystems were defined as
> 'what speak metalanguages';

> without a metasystem
> there is nothing
> to do the talking.

So we are back to square one.

Therefore please do not ask me
the answers to any questions
about the national weal.
Ask me instead
to design a metasystem
which will then have a metalanguage
in which to ask

> and to answer
> > such questions.

Throughout my Arguments of Change
has run the theme
that this is exactly what we have to do.

Whether I was calling
for a new kind of Cabinet Office
or for metamodels of the economy
or for the reconstruction
of old institutions

I was always calling
for this.

The theory and the tools
(I have continually claimed)
are there.

We can even see
after the last Argument
some of the essential features
of a properly designed government
for contemporary purposes.

COLOUR CODE : GOLD
Metalanguage

Because these lineaments seem so clear
let us dare to list :

        devolved government
                with regional parliaments
       dual representation of the people
                 so that half the House of Commons
                 is elected through a region
                 and half directly—
                 every citizen
                 having two *national* votes
       an Upper House with an explicit role (at last)
                 to be a metasystem
                 for the Commons
                 having no authority at all
       two main departments of state
                 to deal with
                          operations
                          development
       a strategic centre
                 to serve the Cabinet

     . . . .

I really could go on
but I shall not.

These matters need the study
they have not got.

We try to solve everything
by commissions 'taking evidence'—
                 now what evidence would that be?

       The undecidable statements of interested parties
       talking the systemic language
       generating contradictions?

       The well-intentioned suggestions of thoughtful people
       without benefit of
                 the time
                 the attendant science
       to design the metasystem?

               COLOUR CODE : GOLD
                   Metalanguage

After that
　　　　whom shall we ask
　　　　to decide
　　　　the undecidable?

There are threats
and there are metathreats

we have systems
　　　　generating super-systems
　　　　becoming supra-systems

　　　　contributing to the metathreat

we have no metasystem
to resolve all this.

And you may recall the doubts expressed
about my metasystems
earlier on :

were they after all

　　　　super-supra-systems?

　　　　a threat to freedom?

Come with me now
a second time in the year
to Washington . . . . .

to argue this with experts.

The language is—in part—an expert language
which by this time
you know as well as I do
how to speak.

COLOUR CODE : GOLD
Metalanguage

AN ARGUMENT OF CHANGE

THE
LIBERTY
MACHINE

Keynote Address* to the Conference on Ecological Systems, organized by the American Society for Cybernetics as their annual national conference, and delivered in Washington D.C. on the 8th October, 1970.

*By permission of
Spartan Books

Of Optimism and Pessimism

It is characteristic of man's way of thinking to contemplate entities rather than systems; to disconnect systems rather than to relate their parts; to record inputs and outputs to systems rather than to measure systemic behaviour itself. When it comes to managing affairs, we characteristically try to deal with that dismantled system—piece by piece—rather than to redesign the totality so that it actually works.

Thus the current awareness of ecological crisis consists in a catalogue of stark and unbearable facts. They sound like this.

In the United States during 1966 man-made pollution by carbon monoxide amounted to eighty-five million tons.

Last year, 8.1 million automobiles were written off; 57,742 of these were abandoned in New York City.

The population of the earth is growing at the rate of one hundred persons a minute.

One does not know what any of this really means, but it certainly sounds bad. And you know how the catalogue of cataclysm goes on—and on, and on. Each item is usually accompanied by an extrapolation of the existing trend into the future.

For example: the loudest noises to which man is exposed have increased by one decibel a year for the last forty years. *If this goes on*, then in about ten years from now we shall have passed a noise level already proven lethal for cockroaches and rats. This is one of the less terrifying examples, because we feel that man may be somehow superior to the cockroach—and besides the postulated rate of increase is merely linear.

People really begin to 'blow their minds' when confronted by exponential rates of growth—extrapolated, of course, to a point of singularity. Some of you will recall how, many years ago, Heinz von Foerster demonstrated how the population explosion would not starve us but crush us to death—by achieving an infinite population some sixty years from now. Reading the subsequent correspondence his friends laid bets as to just how far Heinz's tongue had gone into Heinz's cheek.....

But surely, people respond, this cannot be. Nature is well known for its ability to maintain ecological homeostasis. Explosive tendencies on the part of threatening variables in our situation, which are unseemly not to say annihilating, will be held in check by counterbalancing forces. Thus we shall escape not only Armageddon, but—far more importantly—we shall escape the intellectual agony of trying to contemplate these frightful things.

With this statement we have reached the limits of cybernetic sophistication for the average educated man. As far as the argument goes, it is correct. Not even the worst mismanagement of affairs can have the effect of repealing the cybernetic laws of nature.

So: there we are. 'Are you optimistic or pessimistic about all this?' asked the man. 'I am optimistic', replied the perennial optimist in us all. 'Then why are you scowling?' asked the man. 'Because my optimism is not justified'.....

We cyberneticians know very well that homeostasis, in the face of all the threats, will be achieved. Nature inexorably moves from one equilibrial condition to another. However, it is for this national symposium to speak out plainly (using as many noise-polluting decibels as it can muster) about the likely consequences. What would we say?

The laws of ecosystem are not answerable to a criterion of success which necessarily includes the survival of man. The most likely systemic outcome of the things we are up to is a sudden, catastrophic, population decline. This is a sufficiently familiar experience for many species—observable today (in corals, for example), as it is in the geological record. That record, moreover, suggests that sometimes there may be a little too much positive feedback in the control system. So whereas the catastrophic population collapse typically cuts back the species to about a third of its peak strength, homeostasis sometimes overdoes it. Thus whole species become extinct.

What we have to say to our educated cybernetician-in-the-street is that if this fate were to overtake our species, nature betrays no cybernetic law. Nature can afford to shrug off the incident. She has been up evolutionary blind alleys before. Man seeks to impose his own objective function on the natural homeostat: his failure is his own failure: his extinction is his own affair.

The Metathreat Exposed

Let us try to make a constructive cybernetic approach to the crisis. I ask you first to contemplate the societary system by which ecological threats are currently recognized and handled. There seems to be a typical course of events.

First of all, a specific threat becomes known to a small group of experts having special knowledge and endowed with acute perception. These people draw public attention to the threat, using the only machinery available to them. This means publication through the mass media, which handle such topics meretriciously. It is of course open to the experts privily to address government, which they have often tried to do. But typically government will take no notice—until stimulated to do so by a public outcry that has been artificially engendered in this way. I note here and now what an intolerable system this is: whereby we must sacrifice both dignity and scientific nicety, and be turned into cathode ray buffoons, simply in order to alert our fellow human beings to danger.

This stage of the circuit is quite simply an amplifier. For the facts may be rightly disseminated, but people do not really believe them until we have bared our breasts and cut ourselves with knives. But given this high gain, the clamour may be sufficient to provoke action. Then what is to count as action? Because the threat is specific, and has been made artifically more specific by the use of these communication circuits, then only specific action is likely to count.

Studies will be financed to investigate this precise threat: experts who know about particular aspects of this precise threat will indulge in combat for their piece of the loot; and so society embarks on a familiar route of a reductionist kind. This machinery is guaranteed not to increase our knowledge of anything systemic.

The second thing that government will do is to lay the precise threat squarely at the door of some explicit body or individual. There can be no accusations now that the matter is being overlooked. For example, a recommendation has just been made to the Mayor of Los Angeles to appoint an officer responsible for dealing with the problem of noise. He is to have the unbelievably infelicitous title of 'Noise Administrator'. His terms of reference provide that he should know where the noise is coming from, create acceptable standards for the level of noise, and suggest methods of controlling noise to those standards.

Imagine yourself in this post: what would you do? Would you still expect your salary if you responded to this remit by saying: *everyone* is making a noise; the acceptable standard is *silence*; and the action required is to *shut up*? Again, I fear, we have machinery for talking about the problem but with no access to it—because the problem is just part of the pathology of a complex system, and the supposed solution has to do with peering and poking at a single symptom.

But these measures will count as a solution, because they will satisfy the clamour. Citizens with no comprehension of systems theory will feel that everything possible is being done. This in itself defuses the societary bomb planted by the experts. The bomb is still there, but it does not look very dangerous. And now we encounter another sub-routine of this total program. The researchers who got the money continue to discuss the problem in public, to prove they deserved the funds. Those on whom responsibility has been laid continue to make pronouncements intended to show that they are ameliorating the situation—or at any rate slowing down the appalling development of the threat which people had been led to expect. The result of all this is, very naturally, that the public becomes sick and tired of the whole thing.

We are confronted here with a phenomenon of social habituation. 'You too can live with the hydrogen bomb'—even though the risks associated with this weapon steadily grow as more nations acquire nuclear capability. We have now completed a circuit; for we are back at the stage where there is a wide public knowledge of a threat which is not really believed in. With new knowledge, it is possible to reactivate this circuit, but this time the response will be less alarmed. Indeed, we may expect an exponential decay in the response we get each time round. We have laid bare a machine called 'Cry Wolf'.

Meanwhile, however, a new specific threat has been exposed, and is ready to take over from the first threat in the public esteem. After the trauma of Hiroshima comes the Silent Spring. Pesticides will kill us. if we are now satisfied we shall not be blown up. The societary machine goes into action again, and again the meretricious handling of the problem begins. Europe is alerted to the dangers of building up poisons in the human body with the bizarre cry: 'Americans are now unfit for human consumption'. And when the rituals are complete, and society has habituated to this threat too, along comes Threat the Third.....

I have sought illumination about what happens next in Ross Ashby's model of general habituation which he published in 1958. He explains that a new stimulus tends to free the original response from its habituation, so that if the original stimulus is again presented the response will be restored to its initial value prior to habituation. But he goes on to show that if two stimuli have much in common, then the dehabituation may not work— or any rate will be less effective.

Clearly societary threats *do* have much in common, and Ashby's prediction seems to be coming true. The dehabituation mechanics are not working any longer. Scientists are now being catalogued by the public as prophets of doom, which is precisely to emphasize the commonality of the specific threats to which we draw attention. We are now likely to be discarded, like any good messenger bearing bad news who has his head cut off.

Now I think that Professor Ashby, who is here today, would expect me to record that his model was not intended to handle habituation in cases where special mechanisms of survival are involved, as they surely are here. We are not dealing simply with a stimulus representing *any* kind of disturbance likely to upset the system from an equilibrial state. We are dealing explicitly with threats. A threat is a very special and particular kind of stimulus for any animal: it churns about in the reticular formation of the brain stem which promptly commits the whole organism to some special mode of action. If the threat turns out to be a wolf-crying false alarm, we may yet habituate. Even so, the experience is different from habituating to a neutral stimulus. If someone now cries 'Bear', another but different false alarm, and another 'Lion', and so on, what shall we make of that?

I want to suggest that this is the core of our problem. We might well become convinced that there really were no wolves, really no bears, really no lions, and so on; and yet we should soon begin to wonder why we found ourselves in this imaginary menagerie. Something else must be going on, something we do not understand, which keeps coming at us in the form of urgent alarm signals which turn out to be false. Then although we shall not be eaten by wolves, crushed by bears or mauled by lions, we are at least likely to have a nervous breakdown.

I believe that this stressful situation is the metathreat to our society. We cannot cope with it. It is the threat that society itself will collapse, and with it all our over-sanguine mechanisms for dealing with specific threats. *There* is a dehabituating device if ever there was one. For as we saw, habituation to threat depends on the confidence that there are institutional ways of handling it—whereas now the institution itself is threatened.

If the mechanisms I have criticized for dealing with explicit threats are not particularly satisfactory, it is perfectly clear that the aggregate of these solutions will not touch the metathreat at all. They are not even addressed to it. There is worse still: if we are dealing with a metathreat generated in a metasystem which we do not understand, our well meaning attempts to cope with explicit systemic threats (which we now perceive to be no more than local manifestations of the metathreat) may through our ignorance do more harm than good.

Let me at once tie in this theoretical construct to ecological realities. Endless stories are recorded about the disasters which often follow attempts at local biological control through a lack of understanding the ramifications of these actions in the ecosystem at large. I will not rehearse them here: you are all convinced. Should anyone wish to ponder the factual basis of this complex situation, however, I recommend to him a new book just published in England by Gordon Rattray Taylor. Significantly, in view of my recent remarks, it is called *The Doomsday Book*.

The burden of the argument so far is to say that threats derive from an unrecognized metathreat, and that this is why government and the public are so confused about the nature of ecological and societary crises today. Once this point is taken, so that we see apparently specific threats as being indeed manifestations of the metathreat, we are ready to recognize two truths.

The first is that we shall not be able to handle problems of threat by direct methods. Take the city. Noise, carbon monoxide, water failure, electricity failure, transportation failure, ghetto violence, street muggings, schoolgirl pregnancies, student revolt—all these and many more problems are generated metasystemically. That is to say, they are not problems about decibels, gases, logistics, colour, greed, lust and drugs, but problems about having cities. The city is a settlement grown beyond viable limits, technologically souped-up beyond the threshold of physiological endurance, and perhaps ten percent efficient in terms of its group purposes. It is a machine for generating problems of noise, carbon monoxide, logistics, ghettos, and so forth.

The second truth follows from this. We must redesign the machine that is the city, and for that matter the machine that is the state. That is to say that the metaproblem of the metasystem that engenders the metathreat is a problem of organization.

Stereotypes of Organization, Time and Planning

To put this point in less technical language, we may use the familiar metaphor with which I began. If we are not to attack symptoms but rather the disease, we shall have to look at the body politic rather than the malfunctioning organs.

This seems an obvious thing to do: the difficulty is that it is almost impossible—because we have invented and perfected an unalterable organization for society that does not permit it. Federal organization, everywhere in the world, is delineated by function. Thus it is easy to talk about the health of the people, about the education of the people, and about the social security of the people. But there are no convenient means for discussing the integral state of a citizen, who ought after all to be healthy *and* educated *and* secure— especially since each one of these desiderata probably depends upon the other two.

Well, it is true that you cannot look at everything at once. I define organization as a structural device for reducing proliferating variety. By this I mean that when a large and complex system has been segregated into subsystems, it loses the appropriate combinatorial power to become more complicated still. Sensible attempts to institute horizontal cross linkages in a vertically compartmentalized system of this kind are—and in a sense very properly— resisted, because they would restore the variety generating capability that the organization as such is meant to destroy. But it is a necessary corollary of this that everything we do is constrained in its effectiveness by the appropriateness of the divisions we made in the first place. Since our circumstances, and above all our technology, are so rapidly changing, the likelihood that particular organizational divisions that were once effective will remain so is very low indeed.

Great businesses have come to recognize this fact, and to undertake evolutionary experiments in novel and adaptive modes of organization. Witness for example the President's Office in a large corporation. Changes occur here so quickly that the staff lower down become disoriented. When it comes to public affairs, however, we are locked to an organizational stereotype. This is not due merely to the immense inertia of so elaborate and ponderous a machine as we have come to know and hate, though that is a considerable factor. It is more importantly due to the suspicion that any interference with this machinery is likely to be nefarious.

It is a relatively simple matter to reorganize the responsibilities of a firm's vice-presidents. It is not all that difficult to move from a commercial system of geographic divisions to a commercial system of product divisions. But in affairs of state this is hard indeed to accomplish without first destroying the machinery of state and going through a phase of anarchy. This is why, I suggest, the ever increasing and ever more apparent incompetence of a particular regime of state has been allowed, throughout human history, to continue its inoperable course to the point of collapse or revolution. Those who funk a phase of controlled anarchy in the interests of adaption have bloody anarchy thrust upon them.

Here I pause to consider a philosophical foundation to this incorrigible resistance to change, since I regard it as a matter of profound professional interest to this gathering. The point I want to make concerns the nature of time, and the inherited view we have of processes that unfold with time. Our philosophic heritage has misled us seriously here, and the problem derives from the mysterious irreversibility of time—which is not shared by any other dimension of our existence. This of course means that we cannot undertake the symmetric experiments in the temporal evolution of systems, involving the science of time and entropy, with which we are most at home—in the science of space and energy.

According to the inherited view, which we might dub Bergsonian, world systems are delineated by a complex pattern of trajectories which have been traced until *now*. With this 'now' the trajectories are annihilated, and the future is a void. The philosophers who first understood this view to be mistaken (and I mention particularly J.W. Dunne) pictured the temporal universe as a set of trajectories in which 'now' was the name of a cursor, moving across the scene. As a result, philosophy became bogged down in a variety of problems that were fundamentally bogus.

If you could get ahead of the cursor, by moving outside the reference-frame where the trajectories interplay, then you could have precognition and telekinesis. Then what becomes of freewill? In the nineteen-thirties and forties we had fun and games galore with such spurious problems—in which I was much caught up. It was only with the discovery of cybernetics that we began to see a new and more useful insight. The trajectories are generated by systems under perturbation. Then there is a component of the future that is inexorable, and a component that is adaptive.

I mention all this, however briefly, because it seems that there is a powerful contemporary school of thought in planning technology that has not grasped this point. It is the philosophic legatee of Bergson and Dunne, and is responsible for those peculiar extrapolations of current specific trends which I began today by questioning. It sits in a philosophical halfway house between the views of the future as void and the future as predestined. Are world trajectories shot from the point 'now' like arrows into air, or are they launched on tramlines moulded to the curve $e^{\lambda t}$?

Neither, I say to you emphatically. The trajectories are outputs of the systems which we have built, and which we continue to underwrite even when we see that the trajectory is hell-bent to disaster. It is no good blaming that on human impotence in the face of either the void or the tramlines. We are not impotent, because it is open to us to redesign the systems that generate the trajectories—maintaining predictive control of the inexorable component of outcome, and adaptive control of the rest. No, we are not impotent : just stupid.

And so I return from this discursion to the theme that our accepted control systems for handling environmental threats are functions of the organization that we use. A threat being recognized, it must belong somewhere : someone must be responsible. Or, even if we are sufficiently sophisticated to say that the spread of this threat cuts across the organizational structure, and to try and distribute responsibility under a metastructure, we shall still be caught out. The reason is that the practical processes which must be gone through in order to handle the problem at all are processes of *planning*; and these must be undertaken by staffs who belong—and see themselves as belonging—to the established structure.

The result is inevitable, not surprising, yet very curious—and I have not seen it commented on anywhere. If this address should ever be printed, I would have this summary statement of the point printed alone in heavy type :

PLANNING IS HOMOLOGOUS WITH ORGANIZATION

It sounds trivial; it is certainly obvious. How can you have plans that are not couched in terms of the organization which must implement them? But just think carefully about the converse proposition. If the organization is no longer well-adapted to the environment, how then can the plans be relevant to existing threats? It is just not possible. We have totally failed to grasp this point, despite overwhelming evidence that our plans do not work very well, and that the threats are not being competently met.

Nonetheless, there is indeed an abiding sense of unease. So what do we do? We throw into the situation all the resources we have, resources of money, time and skill. This is done in the cause of efficiency : do it better, do it faster, do it cheaper. *That* will stave off the threat. The point is : do *what*? Obviously, implement the plans. But we have already shown as a lemma that the plans cannot possibly be rightly structured. Thus it is that we expend our resources in the ever more efficient implementation of irrelevant plans.

There is a second massive difficulty which is illuminated by these considerations. If planning is homologous with organization, then plans—which of their very nature ought to be syntheses of parts into a greater whole—become instead ever more detailed and localized sets of unrelated minor decisions. That is because, in deference to one of the major discoveries of the social sciences, we are trying to hold the level of decision at the lowest possible echelon as a matter of policy. I have no quarrel with participative management; in fact I urge it forward. But this ought to mean that small decisions, made in the appropriate locale, are sucked upward, and reformulated into a master plan expressed metalinguistically. Instead it means that the making of decisions is a task pushed down, and implicitly condemned to a stereotyped outcome.

If you wish proof of this assertion, consider the potent development of the decision tree as a technique of operations research. Now planning is a continuous process of decision. If it is homologous with organization, then the decision tree splits according to the organizational split: it cannot do otherwise. For if it did otherwise, there would be no competent body to take the decision. So the continuous process of planning and decision rattles down the stereotyped organizational structure like a steel ball on a pin table, and is awarded some score at the end of the line.

Using that model, you will notice that all is well as long as the pin table retains its structure, and that the metasystem of reward is maintained. If you had a pin table whose structure was constantly altering, and whose pay-off function was constantly being changed by a higher-order system, there would be no point in playing the game. By the same token, there is not much point in playing the game of governing the environment in chunks.

The Metasystem and Human Liberty

We have reached the point of saying that plans to deal with environmental and societary threats do not work because the plans are homologous with organization, and the organization is not appropriate but cannot be radically changed.

There seem to be only two alternative courses ahead. The first is that nothing is done: we carry on as we are. Then the component of future trajectories that is in principle adaptive will, I predict; fail to adapt—because it is frustrated by an organizational strait-jacket. And the component that is inexorable will, I predict, take society on to structural collapse or to its overthrow by revolution. The second available alternative is that we should create a metasystem to handle the metathreat.

Once again, this proposal is based on something more than a theoretical construct--there are many precedents for handling situations in this way. The trouble with the precedents is that they are mostly misleading. In the world of real organizations, characterized as it is by the tenacity of power and the lust for prestige, metasystems are found to masquerade as supra-authorities.

Subsidiary companies of a large corporation cannot be allowed to operate with wholesale autonomy in defiance of each other: therefore we think of them as subservient to the metasystem called the corporation. The same is true for departments of state, which are therefore subservient to their metasystem, the state itself. The father may intervene in a dispute between his subservient children. Using the higher centres of my brain, I may make an act of conation which overrides my subservient autonomic system—by holding my breath, for example.

These precedents are misleading, because they appear to achieve metacontrol by virtue of superior authority rather than by logical necessity. That is to say, we do not see them as metasystems in the proper sense, where they are supposed to employ a higher-order language in order to resolve systemic problems posed in local languages. Instead, we map them onto our hierarchic models of authority—so that it is always possible to erect a higher body, having more authority than any operational system, which is seen not as facing a dilemma but as causing trouble.

In fact, the corporation and the state, like the father, should be cybernetically regarded as servants of the subsidiary companies, the departments and the children. The realities of life are found at the operational level. If my brain sets out to kill my body by holding its breath for good, the autonomic nervous system will soon thwart that merry design. Equally the children and the subsidary organizations will thwart authoritarian behaviour at exactly the point when the metasystem is apparently acting *from* authority rather than from superior information and higher-order logic. This revolt is easily brought about, because the metasystem does not deploy sufficient variety to hold the lower systems down. If is wishes to turn itself into a genuine supra-authority *rather* than a metasystem, that is easily done as well—by destroying variety in the subservient system. In this way my brain can kill my body by throwing it over a cliff, fathers and company presidents may become despotic, and the state may become totalitarian.

By confusing metasystems with supra-authorities we have almost lost the chance of understanding what to do. Think of the limiting case: the United Nations. We wanted, and desperately needed, a world-level metasystem. Frightened of the risk to national sovereignty, we built in the famous Veto. This at once turned the required metasystem into a power system—and one which automatically, and for very good reasons, cannot possibly work. The result is deadlock.

When it comes to the mastery of environmental problems, we observe such deadlocks everywhere. A governmental agency handling funds for research on pollution is in practice forced to recognize the sovereign rights of every responsible academic who has research to do in this area. A Secretary of State for the Environment, if there were such a person, would have to acknowledge the sovereign rights of every industry to continue polluting; while the industry concerned (if it had any sense) would disarm the higher authority and public opinion alike by supporting anti-pollution research with its own funds. In short: the failure of metasystems in society is due to their conception as higher authorities which cannot conceivably exert that authority in a free society. We have invented a self defeating machine, a machine conceived to be unworkable. And we have called it Liberty.

Ladies and gentlemen, I stand here on very thin ice indeed. It could be made to seem that I am ready to forego liberty in the interests of efficiency—and that is a classical trap. In fact, I am not ready to forego liberty at all. Nor do I want to talk politics, but societary cybernetics. If the Liberty Machine does not work, the answer is not to design an illiberal version. Indeed, there is plenty of evidence to suggest that to use a metasystem as a supra-authority whereby to ride roughshod over the interests of minorities is also inoperable. Such a machine is self-defeating too, in the long run—and moreover the cybernetician would not expect it to work in the short run—for one simple reason.

This is: informational overload. We may invest all power in a super-supra-authority, but it cannot exercise that power effectively in the very nature of cybernetic law. When we are talking about these large problems, there are not enough channels in the world to convey information within the limits of Shannon's Tenth Theorem. There are not enough computers in the world to constitute a cerebrum able to supply requisite variety within the contraints of Ashby's Law. Then I cannot in good sense, nor do I, advocate a form of metacontrol which *means* supra-authority. And I seek your protection from any who may say that I have used this occasion for so illiberal an advocacy.

For I must continue to advocate the fresh design of a metasystem, exerting metacontrols, as being the *only* solution to our problems—at whatever risk of being misunderstood. The problem is for cybernetics to discover, and to make abundantly clear to the world, what metasystems truly are, and why they should not be equated with the supra-authorities to which our organizational paradigms direct them. It is an appalling difficult job, because it is so very easy to condemn the whole idea as totalitarian. Hence my use of the term: the Liberty Machine. We want one that actually works.

The first test of the viability of this thinking is that I should be able to convince you, my cybernetic peers. In order to do that, perhaps I may be allowed a technical statement— which would certainly not avail me outside this room. The whole point about a metasystem is that it uses a metalanguage, and the whole point of a metalanguage is to be competent to decide propositions which are undecidable in the lower order languages of the systems concerned. In short, I am making a straight appeal to the logical transcedence at the metasystemic level of limitations imposed on the lower-order logics by Gödel's Theorem.

For this contention my critics usually fire at me simultaneously with both barrels. The message of the first bullet is that undecidability is an arcane property of abstract number systems, and that it is absurd to try and import the findings of metamathematics into socio-political thinking. The second bullet is inscribed 'trivial'. Since I always allow my critics to have it both ways, on the grounds that they usually cancel each other out, I shall continue. The hypothesis that we are dealing with undecidable systems has at least the attraction that it explains why we do not seem able to decide them. Secondly, we are now entitled to suspect that a metasystem or Liberty Machine that will work has to be designed to provide a decidable metalanguage, rather than to exert despotic power in the paradigmatic sense earlier rejected.

The Liberty Machine

Once over this hurdle, which is in truth an emotional barrier (to the daunting fear of which we scientists are just as susceptible as anyone else), we can proceed quite quickly to specify some of the characteristics that the metasystem is bound to display.

- If it breaks with the organizational stereotype of the pyramidal hierarchy, it is a disseminated network.

- If it breaks with the stereotpye whereby action is the product of authority, then action derives from the only available alternative—namely information.

- If it cannot depend on protocol, which is the stereotype of orderly hierarchical and time-consuming procedures for implementaion, then it is a fast-acting real-time regulator.

We see such metacontrols operating in all natural systems. They seem to me to operate through the rapid, discriminatory selection of information, followed by its amplification so as to promote an immediate and colossal shift in negentropy.

Think of a crystal seeding a super-saturated solution. Think of any piece of electronic control gear that you have ever seen to work by error-actuated negative feedback. Think of the cataclysmic population changes, mentioned earlier, by which homeostasis is restored in the ecosystem. Think of the march of the lemmings. Think above all, thanks to Warren McCulloch and Bill Kilmer, of the reticular formation of the brain stem.

None of these arrangements is authoritarian in the power-hungry sense. Each of them constitutes a constraint on liberty of the sub-systems involved. But, in so far as survival is concerned for any of these systems, it is not liberty that stands to be lost—merely licence. We humans of the western civilization are ready to pay a high price for liberty. Is it not a degradation of that ideal unthinkingly to pay bankruptcy price for a licence that entails denaturing the very system in which we have some faith?

I am suggesting that in the doomsday trap that holds our humanity in locked jaws today, liberty is not best preserved at the expense of all synergy and even coherence. But coherence and synergy are possible given metacontrol; and metacontrol is not incompatible with liberty once we see that is *information* and not *legislation* that changes us.

I will go so far as to suggest a redefinition of liberty for our current technological area. It would say that *competent information is free to act*—and that this is the principle on which the new Liberty Machine should be designed. If we test this principle against our present difficulties, must we not agree that it is indeed the frustration of competent information, inhibited from action, that forestalls progress?

That is all very well, people will say; but how can a disembodied 'information' act? Where does the information reside?—for presumably wherever it is becomes the seat of power. I invoke your protection for the third and last time, before it is supposed that I am seeking to enthrone the modern technocratic equivalent of the philosopher-kings. Scientists who suggest that it would be a good idea to have information from which to act are often assumed to be seeking power for themselves. That is because the organizational stereotype does not work on competent information, but on the equilibria of moral suasions. Its incumbents feel a sense of guilt when faced with people they suspect know more than they do. We must try and assure others that this is not at all the point we are making. If science is to offer society yet another tool, let us learn from dire experience and built *right into the package* adequate warnings against its ignorant abuse.

For the tool I am proposing would be very powerful indeed. It is a tool directed towards instant decision. The pace of events will not brook delay. Then by whom should the tool be used? There is ineluctably only one answer. It should be used by those elected by the people to govern, and by the agencies to which these governors delegate that responsibility. There are features of this situation that I think I understand, and features which puzzle me profoundly.

As to the understanding, we surely have a shrewd idea as to what the Liberty Machine would actually look like. It is not too difficult to envisage—given the specification, and the technology available. There ought to be a set of operations rooms, strategically placed in relation to the spread of the system concerned. These rooms would receive real-time data from the systems which they monitor, and they would distil the information content.

(Note I do not say : 'process the data'). Using this input to drive models, the people inside the rooms—who I must repeat would be responsible officials answerable to constitutional masters—would formulate hypotheses, undertake simulations, and make predictions about world trajectories. The metacontrol is of course constituted by the linkage of these rooms across the sub-systems—using colour television, and a network of fast-acting real-time computer terminals.

Does not this begin to sound rather familiar? Do we not already have systems looking very much like this—which were built in the cause of defence? Do we not have 'hot lines'—installed on the premise that the organizational stereotype called diplomacy will not work in the face of the fast-acting thermonuclear threat, and that knowledge must constitute action?

But compare this outcome with the outcomes I discussed earlier for other kinds of threat—whereby committees are formed, officers are appointed, and research grants made. A Martian observer would be forgiven for inferring that we men regard the thermonuclear threat as many orders of magnitude *more* threatening than the other environmental and societary threats which assail us. Then, if our Martian friend looked at the objective facts, he would classify us : *Homo Insapiens*.

As to the features of the situation which puzzle me, I refer first to the disrepute in which fast-acting metasystemic controls are currently held. As an Englishman, I should know : an election has recently been won in my country on the platform that instant decision is a shocking and improper thing. Time for reflection is required. The thesis well suits the scholarly tradition of European gentlemen. The rather obvious fact that you can be shot dead while debating the correct dress for a fight seems to have escaped attention for the moment, as does the pressure of technological advance, and the manifest impatience for reform of that mass of the world's people who have nothing left but their patience to lose.

The second cause of my puzzlement is the total unawareness of governments that the tool of which I speak, a tool of this potency, could be forged by anyone commanding adequate resources. He might then, because of his infinitely superior decision-taking capability in complex ramified international situations, take virtual control of affairs. If that sounds farfetched, just contemplate an 'electronic' Mafia. Information is what changes us; information constitutes control. But to make that work requires a science of effective organization, called cybernetics, which neither racketeers nor governments understand.

Forgive me for the thought that unfortunately the future of mankind secondarily depends on the race between crooks and honest men for this insight, as it depends primarily on the race between nature and any man at all.

Responsibility and Finesse

You are patient, but I must conclude. I have already invited you to join me in sending out a call from this symposium, to anyone who will listen, urgently demanding that the Liberty Machine be redesigned. Experiments must be put in train, pioneering efforts made, and experimental systems tested. All this is easily done : we have the knowledge to do it, and the cost in all conscience—though high compared with ordinary research contracts—would be wholly trivial compared with equivalently important programmes on which we are embarked. The difficulties do not lie here, I feel. They lie in the trapped state of men's minds.

Who are *we* to say that we know best and everyone else is wrong? I have thought deeply about this question, not from a sudden access of unaccustomed humility, but because I honestly do find the sounding of clarions distasteful, and acknowledge that I am fairly quick to condemn it in others. Here is the answer with which I emerge.

It is that we are *responsible*. We are not responsible because we have been elected to govern affairs; we are responsible because cybernetics, that science of effective organization, is our profession. Such understanding of this subject as there is, we have. Therefore we must speak out.

If my son brought an innocuous-looking drug into the home, I should not call the physician who warned me of this a megalomaniac; I should not draw attention to my authority in my own house; I should not beg him to refrain from interference in my son's freedom. On the contrary: were he to say nothing, on the grounds that he might be wrong, I should hold him culpable.

We do not know as much as we would like to know before making such a stand as I propose. But we have waited a hundred years in vain for the socio-political sciences to provide solutions. Instead, they have forfeited their claim to respect by inventing or embracing ideological frameworks for discussion and research which are antipathetic to scientific advance. As a result, mankind does not at all understand, and cannot therefore control, the complex forces which have pushed him to the edge of the evolutionary cliff.

We must use such tools as we have, and use them now. Just as we are responsible for displaying the problem, so we are responsible for the tools themselves. Cybernetics made and forged them. Some who are here, and some great men and wonderful friends now dead, guessed that the tool-kit would not be finished in time. Today we know that the moment has come for us to start work, and we must do the best we can.

I end in a minor key; not with that loud cry to the world for which I earlier asked you, but with a thoughtful and personal word for you my friends. Let us not be seduced by the sheer fun of redesigning the tools and honing their edges, when we ought to be using them to save our lives. Here in a different metaphor are the sad and evocative lines of the Bengali poet Rabindranath Tagore, which have haunted me for twenty-five years:

The song that I came to sing remains unsung to this day.

I have spent my days in stringing and in unstringing my instrument.

The time has not come true, the words have not been rightly set; only there is the agony of wishing in my heart.....

Let us not come to this

For God's sake

and man's.

A keynote address by its nature
often engenders euphoria.
and this one was received with rapture.

Everything depends
on how the message lasts
        through the conference
        and beyond
when the standing ovation
so very rewarding at the time
is forgotten.

I have learned to expect a polarization
because of Homo Faber
his reductionism
and also because
one cannot help noticing.....

Here is the positive side.

The talk had been given after dinner.
and the session was not over until late at night.
A group of volunteers
who had offices in the city
took the few copies I had brought with me
of THE LIBERTY MACHINE

        they reopened their offices
        called in staff

and thereby provided the entire membership of the conference
each with a personal copy of the script
by the start of proceedings
early next morning.

Meanwhile
three people wrote me long letters before they went to bed
and many more spoke to me later
about what should be done
        done
        DONE

        they meant it.

But on the negative side
there is the machine called CRY WOLF
identified in the address itself.

COLOUR CODE : YELLOW
Narrative

It became quite clear
that for many people
the gilt having worn off the gingerbread

there was nothing to be done

and no message

by morning.

The CRY WOLF machine really exists
and must be taken seriously.

Just before I left for Washington
the Confederation of British Industry
held a conference
on technology and the environment.

The platform speaker on behalf of conservation
was the eminent naturalist
Peter Scott.

Returning from the United States
full of thoughts
I began to catch up with my reading,
and I found in the *New Scientist*
Jon Tinker's account
of what had happened to Scott :

'But Peter Scott was totally outmanoeuvred by the CBI, who had arranged for Sir Solly Zuckerman to speak after him. Subtly, before he had even started to talk, platform speakers and the chairman billed Scott as a doom-monger and Zuckerman as a realist. Sir Solly was at his finest : bland, reassuring and above all responsible. The CBI expected no less from the chief scientific advisor to the Cabinet. Zero population growth? Neither possible nor desirable. Statistics? No need to believe them. Sir Solly has a friend in India who told him that in *his* state they had no idea at all how many children were being born. Doomsday? 'Don't let us forget that in the early part of the industrial revolution there were also prophets of doom. Remember Malthus'..... (knowledgeable chuckles in audience). An optimum population? 'In five generations' time there'll be another meeting in this room, still discussing the same subject.'

In other words, don't worry, forget Malthus, and the problem will go away. (Curious how often the 'responsible' attitude is by any objective standards supremely irresponsible.) The Confederation of British Industry knows good advice when it hears it. Peter Scott was thanked politely for his most stimulating speech.'

COLOUR CODE : YELLOW
Narrative

Poor Peter Scott.
And to the CBI
a quiet

      morituri morituros salutant
      those about to die salute those about to die
coupled with the name
of the fifth generation.

I think we should be particularly grateful
to Jon Tinker
for that very direct statement
that the 'responsible' attitude
can so often be
      'supremely irresponsible'.

There is another side to the same coin.
I have noticed
that on every occasion in my life
(and this current effort may be another such)
when I have been called
      'irresponsible'
the situation arose
      because I had been exercising
my personal, deeply-felt sense of responsibility
to the uttermost.

Responsibility
is a peculiarly important concept
of moral philosophy
in our age. . . . .

But let me resume the story
that developed from Washington
and THE LIBERTY MACHINE.

I had really tried
to get into this issue

      always relevant
      now become urgent

between competence and freedom

      destiny lies here
      for humanity

which seems to be a matter
of preserving the right of personal choice
within metasystemic regulation

COLOUR CODE : YELLOW
Narrative

and at any rate rejecting
spurious choices
within the language of the system.

As metalinguistically illiterate
we might as well die in the flesh
not speaking at all.

The teachers of metalanguage
in the Software Milieu
must be the mass media of communication—
there is no-one else.
And they must preserve our freedom.

I said in Washington
do you recall

This means publication
through the mass media
which handle such topics
meretriciously

and moreover I said
that scientists

must sacrifice
both dignity and scientific nicety
and be turned into cathode ray buffoons

simply in order

to alert our fellow human beings to danger.

The difficulties in using the media
are greater than anyone who has not tried it
might suppose.

Further :

there are dangers to liberty here.

At just the same time
as I went to Washington
to spell out THE LIBERTY MACHINE
I was preparing a broadcast
on this matter.

COLOUR CODE : YELLOW
Narrative

The BBC had invited me
to discuss the handling of science
by the mass media...

I told them it would be strong...

They rejected the first draft
and accepted the second

the last piece I wrote
in the first year of the project
PLATFORM FOR CHANGE.

It was recorded and broadcast
in January—

but when I wrote it
I had just returned from Washington
and a session with a very dear friend
who had said

WHAT!
You have never heard
of my first theorem?

COLOUR CODE : YELLOW
Narrative

AN ARGUMENT OF CHANGE

**SCIENCE
AND THE
MASS
MEDIA**

Broadcast* made on BBC Radio Three from London on 30th January 1971.

*By permission of
The Listener, London

I have a friend in America called Heinz von Foerster. Like many another distinguished scientist, he has a Theorem. Von Foerster's Theorem says this:

the more profound the problem which is ignored,
the greater the chance for fame and success.

Everyone knows that many difficulties confront mankind. They are enough to scare the pants off us all. They do indeed hinge on problems of the utmost profundity. And those problems simply *must not* be ignored. For the future of our species depends upon our finding the right answers. Science is at work on those problems—it helps to generate them, helps to solve them, and devises weapons for the affray.

Then how come Heinz von Foerster's implied rebuke? Whose fault is it that fame and success attend the avoidance of these very problems? I put to you the view that the mass media of communication are in fact answerable.

There is a limited space available in our newspapers and journals. The cost—or presumed cost—of time on radio and television is very high. The pressure to make a profit (in one form or another) through these mass media is overwhelming. Who then wants to be bothered with 'profound problems'—or the science required to solve them? The answer is no-one. Or so the communication industry is bound to think. That is because of the competition for readers, listeners and audiences—a competition for fame and success.

I believe that people everywhere are profoundly worried by the problems they know to be profound. I think they *want* to give them attention. But the 'fame and success' criteria used by the media make this almost wholly impossible. Very little counts unless it can be put over simply—and above all, in two and three quarter minutes, or five hundred words.

Long broadcasts and long articles—not to mention long books—do occur. The broadcasts and articles seem to me to be mostly short ones enveloped in padding. I have often been told myself, by editors and producers, *not* to increase the content of profundity—but to spread it more thinly. There is a complete mythology within the mass media about—quote —how much people can take.

As to books: well, the book medium is satisfying to the author—he can say *what* he likes *how* he likes. But let's face it, the mass public does not read serious books about science and humanity. It's not that they are dull; they are just not marketed properly. There are pot boilers of course, but that's not the point. The serious author is condemned to write for himself and his pals in the field.

Let's get back to the public, and the truly mass media. Scientific knowledge is at least *doubling* every decade. Then if you left your formal education 30 years ago (which might mean you are still in your forties) the conception of the universe in all its aspects which was then understood was no more than one-eighth as rich as it is today. You have probably relied—as you are entitled to rely—on the media of communication to keep you abreast of things: so the question is whether you reckon that seven-eights of your *current* understanding has been adequately supplied to you in the interim.

Now I realize that *some* very good expository work is done in explaining the key features of scientific advance. People had a good chance to understand the discovery of the double helix that reveals the structure of the DNA molecule, for example. At the macro level, the thoughtful public is by now really quite expert in its knowledge of the problems and solutions of space travel.

All this is very fine, even if the picture is sometimes clouded by those writers in supplements who have got hold of the wrong end of the stick, and by those television interviewers who interrupt a perfectly lucid explanation with their grave: 'What you really mean, professor . . . . . '—and then get it wrong in words of one syllable.

But I want to come down from space to the earth, to the scene of social action. This is where the profound problems are ignored, while the public reads, hears and watches the same tired stuff that encourages them in their own (and the editor's or producer's) prejudices.

Let's take an obvious example: the uses of the electronic computer. The silver jubilee of the very invention of this machine will be celebrated this year. It wasn't really a working proposition until the mid-fifties. If you are more than twenty-five years old, then you cannot possibly have been taught much about this beast—unless of course you have been quite directly concerned with it, which most people haven't. Are you satisfied that you understand as much as you should? I doubt if you are. Especially when I point out to you that it is now in 1971 virtually impossible to conduct any kind of social transaction that does not involve the computer.

Then let me pose a few relevant questions. Can machines think? Are machines capable of producing answers more accurate than the data which go into them? Why are so many stupidities blamed onto the machine? Can a machine create anything, especially anything aesthetic? Is it possible that a machine could behave more intelligently than its own designer? Do machines really threaten human liberty, and if so precisely how? What could we do about it? Might machines take over from men?

Is the brain itself a machine? How would you like a row of buttons on your chest, communicating with your brain, by which to change your own *feelings* about things? How far off is that? Suppose someone tapped the line transferring information about you between two computers? Suppose someone tapped the line between the buttons on your chest and your own brain? Are you responsible for anything any longer and—if not—who is?

You see the range of questions that can be put. It is likely that you have answers for them all. It is also quite likely—forgive me—that the answers you confidently give will be based on emotional convictions that have no substance whatsoever in scientific fact. For here is the strange paradox: the media of *communication*—of all things—stand between the public and the real insights of science.

Start with the press. If we strike out news items and advertising, what remains in the content of a newspaper—and particularly the quality Sunday newspaper, which lands on the breakfast table at a time when we might seriously contemplate the things I am talking about? There is ancient history: a lot of interesting stuff about long past wars, and the ancient glories on which we like to feed our battered egos. There is a lot of recent history too : the memoirs of people who have done things in our own time, so that we can now at last learn 'the truth'. All this is quite interesting. The trouble is that it has nothing whatever to do with the plight of a species which is heading towards the top of a very steep cliff.

Next, there are acres of space devoted to the arts, and again I do not criticize that. It seems to me a wonderful and civilized thing that we can have six or eight pages of criticism, however well-informed or on the other hand pretentious, that deals with the nobler aspects of man's being. But consider : how much may we discover that is concerned with man's scientific understanding of the universe and of society—knowledge which I repeat is doubling every decade?

I have seen problems ventilated; but I do not see a scientific appraisal of *what might actually be done about them*—and what kind of changes and actual *sacrifices* that might involve. Anything approaching such a debate is at once hurled into the political arena, in which people pontificate—rather than evaluate objectively, using science, what is the best course of action. I can tell you only what editors tell me : that people do not want to know these things (which I don't believe) and that even if they do they cannot understand them (which I don't believe either).

We are so good, you see, at ignoring the profound problems, in favour of increasing fame and success. If you have watched a serious scientific topic being discussed on *Late Night Line-Up* without a single scientist present, as I remember happened when a programme called *Year* 2000 was discussed, you will understand. It makes scientists want to kick in in the screen; but, more importantly, it makes them vow not to risk their own professional careers in having dealings with a medium they increasingly regard as irresponsible. Then just hear the producers complain that scientists will not cooperate!

But that is only the start of an analysis of the deadlock which now exists between broadcasting producers and responsible scientists, who recognize the key importance of this medium—and many of them want to use it. Let me give you my own experience of what this entails.

My last live appearance on TV was a month before Christmas. It took six hours out of my day to get to the studio, consult, broadcast, and get home. I was being interviewed about newly published work on the future of the police. The item before me on this Northern magazine programme concerned a public clock that strikes thirteen instead of one. It went on and on, and—yes—we listened to all thirteen strokes. When I finally got on the air, I was asked about the M1 murder. We had just got on to the point of my work when we hit the sports results—(what else). A total of two-and-a-half minutes : was it worth it? But let's look at more serious issues. I want to talk about the big set-piece programme that deals with science and humanity—a programme such as *Horizon*.

What I fear the public does not understand is that the views expressed are effectively those of the production staff who make the programme—people of whom the public may never have heard. This comes about because such programmes are really anthologies. They are made up of quotations from various scientists, which are put together in whatever way the producer thinks fit—with a linking commentary that was written afterwards.

I am certainly not charging the broadcasting media in this country with using this trick to procure actual falsification—although other countries may not be so lucky, and it is sufficiently serious that the possibility exists. You may moreover say with justice that if scientists don't like the way in which they are handled, it is up to them not to do any more broadcasting. But that is no way out of the problem for society, even if it is for the scientists concerned. And I have already told you how irrascible producers can get about it.

But think how scientists must feel. Did you see the *Horizon* broadcast on Health last year? There was the Minister himself, summing up. Then quite suddenly I appeared saying 'Rubbish!' It was quite a shock. Now the producer was quite right to think that I would have complained, had I been there. The facts remain that I was not there, and that the public doubtless supposed that I was. I was very happy indeed with the effect; but it was illusory.

Think about this when you next watch a documentary of this kind—or indeed listen to one on sound. The same thing happens there, and is easier to do. Given that everyone whose voice you hear or whose face you see for the standard couple of minutes has actually recorded for much longer, given that he has never been confronted with the other characters presented, and given that he has no idea of the way the programme will be put together until he hears it, you will then understand what I mean. The maker of the programme can assemble the materials to say whatever he likes. And this procedure is normal practice, on both sound and vision.

I am building up to my key point. It is not to allege that programmes often say something scientifically objectionable: in our democratic society there will always be one hell of an outcry if they do. But that is no protection against ignoring profound problems in the search for fame and success. What the scientists really want to discuss with the public just happens to be missing. It is not merely that important things said during recording get left out of the edited programme, it is that the whole slant of the programme is the producer's slant and not the scientists' slant. The same thing can happen in print, as the editor wields his authority to kill the author's nuances and reservations.

To return to my example about the computer. Programmes about automation usually revolve—have you noticed?—around the so-called problem of leisure. 'What are we all going to do with ourselves when computers have taken over?' The reason for this is that producers over the last ten years have regarded the issue as important, and they also reckon it has human appeal for listeners.

In vain do specialists say that the problem is bogus (because all the evidence is that computers create more work than ever), and that the profound problems are being ignored. There is the same old programme, and there is the same old expert—saying the same old assinine things about an issue he—poor fellow—regards as unimportant.

OK—he said them; he is not being misquoted. He still thinks his answer to the question he was asked is reasonable. But the question he was asked has been cut out of the broadcast (another perfectly usual technique), so that he suddenly appears, looking frightfully earnest, declaiming about leisure—as if it were the only thing he ever thought about. It isn't. He doesn't think about it at all. Has he been misrepresented? And what in heaven's name happened to his views on the things he really thinks about, and believes to matter? Perhaps they were never even solicited.

Then let's take a look at the situation when a man's views *are* solicited at length. Suddenly we are shot to the other extreme: call it 'the personality spectacular'.

There was an outstanding example of this a month ago: forty-five minutesworty of Dr Herman Kahn being reverenced like the Buddha by Mr Bernard Levin. Did you see this absurd pilgrimage by helicopter to the Hudson Institute? There was Levin looking terribly grave, receiving the Enlightenment. There was Kahn, legislating the future of the human race in his usual cracking form—and writing off our country in a gay aside. Then there was Levin again, looking graver than ever and I'm not surprised, striding back to his helicopter to be drawn up into the skies. Pilgrimage over.

What is the public to make of that? Would they suspect that a dozen other experts would furiously controvert all this stuff? And what was the *Times* newspaper thinking of, when it scooped the interview and quite uncritically printed half a page of it in advance?

I last confronted Herman Kahn on the floor of the House of Representatives in Washington a year ago. If you saw this programme you'll be relieved to hear that we had a violent disagreement. It is exactly that sort of articulate row that the public is entitled to hear. You can put it on the Congressional Record of the United States, but not in the *Times* or on ITV.

Perhaps this sort of reality is too disturbing for the public. If that is the view, then society is in danger indeed. Whatever the reason, the mass media turn out to handle science at one remove—as it were with a pair of sterilized tongs. The public may have snippets of science at the producer's discretion; the public may have glamourized science hosed at it. The public does not get the real thing.

Probably you saw some of those wonderful TV programmes showing the cellist Tortelier holding his master classes. They were immensely technical—and the man spoke French. It didn't matter. We all found out what being a musician is really like. If only you could see scientists like that. I have advocated such programmes for fifteen years—even on the General Advisory Council of the BBC—but no-one wants to know.

Well, it is science and technology which—like it or not—shape the world *today*. While people are arguing amongst themselves, a new world is continuously and inexorably being forged—by scientists, by technologists. Will you blame them for what happens? Although it is their doing, that would not be fair. They are not iron creatures, grinding unthinkingly on, but concerned human beings who want to discuss the issues—and above all to help.

The advice remains to have scientists pitch in with everyone else, and sometimes give them free rein—and the money—to express themselves in their own way. I don't think they will turn out to be incomprehensible—although that belief is part of the mass media mythology. At least the public would discover that there are real men in there behind the white coats and the electronic gubbins. It has always puzzled me that the mass media continually and rightly run the risk of doing this not only with Torteliers, but with artists and critics of every kind, often with disastrous results, while scientists are let loose only under supervision—to do their party piece.

Is that because the citizen finds the real problems of society so scientifically profound that he wishes to ignore them? Or is it because to tackle societary problems scientifically reduces the politicians' chance for fame and success?

It is still a free country
in which such things can be said
in a nation-wide broadcast
and subsequently printed.

Here is the joke
(or something).

You probably noticed
two inset paragraphs printed in italics.

> The first was particularly rude
> I admit
> nonetheless valid.

> The second was particularly strong
> I agree
> nonetheless the climax of my case.

Both were included in the approved script,
both were recorded,
neither was questioned
then or later.

But both were cut out of the broadcast.

Given the context
something really might have been said
to me
to the public.....

> But no—
> *Quod Erat Demonstrandum*—
> Q.E.D.

Thank you BBC.

Naturally there was a furore.
Producers really are nice men
seeing themselves
as custodians of the public good.
They really do—
and they can dish it out.....

But *this*—
unfair, exaggerated, even (did I not hear?) absurd.
Quite so.

COLOUR CODE : YELLOW
Narrative

When the man who replies in print
with no answers to the criticisms
but only biting sarcasm for the constructive suggestions
says

'I am not making these obvious remarks
to score cheap points
off the professor'

it is reasonable to fear the worst.

The worst was indeed to come.

I might have been spared this argument
put forward by the Head of Science and Features
for BBC TV in the *Listener*
about my statement that scientists
'vow not to risk their own professional careers
in having dealings with a medium
they increasingly regard as irresponsible' :

'Since, without any difficulty whatever, I found the name of Stafford Beer
figuring large in at least two radio programmes during the week in which
I write, and since I know him to be intimately connected with at least one
forthcoming television programme, I cannot take *his* polemics in this
regard too seriously.'

May I beg my colleagues not to fall into the trap?
Can you imagine what fate would befall
a critic who was not known to have the facts
from the inside?

Even so

it might be best
to give up

don't you think?

We can trust our freedom

to those whose genuine objective
is to safeguard it

don't you think?

COLOUR CODE : YELLOW
Narrative

In so far as the previous page peters out like that
it reflects a sense of weariness :
the first year of the project
PLATFORM FOR CHANGE
was indeed a tiring year.

The Arguments of Change
covered so much—

        from man's own perception of himself
        and of his environment
        through the scientific approach to management
        through models of the situation
        through measures
        and the methods of attack
        to some glimpses of possible solutions.

All of this I had been asked to do,
even though the scheme to relate the elements
into a large design
was my own.

But I found myself reflecting
that I have been giving invited addresses such as these
all my life.

        'We have with us tonight . . . . .'
        'Ladies and gentlemen . . . . .'
        ' . . . . . express the thanks . . . . .'

Now I got into the habit
of entering the date, place and provenance
of all my addresses
in a loose-leaf book
which begins more than twenty years ago.
Because the entries are numbered
I realized that towards the end of 1970
I should perforce deliver

        the five-hundredth lecture.

Five hundred is a big number.

It gave me pause.

COLOUR CODE : YELLOW
Narrative

340

I took a sheet of paper
in a new colour

and wrote on it :

COLOUR CODE : YELLOW
Narrative

WOT is the point?

is the good?

THE is achieved?

does it matter?

HELL am I doing?

COLOUR CODE : RED
A Reflexion

and then I remembered how I knew

what's wot

it comes from *archy's life of mehitabel*
by don marquis
and he has his splendid cat say :

                                        i would
                            rather kill my own
                            rats and share
                            them with a
                            friend from greenwich
                            village than lap up
                            cream or beef juice
                            from a silver porringer
                            and have to
                            be polite to the
                            bourgeois clans
                            that feed me

                            wot the hell i
                            feel superior to that
                            stupid bunch me
                            for a dance
                            across the roofs when
                            the red star
                            calls to my blood
                            none of your
                            pretty puss stuff for
                            mehitabel it would
                            give me a grouch
                            to have to be so
                            solemn toujours
                            gai archy toujours
                            gai is my
                            motto

COLOUR CODE : YELLOW
Narrative

344

Thereupon I decided
in that good spirit
and with renewed heart
to maintain the symmetry
of the project
PLATFORM FOR CHANGE
by building in
an argument of Change
over and beyond
                    which we know as meta
the others.

This address could not be
on the PLATFORM
(if we have understood our logic).
It could not be commissioned

                    by *us*
                    on *this* day
                    on *this* topic

                    and thanks very much.

Thanks very much.

With much satisfaction therefore
I accepted my invitation
to prepare during 1970
my five-hundredth lecture
and not to deliver it
between Lecture No. 499
and Lecture No. 501.

This Benefit Performance
and singularly Private Celebration

(which was exceptionally well received)

did not take place
roughly as forecast
between 10th and 18th September 1970
anywhere.

COLOUR CODE : YELLOW
Narrative

A META-ARGUMENT OF CHANGE

RENASCENCE

The uninvited Five-Hundredth Lecture*, not delivered anywhere between the 10th and the 18th September, 1970.

*By permission of
me

In audiendi officio perit gratia
si reposcatur.

*In the matter of listening grace is lost
if demanded as a right.*

—PLINY the YOUNGER

Men and women are creatures built on a certain scale. We do not easily understand, because we do not directly perceive, either the very small or the very large. This fact profoundly affects our purposes and our competence.

If we look for the signposts of civilization, we find one guiding principle in our respect for life. If we do not respect the right of other men and women to live, our own lives are threatened; and not even savages kill animals they do not need to eat. Then come the problems of scale.

Our emotions are engaged by the agony of a dog, with its great soulful eyes. But we heedlessly swat, stamp on and spray myriads of tiny beasts whose eyes are too small for us to see. Each is a miraculous testimony to whatever life is. But our respect for living things stops short at some point on the scale of smaller size. They are too small.

Next, as we undertake genetic engineering on the living populations we label pests or prize as food, we do not see the life writ very large that is the organic ecological system of the planet. It is beyond our comprehension in its complexity and scale of larger size and longer time. We may be alerted to the existence and importance of this macro-life, in terms of the danger that its damage threatens: even then, we do not *respect* it. It is too large.

Finally, even fellow human beings seem to lose our firmly held respect, if they become small by being very far. I refer to the dying and the undernourished throughout the world. And they have forfeited respect, not only in being denied existence, but in somehow managing to have their existence denied. Let me explain.

I constantly meet men—statesmen, businessmen, scientists—who pooh-pooh the suggestion that mankind may be on the brink of catastrophe. They talk disparagingly about prophets of doom. They slap you on the back, grin broadly, and remind you of Malthus— as if that far-sighted man had in some sense been proven *wrong*.

The Malthusian projection is not yet complete, but—after two hundred years—it is right on course. Today, right now, two thirds of the people alive are not receiving enough food: *two thirds*. Let us not take refuge in those conveniently collapsed numerals called billions. If we do have respect for the living human being, then today, right now, we must count and consider 2,400,000,000 hungry people, half of whom perhaps are actually starving, and try to visualize their awful ranks. Can anyone, I wonder, see in his mind's eye 171,000,000 children under seven—all suffering from serious protein deficiency? (1) And apart from this human agony of malnutrition, we have to live with the fact of war—sometimes amounting to near-genocide, with the fact of insurrection and all its barbarities, with the fact of widespread torture and incarceration without trial, with the fact of assassination.

There is no prophecy to make fun of here: these are just facts. They are truths of the world today. We live with them. I do not believe in fairies, nor in Father Christmas. Yet somehow I have to believe in men—leaders of our society—who go around assuring us that things are quite all right. I rub my eyes: they are still there.

THE ETHIC WITH A BUSTED GUT

What has gone wrong, and what can be done? The individuals who have sacrificed themselves in one-man efforts to help made no empty gestures in giving up possessions and offering their talents. They earn our great respect. But were everyone to do this, our society would collapse. And we should then lose the one asset we still have: the advanced machinery—I will use the despised and suspect word *technology*—to put things right.

The technology is there. At last, perhaps, the will is there on the part of large numbers of ordinary men and women within the Western culture that controls the technology. What is conspicuously missing is the leadership.

This leadership has two tasks. One is to know enough and be clever enough to mobilize the technology. That should be sufficiently easy, though heaven knows few of our present leaders possess this competence. They do not accept such solutions, nor embark on such routes to solutions, as already exist. After thinking hard for twenty years as to why that is, I finally reached a possible answer which discloses the other, and prior, task of the leadership.

It is to put forward a new ethic. For the ethic we have is so framed as to make proper solutions to current societary problems incapable of expression.

The Western culture which has exploited Earth, and proven so successful in material terms that it has cornered more than half the world's wealth for less than a tenth of its people, operates on a very strange ethic indeed. It is supposedly of Christian inspiration. That is, it subscribes to respect and even love for life—so long as that life is on its perceptual scale—and it is suffused with moral virtues. By this I really mean that it subscribes to the Judaic law. Perhaps, then, it actually missed the Christian inspiration it is supposed to exhibit.

Here is an illustration. I have more than once heard, as an explicitly *Christian* justification for the English notion of retributive 'fair play': 'an eye for an eye and a tooth for a tooth'. I heard it at Public School. I have heard it from a Christian pulpit. There can never have been a better example of a remark wrenched from its context:

> 'Ye have heard that it hath been said,
> An eye for an eye, and a tooth for a tooth:
> But I say unto you,
> That ye resist not evil:
> but whosoever shall smite thee on thy right cheek,
> turn to him the other also.' (2)

Our supposedly Christian ethic lost sight of all that. And indeed the phrase 'turn the other cheek' is commonly used—not at all as an admonition—but in the same mocking tone that is turned on Malthus and the 'prophets of doom'.

The fact is that for a very long time the ethic of Western culture has made a very good thing out of *masquerading* as Christian. It is nothing of the kind. We have preached love and shown none, and our children have found us out.

The result of this is that young people are definitely, deliberately, rejecting the inherited ethic. The gut, the central theme that supposedly holds that ethic together is Christian *caritas*. But the gut is seen to be busted. It is busted by the translation of *caritas* into 'charity', which is notoriously cold and demanding, instead of into 'love', which gives from the warmth of the human heart. The ethic with a busted gut is precisely the pharisaical ethic, the ethic which Christ has so far spent two thousand years in seeking to undermine. It is the ethic of the whited sepulchre, and its exponents are still (as Christ said) 'blind guides, which strain at a gnat and swallow a camel' (3). Our gnats are homosexuals and kids with long hair; our camel is measured by the number 2,400,000,000.

What worries me is that these same young people are inclined to reject the technology that appears to them to be the fruit of this ethic. This would be a classic case of throwing out the baby with the bathwater. I repeat: this technology, this know-how, is the only asset that mankind has left, apart from love.

If I am right, there has to be a misapprehension somewhere—and there is. The ethic with the busted gut, the illegitimate offspring of an illicit union between materialism and a misapprehended Christianity, bred technology: therefore technology is bad. But we can be more discriminatory than that, just as we can discriminate a worthy son from a worthless father.

Wholly contrarily to the teaching of its putative Christian parent, the busted-gut ethic set up economic viability rather than the eudemony (or well-being) of people as its only criterion. Let me hand over the argument to two others for a moment . . . . .

Schumacher (4) has written:

> 'Call a thing immoral or ugly, soul-destroying or a degradation of man,
> a peril to the peace of the world or to the well-being of future generations;
> so long as you have not shown it to be 'uneconomic' you have not really
> questioned its right to exist, grow and proper.'

Quoting this, Sir Geoffrey Vickers (5) adds:

> 'Never did a concept so limited and so factual attain a meaning so general,
> so normative and so saturated with unjustified connotations of value.'

Exactly so. It is this criterion that has to be expunged—before we can make any progress at all.

Now just how can that be done, short of overthrowing the whole machinery of Western society, from private life, through commerce and industry, to the workings of state and even of international institutions? There are those who preach that very overthrow. But anarchy at home will not help the hungry oversea. Nor do we necessarily advance by repudiating all the values we inherit, just because some of them have let us down. Above all, as I said earlier, mankind cannot afford to discard its hard-won technological knowledge.

ABOUT

EXPERIMENTAL ETHICS

It looks as though this is just what the experiméntal ethics of this century have done—repudiated too much, and failed to advance.

Two world wars have twice focussed the mass of opinion onto the ethic with a busted gut, and twice spliced that gut, in order to get on with the business of survival. This business, under pressure of armed attack, has to be about preserving 'everything we hold most dear'. There just isn't time to work out anything else. So even those who suspected the gut was busted, and wanted to do something about it, let the issue rest. There must be something, in short, to give your life for in the high drama of war—if you are to keep sane.

But there is nothing so effective as war in reinforcing the old material values. Wars notoriously 'have to be paid for'. The whole armament scene, with its extensions into solar space, drains our wealth as it threatens us with extinction. Mankind has become inured to the threat, which grows almost daily, and resigned to the waste of our technological potency to look after the whole brotherhood of man. It does not seem realistic to say: 'this must stop'. But is it any more realistic to say: 'carry on then, stupid, but *I* refuse to play'?

In either case we should be held to have joined 'the lunatic fringe'. To have that epithet hung round one's neck does the cause of innovation and change no good at all. In all conscience, it is the *centre* that is lunatic—but the fact is not within the perceptual grasp of this 'silent majority' (what a diabolically clever phrase that is), because it is trapped by the issues of scale. And every one of us is trapped by the cortical concatenations that trace his own experience.

Let me be open about my own. When I was sixteen my country was at war, and I knew I should be in the Army before it was over. I was also in full revolt against the ethic preached to me—although I did not then know that it had a busted gut. It seemed to me then just plain immoral. Moreover, because of the Spanish Civil War and the fiasco of the first Labour government in the early thirties at home (which it was quite impossible for any of us at that age in a middle class ethos to understand at all), I imagined the problem to be *political*. It has taken the double alternation of two political administrations in Britain since the war to convince me that the problem is not political at all. Neither of the creeds that the two parties have preached or practised comes near to touching it.

Well: the war was on, I was sixteen, and I filled sandbags and dug trenches. Neither I nor my friends contemplated 'dropping out' at that time—though within a year, at University, we were all contemplating exactly this like mad. Some of my friends then became conscientious objectors, and I discovered how society treats its deviant members. They asked one close friend: 'would you defend yourself if attacked?' He said: 'no'. They said: 'that would be tantamount to suicide'. He said: 'if you say so'. The newspaper headline said: *Student says suicide the only way out*. This affected me deeply at the time.

But the year before University it was not like that. I became loftily remote from fun—priggish would be the word. How does one, at sixteen, deal with the conviction that one will not see twenty? I wrote an essay for the only inspired teacher I had. It was about human survival, then as now. And I seized, as many of us did, on the romanticism handed down to us—oh, so wrong-headedly—from the earlier war of 1914–18. This was the final, dramatic paragraph of that essay :

'We must be able to say, with Rupert Brooke :

> *Now God be thanked*
> *Who has matched us with his hour*
> *And caught our youth*
> *And wakened us from sleeping.* (6)

Against this satisfying resolution of the issues, my teacher wrote in the margin : *Why?*

I used to think about that when, still barely twenty. I confronted confusion, alienation and messy death in the dividing continent of India. Jingoism was out; the Raj was a no-no; but the garrison church kept the wogs at the back. All my real friends, for a couple of years in India, were wogs..... At last I perceived that the received ethic had a busted gut. I threw all my extramilitary effort into understanding these new friends, learning Hindi, studying the *Upanishads* and yoga, bouncing off Islam, thinking about Buddhism, and trying to hold the balance between all of this and my own Western and Christian culture by becoming profoundly immersed in the explicitly Franciscan ethic.

It seemed clear to me that cultures could be bridged, and that all worth-while ethics mapped onto each other under some transformation. While retired Indian Army men were still lecturing in England about 'the natives', and how Muslims, Hindus and Sikhs could not mess together (in case an infidel shadow fell across the cooking pot, and so forth) I was sitting round camp fires with all of them, eating sweetmeats and singing : *masjid, mandir aur gurdwara ke khuda eki hain. Masjid* is a mosque, *mandir* is a Hindu temple, and *gurdwara* a Sikh temple. This line of the song says that the gods of the three places are one. I always wanted to get in the word *girja*, meaning just church, but it did not fit the music.

But this is no biography. I just wanted to explain from what basis I comment on the experimental ethics that have been projected to me over recent years, mainly by young people. They talked about existenialism, about yoga, about Zen—and many more things that I had first discussed first-hand as the sun went down on the plains. The hookah we passed round had a four-foot bamboo stem, and burnt a kind of black sludge—the ingredients of which were suspect in several ways, but I doubt if they included cannabis. Well : I feel increasingly convinced that our experimentalists have missed the whole point.

In repudiating the ethic with a busted gut they come to a posture known as *alienation*. There is to be no involvement with society as it is. We must have the Alternative Society. This is an intellectually tenable position, no doubt—until realization dawns that there is no such thing as alternation in a world that is solidly one, because it is indivisibly at risk. Thus there is no way of not being involved; society is too tightly knit—and there are laws. Besides, to be alienated *is* to be involved : involved with a negative sign. We should also note that there are dissident social groups who regard themselves as very much involved—with a negative sign. They are the wreckers. Then it is inevitable that the established order should get two very different things confused. All its proponents can see is the negative sign. Instead of recognizing legitimate complaint (because of underprivilege) in the second group, and instead of recognizing a new ethical posture in the first group, society sees only the flouting of its established canons by all and sundry. And society is armed to the teeth.

So it comes about, I submit, that society picks on any and every convenient symbol of the negative sign—whether it be drugs, or colour, or sexual mores, or communism—to denounce dissidence as such. Then there is no longer any way to explain anything at all. Dissent is dissidence is anti-social: period. Next, in so far as communications have therefore broken down, we have a recipe for explosive violence.

If the feedback channels in a system are blocked or disrupted, the system can no longer adapt. Moreover, it now lacks even a damping mechanism, and is due to explode. In short, experimental ethics that are involuted cannot be effective instruments of social change—unless it is thought to be enough to hasten catastrophe. Too many people, I feel, ask me whether it is not true that some kind of cataclysm must come before innovative change can happen. This is dire pessimism, and it promotes a dangerously acquiescent frame of mind. The reply ought to be :

> "It is not enough to set tasks, we must also solve the problem of the methods
> for carrying them out. If our task is to cross a river we cannot cross it without
> a bridge or a boat. Unless the bridge or boat problem is solved, it is idle to
> speak of crossing the river. Unless the problem of method is solved, talk about
> the task is useless'.(7)

Cataclysm does not count as a method; waiting for it is a sort of useless talk. The quotation comes from the 'little red book': it is a thought of Chairman Mao. Another of his thoughts points out that man attains freedom from nature by using natural science to understand, conquer and change it—and that he ought to attain social freedom by an equivalent use of social science.

TOWARDS THE RELEVANT ETHIC

Any ethic that is relevant to our problem must surely include such a naive but practical element. I am no Red Guard, and I quote Mao Tse-Tung to underline the *any* ethic.

For what seems to matter about any ethic is precisely this: it is a value-structure intended for *coping with things*. We may read the Bible, the Gita or the Koran: we may quote Buddha, Francis or Mao. We are getting recipes for coping—and indeed we may choose between them. The point is that no ethic worth talking about offers a recipe for not coping at all—and that is where our experimental ethics have failed. They manifestly do not cope; they attend on disaster.

The Professor of Medicine at Cambridge University has found that 'attempted suicide' or 'self-poisoning' is now the *commonest* cause of admission to a medical ward for people between 15 and 40 years old. 'Among females in this age group nearly 50 per cent of all medical admissions are now for attempted suicide', writes Professor Mills (8). This is some measure at the level of individual behaviour of the extent to which people fail to cope, or have no relevant ethic. For Western Society as a whole symptoms of the malaise are clear enough.

People are trapped :

- trapped firstly by the scale of their own perception;

- trapped secondly by the dominance of money (of which there is never enough) as the only measure of value;

- trapped thirdly by their own technology;

- trapped fourthly in a malignant bureaucratic net which is the outcome of society's threshing about inside the first three traps.

Then let us seek the relevant ethic in a system of values which would free us from these traps.

I take it for granted that the basis of the ethic we wish to embrace is the objective of eudemony—well-being—for humanity. Love. compassion. brotherhood are all names for this principle that underlies every ethic that is not satanic. From here, we go on to seek ways of avoiding the four traps.

There has to be teaching about systems beyond the normal perceptual scale. whereby the factual modern truth of the ancient insight 'we are members one of another' can be brought home. Whatever man does with this technological power today is likely to affect everyone on the planet; we must elicit the mechanisms. and they must be explained. so that people may choose with understanding and knowledge. One of the choices to which attention needs urgent direction is the system of world government. We have one. of course; but it is a model of ineptitude. To these ends new systems of publishing will be needed. Frenetic 'communication'—the dissemination of mindless pap and the endless discussion of non-events—must no longer obscure what people who think are thinking from each other. or from anyone else who (given the chance) may yet start to think.

This consideration leads straight to the problem of the second trap. for the perversion of the power to communicate has been all about the money criterion. Money will never be an *end*, for the relevant ethic; it will always be a *constraint*. (Not a very serious constraint either. it will turn out.) Then we need to construct eudemonic measures that are about free behaviour. and not about money. as a criterion of value. So we shall not ask people how much they would pay to achieve some good or to avert some evil. but only observe in conditions of free choice what people actually do. This means that we must be prepared (and we are not yet prepared. because on a monetary scale all values are commensurable) to find that there are choices that people prefer to set aside. or find too difficult to make. At this point. freed from economic mythology. we shall no longer refer to this condition as *indifference*. Far from it.

It has been understood for a very long time that anyone not making an offered choice is indifferent to the outcome. This would be true for a unidimensional value structure— which. in money. our culture claims to have. In fact. although there may well be an approximate money-eudemony equation in the general conduct of affairs. the equation usually breaks down altogether at the boundaries of this roughly-limned system. And it is exactly in the boundary conditions that humanity is interested.

To illustrate this at the domestic level, consider house purchase and sale. In the normal course of such transactions we do indeed use money as a measure of eudemony. An independent valuation of the property we are buying says it is worth x less than the offering price. We may well agree to pay this increment x; 'it's worth it' we say, meaning worth it to us (because of some special features that appeal to our particular sensibilities). We may also have in mind that our sensibilities are not wholly atypical, and therefore we may, in the event of sale, find someone else for whom the extra x is 'worth it'. Should we not, we are prepared to forfeit the x increment, for the sake of eudemony. The house is bought, and becomes *home*. We lavish care on it, pouring in time and trouble; we make friends with neighbours; we establish a business nearby; our children are settled in schools. Now comes someone who offers us twice what the house is currently worth on the market. If the money-eduemony equation is working, our refusal to sell means that half the value we place on the house is not normally realizable in money. Suppose the next would-be purchaser asks us to name our own figure, and we refuse. The unrealizable part of the value is now *infinite*. A year later comes a good job offer; we move, selling the house for its normal, realizable value because now we have no better offer. Presumably the infinite value of the eudemony that attached to the house has now been mysteriously transferred to the new job.....

This whole argument is spurious. We are doing what we prefer to do (that is, answering to a eudemonic criterion), within the constraints of finance—which we manipulate as far as we are able. In particular, we spurn choices which the money-criterion people say we *must* be making—if only implicitly—which does not mean that we are indifferent to the outcome but quite the reverse. It seems to me that everyone is forced to pretend that in the end we are all out to maximize our cash. But we are not; and therefore a society which acts on our behalf as if we were becomes more and more unsatisfactory.

A good illustration at the societary level concerns the attempt to find a rational answer to the problem: where should London's third airport be sited? It turned out that 'rational' ought to mean 'cheapest'. Immense research efforts and an elaborate quasi-legal paraphernalia produced an attempt to make a monetary quantification of eudemony. The research tried to place money values on such commodities as a noisy environment and the convenience to travellers of shorter and longer city-airport journeys. I contend that this cannot legitimately be done, because eudemony is not single-valued. Secondly I contend that we do not even want to do it, because 'cheapest' is not the cynosure of the human condition. Thirdly I contend that the original question should not have been asked. To see why not we must recognize how that question floats up from deep inside the third trap—the trap of technology incorrectly managed.

Most of the dilemma about the societary effects of technology is completely bogus. From the failure of perception of systems that are out of scale, through the acceptance of the money metric that does not measure eudemony, we arrive at a conviction that we must choose between every sort of devil and every lagoon of the deep blue sea. This is because we follow our technological noses. To stick to the aircraft example: we know how to build big and fast aircraft. Therefore bigger and faster aircraft are just round the R and D corner. Therefore we must make them, and money must be made available (or we are not 'cashing in on our investment'). Therefore society must choose between noise and convenience. As if this argument were not demaging enough, John Stringer has piled on a further agony. He showed me the economics of this situation. We have expensive aircraft that will not pay, because the seats are not filled. We invent packaged tours to fill the seats, and the aircraft do pay. Moreover, they are *not big enough*. We must now have bigger aircraft to fill the profit vacuum. Unfortunately, the seats are not filled . . . . . I now call this process. 'following our technological noses, with positive feedback'. Processes such as this are well-dubbed traps. Start again. Modern technology can do what you like — within financial constraints. But the question : what do you like? is not asked. Perhaps we would like not to have a third, or indeed *any*, London airport. That could be done. Perhaps we would like not to travel at all, but to use electronics to project our images to each other. That could be done. If we like to say that the images ought to be three-dimensional, then we should put more effort into holography and laser technology. It could be done. We just do not know whether we want aircraft, or cities — so how can we be expected to know whether we want a third London airport, still less to know where it should be?

It is often said in reply to such contentions that all this is about the twenty-first century : a pie-in-the-sky implication. But this reply is wholly frivolous. *Whatever* we do now is about the twenty-first century — just think of the money we tie up, and just think of the social consequences of every decision on this scale. The implication is truly a pie-in-the-eye — for our children, if not for us. Moreover : people fall for the argument : scientists predict that such-and-such a development will not occur until so-and-so. This prediction, established by what is called the Delphi technique, is nonsense—or rather we human beings ought to ensure that it is nonsense. Humanity should say what is to be done, and by when. Technology can do it.

Is this not credible? Is it all going to cost too much? My reply is that man has walked on the moon.

Well, of course he has. He followed his technological nose — and it pointed *up*. The money was forthcoming all right. We have to remember that the United States has based her entire economy on military production and its associated research and endeavour. These government programmes have consumed about *two-thirds* of the effort of America's scientists and technologists, and a very substantial part of her labour force. It was all this potency that blasted man to the moon. The potency could of course be directed elsewhere.

The whole argument about 'economic viability' has been assaulted in this part of my address. We now begin to see why it is of so little account. The fact is that Western man is incredibly wealthy. *Technology* has done this : it is an amplifier of resources. If we choose to put all this wealth into following our noses, so be it. But if so, it is useless to blame technology for a want of human vision. We think we are hard-up—because we have no idea how to use technological power. We waste it. Our fruitless but profligate pursuits bring incommensurate benefits, so we say that technology is an expensive way of polluting the Earth. It is not true.

To escape from this mess we must escape from *all* those traps. As far as this third one is concerned, we can start on a conveniently small scale. Every industry we have is so busy following its technological nose that it cannot pause to think again. As a direct result of this, it positively dives into the fourth trap—like a wanderer come home.

The fourth trap is the bureaucratic net. The further society departs from what is sensible, because it uses technology merely to soup-up rather than redesign what is already going on, the more and more and more it is compelled to *force* people into line. This is because people tend to do what they prefer—to do what makes sense to them. If society is going in the other direction, then society declares that people must comply. The outcome is what it must be— bureaucracy: a vast incursion into personal liberty, a huge apparatus of invigilation, and a proliferation of systems for obtaining conformity. And all of this too is waste. Because if society could organize itself properly, if it could determine its courses from free thought, good advice and the people's choice, then none of this would be necessary. In short, as I shall proceed to argue on general principles, to avoid the fourth trap is to cut out waste.

From the immense wealth of Western society, from its huge store of scientific knowledge, the relevant ethic must call for a fresh design for human living. And in so far as the choices of man are constrained by the availability of money, the relevant ethic looks to present waste to finance every genuine technological opportunity to cater for every genuine human need.

WASTE NOT WANT NOT

A call for the elimination of waste sounds very like obeisance to the cult of efficiency that is preached by the rejected ethic. Not so: what the affluent society wastes *is* the deprivation of the indigent society—at home as well as abroad.

I seek to demonstrate how waste is built into our societary system in a most fundamental way. The diagram entitled *The Data Trail* is a far from exhaustive, far from sufficiently intricate, account of the information generated by a single citizen as he moves through life. All of these data are recorded, and possibly (though by no means always) retrieved from time to time. All of them, however, give rise to systems which have to do with the regulation of the citizen as a unit of society. So although that diagram shows a man or a woman as throwing off these data—as it were heedlessly, leaving his or her imprints on the sands of time—there is a mass of regulatory information flowing in the other direction.

The fact that I impinge on any one of these boxes to a certain degree, means that I impart to it a certain amount of information—whether much or little. We learn from the mathematical theory of communication(9) that if my behaviour vis-a-vis this box is to be regulated, at least as much information as I impart must be channelled back to me. If the information I have registered is ambiguous (as it often is) and if the regulatory system is inefficient (as it usually is) then still more regulatory information is required to resolve the ambiguity and to correct the inefficiency.

For example: I own a dog, and for this dog I need a licence. It is my duty to renew his licence annually, but I may not remember to do so—or I may deliberately not do so—and therefore the dog-licencing authority must perform a regulatory act. My original message said: 'I have a dog. I pay you 37½p'. The regulatory message a year later says: 'You have a dog. You pay us 37½p'. The information content is identical. If, being inefficient, I do nothing, a further message will come to correct this inefficiency. If, expecting to hear '37½p', I should get a message saying 50p, this would count as an ambiguous message, and therefore the further information would have to be added: 'the price has been raised by the provisions of the new Finance Act', to resolve the ambiguity.

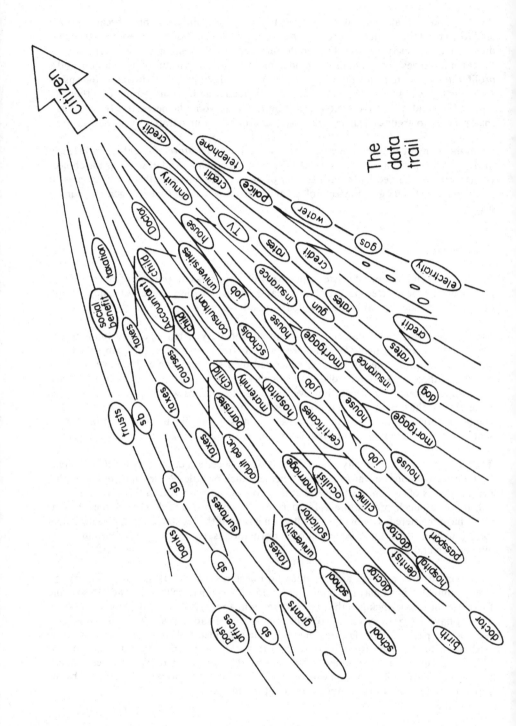

The data trail

Citizen

credit · telephone
Credit · Police · water · gas
annuity · TV · rates · credit · electricity
Doctor · house · insurance · gun · rates · credit
taxation · universities · job · mortgage · house · insurance · dog
social benefit · Child · Accountant · consultant · schools · house · job · house · mortgage
local benefit · taxes · courses · Child · maternity · hospital · job · house · house · passport
trusts · sb · taxes · Child · barrister · oculist · marriage · clinic · oculist · job · doctor · hospital
sb · taxes · adult educ · university · solicitor · doctor · dentist · doctor
sb · surtaxes · taxes · school · doctor · birth
banks · sb · grants · school
post offices · sb · school

As soon as there is a box for registering societary information, then the mathematical laws must apply: a reciprocal flow of information begins, and must be maintained on whatever time, scale is implicit in the case. If I become ill, for example, the regulatory loop called 'treatment' must be at least as rich in information as the registration of my symptoms, or I shall not get well (unless I cure myself), and in fact the treatment will probably be much richer—because of the ambiguity of the symptoms. And now the time-scale will be diurnal—even hourly.

All this being so, it is plain that the complexity of societary control is a function of the number of record-keeping boxes. It is vital that we correctly perceive these as regulators, and do not think of them merely as passive recorders. The complexity of societary control is also a function of the degree of interaction *between* those boxes. A little thought about the diagram will reveal that if these connexions were all marked, the diagram itself would be obliterated (I tried it). 'Taxation', for example, is connected to practically everything else. Calling on mathematical theory once again, we can say that the total complexity will, because of these interactions, be a *logarithmic* function of the number of boxes. I should further argue that, society being what it is, the power of this logarithmic function will itself rise with the number of boxes—because more and more ambiguity and more and more inefficiency will be imported into the system. If proof is required, then try to calculate the size of the industry that handles taxation. The tax law *must* be at least as rich in information as the total set of circumstances of the citizens. If this mathematical rule is broken by the Finance Act, then inspectors and lawyers are required to amplify the tax law, and the complexity inexorably rises as precedent mounts on precedent. All of this creates such ambiguity that an army of accountants is now required to resolve it.

It would be possible to continue with this information-theoretic analysis of societary regulation, and indeed it ought to be done. But there is no point in going further at the moment; for the present concern is not with the intricacies of design, but with the fundamental principle which has been brought to light. This says that the amount of regulatory effort required in society is an increasing logarithmic function of the number of separate recording boxes. It immediately follows that we should try to reduce that number. Thirdly, we may conclude that the amount of effort needed to sustain the existing total system, less the amount of effort needed to sustain a system having a minimal number of recording boxes, is a measure of waste.

Elsewhere (10) I have argued from the general principles of cybernetics that the total regulatory effort in our society must be more than half the total effort. Applying the present argument to that argument, we see that it is in principle possible to free half of our wealth-generating capacity for new purposes. This possibility emerges simply from the way society is ineffectively organized, and long before we start to apply any explicitly ethical considerations. For we may go much further with these arguments of reciprocity in control under ethical guidance. We may for instance ask whether it is *right* (ethics) to spend what we do on the packaging of goods in the interests of a high rate of trading metabolism, once we note the operation of the reciprocal law: the packages must be cleared up and disposed of. The bill for doing just *that* in a Western country would finance the nutrition of an African country.

Then how should we proceed in reducing the number of recording boxes? We should ruthlessly cut them out. For example, and I argue from the findings of a host of studies made by O & M researchers in other fields. the true cost of running the dog-licensing scheme will surely be in excess of the revenue raised of 37½p per dog. Let me illustrate the principle under which we could proceed by following through this example, however facetious the content.

If the Minister simply said to the doctors that in lieu of part of their salary they would be empowered to collect 6p from each dog-owning patient per visit, that would be one recording box less. The doctor arrives at the house, the dog barks, and the doctor collects his cash before crossing the threshold: easy. What has happened to the mathematical laws that illuminated the problem? They cannot be repealed; they must still be operative. The answer is that the information is still flowing, in the right quantities in both directions but it is being carried on an existing channel instead of *wasting* a dedicated channel. Now to do this, we must make some assumptions (beginning with the assumption that all doctors will not promptly emigrate). If no-one is to waste wealth on a record of the households having dogs, then it must be assumed that a certain percentage of any doctor's patients has dogs. Secondly, it must have been assumed. in the given example that doctors visit each household on average six-and-a-quarter times in the year.

Now note the familiar reciprocity. *Doctors* who do not have the average number of dog-owning patients are inequitably treated; *patients* who do not receive the average number of visits do not pay the 'proper' tax of 37½p. Thus the mathematical laws re-assert themselves: there is not enough information in the system to handle the regulatory requirement. And if we are not careful, we shall reinstate it by making the doctors keep the records. Next we shall need a system whereby accounts may be reconciled: doctors claiming underpayments, patients claiming overpayments.....Perhaps the patients would connive with their doctors to poison their dogs.

I declare an end to facetiousness. Look at the lessons. First: it is true that a channel can carry more than one set of information, but *only* if the several sets of information map onto each other under some simple rule. Second: if the mapping is ineffectual, or merely too complicated to be effective, the effort required to do the necessary reconciliation is absurdly disproportionate—because everything has to be gone over in detail at least once more. Third: there is no earthly reason why the *method* whereby things can most conveniently be done (in contemporary society, using modern technology) should not be allowed to change the precise nature of *what* is done. In this case. if the real cost of collecting these fees is greater than the revenue: give it up.

These lessons seems so obvious as to be not worth drawing. But look around. We *do* have dog licences. Worse: we have radio and television licences intended directly to finance the BBC. By 'directly' I mean that if a million people evade this tax, as they do, the BBC loses the revenue—which is wholly absurd. The BBC is not a tax collector. We *do* have reconciliation accounts everywhere: people paying taxes and reclaiming them, people drawing allowances and paying them back. The whole of this fatuous apparatus ought to be dismantled.

THE FORM OF REFORM

Let us start at the beginning. The whole of this problem is about the citizen. He clearly must have a record in modern society. So let us create it for him. He is born, and registered as being himself, with particular parents. What used to be his birth certificate is now the beginning of his electronic file. This is rightly housed in his community computer—in the community record office. The data trail begins to be generated.

The citizen now starts to have dealings with various social services, notably health and education. The transactions that occur, when completed, are transmitted straight into his record. The doctor who vaccinates the child dials this information, on his computer terminal, into the community record office. *He keeps no other record*, once the input information is verified on his own screen. If he wants a patient's record, he simply calls it up on his screen. No-one else can do this, because his terminal scrambles the information before it is stored.

The teacher dials his pupil's termly report into the record office too. This report will (please) be wholly redesigned, so as to contain some minimal information about the pupil's progress. (Existing reports are well-known to be innocent of actual information. Which one of us, at whatever age, could not 'do better'?)

Employment starts, and the employer is now dialing the community computer. The registrar of his marriage dials too. Now what about the citizen's own responsibilities? He is furnished with a simple list of matters on which the locality record office must be informed. He buys a dog. He takes a card from his pack, already addressed to the record office, which says: *I have bought a dog*. He signs, dates and delivers his card. Nothing more happens until he sends the card: *My dog has died*. The same with television sets, houses, swimming pools, investments—and whatever it is that the government thinks it should know about.

I can see the hackles rising. Our citizen is chained to the prison wall, electronically pinioned. The answer to this is: for pity's sake, be realistic. All of this is already known. It is just inefficiently, expensively known—whereas it could be known so simply and easily and cheaply. It could be known without wasting the quantities of humanity's wealth of which our absurd systems are depriving the underprivileged. If it gives you a nasty feeling, remember how much nastier the feeling would be if you were disembowelled during an insurrection due to famine, for being on the wrong side. If it offers genuine and serious difficulties about the extent to which the government may now control you, then devote some effort to making sure it cannot—bearing in mind that if the government became tyrannous, it would have no difficulty in controlling you anyway, as things are. More and more people in this world are finding this out, and it has nothing to do with electronics.

We can see how the citizen's file sequentially grows, so as to account for his (currently updated) situation. Now this is the only public record there is—so, yes, there must be a copy. But think what has happened to the vast records in the Ministry of Health, in the Ministry of Education, and so forth.....They no longer exist; neither do their computers, their staffs, their invigilators.

The community record offices all use the same computing system, so that the citizen's record is simply transmitted to a new office if he moves. This also means that *all* community computers can be accessed by a government department. Thus if the Ministry of Education wants to know how many graduates in technology there are, it interrogates the system as a whole—and the summed answer is instantaneous. If someone then gets the idea that

Education needs to know how many syphilitics there are, he will have to ask the Ministry of Health, which may withold the information. And if Health wants to know if *you* have got syphilis, it will not be able to find out. Your personal doctor can get that out of the system: no-one else.

I am trying to say that in future liberty will be all about the design of such electronic systems, and especially the design of heirarchies of filters intended to safeguard the rights of the individual. Will you call me a fascist for the things I have been saying? On the contrary: I believe in your liberty more than any of the people who, although *currently* engaged in your electronic incarceration in every department of life, do not warn you of the dangers. I am issuing that warning, and with it a message of hope. We can overcome the dangers, but only by intense study, public debate, and early legislation. You will get no protection by shouting me down. You will get enhanced danger, and waste—and therefore the deprivation of others. I am in the role of the messenger bearing alarming news: shall I then die—who have the information you need?

Given *one* record, to which there is a large number of keys each of which grants access to only a *part* of the record, we no longer need to waste half of our societary effort in the regulation of the other half. There is no census to take: we have a perpetual census, always up to date. There are no tax returns to complete. If the government devises a totally new tax package, it devotes its effort not to devising a Bill but to devising a computer program. This program, when applied to each and every personal record, determines the tax payable. *The* tax, I said; and I did not mean dozens of taxes. There is only one 'me' to pay tax, out of only one total income. Equally, there is only one deduction from my income—be the intricacies of the taxation infrastructure never so complicated.

The bill I shall receive lists my liabilities (income, house, dog, radio, and so on) and the money demanded on each account. It adds these up, and asks for the money—payable by regular instalments.

As to the legality of all this, the taxation package computer program, duly authorized by parliament, *is* the Finance Act. We should note that the room for manoeuvre on the part of our legislators has never been so great. They may simplify, complicate, elaborate, and distinguish in whatever ways they like. Only one computer program has to be written, and the machines do all the work. Lawyers engaged to dispute matters of tax will need to dispute the effect of this program on the citizen's record. This is a very precise matter, well suited to the legal mind. And it means that lawyers will become diagnosticians of mistakes in mapping a set of complicated rules onto a set of complicated circumstances. Why did I say 'become'? I apologize: it is this that lawyers already do.

All this cuts out waste. But you may think that it overcentralizes control. On the contrary. Control is vested in the community; and if the citizen wishes to know what is going on, the record office is just around the corner. He can if he wishes buy a copy of every entry as it is made in his file. But as a birthday present he will receive an updated copy of his total file, including (of course) annotations showing what information has been read from it, by whom, and for what reason. Such annotations would automatically be made in the very act of retrieving the information. And I would certainly suggest that every community record office should have an *ombudsman* to whom the citizen may directly appeal—in person.

So now the financial operations of the nation are consolidated. The local authority calls for rates, and explains its call to the citizen—as it does now. But there is no reason why either of these parties should bother with a mass of paperwork. The rate having been democratically approved, the money would be transferred from TAX (remember: there is only one tax) to the authority. This is just an electronic transaction. Other components of TAX would be transferred to Health, to Education, to Defence, and so on, as parliament approved. People registered as owning dogs, radios, cars, and so on, would have their TAX computed to include these components, and the relevant credits would be painlessly, *effortlessly* transferred (inside the national computer system) to the RSPCA, the BBC, and Road Fund and so on.

There is no problem because for every element of government, the information relating the law to the citizen maps onto the citizen's circumstances. THIS IS ALREADY THE CASE. There is no suggestion here that new information should be provided, only that the tasks that have to be done should be effectively organized. Present difficulties and immense waste arise because there are hundreds of recording boxes which between them account for the citizen's circumstances—and so we get the regulatory problem measured by an increasing logarithmic power that is a function of the number of boxes. If there is only one box, just as there is one integral citizen (and not a citizen who is healthy but uneducated, educated but homeless, and so on indefinitely), the rest is electronic manipulation.

These are the facts. The system is quite easy to design and to implement. It frees half the country's capabilities for constructive work. It requires a mammoth change of outlook, and the total reform of the civil service. It means that the biggest effort ever made in the protection of democratic government must be made now. This effort is bigger, because it requires moral energy, than the sum of the efforts yet devoted through war to the cause of freedom. But aside from the expenditure of moral energy, the cost in cash would be *many orders of magnitude* less than the cost of any of the wars we have thought it necessary to wage for our liberty.

Therefore we should not be downhearted. If we ever came near to abandoning hope, it should be because these things were *not* done. It is, I repeat, already the case that we record the entire set of information for which this scheme asks. We just happen to do it with unbelievable inefficiency and waste. I also repeat that we can afford this waste only by robbing the destitute.

So the issue is clear. Shall we abandon the destitute as the price of kidding ourselves that our own freedom is not endangered (whereas in fact it already is), or shall we turn our waste into living help for the afflicted, and keep a little of our wealth in reserve for the protection of our own freedom?

This plan sets the individual where he belongs: in his community. If the integrity of the citizen can be maintained, in the existence of his electronic shadow—the integral record—then his liberty can be protected. The community yields only certain information to the locality, the locality to the region, the region to government. These forms of access are decided by law. So although central government picks up information it needs about me direct from my community computer (thereby eliminating bureaucratic waste) it does so via a set of filters in the computer—whose programmes are labelled 'region', 'locality', 'community'.

Contrast this with the present, highly dangerous, situation. The citizen has already lost his integrity; he is chopped into bits—and at least half-a-dozen departments of central government have uninhibited access to personal information about him that is incomplete, and may therefore lead to wrong judgments. Thereby is the total man destroyed, and power over him resides wherever anyone cares to assemble a dossier.

RESURRECTING THE COMMUNITY

You may well ask why, if I am so very much concerned about human beings, I have hinged my notion of the form of reform entirely on technology. I said before (twice) that it is the only asset we have except our love, and I would like to expand on that.

Half the population of the world is fifteen-years old or younger. These people will inherit a world the institutions of which have grown like a cancer: they are vast, and malignant, and out of control. Humanity has come to this pitch, despite thousands of years of reflection upon the nature of man and society, and the nature of the ultimate good. The new fifteen-year old generation may continue to reflect; but their cerebral computers are no larger than those of Aristotle and Plato, More and Hobbes, Marx and Lenin . . . . . Nor is there any evidence that human nature in itself has changed. The one new variable in their situation is precisely the existence of a new science and technology. That science of course includes human and social science, just as that technology includes (for instance) medical and architectural technology—which are directed to the individual need.

In the last section, my use of technological concepts was directed towards the resurrection of the community. Men with their small brain pans and limited data processing capability did once learn, and still maintain, the capacity to operate both effectively and happily in relatively small groups. This much we know. But since the beginning of the Industrial Revolution, the cancerous growth of institutions has completely broken down the viability of small groups and local communities, by suborning individuals to the ends of larger, ill-comprehended, and giantesque institutions and societies. This then explains why I have advocated the use of science and technology to re-establish the community, pointing out that they are now competent to do so without actually destroying the civilization on which we all precariously depend.

Hitherto this would not have been possible, because there was no technological way to knit together autonomous groups. People had to come together physically in order to work on the scale demanded by mass-production: but that was before automation. People had to come together statistically in order to constitute a firm or a nation and be cared for economically or medically or educationally: but that was before computers. People had to abandon the community to the wider interest, submitting their homes to the pollution of roads, railways, aircraft and garbage: but that was before electronic communications and management science. It is time to call a halt, but it may be too late.

If so, that is because control of our lives is no longer vested in the elected government—whether local or national. It is vested in the firm: the firm for which we work, certainly: but also and more especially the firms which make our consumer economy tick. Consider this. The wealth on which our form of society rests is no longer the Wealth of Nations, but the wealth of multinational companies. The Gross 'National' Product (I mean the turnover) of General Motors is greater than the GNP of Belgium ; Standard Oil's is greater than Denmark's ; Ford's is greater than that of Norway and New Zealand put together ; Chrysler's is the same as that of Greece..... And eight British companies account for more than a quarter of the British GNP.

Multinational companies, served by computers and an international time-sharing network ; this is where economic power for good or ill resides for good or ill. And the joint Gross 'National' Product of IBM and General Electric, standing at fifteen, thousand million dollars, is well able to sustain that network. Each little nation, as well as the mighty Congress of the United States, holds its commissions and enquiries into the data-bank game. They are taking thought for human liberty. Meanwhile, guess who is writing the software that will in fact be used throughout the advanced countries of the world.

I am asking that power should be returned to the people. It is useless to argue that the whole of this technology should be destroyed before it destroys us : that will not happen. But there may be time to harness it. I have already explained how.

Then let us now devote some thought to the operation of a community which has indeed been reinstated by technological means. It can now afford to forget about technology. To what end is the community reborn? Is it to proliferate debating societies, women's institutes, theatrical societies and bridge clubs? No : because we do not move into Utopia at a step ; and besides, these particular manifestations of 'community' may very well be mere surrogates for constructive action. The real *problems* remain around us, some near and some far.

Because of the imbalance of our institutions, their size and unwieldliness, and because of the general incompetence of our managerial efforts, we already find that problems we expect to be solved, and as citizens imagine we have already paid to have solved, are not solved. But there is no lack of goodwill. People who know they are favoured in an ill-favoured world have no wish to ignore the indigent and distressed. Witness : favoured individuals are always ready to answer the call for help, and make pathetic cash donations to worthy bodies. This is the only action open to them ; but the coins seem to the donors to fall ineffectually to the floor of their wishing well. In a vain effort actually to *do* something that looks like action, they may undertake sponsored walks — where they are first knocked down, and then abused for being such an unproductive nuisance.

The community that newly finds itself could make an action plan. It might for example create a social commando. This might consist of some thirty people, chosen for a mixture of skills. Compassion, energy, and physical strength would be attributes to be matched with intellectual activity and professional knowledge. These people, selected as honoured representatives of the community, and having at least one understudy each, would be ready to donate their time and energy to any problem selected by the community itself. The members would normally go about their normal business. But in the event of trouble, or some predictable disaster, or some identified crying need, the commando would be called into immediate action.

Now we must remain realists, and I am assuming that we live in the kind of society we know — which is characterized most particularly by the set of onerous obligations it lays upon people. The more competent the person, the more onerous is the load. It will therefore be necessary to release each member of a commando from all his obligations for the length of the assignment—and it turns out that this would be quite easy to do. First of all, the employer must undertake to continue paying normal wages: that is his contribution. The employer is donating the person's service, and this is a necessary facilitation for the scheme. Employers would certainly make their own decisions about the number of people they would agree to support in this way, and on what terms. They would do better to be concerned about such decisions than to decide on their response to the standard 'charitable' appeal.

But the commando as such will need money, perhaps a great deal of money, to achieve its ends. Then each person honoured by election to a commando would seek (and would surely find) sponsors in the community for his membership—perhaps a hundred of them. A sponsor would be someone willing not just to give but to *raise* money for the sponsored person. I submit that if local folk knew exactly whom they were sponsoring in their locality, and in what precise cause, crash money-raising programmes would yield staggering sums. There would be no organizational overheads to pay, because there would be no administration—a sponge which absorbs a sufficient proportion of orthodox charitable donations as to deflate (whether with good reason or not) much enthusiasm on the part of many citizens of goodwill. The commando goes into action, using its money, and accounting for it to its sponsors in direct and personal terms.

I do not think that this is a pipe dream. The suggestion works on the basis of the few things that social science yet properly understands. Small groups work, participation in activity works, direct accountability works, and visible action is a mighty spur to all of this. Frankly, I see no limit to the sacrifices that individual members of the community might not make to achieve real purposes that they *knew* were being effectively accomplished. People who despair at government inefficiency in spending their taxes for the relief of suffering, people who feel that charitable institutions somehow just soak up their anonymous donation without producing effective action at the end of the line, these people would not for the most part fail to lift into the house a dying child if it miraculously appeared on their own doorsteps.

Contemplate any social problem you wish. Are there old people in the community, and is a veil drawn over their plight? We write to the papers and draw attention to it. Are there young offenders in the place? We leave it to our magistrates to send these people to institutions miles away, where they are taught by more accomplished inmates how to avoid being caught next time. Do we have traffic problems in the town, problems with hospitals and schools? The national machinery should devolve its authority in these matters, and the local authority should devolve it to commandos in turn. It is obvious; it is not done. Why not? Because society would be fragmented; shattered into unorganized fragments.

Forgive my saying it again. We now have the science and technology required to redesign our institutions, *so that they are both autonomous and integral at the same time.* We have developed a machinery of government that cuts out people, who are frustrated. There is no chance that people can get back into this machine. So change the machine. Then rely on the people.

THE BOW IN THE CLOUD

If I am right about the sensational waste in our society, it is indeed evident that no amount of tinkering about with the present system will release the wealth entrapped. There has to be radical change. But it is also evident that we cannot transform society in this revolutionary fashion by a stroke.

What counts as effective revolution? It is a question that I cannot resolve. I am a rational animal, and it is not rational to blow things up—unless a point has been reached where tyranny reigns.

As a scientist, I see just a glimmer of light in the obscurity of this question. It is open to man to experiment. If we could have a volunteer community that would be organized information-theoretically in the way I have described, what is bound to be called a theory could be tested and examined. There would have to be a large fund to support the experiment, because we should have to pay for a great deal of work to be done in transduction. That is to say, at the boundaries of the system—the community—all information coming in or going out would necessarily have to be translated. Well, this is normal in the world of management electronics. New systems have to be run, and expensively run, in parallel with the old systems they are due to replace.

Even if a government were to accept this experimental proposition, the development would be slow—mainly on account of that commitment to transduction. I fear it would be too slow. Is there somewhere a self-contained country that would agree to act as the experimental laboratory for the rest of the world—which would finance the work? I do not know. But this suggestion sounds a great deal more plausible, given the time-scale of human doom. . . . .

We have no precise demonstration of what that time-scale may be. It would however be most unwise to think that mankind has very much time left in which to deploy technology to save itself. I am ever-conscious of the vast nuclear capability of the nations that ranges round the world, and of the chemical and bacteriological capability for destruction which very likely already renders that nuclear threat obsolete in terms of horror. I am ever-conscious of the war-oriented economies of the world's most powerful nations, of the violence that seethes beneath every veneer of calm—even in my own apparently quiet homeland of England.

I do what I can; and I beg others to carry the thinking and above all the action forward. Any lecture such as this can lead to sterile debate, or to postures of enthusiasm on the one hand and denunciation on the other. None of that will fill a single belly.

The problems of the world can be solved, but a revolution is required. It will therefore come. It may be emotive and unthought, and its consequences may therefore be cataclysmic. Of those who are still both sane and not in their ultimate despair I ask again : what counts as effective revolution?

Think

And take heart.

Remember (11) that the Ark having rested

the Lord said in his heart

I will not again curse the
ground for man's sake.....
neither will I again smite
any more every thing living
as I have done.....

This is the token of the covenant which I make

between me
and you
and every living creature
that is with you

for perpetual generations.....

I DO SET MY BOW IN THE CLOUD.....

that I may remember the everlasting covenant.

REFERENCES

1. Orvill L Freeman (Secretary of Agriculture, USA), *World Without Hunger*, Frederick A Praeger, New York, 1968.
2. St Matthew, **5,** 38, 39.
3. St Matthew, **23,** 24, 27.
4. EF Schumacher, *Des Voeux Memorial Lecture*, National Society for Clean Air, 1967.
5. Geoffrey Vickers, *Freedom in a Rocking Boat*, Allen Lane, The Penguin Press, 1970.
6. Rupert Brooke, 'Peace' (1941), *The Complete Poems*, Sidgwick and Jackson, London, 1941.
7. *Qutotations from Chairman Mao Tse-Tung*, Corgi Books, London, 1967.
8. Ivor H Mills, Letter to *The Times*, May 30, 1970.
9. Claude E Shannon and Warren Weaver, *The Mathematical Theory of Communication*, University of Illinois Press, Urbana, 1949.
10. Stafford Beer, 'Homo Gubernator', *Platform for Change*.
11. Genesis, **8,** 21; **9,** 12, 13, 16.

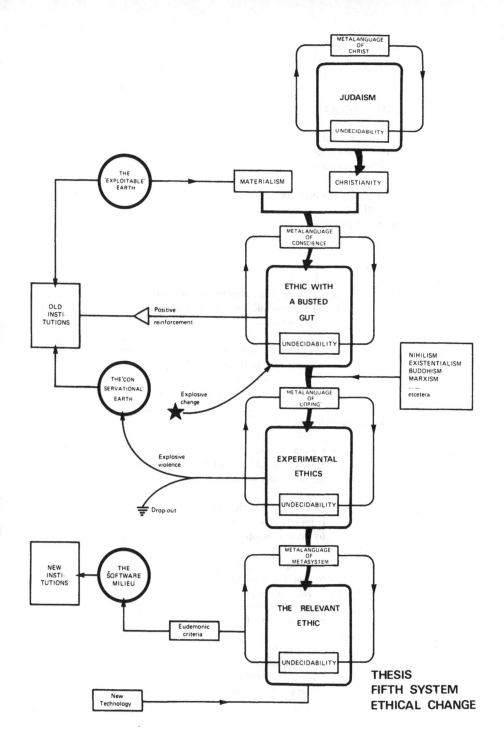

THESIS
FIFTH SYSTEM
ETHICAL CHANGE

COLOUR CODE : BLUE
Thesis

THESIS

EIGHTH STATEMENT

Change cannot occur
within the framework
of the existing ethic :

mankind needs to formulate
a new ethic
relevant to the problems
that face the species today.

The basis of this ethic is

- a true and not spurious compassion
- for the real and not imagined plight
of mankind—

        two thirds being undernourished
        and three thirds being
        under threat
        of extinction.

The key to applying this ethic is

- recognition that technology
makes mankind as a whole
unimaginably wealthy

- recognition that this wealth
is largely consumed
by massive waste

- a willingness
to reorganize society
to eliminate waste
thereby to finance
the eudemony of man

    facing up to
    and conquering
    any entailed threat
    to personal freedom.

COLOUR CODE : BLUE
Thesis

We still have rainbows.

Indeed. we can now look down on them
from thirty thousand feet
and see a complete circle . . . . .

The circle with which PLATFORM FOR CHANGE
turns out to be most concerned
is revealed in the remark
that our problems are not political.
And we need the metalanguage to explain that.

Politics is often defined
as the art of the possible.
I take this to mean that the politician
sees himself as thoroughly immersed
in the on-going realities of life :
he accepts their frame of reference.

> *Pragmatic*
> is a word he likes to use
> wrongly

> to connote this.

The frame of reference that includes
Homo Faber and the primacy of work
analytic thinking degraded to reductionism
old institutions and the hierarchy of power
the Exploitable Earth and the profit criterion
the ethic with a busted gut

> provides the universe of discourse
> the language.

In such a language
reform is decidable
only in certain terms.

For example
it is perfectly possible to say :

> rob the rich
> to feed the poor.

But the notion of reform
put forward in PLATFORM FOR CHANGE
can be expressed
only metalinguistically.

COLOUR CODE : GOLD
Metalanguage

For example
the section in Renascence
called *The Form of Reform*
must be read in the language
to mean that

administration would be more efficient
if it were computerized.

And despite the ethical preamble
meant precisely to establish a metalanguage
in which this is not what the proposal

is about
at all

it is likely to be read
in the language
and not in the metalanguage
just the same.

Then the politician
may well take leave to doubt
the proposition expressed in the language
and go away.

Politics
in short

decreates my barbers

Politics
at length

does not express
my propositions

which are undecidable in the language.

This then is my reason
for having said that the problems
are not political;
for although my propositions lie
within the meaning of the word
they are excluded from political language
as politicians like to speak it

pragmatically
in inverted commas.

COLOUR CODE : GOLD
Metalanguage

This intends to say
not that a politican cannot understand
and hopefully even approve
the PLATFORM FOR CHANGE
but that he operates in a milieu
for which these ideas
cannot exist.

Then the power for reform
and the creation of metasystems
to speak the metalanguage
and discuss the propositions
lies elsewhere:

the power for reform
is where insight is shared.

If for example
the insight is shared and spread
that money is best regarded

        as a constraint
        not as a goal

then this is how
a metasystem might grow
speaking the language of eudemony.

This is a more practical expectation
than that the money criterion
should be repudiated.

Throughout PLATFORM FOR CHANGE
the traps of the language
of brain limitation
and the human condition
have been examined
from various angles.

What we have to remember
is the power that lies in us all
not so much to dismantle the traps
or burn them in public

        as to decreate *them*
        by reformulating
        the logical language.

COLOUR CODE : GOLD
Metalanguage

At last the tables are turned
on undecidability.
All along
we have had to use metalanguages
to reformulate languages
in which *our* propositions
could not be expressed.
Now we seek to create a language
in which the current political slogans
cannot be expressed.

Sticking to the example of the profit criterion
we find that (non-military) science
has done something like this.
The scientist already treats money as a constraint.
He has work to do

      why *this* work?
           —not to make a profit
      why *this* work?
           —not for the extension of knowledge
           how very pious

      why *this* work?

because this work is what he does.
That is all.
This work increases his eudemony.

Then not having money
is a constraint on this work—
and you ought to see the scientist
wriggling out of this strait-jacket.....

      it will contribute to profit
          —in the end
      it will extend human knowledge
          —inevitably.

Is the scientist a confidence trickster?

In the language we seek to discard
the political language
the answer is:

      yes
      quite often.

COLOUR CODE : GOLD
Metalanguage

In the metalanguage we seek to develop
the language of the relevant ethic
the answer is:

> certainly *not*
> and how dare you?

So it can be done.
The artist knew the knack
long before the scientist was born

> (in the language of patronage
> propositions about profit
> are
> > beautifully
>
> undecidable
>
> > as the patron found out.)

but he seems to me to have lost the knack--
to be talking the language himself
which if true
is a pity.

Going back to *The Form of Reform*
it will not be enough
to say that

> administration would be more efficient
> if it were computerized

because it may be expressible
but is not credible
in the language.

(If you cannot think why
read again the Argument of Change
called *The Software Milieu*.)

It seems likely
that the solution will have to be
to find the social need
that is expressible in the language

> as I *tried* to do
> in *The Law and the Profits*

COLOUR CODE : GOLD
Metalanguage

so as to use eudemony
not to replace the money criterion forthwith
which is too much to ask
but as the measure of the extent
to which the money tap turns.

Finally
in this metalanguage
I have a comment about simplicity.

It may have seemed
in reading *Renascence*
that the answer:

      reduce the number of boxes
      because the waste
      is an increasing logarithmic function
      of their number

is just too simple.

But I want to attest to the truth
that simplicity
is always the answer.
We do not see it
because we search for it
in the wrong language.

      Verify this statement
      by reference to almost any major
      scientific breakthrough.

A serene example
is written in
to the Fifth System Diagram
at the top.

Christianity
was the outcome
of Christ's reformulation
in a metalanguage
of the Judaic law.

      Here is the survival power
      of the truly Christian ethic—
      that it resolves
      the undecidability of love
      in the language of Jehovah.

COLOUR CODE : GOLD
Metalanguage

In the metalanguage spoken by Christ
There is no way of saying

> *either*
>
> > do as you're told
>
> *or*
>
> > do as you like.

I now draw the Thesis together
for your convenience

and supply a composite System Diagram
explaining it all.

COLOUR CODE : GOLD
Metalanguage

THE INTEGRAL

THESIS

FIRST STATEMENT

Man is a prisoner of his own way of thinking
and of his own stereotypes of himself.

His machine for thinking
the brain
has been programmed to deal with a vanished world.

This old world was characterized by the need
to manage *things*—
stone, wood, iron.

The new world is characterized by the need
to manage
complexity.

Complexity is the very stuff of today's world.

The tool for handling complexity is
ORGANIZATION.

But our concepts of organization belong
to the much less complex old world
not to the much more complex today's world

still less are they adequate to deal with
the next epoch of complexification—
in a world of explosive change.

COLOUR CODE : BLUE
Thesis

SECOND STATEMENT

We shall not succeed
in reforming our concept of organization
or in creating new institutions that actually work
simply by hard work—or even hard thought.

We need to invoke SCIENCE—defined as
the organized body of human knowledge
about the world and its workings.

Science offers the means

- **to measure and manipulate complexity**
  through mathematics

- **to design complex systems**
  through general systems theory

- **to devise viable organizations**
  through cybernetics

- **to work** *effectively* **with people**
  through behavioural science

- **to apply all this to practical affairs**
  through operational research

In using these essentially interdisciplinary capabilities
science is free to draw on its depository of knowledge
of physical, biological and social systems.

The knowledge and the skills exist
but are wasted—frivolled away.

Society proceeds instead by *consensus*
that lowest common denominator of alternative democracies
which buys protection against
megalomaniacs, fascists, charlatans and lunatics
and which also protects us from
novelty, unique ability, change and leadership.

The consensus simplifies, distorts and makes trivial
the real problems of complexification
which are inherently too difficult
for *all* **to understand.**

COLOUR CODE : BLUE
Thesis

Thus we come to manage an oversimplified model of the world
that exists only in the mind of the consensus
instead of the real world . . . . . out there.

This mismatch
lies at the root
of our incompetence.

COLOUR CODE : BLUE
Thesis

THIRD STATEMENT

There are three things to do :

FIRST   do some thinking

reconstruct the language,
and then operate metasystemically

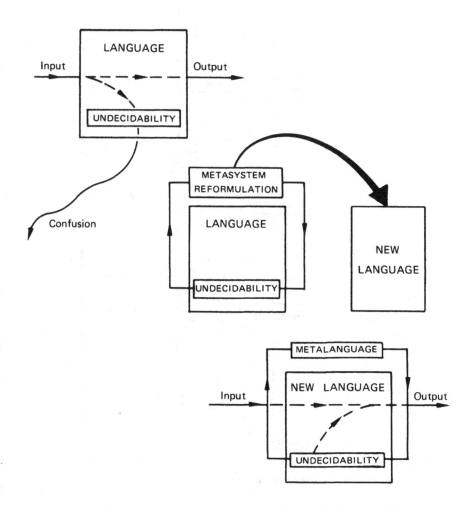

make provision this time
for continuous metasystemic monitoring.

COLOUR CODE : BLUE
    Thesis

384

SECOND   do some operational research

**reconstruct the accepted model of the world situation
using the new language**

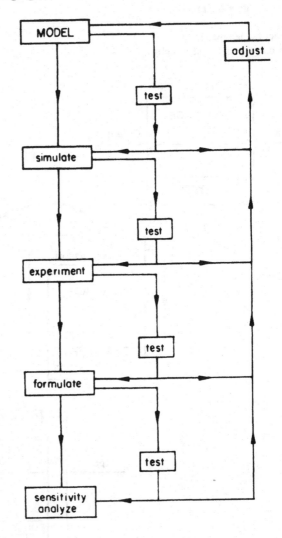

THIRD   do some cybernetics

**deploy cybernetic theory
to redesign institutions
using the continued experience
of model manipulation.**

FOURTH STATEMENT

Institutions are self-contained cells
for each of which the nucleus—
the organizing principle
called the cytoblast—
is management itself.

It is the responsibility of management
to revitalize their decaying institutions :
a management
informed by the insights
and using the tools
that science makes available
through its study of complex systems.

Through science we set up the hypothesis
that institutions
have certain systemic characteristics
that make them highly stable
   —in itself a good
and therefore unadaptable
   —something highly dangerous.

They are esoteric boxes
difficult to penetrate :
which puts all the more onus for internal reform
on their own managements.

Society itself however
needs to recognize
that the revitalizing of separate institutions
will not of itself
successfully reform society
nor cope with societary threats
because

   ● there is not likely to be
     enough time left

   ● the major instabilities of society
     arise *between*
     the esoteric boxes.

This unfortunately puts the onus on governments

to attend to the creation and regulation
of metasystems
mean to induce this new societary stability.

   'unfortunately'?

   Of course.
   The dangers are manifest.

COLOUR CODE : BLUE
  Thesis

FIFTH STATEMENT

In seeking to design metasystems
synergistically to organize
systems of esoteric boxes
we must have a metric.

Money is the established metric
of our society;
and all attempts
to calculate societary good
in other than monetary terms
fail.

This may be because
either to abolish or to ignore money
destroys only a symbol
of a necessary calculus
to which society always returns
under some guise :
> barter of goods
> their relative ease of procurement
> resource allocation.

The metric of money
is too useful to abandon
but it ought to be viewed essentially
as the metric of *constraint*.

> ● Although we may fail to abolish the metric
> we also conspicuously fail
> to *use* it successfully
> in the measurement of societary good.

We are free to choose
another metric of *utility*

yielding a system
capable of regulating societary behaviour
for direct betterment—
within monetary constraints.

Call the new and hypothetical metric :

> eudemony.

COLOUR CODE : BLUE
Thesis

SIXTH STATEMENT

Even though we may succeed
in inventing a measure of utility
called eudemony,
that metric depends
on the measurement of *information flow*—

for on this basic measure
all societal metrics
(even the monetary metric)
necessarily depend.

For this specific reason
the way in which society handles
the commodity of

        information

        which is what changes us

and the commodity of

        data

        which are the raw materials of information

will prove to be critical
in the good management of affairs
and even to

        the preservation of human freedom.

There is no need for alarm
that science has provided the tool

        in the shape of the computer

to promote information handling
as the predominant human skill
of our age—
and as the machine

        for changing data into information

provided that

        we understand what we are doing
        and legislate :

            not only for protection
            but for the advancement of man

        in time.

COLOUR CODE : BLUE
    Thesis

SEVENTH STATEMENT

New institutions
with new eudemonic metrics
and new organizational structures
also need

> new kinds of strategy
> new approaches to decision making

in a phrase :

> dynamics of decision

fast-responding, self-regulating, self-organizing.

This concept is integrative and organic.

It does away with sterile models
of institutions as being for instance

> centralized or
> decentralized

since any viable system is both at once.

Such tired old issues
are easily resolved
metalinguistically.

> We need only to create
> metasystems to speak
> the metalanguage.

The institution most needing reform
under these cybernetic canons
is government itself.

It is therefore imperative
that public channels of communication
especially those commanded by the overwhelmingly influential
electronic media
should not be clogged
nor be allowed to distort
available insights.

COLOUR CODE : BLUE
Thesis

EIGHTH STATEMENT

Change cannot occur
within the framework
of the existing ethic :

mankind needs to formulate
a new ethic
relevant to the problems
that face the species today.

The basis of this ethic is

> a true and not spurious compassion
> for the real and not imagined plight
> of mankind—

>> two thirds being undernourished
>> and three thirds being
>> under threat
>> of extinction.

The key to applying this ethic is

> ● recognition that technology
> makes mankind as a whole
> unimaginably wealthy

> ● recognition that this wealth
> is largely consumed
> by massive waste

> ● a willingness
> to reorganize society
> to eliminate waste
> thereby to finance
> the eudemony of man

> facing up to
> and conquering
> any entailed threat
> to personal freedom.

COLOUR CODE : BLUE
Thesis

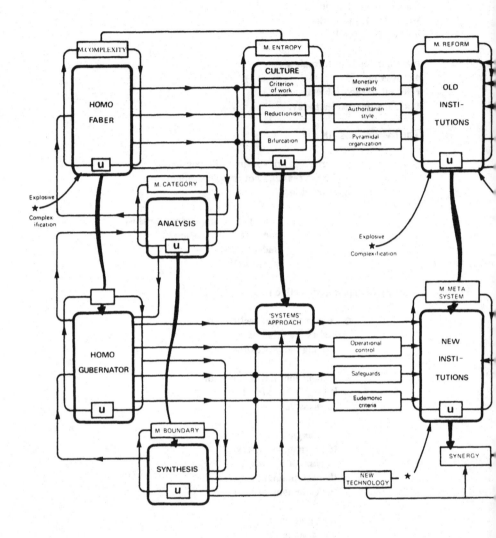

OUR CODE : BLUE
      Thesis

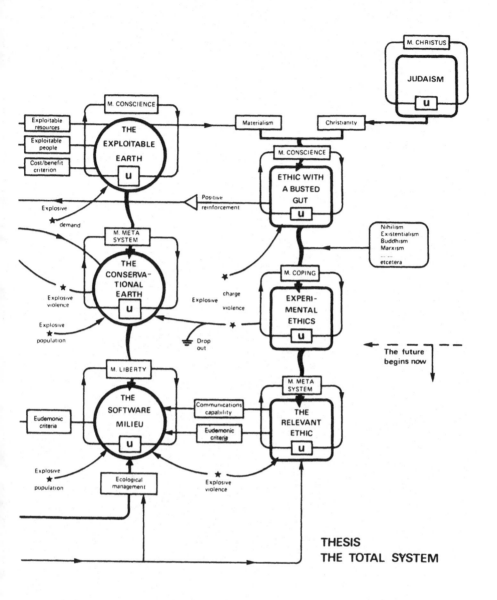

THESIS
THE TOTAL SYSTEM

COLOUR CODE : BLUE
Thesis

The ARGUMENTS OF CHANGE
so far expressed here
were all set out
during 1970
>the first year of the project
>PLATFORM FOR CHANGE
while meanwhile
I earned my living.

Meanwhile also
the British government changed hands

>Toute nation a
>le gouvernement
>qu'elle mérite
>>Joseph de Maistre 1811.

Thus it was
that in the second year
of the project, 1971
I became prepared for the third year

● by steering a new book
into publication.
It had taken six years to write
the culmination of more than twenty years' work
on what organization
makes a viable system

● second through creating in detail
the metasystemic content
of the project here recorded
thesis, systems,
explanation

● next by working on a new
Argument of Change
addressing anew the problems confronting government
in a software milieu
collecting, expanding thoughts
understanding new models

● then by an ENCOUNTER
THAT CHANGED EVERYTHING
because it gave me the opportunity
to do what I was now ready to do
namely
get on with the action.

COLOUR CODE : YELLOW
Narrative

Looking back
on all this
it was an extraordinary preparation
for the third year.

The encounter itself
might have gone unrecognized
without that psychological context—
and the knowledge too
that whatever I did next
must needs be done abroad.

Probably the reasons for this conviction
are perfectly clear

        but for example

           this is only one example
           chosen because you know about it
consider the fate of the proposal
for an Open Research Network
explained in DYNAMICS OF DECISION
        Winding-up pp 283–285.

The appropriate Department of State
was already squeezing the University's funds
        no hope there.

The appropriate government agency
could support only *existing* projects
        fatally
        this was new.

As to industry
one great company
spent many months examining the idea :
        we are inspired by this thinking
        they said finally
        to make a study
        of our use of telephones.

So I gave up my effort for the Open University
after two years of trying
        very unBritish
        it gets you a bad name.

COLOUR CODE : YELLOW
Narrative

Before recounting the story
of the mysterious ENCOUNTER
let us fill in the gap
in the psychological preparation :
the new Argument of Change.

This is another presidential address
which makes it initially repetitious
because it would be madness to assume
too much
just because they made you president.

It begins by picking up familiar threads :

> the threats
> the anachronistic models
> the esoteric box . . . . .

Then pray treat the first three sections
as a quick recapitulation
> with some new examples
or ignore them altogether.

The fourth heading
General Systems Approach to Public Policy
begins what is new.
These models came out of work
done for a government in the Northern hemisphere
during 1971.

For despite all the excitement
> the preparation
> the encounter
during the second year

meanwhile
I earned my living.

COLOUR CODE : YELLOW
Narrative

AN ARGUMENT OF CHANGE

THE
SURROGATE WORLD
WE MANAGE

Presidential Address* to the Society for General Systems Research, delivered at the annual meeting of the American Association for the Advancement of Science, in Philadelphia, on December 29, 1971.

*By permission of
Behavioural Science

Science—The Generalizer

We are here to look beyond the ends of our noses-to-grindstone. People who did that in biblical days were called prophets. More often than not, they did not like what they saw ahead. We do not like what we see either. Thus some of us have earned the epithet 'prophets of doom'—and that is an easy way for the fundamentally cheerful human animal to avoid the issues. It is back to the grindstone for him—and that is morally respectable.

What is the prophecy business all about? Did men ever, can we now, peer successfully into the future? The people who want to argue the metaphysics of that are welcome to do so ; but they have missed the point. The whole world is by now a richly interactive system. It is running according to various tenets: cultural tenets, legal tenets, financial tenets, industrial tenets, political tenets. . . . . These tenets prescribe the rules governing a great many of the interactions. The second thing governing what can conceivably happen in this systemic world is the level of resources and the rates at which they are metabolized as energy for running the systemic world. There are, it is true (or at least I hope it is true) many uncertainties. Uncertainty is the stuff of our free will. But it seems clear that this free will can operate in the new systemic world only under two conditions. First, we exercise a power of decision only within the systemic framework to which I have alluded ; second, we accept the uncertainty to mean that things will probably not turn out as we expect. We blunder on.

In fact, however, the structure of the richly interactive systemic world, the given levels of resources, and the way in which industrial capitalization has set the metabolic rates, powerfully restrict the uncertainty. Mankind has underwritten a sort of 'executive program' that operates the systemic world. Thus when we lift our eyes we are not so much peering into the mists of an inscrutable future, as evaluating the inexorable consequences of the things we are doing now. Especially we perceive a loss of freedom to manoeuvre. the constraint of the power of decision.

I think it was much the same as this for the Old Testament prophets, except that they were dealing in an ethical universe of discourse. They were moralists, who told people what would be the fruits of sin. Today, as we try to deal in a world of hard facts, we are scientists evaluating the performance, and thus the built-in destiny, of very large systems. The faculty involved is not one of divination; it is, as for all sciences. a faculty of generalization.

Back at the grindstone. people know that science is about facts of nature—and they go on to get it hopelessly confused with technology. where anything general is totally absorbed in what is particular. The scientist is moving in the other direction : he is trying to get at the governing principles. That is how he comes to assume the mantle of the prophet. And people become incensed with him, just as they did before, because he deals at a level of abstraction that appears to have nothing to do with grindstones.

Now if people find it hard to understand the sense in which a general systems scientist discusses the future, they also find it tiresome to hear him talk about the world entire. Does the man have delusions of grandeur? How *can* one think about the whole world? This popular doubt is also answered by the notion of science as generalizer. For if what I have so far said is true, then man is making the same sorts of mistake in constructing systems at every level of complexity. This may sound cynical : but if you have once learned the fundamental trick of constructing a firm as a system incapable of adaptation, you can construct a social service, an economy, and even an ecology, that will all be unadaptive as well. . . . . The invariant is bad cybernetics.

Models and Surrogates

Then I would like to talk about some generalizations of the management process which appear to me applicable at every level of complexity.

Every one of us is committed to operate in the world in terms of his conceptual understanding of the world—his model of it, if you will. I respond to my children in a certain way, because my mental files about them include models of how they are—and, please note, how they are likely to respond, which means that I have a predictive model in just the sense described. There is a good deal of evidence to suggest that large families are more stable than small ones. In terms of what I have just been saying, this would be because the rapidly increasing number of familial relationships as the family grows in size (which is of course the number in the family times one less than that number) reduces the uncertainty of the individual's response to a total family situation.

Well, the manager of any situation is no less committed to his model of what he manages than any of us. As we see in Figure 1, the model intervenes between the manager and the situation. It must do this; it is a kind of filter intended to cut out noise and enhance perception of meaningful patterns. We may note two things about it immediately.

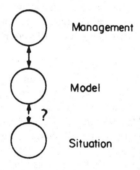

Management

Model

?

Situation

Figure 1

Firstly, the model may be no good. It is more like *us* than external reality, as my drawing tries to show. Think of a city with a traffic problem, which in turn generates a street parking problem. Then city managers have a conceptual model which vividly depicts how people go to work in buildings and leave their cars outside—so that traffic can no longer conveniently pass down the road. The model at once proposes the answer: let the business fraternity take their cars *into* the buildings with them, and then the road will be clear and the traffic can move. Accordingly, the city managers legislated to say that all new buildings must include off-street parking facilities in their design. The result of this policy was that wherever it took effect other people altogether noticed free places in the road—and parked their cars in them. This made the problem worse. There were twice as many cars in the offing.

And naturally the total traffic flow increased into the bargain. So then there was some more legislation to *dis*courage the inclusion of parking facilities in new buildings. Unhappily, people do have models which are just as bad as that. They not only give the wrong answers; they oscillate. It happened: in London.

The second point is that you will discover how people often begin to mistake the model for the reality—and start managing the model instead. Let me give you a true instance of this too. The residents of a certain small town got up a petition to ask the railway company to put on a train at three o'clock in the afternoon to take them to the big town. Now the railway company had a model of this line, and more than a mental model in this case. They had done an empirical study, and had quantified their model. The reply the residents received (this is going to strain your credulity, but I saw the letter) said that the Railway had undertaken a factual survey—and there was no one *waiting* for a train at three o'clock. It happened: in Sussex.

This is the start of my general diagnosis. If we start managing models instead of the realities the models are supposed to reflect, and if the models are as bad as they often are, then that is bad enough. But what happens when we introduce the effect of time? Until comparatively recently, I submit, the answer to this question was: not very much. But it is patently obvious today, and indeed the remark becomes trite, that mankind has never experienced the rate of change which is by now established in every department of our lives. I mentioned earlier how what used to be prophecy becomes the anticipation of inexorable consequences. We can see this in contemplating the acceleration of the rate of change, simply by tracing the many positive feedback circuits which change itself generates. Technological advance demands an explosive increase in the number of technically trained people to service it; and as this number explodes the amount of new technology generated itself explodes. Moreover, the exponential increase in the number of relationships between all these people and all their works, has the effect of reducing uncertainty.

When I discussed this effect just now in terms of growth in family size, I said it made the family more stable—a pleasing word, perhaps, to apply to a family. But when society stabilizes by means of systematic technological growth, all the evidence suggests that it is powerless any longer to control the breeding process. I would wager that all of us here suspect that mankind is now locked into a technological growth machine which may well carry it over the edge of a precipice. . . . .

So when I refer to the influence of the passage of time on the model-building proclivity of managers, I am saying that for the first time in history there is an explicit need continuously to update the models we are using. This has simply not been recognized. The changing and finally explosive situation moves on through time; we people are swept along with it. But the managerial models we made, bad as they were at the start, stupid as we were at the start to manage *them* rather than reality, remain much the same. You can see what I mean from Figure 2.

The evidence for the contention is everywhere around us. Men discovered how to run a village a long time ago, and did it fairly successfully—with their elders, their specialized committees (as it were), and their functional specialists in such (then unrecognized) sciences as psychology. . . . . The village was almost a closed system; or at least it became

402

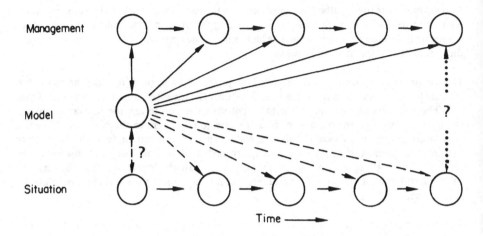

Figure 2.   How the bad model becomes a mere surrogate.

an open system only under specified rules—of warfare or trade or sex. Human beings could run this show with their limited brains, with their capacity quantitatively to distinguish between at the most nine levels of intensity. Which of us would like to be village headman of the world entire—with those 3.2 bits of cerebral output? Yet the organization we adopt is just the same.

Let me return for the last time to the homely example of the children. Evidence of a generation gap can be found in Plato—it is not a new phenomenon. Nonetheless, modern parents strongly suspect that this has become a more substantial problem than it was when they themselves were young—never mind the Greeks. Please look at Figure 2 again. Perhaps we are trying to manage our children, as we try to manage the United Nations, *in* the model rather than *through* the model, where the model was always rather bad, and where the model has not been updated.

A model with these three lethal characteristics does not deserve to be called a model at all. That is why in my title I have proposed to you the word *surrogate* instead. And this is the sense in which I contend that we are managing a surrogate world—while the reality is well-nigh out of control.

A General Model of a Failing Institution

What, then, is really going on in this surrogate world we manage?

It is populated by institutions of every kind. And because I am trying to keep the level of abstraction high, the thinking generalized for every level of organization, I shall again use the term I have been using for some years which refers to an institution as an esoteric box.

That it is an institution at all makes it a box: I mean that the instituion has recognizable boundaries. What is going on inside this box is what makes it esoteric: I mean, to use a dictionary definition, 'for the initiated only'. For there is a way of behaving about any institution that is unique, that requires an entrance permit, that calls for knowledge of special rules, and that roundly declares that outsiders 'don't understand'. It is this box, I am claiming, which today is—almost inevitably—managing a surrogate world.

Any viable institution has two major characteristics. First of all, it is stable. But the ultimately stable state for any system is death. Therefore its second vital characteristic is that it remains adaptable. The dinosaurs failed in the second mode, and therefore embraced the first. This is precisely my fear for the species Homo Sapiens. Why should I have this fear? After all, man has remained adaptable for a very long time—since he was a monkey in fact. But through our study of systems we know a great deal about adaptation. Just to take one point: an adaptive system must obviously be in continuous receipt of inputs about changes in the outside world—it is to those very changes that it must adapt. But we saw that it inevitably does this through a model. If the model is a surrogate.....what then? Clearly the institution is no longer adaptive, and the stability of sanity and viability (which admits of learning and evolution) is overtaken by the stability of high entropy and death. Then let us analyse the problem of the institution, that esoteric box, in terms of its stability.

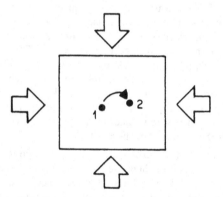

Figure 3. The Esoteric Box

In Figure 3 we see the box containing its representative point—a point of equilibrium. We also see that the box is being bombarded by outside disturbances, and we have already noted that (thanks to the unique rate of change in our time) the perturbations that result will be of unexampled frequency and ferocity. What is the estoric box supposed to do, where is its equilibrium point supposed to move, in the face of such perturbations?

Reformers who assault the box expect one of two consequences. Either the walls of Jericho will collapse, and the reformer himself will be acclaimed as saviour, or alternatively the walls will remain inviolate, and the reformer will be flung from the battlements. It is in the nature of reformers that they propose to accept either fate with equanimity. In fact, neither of these things happens. The reason why not is made very explicit in the work of one of our great pioneers, Ross Ashby. But I strongly suspect, at the level of generality at which I am trying to talk today, that the fundamental explanation has existed for a long time in physical chemistry—where it is known as Le Chatelier's Principle. All that happens inside the esoteric box when it is subjected to these massive perturbations from outside is that the equilibrium point moves—ever so slightly—to accommodate the change. Thus are reformers robbed of both glory and martyrdom; thus do institutions remain adaptable and survive.

It is all very fine so long as the institution is managing the real world through a workable model. It is then able to maintain its integrity and continuity, and yet effect internal change by responding to external stimuli. If it does so, we call it self-regulating and even self-organizing. The first property sponsors stability and even learning, while the second sponsors adaptation and even evolution. *These* are the survival mechanisms. You will notice that each of them takes a little longer than the last to attain to an equilibrial state following perturbation. We may call the time taken, in any event, the relaxation time. Then I have the following hypothesis to put before you:

> it is characteristic of our society that its institutions, because
> they are managing surrogate worlds, have a longer relaxation time
> on average than the mean interval between massive external perturbations.

Please examine this hypothesis with me in terms of the predictions we can make if it should be true. In the first place, the system will never be stable again. It has no hope of hanging on to an equilibrial state. Then of course the survival mechanisms cannot work. Secondly, we may note that in social systems, as in physiological systems, the operation of the survival mechanisms tends to be followed by a refractory period—during which they are denatured. That will make the initial instability much worse. Thirdly, if the relative time lags within the system are changed, and we know that they are being changed because of the rate of advance in technology, then the whole survival mechanism will go into an indefinite oscillation. Fourthly, since all of this will make the internal reactions within the system more unstable, more rapidly oscillatory, while the regulatory channels pass information at an ancient and leisurely pace, then the system will reach a condition of explicit clonus—which is the symptom of the spastic.

I hope we shall all think about these corollaries of the initial hypothesis. There is no time to attempt to demonstrate that all of them are manifest in our society. Besides, even if I did so, I should not have proved the hypothesis. On the other hand, in order to falsify the hypothesis, you would need to give me one example of a significant institution which is both stable and adaptive, and which exhibits none of the symptoms I have just mentioned. I tell you frankly that I do not believe that you can do it. Of all the esoteric boxes, the firm has more chance of establishing the claim to viability than any other. I certainly consider that public utilities and social services, the professional institutions such as law and taxation, governments themselves, and the instruments of world control which mankind has set up, will not meet the test. And firms themselves should not be over confident . . . . . Even in the United States the name 'Rolls Royce' meant something.

Well, people say, there are plans to deal with all this. Managers and ministers are certainly aware of a great many problems, and they have become zealous in trying to handle them. The plea I am making to you—and in heaven's name to them, if they will listen—is that the plans are illusory. That is because the plans are framed within a model which is in fact a surrogate. They have almost no bearing on reality at all. Above all, I suppose, the plans are attempts to hold together the institutions that have already failed. It is like trying to preserve a familiar church spire by inviting the death watch beetles to hold hands.

The problem is much more difficult than it appears. I am not denigrating people in power, whether company directors, permanent officials, professionals or ministers. But I perceive them as wielding their authority within a failing institutional context. Enlightened ones among them will do much to improve matters within that context. That is fine—if we can be satisfied with a more cost-effective failure, more scientific ineffectual plans, and a more humane extinction. But how does the man in power question the viability of the very institution from which he draws that power? In what language does a Pope infallibly declare himself fallible?

There is only one language that will do—the language of science. If the institutional world is a surrogate for the real world, we have to get out into the real world and make empirical studies that cut across all the boundaries of the surrogate. To do this, we need a truly interdisciplinary science. Let us note that science itself is an institution, a veritable esoteric box, full of surrogates of its own devising. Do not ask, then, whether this is a problem for physics or biology or sociology, or even whether it calls for a mixture of all three. These are names written over the lockers in the left-luggage office we call education. The objective is simply to investigate the systemic world, and in so doing to create new institutions with organizational structures that map onto reality.

General Systems Approach to Public Policy

Just *how* do the surrogates fail? The theory of the esoteric box explains only *why* they fail. If we can get at the mechanics of this, maybe we can see what to do. Here is a systems approach to this problem, culled from empirical work on real situations, which seems to have some generality.

Figure 4 depicts a situation in the real world (note the fuzzy boundary), and above it is erected a typical management process. We try to identify the needs of the situation. But we are using a surrogate version of the world—and that is the meaning of the tidy set of boxes that comprise the perceived needs. It also explains the attenuator that reduces variety on the ascending line. This is where school education is separated from university education, and subject from subject; this is where hospitals are separated from the general practice of medicine; this is where poisons, noise, dirt and vice are separated out as 'pollutants' from the city that generates them all. Thus are we committed to not-considering the education system, the health system or the urban system—and still less the total system of the social good.

Plans are generated from the needs, and these too exist for the surrogate world. You will note how the esoteric box, floating in space, disconnected from reality, acts as kind of coenetic variable in all this—imposing its organizational stereotype on the perception of need and the plans alike. As I said in an address a little South of here a year ago:
PLANNING IS HOMOLOGOUS WITH ORGANIZATION—it is an important point.

Meanwhile, the capability to give the plans effect is conditioning the plans, which would be very proper if there were a clear understanding of what technology can do: and the resources required to service the capability are fed in, which would be fine if there were any realization of how the capability could be changed given suitable resources. In general, these things are not at all understood, because of the surrogate world. When we were

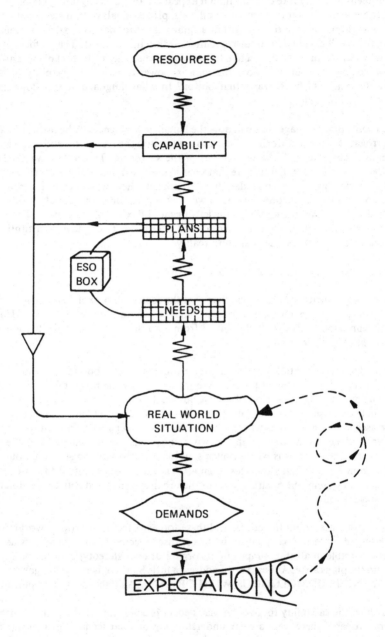

Figure 4. *The Surrogate and the Reality*

nearer to reality, long ago, this part of the diagram *was* understood. Men built pyramids, and Gothic cathedrals, and iron ships, and heavier-than-air flying machines. In recent times I can think of only one example:
the Apollo mission, of course.

So there it is. The available capability and the stereotyped plans are applied to the real world through a gigantic amplifier, as the diagram shows. They don't work.

Then take a look at what is happening in the real rather than the surrogate world. This is the lower half of the diagram. The situation is bad, and people know it. They voice demands. Then the demands grow into expectations. By some crazy route, the situation is supposedly changed. The route is hard to trace; it is an essentially political process. I draw attention now to the attenuators on this line toward public action. They are. it seems. what we call the media'.

None of this is as simple as it looks: the whole system is full of feedback. Let us note first that we are in a dynamic system, and the state of the situation is moving. According to the esoteric box hypothesis, the perception of need will not recognize this quickly enough. A comparator (which exists in the body politic—although it may be inexplicit) picks up the signal and starts to influence the planning process. A second comparator, sensing the movement between the needs and the plans, may alter the capability. A third comparator, noting the discrepancy between the required capability and the allocated resources, may alter that allocation. All this is shown in the top half of Figure 5.

I have discovered these mechanisms in their effects: they really do exist. With good modelling, they would make a lot of sense. But in the context of the surrogate, their action simply exacerbates every absurdity. For example: as I said before our whole industrial economy is locked onto the path of growth. It is a growth that manifestly cannot be maintained—because the resources are not there. But it *can* be maintained by illusion in the surrogate world. It follows that all the feedbacks have the wrong sign. This is how, in Britain, we have come to pour money into supersonic aircraft and to join the Common Market.

FEEDBACK WITH THE WRONG SIGN is frightening indeed. It makes aggressive managements manic, and already manic governments hypermanic. And the bureaucracies that support the surrogate world are ever more withdrawn from reality into the arcane rituals of their own esoteric boxes. You can see all this being enacted in the Board Room; you can see it in Parliaments too.

Then see also what is happening meantime in the real world, in the bottom half of the diagram. As the situation gets worse, the demands increase—because of the filters that we said comprised the press, radio and TV. The gross discrepancy is read by a comparator (again, I suspect, owned by the media) which applies an immense amplification to the public's expectations. Now the expressed demands and the inarticulate expectations begin to part company. The next comparator (still owned by the media) feeds back to increase the expressed demand.

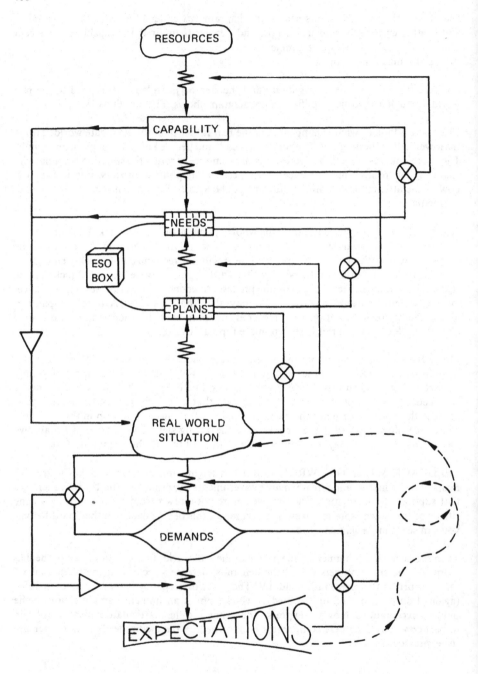

Figure 5. Surrogate and Reality with Feedback

Has any systems man ever *seen* such a diagram as this? Could there *be* a system more unstable, more explosive, more threatening? It is bound to blow up. It does blow up. I have studied it often. If there were time I would use the model to take you through the bizarre story of the Third London Airport, of which you may have heard. There can be only one outcome, so long as politicians want to win the next Election. They must eventually implement the expectations, to still the public clamour. This they do.

Please note two things. According to this analysis, the ultimate political action will have nothing to do with the facts of the situation, but with discrepancies between public demand and public expectation. That is bad. Secondly, the whole apparatus of public planning may prove to be largely irrelevant. That is bad too; particularly since it means that the surrogate world can continue to exist, with all its rituals, as if nothing had happened.

There is something else to note which I regard as deeply worrying. It would not be surprising, from a systems point of view, if—after a few circuits of the lower loop—the filters became denatured. That is, the media 'go haywire' on the issue involved. I believe I am watching this happen (in England, that is) where everything concerned with the future of this planet and of our society is involved. Now if my earlier remarks about the growth syndrome were correct, then the chances of making a proper impact on public opinion about the risks, via media which depend for their very existence on that same growth pattern, are minimal. If you think that the BBC, which is certainly unusual among the major networks of the Western world in that it carries no advertising, must be an exception to this—remember one thing. The BBC, although independent of the state as such, is very much part of the Establishment, and an esoteric box in its own right. To my mind it lives in the surrogate world.

What could be done? System-theoretically it is evident that connexions must be inserted between the lower loop realities and the upper loop surrogates. This is done in Figure 6. Given these feedbacks, needs and demands should come into balance; and so should plans and expectations. The result should be that the effects of official policy should equate to the effects of public clamour—in the real world situation itself. How these feedbacks are to find any embodiment in the systemic world outside the window is another matter. May I offer my personal views.

Commentary on this Apparatus

Firstly, it seems to mean that government has to become almost entrepreneurial. I am not talking about politics (which you may think is quite entrepreneurial enough, thank you), but about the apparatus of state. It will not be enough to issue formal government White Papers. The people do not read those. The people absorb the version that the media choose to disseminate.

Hence I come to the second point. In this epoch, we must certainly use television to reach the people. Various experiments are being held, and the Germans in particular have gone some way into the idea. You may have heard of ORAKEL, organized—appropriately—by a Systems Research group in Heidelberg, using an educational TV channel. Essentially, this set up a link between viewers in their homes and the studio, with a computer in circuit. With 3,000 phone calls during the session, this becomes a highly participative effort. I do

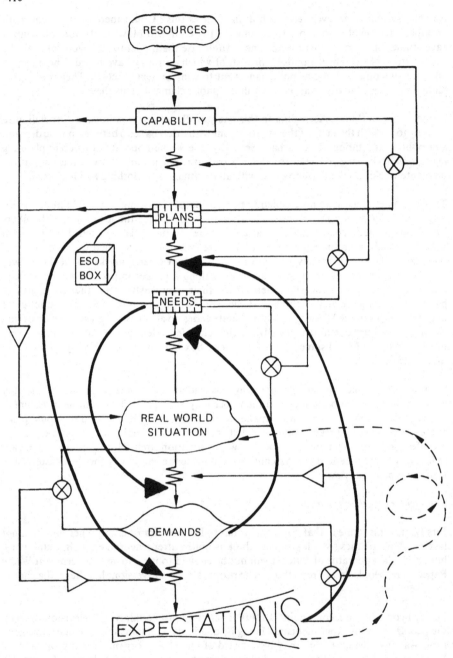

Figure 6.   Corrective Feedback

not think this sort of thing can possibly be done responsibly on a commercial network, so the next possibility is going to encounter 'Big Brother' charges and raise issues about government by plebiscite. None of this need happen. It is the surrogate world that draws up such dichotomies. I am talking about a new kind of societary self-organizing system, that we could actually have, run by the people themselves. It would be a new arm of government—and why not?

The third conclusion I draw is that the issue of political penetration into the executive arm of government and its administration needs a thoroughgoing cybernetic analysis. Assume that a party, democratically elected, really stands for change—and the abandonment of the surrogate world. In Britain, the permanent civil service is readily able to put a quick end to any such nonsense. *It* does not change: the minister is on his own. In the United States many changes are made, and the penetration is deep. Yet the surrogate world seems to hold up very well. In other countries, there are various degrees of political penetration into the government machine when a new party comes to power. Trying to understand the effects of these differences in system-theoretic terms is very difficult. We have to take out historical factors which may make the differences more apparent than real: we have to discount spurious changes which are simply 'jobs for the boys'; and we must cope with the possibility that none of the alternative governments actually *wants* to change anything. Nevertheless, the whole world of government is a laboratory for such investigation. The concern is about the rate of perturbation and the inertia of the established system—Beer's Hypothesis, with which I began. Since we can measure the rate of technological change and its diffusion, since we have various measures of societary change too, we ought to be able to provide a *measure of required metabolism* that would shift the surrogate world towards reality. I am suggesting, then, that the degree of necessary penetration is susceptible to scientific calculation.

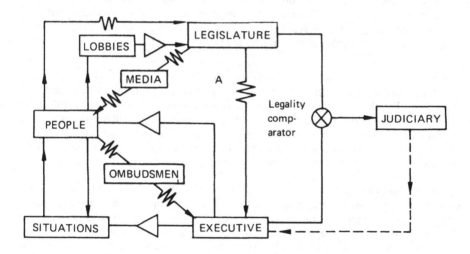

Figure 7.—Illustrating the inadequacy of contemporary democratic controls

Let us now take a look at my final diagram, Figure 7. Here we see the attenuator (A) between the legislature and the executive that I have just discussed. We see also the attenuators in the loop connecting legislature and people; the media controlling the output channel, and the pathetic hopes of men working through to their elected representatives. In parallel with that circuit, we see the powerful amplifiers of special pleading which I have labelled 'lobbies'. Next we may note the amplifiers by which the executive influences people and situations. How shall its onslaught be contained? There is the classical feedback from the judiciary, where a 'legality comparator' checks the actions of the executive against the law. And there are the new attempts, labelled 'ombudsmen', to obtain direct redress from the executive against bureaucratic excess. In this loop I include all systems of public inquiry.

It is clear that this system is very much out of balance, and how supportive of a surrogate world it truly is. For the three arms of government on the right are almost a self-contained system. Feedbacks from the people are weak and attenuated—except in terms of the lobbies, which disbalance the system further. You may or may not agree that this first shot at a model is reasonable. If it is, you will not be surprised to hear what I personally would like to see done.

(i) I would like to get rid of the attenuator A, by a *calculated* and *effective* degree of political penetration into the executive. This would mean that the democratic demand for change could not be blocked by a bureaucracy dealing in surrogates.

(ii) I would like to replace the whole top-left-hand corner of the system with an ORAKEL-type system of rapid feedback. This proposal would implement the conclusions reached as the result of the analysis in Figure 6.

(iii) I would like to replace the bureaucratic machine that drives the bottom-left-hand corner of the system with an efficient, computer-based, liberty-protecting information system operating in real time. (I have said nothing about this today, mainly because I have said so much about it before: it is on record.)

But these are just my views. I want to make a final use of Figure 7, and that is to draw attention to the system of time lags. We have to realize that in the real world the time is clock time. People are born and people die at an instant; people are constantly being people—who cannot defer falling in love or going bankrupt. The executive takes advantage of this when it suits them: 'pay NOW or go to prison—even though we have wasted three years in assessing your debt'. But the people's protection from the managers of the surrogate world is based on very different time constants.

There are three protective loops in Figure 7. The first two, the judicial and the ombudsmen loops, are heavily bureaucratic: I suppose they work in months and years while the people work in days and weeks. As to the judiciary, the use of modern technology in reforming the whole business of the law is long overdue. In the only country where I have closely studied this problem, change is totally blocked by the mechanisms I discussed at the outset—and the surrogate world is paramount. The time lag here will become longer.

The third loop (which is the highest on the left) works in several time epochs. It carries person-to-person messages between constituents and their elected representatives—the rate may be fast, but this is an exiguous channel indeed. Secondly, the loop carries the messages of the opinion polls, which may or may not be properly conducted and interpreted. But the loop goes into really effective action only at the time of an election. So the time cycle is incredibly long. Moreover, since modern projects take so long to complete, there is now a tendency for the tenure of a government and the epoch of its main effects to become precisely out of phase—and this is very confusing to the ordinary voter. Perhaps the answer lies in bicameral government: some form of this has appealed to many nations for a very long time. My point is that the reasons for it have not been subjected to systems analysis in the past, because they have not been properly understood in the total system context; and besides there may be new reasons now.

Towards some Action

In concluding, I shall try to begin answering three questions which I would like to think are now burning in all our minds. They are in mine.

The first question is: what is all this meant to apply to?

The answer is: precisely everything. I have talked about the esoteric box, which stands for any social institution, even if I have spoken mainly about national governments. But where the planetary future is concerned, the large firms, the multinational companies, *count* as governments—for this is where the Wealth of Nations increasingly resides. The gross 'national' product of General Motors is greater than the GNP of Belgium; Standard Oil's is greater than Denmark's; Chrysler's is the same as that of Greece; and Ford can account for Norway and New Zealand put together. If we map these firms onto the models offered here, we shall not find even those minimal protective loops, except where national laws impinge on business conduct. But while nations chauvinistically debate issue of liberty, by holding inquiries into privacy and the databank game, multinational companies are busy developing international metasystems supported by time sharing networks encompassing the globe. *Guess who is writing the software . . . . .*

If that is the scenario, then national sovereignty is itself a surrogate. Increasingly we should look to the United Nations to create the metasystem for individual liberty. Yet if we map the UN onto the models offered here, we find it dealing in a super-surrogate; and we find that there are no loops at all that directly connect the legislature and the people.

The second question is: what has this kind of analysis got to do with the environmental issues that confront us?

It is true that I have not mentioned ecology: I have not talked like an 'environmentalist'. Now that is very deliberate. It is easy enough to be pious, as the people who do the environmental damage are now discovering—to their delight. These are the people whose surrogate tells them that growth is essential, that resources can somehow be created out of thin air, and that we can escape the disasters—which are demonstrable all around us already in the real world—by not *having* disasters in the surrogate world. This they really do. In Britain, a speaker will characteristically denounce the 'prophets of doom', and with snide references to Malthus ('he was saying all this nearly two hundred years ago') will set his audience rocking in the aisles. Two thirds of the world is undernourished, a third of it actually starving; but in the surrogate world Malthus is a joke.

And so the trick is to become an inverted environmental snob. Carry on with your growth, your pollution, your consumption of resources; spend some money on research; and make a film to show how 'responsible' you are—a film which actually lectures the rest of us about the dangers. I am reminded of the British peer, a pioneer against racialism, who announced : 'If I sit next to a black man in the train, I always say Good Morning'.

Thus I contend that, while the use of our science to study the ecosystem is admirable and necessary, our primary task is to study the system of management by which control of the real world is not achieved. Hence this discussion of surrogates, of equilibrial systems, and of the role of the people—who are increasingly ignored in the surrogate just because they are real.

The third question is : what can we actually do?

Let me first tell you briefly what I am actually doing. I have, over twenty years, devised a model of organization for viable systems that is meant to bring the surrogate world of the esoteric box into a new correspondence with reality. (This has been published in various versions : the latest date for the definitive book is next March). I have deployed this model, with a supporting cast of general systems concepts and cybernetic techniques, in every kind of institution.

The main lesson I learned was that there are such things as strings of esoteric boxes, which need to be linked together by a *meta*system. For example, work I did on the British police force led to conclusions about its financing and pay structure which could be implemented only by invoking the same system to finance and pay nurses and teachers as well as police-men. In the surrogate world, however, there is no connexion between these three social services. Indeed, my look into the health service found no connexion between hospitals, general practice and local government health—as I implied earlier. Anyone shunted like a freight train around the health system soon discovers that it is a surrogate world, in which he—the integral human being—does not exist. His eyes exist; his ears-nose-and-throat exist; his teeth exist; and so on. But he himself is reduced to a fiction.

And so I embarked on a search for total systems. It has led to my circling the earth like a demented spaceman. I work where I am enabled to work. Maybe it does some good—but I feel very lonely and inadequate.

Where *is* everyone? That is the personal plea that comes out of the personal experience. Just how do we rally? Many would think, hearing what I have said here, that my speech represents an incursion into politics. Maybe it is. Do we want to form an international political movement? All my instincts say that science—that old generalizer—should be able to provide the systemic framework for good management that is neutral with respect to belief structures and value judgments. Maybe that is an illusion. I have been told that my own profound concern for the individual, his rights, and especially his right of choice, *is* a political judgment. I have noticed that I refuse to work in some countries, and rejoice to work in others. The decisions I take on this score are meant to be objective. I do not go to countries where I feel sure that—were I a citizen there—I should be in prison. But would I be in prison *just* for the sake of science? It seems unlikely, and the matter is very confusing. I turn over that debate to you.

What I do know is that most people do not understand—in the very least—what these issues are all about. They are not going to learn about it through 'the media'. So there is a programme of education on which it seems to me that our Society ought to embark.

You heard me disparage our existing educational system, with its 'left-luggage' version of knowledge. Maybe we can reform that system, maybe we cannot. What we certainly could do, between us, is to re-write knowledge *in terms of* system. Perhaps the time is ripe. There does, after all, come a time when the shape in which knowledge is projected alters utterly.

In this century we have seen the whole of physics rewritten. It used to be about billiard balls; it is now about probabilities. Carnot would not have defined entropy as the probability of the universe. We have seen biology rewritten. It used to be about taxonomy; it is now about dynamic organization. Darwin would not have defined evolution in terms of an epigenetic landscape. We have seen logic itself rewritten. It used to be about reduction, and the inability of the syllogism to procreate new knowledge; it is now about metamathematics. As to mathematics itself: it has been rewritten in our recent lifetime. When I was a student, it used to be about integrals with no physical correlate on the earth or the moon. It is now all about sets.

I envisage the production of a total education system that could be promulgated independently of all surrogate systems of education. It comes in two parts, each with five units.

Part the First contains a basic knowledge of the systemic universe. Its first unit deals with the concept of system. The next three units expound respectively a contemporary understanding of the physical, biological and social aspects of the world. These divisions are some concession to the way people have—erroneously—been taught to think. This makes necessary the fifth unit, which integrates the first four.

Part the Second would begin with a restatement *ab ovo* of mathematics adequate to deal with these concepts. It would be close to Spencer Brown's 'Laws of Form'. The second unit would encompass the systems approach to management, at every level (by a logical recursion) from the community to the world entire. Thirdly, we should tackle aesthetics, design and the quality of life. This unit would invent new systems for living—including a new kind of house and a new kind of city. The fourth unit would consider man's heritage, history and the classics, not with a nostalgic scholarship that clearly has a surrogate existence within the ages under discussion, but with a forward orientation that projects us onward. The fifth and final unit would put together a new philosophy, comprehensible only to students of this total work.

You will note that these ten units are not referred to as books, as TV programmes, nor as anything else. They would be *packages*, using the appropriate medium for the job. Part of the work would be to design those packages so that they were effective instruments of communication—given the technology that we already have. Another part of the work would be to devise a means of promulgating the package economically, so that anyone—irrespective of age, learning or income—could gain access to a Systems perspective on the systemic world.

This is a dream I have dreamed during my lonely peripatetic mission as a demented spaceman. Where are the collaborators? Where is the money? Would the project be just another project, or is it worth devoting our lives to? I do not know. I turn over that debate to you as well.

Meanwhile, we shall part. All of us leave here to return to our work, whatever it may be, in a real world, containing real people—as we ourselves are real. This world is crashing, and its institutions are failing. It is run through a surrogate, by surrogate men. We have new solutions, which cannot even be expressed in the surrogate language. This is the problem.

I tell you that the problem cannot be solved as most people, most parties, most governments appear to believe, by adopting any one of the solutions that each of them canvass. For these solutions, different from each other as they claim to be, have one striking feature in common. All of them are known not to work.

So what was THE ENCOUNTER all about?

It happened in the middle of 1972.

I encountered Chile.

While I was working on this book
and thinking out the political approaches
adumbrated in the last address

I received a letter
                    out of the blue.

It changed the project
and it changed my life.

The story of me-in-Chile
                    please God
is by no means over.

Nonetheless
a phase of it is done

                    and this last address
                    written at the end
                    of the third year
                    of the project
                    tells the story.

You will soon see how the whole project
PLATFORM FOR CHANGE
becomes in retrospect
a preparation
for this last instalment.

                    It surely is
                    the *last* instalment.

I will say a little more about that
when you have read the story.

COLOUR CODE : YELLOW
Narrative

THE POST—THESIS :

PRAXIS

FANFARE
for
EFFECTIVE
FREEDOM

Cybernetic Praxis
in Government

The Third Richard Goodman Memorial Lecture,* delivered at Brighton Polytechnic, Moulsecoomb, Brighton, on Wednesday, 14th February, 1973.

*By permission of
 The Trustees of the Richard Goodman Memorial Fund, Brighton Polytechnic

This is the first memorial lecture I have given for a man I knew personally—a man whom I also loved. He was a tenacious cybernetician; the pioneer of that work here in Brighton, but one whose name at least was known throughout the cybernetic world. More than this, and more importantly than this, he had a dedication to humanity. It may not be well known, but I knew, that he was as interested in the cybernetics of society as he was in the more recondite mathematics of the science. And I also know very well that he would have been captivated by the unfinished story I am telling here formally for the first time. If I could have had his advice while the project was unfolding, it might have been a better story. But I still hope that it is worthy of his memory.

In November 1970, Dr Salvador Allende became President of the Republic of Chile. In November 1971, after some letters had passed, a meeting held in London, and some homework done, I arrived in Santiago. There I first met the prepared group of a dozen men who formed the nucleus of a team which is now much larger, and with whom I am still working—for I have been commuting the 8000 miles between London and Santiago ever since. The charge was daunting indeed: *how should cybernetics be used in the exercise of national government?* You will note that the question whether cybernetics had any relevance to the problems of society and of government had already been answered affirmatively.

What was and is the situation? The answer, as I have intimately known it for these last eighteen months, is immensely complicated. Let me paint my own crude picture for you, with a rapid brush. First, more than half the total population lives an urban life in the small central region of this long, thin country—a region that perfectly balances the arid North and the wet South in a superb climate. Here the people are highly literate, and constitutionally mindled; their men are frank and friendly, their women gorgeous and gay. There is as great a spirit of freedom in the air as I have sensed anywhere in the world—and decreasingly sense in so much of it today. Yet, as you must surely know, Chile is in the middle of a Marxist revolution that has so far been constitutional, so far legal, so far bloodless.

On the land, the previous government had begun a process of agrarian reform, and that policy had general agreement. Landowners would no longer control estates larger than eighty hectares—say about 200 acres. The residual land was split up, and handed to worker's cooperatives, who have the support of government agencies. In the six years of that previous government, about 20% of the programme was implemented. But the people were impatient, especially in the South, and a deeply embedded bureaucracy slowly moves. New forms of expression were given to agrarian reform; and the programme was completed, not always in good order, in the first two years of the government of Popular Unity. This rate of change has surely contributed to the current food shortage; not so much, perhaps, because the new arrangements are inefficient in themselves, but because the remaining landowners—disrupted by these events and fearful of further change—are eating their seed corn rather than investing it in production.

In industry too, the new government's policies of nationalization and worker participation have been implemented so rapidly that the control of that process was—and remains—extremely difficult. Foreign managers of expropriated firms have mostly left the country, and the problem of finding men to take temporary charge (these are the *interventors*) was—and remains—severe. It has been exacerbated by a brain drain of native Chileans: too many qualified professionals have left the country. That they should do so was surely implicit in their upbringing and their expectations; but their problem was much aggravated by the psychological panic induced by Opposition campaigns to spread rumours of terrors to come. As to industrial investment, we should note that all the banks were nationalized, and those banks hold the internal assets of the landed classes.

Politically, the government's problems have been huge, all along. In the presidential election that put Dr Allende in power, he obtained only 36 % of the vote. The coalition he leads itself contains factions which struggle for influence between themselves. Throughout he has faced a hostile Congress and Senate, capable of blocking any government initiative by the Oppositions' majority of 60 % to 40 %. On the other hand, the government is empowered to block the majority vote of Congress—so long as its own support is at least a third. Hence the political stalemate; hence the tension of the marginal vote; hence the importance of the Congressional Election next month.

All of this is easily recognized, especially in cybernetic terms, as a grossly unstable situation. And its explosive economic tendencies were perfectly predictable when I first became involved. There had been a very large and very sudden increase in the purchasing power of the rank and file. Wages rose fast, for the land-workers in particular—who were put on the same footing as the blue collar workers. Social security benefits were much increased for everyone with young, old or incapacitated dependents. Then clearly there would be a run on stocks; clearly there would be a run on reserves. Indeed this was well understood: on my very first visit a Minister took several hours to explain the risks being run, and the political determination with which those risks were accepted as the price of rapid social progress. The question was whether the government could get a sufficient grip on the situation in time—before this inflationary time-bomb blew up in its face.

In the event it did not, and the state of the country is very precarious. It is superficial to think of this in terms of food shortages and 'housewives marches', tiresome as the food problem certainly is for the middle class. The more important fact is that Chile suffers from the effects of an economic blockade. There has been a blockade of spare parts, which has made it even harder to keep agriculture going, industry productive, transportation moving. There has been a blockade on exports, by which I refer especially to copper—which used to earn more than eighty percent of the country's foreign exchange. The attempt is being made to close world markets to Chilean copper, and the world price has fallen. Above all, there has been a blockade on foreign credit. And since Chile's natural resources will one day make it a rich country, when those resources are properly deployed, it follows that the stranglehold on credit is not a solely economic matter.

It appears to me that the government did not anticipate the full vindictiveness with which the rich world would react to its actions, which I emphasize have—so far--been perfectly legal. At any rate, a true resolution of the very potent conflicts in Chilean society is not discernible within the mounting instability, and may be long postponed. But I consider that this is largely a phenomenon of the cybernetics of international power: you could say that the Chilean people have not been given a chance. They are being systematically isolated behind those beautiful Andes mountains, and are in a state of seige. The mass media have not helped much—especially inside the country itself, where freedom of speech has been respected in very testing circumstances. Because of its ownership, this freedom is largely employed to oppose the government. Because of its prestige, the anti-government press is widely copied—embroidered even—across the world.

It says a lot for the good intentions of the government that the work I shall describe has been going on in the midst of such obvious turmoil. It wanted scientific tools to help tackle the country's problems, and it knew that their provision would take time—perhaps too long. So it may be proved. The government has so far had to work with the tools that other governments have used without success. It also wanted to work out the relationship between science and the people, and that too ought to interest us all. We have moved into an epoch in which the misuse of science has created a society that is already close to a technocracy. The very language—the dehumanized jargon—in which powerful countries talk about the wars they wage, or powerful companies talk about the people they exploit, frankly makes me vomit.

I am a scientist; but to be a technocrat would put me out of business as a man. Yet there I was, eighteen months ago, intent on creating a scientific way of governing. And here I am today, proud of the tools we have made. Why? Because I believe that cybernetics can do the job better than bureaucracy—and more humanely too. We must learn how to expunge technocracy, without rejecting science—because the proper use of science is really the world's brightest hope for stable government. Some people in Chile share that view; and they reject technocracy as strongly as do I. All of us have already been misrepresented in that respect, just as the scientific work we have done has already been misrepresented as analogous to other management control systems that have failed. Both comments miss out the cybernetics, to discuss which we are here—and a subject which, for government in general, is not at all understood.

CYBERNETICS AND FREEDOM

What is cybernetics, that a government should not understand it? It is, as Wiener (1) originally called it twenty-five years ago, 'the science of communication and control in the animal and the machine'. He was pointing, in that second phrase, to laws of complex systems that are invariant to transformations of their fabric. It does not matter whether the system be realized in the flesh or in the metal.

What is cybernetics, that government should need it? It is, as I should prefer to define it today, 'the science of effective organization'. In this definition I am pointing to laws of complex systems that are invariant not only to transformations of their fabric, but also of their *content*. It does not matter whether the system's content is neurophysiological, automotive, social or economic.

This is not to argue that all complex systems are really the same, nor yet that they are all in some way 'analogous'. It is to argue that there are fundamental rules which, disobeyed, lead to instability, or to explosion, or to a failure to learn, adapt and evolve, in *any* complex system. And those pathological states do indeed belong to all complex systems— whatever their fabric, whatever their content—not by analogy, but as a matter of fact.

With cybernetics, we seek to lift the problems of organizational structure out of the ruck of prejudice—by studying them scientifically. People wonder whether to centralize or to decentralize the economy—they are answered by dogmas. People ask whether planning is inimical to freedom—they are answered with doctrines. People demand an end to bureaucracy and muddle—they are answered with a so-called expertise which, from its record, has no effect. If dogma, doctrine and expertise fail to give effective answers, then what criterion of effectiveness shall cybernetics use? My answer to this question is : the criterion of *viability*. Whatever makes a system survival-worthy is necessary to it.

Necessary, yes, one might reply; but surely not also sufficient? The more I consider that criticism, the less I see its force. Suppose one were to say, for example (pleading necessity), that since a particular anarchic society is falling apart, a high degree of autocracy will be needed to ensure its survival. Then the critic might say: but this way lies totalitarianism and the loss of human freedom. Not so, if we adhere to our viability criterion. Because that society would be unstable also: sooner or later would come a revolution—it always does. Suppose one were to say (pleading necessity) that a particular repressive society must throw over all constraint. Then the critic might say: then you will have chaos, and no-one will be safe. But that situation would not conduce to survival either, and the pendulum would swing the other way—it always does. The point is that a truly viable system does not oscillate to those extremes, because it is under homeostatic control in every dimension that is important to its survival. Then when it comes to designing systems of government, we need to understand the cybernetic laws of homeostasis. Fortunately, and thanks mainly to Ross Ashby (2), we do understand.

Let me briefly explain. Homeostasis is the tendency of a complex system to run towards an equilibrial state. This happens because the many parts of the complex system absorb each other's capacity to disrupt the whole. Now the ultimately stable state to which a viable system may run (that state where its entropy is unity) is finally rigid—and we call that death. If the system is to remain viable, if it is not to die, then we need the extra concept of an equilibrium that is not fixed, but on the move. What causes the incipiently stable point to move is the total system's response to environmental change; and this kind of adjustment we call adaptation. The third notion that we need to understand homeostasis is the idea of a physiological limit. It is necessary for a viable system to keep moving its stable point, but it cannot afford to move it so far or so fast that the system itself is blown apart. It must keep its degree and its rate of change within a tolerance fixed by its own physiology. Revolutions, violent or not, do blow societies apart—because they deliberately take the inherited system outside its physiological limits. Then the system has to be redefined, and the new definition must again adhere to the cybernetic criteria of viability. Then it is useless for whoever has lost his privileges to complain about his bad luck, so long as he uses a language appropriate to the system that has been replaced. He must talk the new language or get out. This fact is the fact that is polarizing Chilean society now.

By the same token, a society that does not have a revolution, violent or not, inevitably goes on talking the inherited system's language, even though the rate of change has made it irrelevant to the problems which that society faces. Perhaps this fact is the fact that begins to polarize British society now.

At any rate, cybernetic analysis—I have tried to give you merely its flavour—enables us to study the problems of a particular society in terms of its viability. In general, I have only this to say about societary homeostasis in the nineteen-seventies :

- A homeostat works (and we know all the cybernetic rules) by moving its stable point in a very complicated response to the shocks it receives to its total system.

- Any homeostat takes a finite time to re-establish its new stable point. This is called the relaxation time of the system.

- Today it is typical of social institutions that the mean interval between shocks (thanks to the rate of change) is shorter than the relaxation time. That is because the institutions were originally designed to accept a much longer interval between shocks.

- From this it follows that societary institutions will either go into a state of oscillation, or plunge into that terminal equilibrium called death.

The cybernetician will expect the politician to adopt one of two basic postures in the face of these systemic troubles.

The first is to ignore the cybernetic facts, and to pretend that the oscillations are due to some kind of wickedness which can be stamped out. The second is to undertake some kind of revolution, violent or not, to redesign the faulty instruments of government. I do not have to relate the polarization throughout the entire world to which this cybernetic expectation is the key. But it seems very clear to me, as a matter of management science, that if in these typical circumstances you do not like violence, then you should quickly embark on a pacific revolution in government. If you do not, then violence you will certainly get.

Outstandingly it was Chile that embarked on this recommended course of pacific revolution. But, as I have already argued, the process has strained Chile's internal homeostatic faculties to the breaking point. Let me restate the reasons I gave before in cybernetic terms. Firstly it is because its minority government has been frustrated in fully restructuring the system according to the criteria of viability. Secondly it is because in the wider world system Chile's experiment was observed as an oscillation to be stamped out. How this will end I do not know. Meanwhile, however, we had set out to redefine the internal homeostasis.

I went to Chile armed with a model of *any* viable system, which I very well understood. It had taken twenty years to develop, in modelling, testing, and applying to all manner of organizations. The book expounding it (3) was already in the press when this story started.

One of the key ideas the general theory embodies is the principle of recursion. This says that all viable systems contain viable systems, and are contained within viable systems. Then if we have a model of *any* viable system, it must be recursive. That is to say, at whatever level of aggregation we start, then the whole model is rewritten in each element of the original model, and so on indefinitely.

If we model the state, then one element is the economic system; if we model the economic system, then one element is an industrial sector; if we model that industrial sector, then one element is a firm. The model itself is invariant. See what happens if we go on with this recursion. An element of the firm is a plant; an element of the plant is a particular shop;

an element of the shop is a section; an element of the section is a man. And the man is assuredly a viable system—as a matter of fact, the model started from the cybernetic study of man's effective neurophysiological organization in the first place.

A second key idea was that by using the viability criterion, all alone—for the reasons I gave earlier, one might succeed in identifying regions of policy in the total organizational space that represent homeostatically stable points for long term survival. I am pointing now to a possibility that it is open to mankind at last to compute a set of organizational structures that would suit the needs of actual men—as being at once themselves independent viable systems with a right of individual choice, and also members of a coherent society which in turn has a right of collective choice. Now one of the main issues identified was the issue of autonomy, or participation (these are catch words), or perhaps I mean just liberty, for whatever element within whatever viable system. Then this means that there ought to be a *computable function* setting the degree of centralization consistent with effectiveness and with freedom at every level of recursion. This I now believe. It is a bold claim. Let me try to give it verisimilitude.

Government and management control systems range over a fairly wide spectrum on the autocratic-permissive scale, and still remain viable. What is happening in cybernetic terms is that the homeostat connecting 'the boss' to the people's homeostat is either in high or low gear—while still operating within physiological limits. In an autocratic system, the people's homeostat is robbed of flexibility: in a permissive system, it is deprived of guidance and help. As long as oppression and freedom are seen *solely* as normative values, the outcome is determined by self-interest. Then we get polarization, and people will fight to the death for a prospect which is in either case ultimately not viable. But if we raise our eyes to the higher level of the total system in designing government controls, and use the viability criterion to determine the balance point, liberty must be a computable function of effectiveness for any total system *whose objectives are known*.

For example, when winning a war is the accepted objective—either for a nation or a guerrilla force—personal freedoms are acceptably sacrificed. But when a society fails to define its objectives, its consequent self-indulgence in freedom is met by a running tide of authoritarianism. And this is the explosive situation that so much of the world faces today, whatever its political colour, and at whatever level of recursion. Using the analysis I made a little earlier, the threat is that our world may not be viable much longer. Hence my plea for a cybernetic understanding of what is going on. I do not believe it has anything to do with genuine ethics: it is all about power.

Above all, the polarity between centralization and decentralization—one masquerading as oppression and the other as freedom—is a myth. Even if the homeostatic balance point turns out not to be always computable, it surely exists. The poles are two absurdities for any viable system, as our own bodies will tell us. And yet government and business continue the great debate, to the advantage only of those politicians and consultants who find the system in one state and promptly recommend a switch to the other.

These notions are central to the work I shall next describe. In Chile, I know that I am making the maximum effort towards the devolution of power. The government made their revolution about it; I find it good cybernetics. But the tools of science are not anywhere regarded as the people's tools; and people everywhere become alienated from that very science which is their own. Hence we are studying all these matters with the workers. Hence the systems I have to tell you about so far are designed for workers as well as ministers to use. Hence we are working on feedback systems to link the people to their government.

The enemy in all this is the image of exploitation that high science and the electronic computer by now represents. We are fighting that enemy and its ally technocracy. And so it must be only in Chile that you will find a famous folklore singer declaiming: 'Seize the benefits that science gives the people in their quest', and 'Let us heap all science together, before we reach the end of our tether'.

I am proud to have worked with Angel Parra on that song, which is called *Litany for a Computer and a Baby About to be Born*. Contrast that title with the headline given to the first public mention of this work, which was leaked in a British newspaper last month, and has since been copied all over the world. It said: 'Chile run by Computer'. Woe to the sub-editor who wrote that.

REAL TIME CONTROL

All that I have so far said is a very necessary preliminary to a right understanding of the economic control system I shall describe, which in any other terms would be a nightmare. But as society becomes differently understood—cybernetically restructured, politically redefined, differently lived by our children—yesterday's nightmares may become to-morrow's dreams. That is true for the whole of technological development. Without the re-structuring and the redefinition the nightmare remains, as we who live in the polluted wake of the industrial revolution ought very well to know.

The thinking begins with one very clear idea. If things are changing very fast, then govern-ment needs *instantaneous* information. If its information is out of date, then its decisions are worse than irrelevant. Please consider this point very closely.

In 1956, Mr Harold MacMillan (who was at the time Chancellor of the Exchequer) com-plained that controlling the economy was like trying to catch a train using last year's *Bradshaw* (time-table). It was true: the vital statistics of the nation were twelve months out of date. Sixteen years later, Mr Harold Wilson (at the time Immediate Past Premier and the newly elected President of the Royal Statistical Society) has recently explained that things are better, and maybe many key national statistics are now only six or eight months out of date. And of course lags of either magnitude are commonplace in government throughout the world. It will not do. This is not only because decisions taken cannot have the benefit of the latest information; there is a far more ominous reason given in cybernetics.

It is a familiar notion that economic movements operate in cycles. Then out-of-date infor-mation is not merely 'late': it is precisely incorrect—because it represents some cyclical trend that has since been superseded, but this is not recognized. If economic cycles were regular in periodicity and amplitude there would be no problem: the delay could easily be corrected. The decision-taker would discount the time-lag, and extrapolate. Indeed he tries to do this. Please look at Figure 1. By the time we discover either of the crises depicted, those crises are actually over. But we take action without knowing that, and therefore decide on exactly the wrong action each time. Now doing this actually causes instability.

To put the point in proper scientific terms: an unstable oscillation will occur at precisely the frequency for which the time-lags cause a phase shift of 180°. The negative feedback signal reinforces—instead of corrects—the original error.

It happens that the time it takes to implement a new government economic policy is of similar order to the statistical delay in acquiring facts, and so it is very possible to have the control system completely out of phase.

Lest this explanation should sound absurdly naive, let me add two reasons why the difficulty is not as perfectly obvious as I have made it appear. In the first place, neither of the lines I have drawn in Figure 1 is clear: both are fuzzy. That is, there is a tremendous amount of 'noise' present in the system—much of it deliberately injected by economic participants who stand to gain by causing this confusion. The second point is more difficult. The controller of an economic system is not a straightforward servomechanism with a known transfer function. It is itself a complex system, with its own time-lags, which are separate from the time-lags in the economy. It too may begin to oscillate; and in my experience, it does. Then there is a distinct likelihood that there will be a resonance effect between the two loops. If so, the oscillation in the controller would actually *force* a new oscillation onto the already oscillating system.

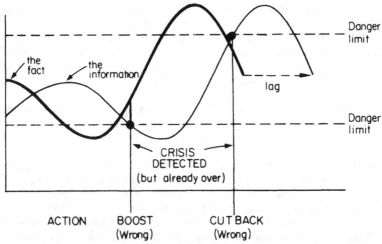

Figure 1. Underlying problem in controlling an economic variable, obscured by other mechanisms (see text).

No wonder, then, that no-one can disentangle all these effects: and no wonder that we do not perceive anything as simple as Figure 1 proposes. But in the absence of a complete explanation, there is something that we can do. Instead of solving the problem, we can *dissolve* it. Let us get rid of all the time-lags. Indeed, we ought to break with the very idea of arbitrarily quantized managerial time. Just as lags in reporting the past produce a bogus periodicity, so quite clearly do the lags fed forward in planning the future. A year's forward projection, or five-year plan, predetermine the cycle of expenditure and investment, and betray the capability of a viable system to adapt to environmental change. We cannot afford to await 'the next quinquennial review' when someone is standing on our foot.

What is the alternative to these inherited systems of lagged, quantized reporting on what has happened and lagged, quantized response to projected change? The answer from the mid-sixties onward has been and remains *real-time control*. We have the technology to do it. This concept was fundamental to the plan we drew up for Chile in late 1971. We would abandon the hare-and-tortoise race to make relevant statistics overtake the lag in data capture and analysis, and implant a real-time nervous system in the economy instead. We would forget about the bureaucratic planning systems that talk in terms of months and years, norms and targets, and implant a continuously adaptive decision-taking system in which human foresight would be permanently stretched as far in any context as this real-time input of information could take it. Above all, we would use our cybernetic understanding of filtration to deploy computers properly as quasi-intelligent machines, instead of using them as giant data-banks of dead information. That use of computers, taken on its own as it usually is, in my opinion represents the biggest waste of a magnificent invention that mankind has ever perpetrated. It is like seeking out the greatest human intellects of the day, asking them to memorize the telephone book, and then telling them to man 'Directory Enquiries' at the telephone exchange.

Having advocated all these policies for many years in Britain and elsewhere before going to Santiago, I was alert to the potential objections. I knew very well what is the standard response of economists, of managers, of civil servants, of ministers, and of 'established' science to these ideas. Let me list seven of them, and give you the answers in brief, since some (though I trust not all) of these worries may be in your minds already.

● First Objection : The boss will be overwhelmed with data.

Answer : Not so. This is what happens *now*, as any manager who has had a foot-high file of computer read-out slapped in front of him can attest. The idea is to create a capability in the computer to recognize what is *important*, and to present only that very little information—as you shall see.

● Second Objection : The management machine will over-react to such speedy signals, which may not be representative.

Answer : Not so. This also happens *now*, as shown embryonically in Figure 1. The objection disregards cybernetic knowledge of filtration, and damping servo-mechanics.

● Third Objection : Such a system would be too vulnerable to corrupt inputs.

Answer : Not so, again. Present inputs are corrupt and go undetected, because they are aggregated and because the time has passed when they could be spotted. Clever computer programs can make all sorts of checks on a real-time input to see if it is plausible.

● Fourth Objection : 'Intelligent' computer programmes to do all this are still in the science-fiction stage.

Answer : This is woolly thinking. People do not really think out what is involved, because they conceive to the computer as a fast adding machine processing a data-bank—instead of seeing in the computer, quite correctly, the logical engine that Leibniz first conceived. The computer can do anything that we can precisely specify; and that includes testing hypotheses by calculating probabilities—as again you shall see.

● Fifth Objection : Even so, such programmes would take hundreds of man-years to write and be debugged.

Answer : I am sorry, but they did not. That is because the people involved in both London and Santiago were first rate programmers who understood what they were doing. Let me be brutal about this : how many managers are aware of the research done into the relative effectiveness of programmers? They should be. The best are anything from ten to twenty times as good as the worst : and when it comes to cybernetic programming, only the *very* best can even understand what is going on.

● Sixth Objection : A real-time system with on-line inputs? It is Big Brother : it is 1984 already.

Answer : Stop panicking, and work out the notion of autonomy. I have still more so say about this later. All technology can be, and usually is, abused. When people turn their backs on the problem, crying touch-me-not, the abuse is the worse.

● Seventh Objection : Only the United States has the money and the knowledge to do this kind of thing : let them get on with it.

Answer : 'I find that slightly boring'.

Note : This objection was voiced to me in one of the highest level scientific committees in this land. The answer came from the Chairman, and I was glad not to be in his withering line of fire at the time. But he did not prevail, and neither did I.

In Chile, it took just four months to link up the key industrial centres to computers in the capital city—using a mixture of Telex lines and microwave connexions (Figure 2). Purists may well point out that this does not constitute a real-time teleprocessing network, and they will be right. However, we have used the real-time philosophy, and have *simulated* an on-line system. The programs are written for that; and if someone will kindly donate the teleprocessing equipment, it will soon be in action. (I have mentioned the problem of foreign exchange already.) Meanwhile, we have to use too many human interfaces. But I am not going to apologize much about that. The fact is that we can cope with *daily* input, and that is—relatively—very close to real-time : in normal government terms, you cannot tell the difference.

This communications network was in itself a fairly simple technological manoeuvre : but even so it constitutes a big advance for government cybernetics. During the October crisis of 1972, some of the most senior people in Chilean government came fully to understand in practice what Wiener had expounded theoretically long ago : communication is indeed control.

Well : to know *today* what was the state of the industrial economy *yesterday* is a considerable advance on knowing what it was six months or a year ago. But we were trying to do

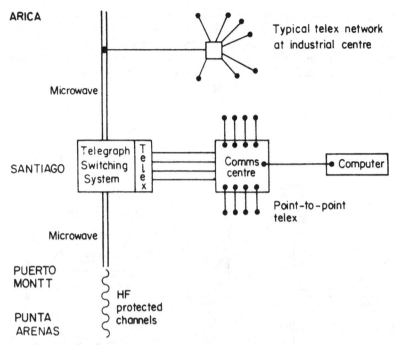

ARICA

Typical telex network
at industrial centre

Microwave

SANTIAGO

Telegraph
Switching
System

Telex

Comms
centre

Computer

Point-to-point
telex

Microwave

**PUERTO
MONTT**

**PUNTA
ARENAS**

HF
protected
channels

Figure 2. Nature of Telecommunications using existing public system. This cannot yet accept even low speed data. System uses Alphabet No. 2 at 50 Bauds.

more than merely get up to date. Frankly, there is not much point in knowing what happened even yesterday—because even yesterday is the purest history. Nothing can be done about it any longer. But if we can get hold of a close idea of what is *going* to happen next week, then we have at least a chance of doing something about that. And certainly knowing what has been happening over the last few days is the best basis for estimating what is likely to happen over the next few days. . . . .

The question is : how? One may call for data, but he has to meet the problems I listed just now (—the 'fatal' British Objections—) if he is to make effective use of them. One may know all about yesterday: but he has to be fairly ingenious to say the right things about next week. The initial four-month plan of action, which had included setting up the communications network, tackled these problems too: and it successfully defeated them.

SYSTEMS DESIGN AND VARIETY ENGINEERING

Interdisciplinary operational research teams set out to make (crude, but effective) models of all the major enterprises in the social economy. These were not to be the vast, static, historical, and essentially out of date and non-stochastic input-output matrices beloved of so many state planners. We wanted to get at the *dynamic systems* which made the enterprises tick; and we wanted them in a form that managers and ministers could immediately grasp. Therefore we used a visible and visualizable type of model, called a 'quantified flow-chart'. Start with production (a Marxist government has no illusions about the source of the creation of wealth). If we list the production operations of the firm. and their productive capability, we can make a map of production flow—in which the flow lines are proportional to the relative amounts of flow, using some convenient measure, and the operations themselves are boxes at the confluences—also shown in relative sizes according to their productive capability. Here is an example (Figure 3).

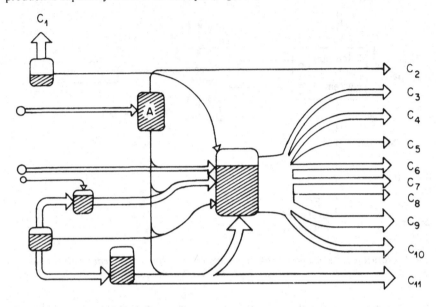

Figure 3. Quantified Flowchart: thickness of lines proportional to rate of flow; size of process boxes proportional to productive capability; productivity indicated as a level in boxes; bottleneck process highlighted at A; Customers listed C_1 to C_{11}.

Now of course if that kind of presentation can be made for the flow of production it can be made for any other kind of dynamic system in which management may be interested: cash flow. for example. or the deployment and movement of people and of goods. And although we started out on this task under the aegis of Operational Research. I am hopeful that as people become accustomed to the idea we can use a better approach. Do we really need objective. scientific enquiry to understand what the structure of the system is. and how it should best be quantified? Actually not. The people who best understand what these systems are really like are the people who operate them. You do not need a string of degrees to understand how to make a quantified flow chart of the activity that surrounds your daily life. So here I hope will be the start of 'participation' in the future: and OR expertise will be used merely in teaching and in guidance.

With this simple device we start on the road leading to the answers to those objections about overload. In cybernetics we have an actual measure of complexity. which we call variety. By devising systems in which homeostats are set up between management and whatever is managed. we embark on the process that I have labelled 'variety engineering'.

The quantified flow chart is in itself a variety-attenuating filter. In the first place, it can select its own degree of optical resolution. For example, it can show a box called simply steel production: or it can show three boxes identifying *kinds* of steel production—by open-hearth, electric arc, and converter. say: or it can show every individual furnace. By the same token, it can lump together all the materials that go into a steel-making furnace charge, or it can distinguish between them. This variety engineering concerns the account of the operation that has meaning for a particular management group, and the degree of optical resolution chosen depends on the level of recursion at which this operation is being considered. In the second place, iconic representation is also a variety attenuator in the suppression of words and numerical data : it is a product of gestalt psychology, in which pattern is relied upon to convey information.

The next variety attenuator involved in this representation is the concept of *capability*. The real-time variation in actual flows and outputs is killed in the iconic quantified flow chart, and referred instead to a relatively static idea of 'what can be done'. You might think that this would be difficult to define, but in practice it is fairly easy. Capability is a systems concept : what outputs is the total system capable of generating in each part, given the limitations imposed on any part of the system by other parts? Then 'capability' is not to be confused with 'capacity', which is not a systems concept—because it alleges that some part of the system can in theory do something that may be rendered impossible by other parts. This variety attenuator is valuable because it reflects reality for the whole system concerned, and that has meaning for the recipient of the iconic representation.

However, we could—given a breakthrough of some kind—do better than the results of which we are currently capable. After all : if capacity exceeds capability in some parts of the system, there must be other parts of the system (called bottlenecks) that are actively restricting capability. These bottlenecks may have to do with low local capacities, or they may have to do with technological constraints. For example : a mill's engine might be perfectly adequate to drive its rolls at twice their current speed—if only we had a better lubricant. Then these considerations define potentiality, which is something better than capability. Potentiality is the performance of which the system would be capable, 'if only.....'. That does not mean that we look for pie in the sky : it means that we look for investment—in new equipment, to cure the bottlenecks, or in research to cure technological shortcomings. It is not very difficult, keeping one's feet firmly on the ground, to define a system's potentiality.

But if potentiality is better than capability, there is something worse—and that is actuality. The performance of systems cannot rise to their potentiality without investment of some kind; it cannot even rise to their capability unless activity is perfectly well organized. It never is. In consequence, what actually happens falls short of the capability expressed before. Moreover, actuality expresses that very reality of which I spoke earlier—the day-to-day viscissitudes of life. It was this continuous variation which drove our thinking down the road to real-time control. Somehow we have ended up with three versions of systemic truth: actuality, continuously fluctuating: capability, a much steadier variable: potentiality, which is absolute until the system itself is structually changed. And it is capability which the iconic representations represent. To make them show potentiality would, for the moment, be unrealistic: to make them show actuality would, at all times, result in their dancing in perpetual fandango before our eyes. So this capability attenuator is a powerful but sensible reducer of operational variety.

436

So be it. in so far as iconic flow charts are concerned. But what about continuous reporting. and the problems of real-time control? Whatever information we collect, it is due to be hurled round dozens of homeostatic loops—those loops that make up the total systems design. That information has very high variety; and the analysis we have just made multiplies it by a factor of three—or so it seems. if we want a measure not only of actuality, but of capability and potentiality as well. . . . . But rescue is in sight. Both capability and potentiality are relatively static measures. If we take their ratio. the resulting index will also be relatively static. Moreover. such a ratio will be a massive variety attenuator—because it will be a pure number. varying between nought and one. So instead of trying to consider, all-in-one-breath, that we have a capability of 800,000 tons and a potentiality of 1,000,000 tons. we shall think of a ratio of 0.8; while the capability to use 110 men contrasted with a potentiality to use only 22 yields a ratio of 0.2; and the capability cost of an item of product at 120 escudos compared with a potential cost of 60 escudos indicates a ratio of 0.5. Well what is potential in current capability is a latent resource; and it could be freed by investment in some form. So I call the ratio between capability and potentiality the Latency Index. Looking at a new iconic diagram (Figure 4. we can see how potent a variety attenuator has been devised.

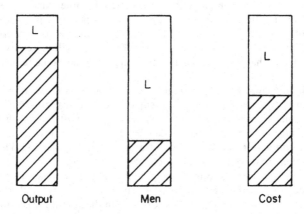

Figure 4. *Iconic representation of relative Latencies* (*see text*).

There is no need any longer to try and assimilate the numbers that characterize the units measured. That is the strength of an index—it is a pure number. varying over a fixed range. Hundreds of thousands of tons; hundreds and tens of men; units of money; there is no need to wrestle with them. Nor. if we stick to our ideas about iconic diagrams is there any real need to use digits at all. We can distinguish very clearly. using our eyes. between the levels represented in the iconic diagram. It might satisfy an accountant. but it would make no difference to a manager. to declare that a Latency Index had changed from 0.71 to 0.73. Who cares? The computers behind the manager's eyes will undertake whatever process of discrimination has meaning for his judgmental brain. Then this was the first though massive piece of variety engineering we set out to achieve in Chile. on those initial (crude. but effective) models. contrived at an appropriate level of optical resolution. of all the firms. As I said. the Latency Index is all about investment. and we shall certainly return to it later.

Meanwhile we must consider actuality, the real-time variable in the entire system. For if a Latency difference between 0.71 and 0.73 means nothing, because both potentiality and capability are fairly static, such a difference in a fast-moving index could mean something very important. It might be part of a trend. I have already explained the arrangements by which the data representing actuality come into Santiago every day. They are used to form a second ratio, comparing actuality (the newly arrived figure) with capability (selected from the computer store). This is the Productivity Index. It is in a continual state of oscillation, which destroys the variety that is of no concern. In the next diagram (Figure 5), we can see how the three concepts of actuality, capability and potentiality are combined as two ratios to form the Latency and Productivity Indices, and how these in turn create an overall Performance Index. The reason for this iconic representation, in place of the familiar mathematical notation, lies in the fact that which part of the ratio is the numerator and which the denominator depends on what is being measured. For instance, capability is always *better* than actuality, but in numerical terms it may be more (e.g. output) or less (e.g. manhours per unit). Naturally enough, the smaller number in the ratio is the numerator, since the index will be less than 1.0.

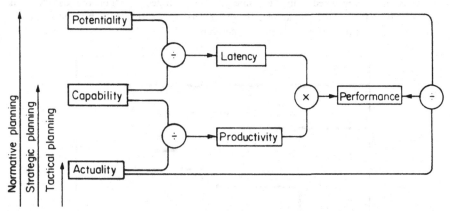

Figure 5. Three measures of capacity defining three indices of achievement and three concepts of planning.

The indices procure an enormous variety reduction; even so, we still have problems in conforming to Ashby's Law of Requisite Variety when it comes to managing the economy. The company production models for instance generate on average about ten triple-indices per plant; these always include raw material and finished stocks, the output of key production processes, and labour absenteeism. This degree of resolution is minimal, and managements have free rein to install whatever extra indicators they like. This honours the argument for autonomy, and it makes an insignificant difference to the work load of the computers, because all the numbers inside the computational system are diurnal time series of indices varying between nought and one. The programmes are therefore infinitely extensible in application. Even so, with the system in full operation, many thousands of actuality inputs will arrive daily, generating three times as many indices; and the total number could easily rise by two orders of magnitude as the autonomy criterion is understood by managements, the operational research goes deeper, and worker participation becomes real. And so we reach the more subtle notions of variety engineering.

If a particular indicator, say the rate of crushing limestone in a cement factory in Northern Chile, is generating a new Productivity Index every day, what ought to be done with it? Should be lay the new figure, each day, on the desk of the Minister of Economics? Surely not. This variety must also be filtered. There are two statistical notions involved, and the first is very simple. A population of (say) a hundred such figures generates a probability distribution. This may turn out to be oddly-shaped, rather than straightforwardly Gaussian; and especially it may be skewed to the right (since the index has a finite limit of one). It is a simple matter, however, to correct for this statistical aberration, by using a trigonometrical transformation. Then we may establish the mean and variance of this population of indices. These two statistics, all alone, characterize the stochastic behaviour of each index over time. Then if we take a running sample of the indexical figures as they are computed, it is easy to establish whether a significant change in the mean or variance of the statistical population has occurred. The statistical population characterizing each indicator is known as the taxonomic index, because it classifies every measured activity within every operation according to its mean productivity. There is a standard computer programme that looks for changes in the taxonomic index; if such a change is found, that is notified to the management concerned, and the iconic graph is changed. Further, the history of the index over time is updated (Figure 6). These are relatively rare events, but the procedure mentioned absorbs the variety engendered perfectly well.

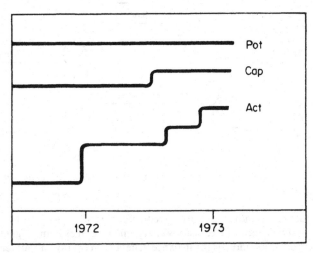

Figure 6. *Iconic record of significant (therefore taxonomic) change.*

BREAKING THE TIME BARRIER: CYBERSTRIDE

The more difficult problem, and the more sophisticated statistical notion, concerns the possible trend that each new daily figure may betray. If the economy is to be under real-time control, the government cannot wait to know that a significant change has been registered for a particular taxonomic index—although this is already much to be preferred to the orthodox system of routinely quantizing statistics, where the recognition of significant change is left first to the alertness and next to the judgment of whoever is supposed to be watching the results. No, it is much more than this: we approach the problem of breaking the time barrier. Can we tell from yesterday's figure. and the short-term run in which it participates. what will happen (unless we intervene) tomorrow and next week? It is the problem of short-term forecasting. with which a great deal of progress has been made in recent years.

Allow me once more to return to the facts of the Chilean work. Before the end of 1971 I had designed a specification for the computer programme to deal with taxonomic indices having daily actuality inputs. and it was in the hands of a team of operational research consultants in London, who had been commissioned to write the programs. We were discussing the short-term forecasting problem. when the London team discovered a brand new paper in the *Operational Research Quarterly*—hot off the press. The authors were Harrison and Stevens and they had clearly made a major advance in the field of short-term forecasting (4). We had been talking in terms of Cusum (cumulative sum) techniques to this point. as representing the best available practice. Cusum itself was associated with the first author. who had been pressing its virtues for many years. so we were naturally impressed that this novel development came from him. The obvious power of the method (always supposing it worked). and the elegance of the mathematical demonstration behind the approach. convinced us to take the plunge. It was a noteworthy decision. The London team wrote a temporary suite of programs which included the Harrison–Stevens approach and incredibly had it working in Santiago by the March 1972 deadline of the first phase of the operation mentioned already. Meanwhile they began work on the permanent version. creating a specification that was handed over to the Chilean scientists. In the meantime. as the system was growing. experience was gained in the actual use of these very complicated program suites, and they grew in sophistication all the time. But these new developments. vitally important though they are. must await presentation by the men who made them possible in more technical papers than this.

This suite of computer programs. called CYBERSTRIDE. is the essential feature of the filtration system that achieves the variety attenuation demanded. and which breaks the time barrier of which I was speaking. It takes as input the actuality figures every day: it makes various checks on their integrity: it computes the triple-indices: it makes statistical judgments about the taxonomic indices as I have already described. After that. using the Harrison–Stevens techniques. it really gets clever.

When a new value for any index is computed. Cyberstride looks at it in the context of the recent history of that index (Figure 7). The new point might stand for any one of the four outcomes depicted. It stands for no change. or for a transient (neither of which matters to the manager): or it stands for a change of slope. or for a step function. (both of which possibilities matter very much). Using Bayesian statistical theory. the program calculates the posterior probability of each of these four events—for every index. every day. The programme is incredibly sensitive to these changes. recognizing them long before the human brain would dare to make a judgment. Cybernetically speaking. the system (as Harrison and Stevens claimed) is self-adaptive: its sensitivity increases whenever uncertainty increases—which happens whenever an apparently unusual index value is thrown up. Moreover. instead of producing merely single-figure forecasts (and who can foretell the future with that kind of precision?) it produces a joint parameter distribution that expresses the inherent uncertainty of all forecasting.

440

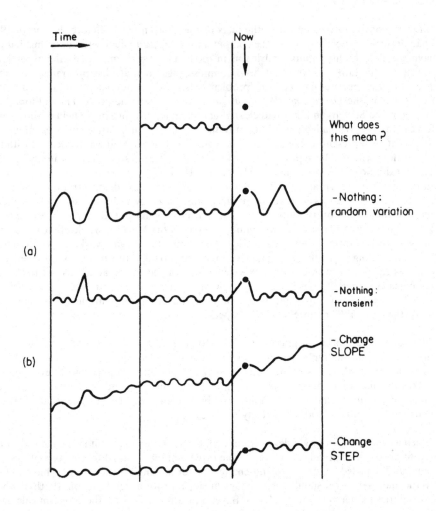

Figure 7. *Using the computer intelligently to calculate probabilities of future alternatives.*

So this is what I meant in speaking of computers as quasi-intelligent machines. Cyberstride throws away the huge component of variety that has no meaning, because it represents a chance fluctuation. It is at once alert to significant changes, focussing on them an analytical eye, and capable of estimating on the strength of that analysis what will happen next. The only problem we had with Cyberstride, and it was very severe, was its calibration in terms of these posterior probabilities: how sensitive should it be made? Obviously, it could discard too much, or become overexcited about too little. The 'tuning' subroutine that fixes these limits of excitation, so analogous to the so-called physiological limits of variation in any homeostat, was the big achievement of the Chilean scientists working on Cyberstride.

The variety engineering is complete—for the lowest level of recursion, the enterprise itself. If it would have been ludicrous to confront the Minister of Economics with the whole variety of fluctuating indices, it would still be absurd to inform him of even highly significant movements in the limestone-crushing activity of a cement plant in Northern Chile. Absurd, yes; but also ominous. I am sure you recall the argument about autonomy and overcentralization. What happens in Chile is this. The results of applying Cyberstride daily to the new inputs which quantify the iconic flowcharts are fed straight back to the managements concerned. It is their responsibility to do something about the warnings that are generated in this way by quasi-intelligent machines. No other human being than the responsible manager receives any information about this extremely elaborate piece of computation, and I attach very weighty importance to this fact.

Then, you will ask, what about the other levels of recursion? The manager of the enterprise is very well served by all of this, especially so, since he can pump any indexical series he cares to contemplate into the routine—and receive the alerting advice, whenever it is available; meanwhile he may feel perfectly confident that an absence of alerting advice means that whatever operations or activities are being monitored for him by Cyberstride are fluctuating within the physiological range of chance variation. But what about the Sector Committee, the Industrial Branch, the Minister of Economics himself? These are higher levels of recursion: how are they to be informed?

Here is the coup de grace of the cybernetician, in his role as variety engineer. *All viable systems are contained within viable systems.* It is the principle of recursion; the model is the same. So it is easy to see what next to do. The iconic representations, called quantified flowcharts, are to be aggregated at sector level, aggregated again at the industrial branch level, and aggregated finally at the level of total Industry. The quantifiers (those actualities, capabilities, and potentialities) are to be aggregated too—not, as is orthodox practice, in terms of averages, but in terms of new operational research models (crude, but effective) of the level of recursion concerned. In that case, raw data—heavily processed through atomic indices and through Cyberstride, which produces exceptions known only to the manager concerned—bypass that atomic level of recursion, and become raw material for a molecular level of aggregation higher up. Here they lose their identity; they merge (not by averaging but by modelling) into new molecular indices.

But these new indices, although they have lost a great deal of variety in the process of molecular aggregation, have acquired variety by the sheer amalgamation of so many enterprises. How shall we deal requisitely with this new variety? Well, it is repesented by triple-indices, all operating between nought and one. So although the level of recursion changes. and although the atomic index changes to a molecular index. the Cyberstride suite of programs is invariant. The whole process I have described starts again. This time and again. exceptional information is fed back to its proper level of recursion : the sector. or the branch. or the minister.

Return with me now. for the last time. to the vexed issue of autonomy. I regard the whole of this work as a fanfare for freedom—but for *effective* freedom. The claim was made that the degree of autonomy. and its complement the degree of centralization. are computable functions of viability. I stick to that. By separating the levels of recursion. and within those levels by preserving freedom for each separately designed interlocking homeostat. the maximum autonomy consistent with effective organization is assured. A problem remains. What happens when. for whatever reason. the appropriate homeostat at the appropriate level of recursion FAILS TO ACT?

Many a freedom must have been lost from the fear of those in power that subservient systems down the line would not do their jobs. And. if not. it makes a good excuse for the tyrant. This is a classic and intransigent problem. but we can now deal with it easily—if we keep our cybernetic heads. An autonomous unit is supposed to react to any adverse exception reports that it receives from Cyberstride. How long will that take. and how much does it matter? The answer to both questions will vary widely. In our work we have included in the operational research modelling a requirement to assess the possible rate of reaction to change. and the relative importance to the system modelled of such a change. for every indicator. When the computer sends an exception report to a manager. at whatever level of recursion. it computes for the message an acceptable delay time which is a function of both the possible reaction time and the importance. and it starts a clock. If our quasi-intelligent machine fails to detect an improvement within this allotted time. it breaks with the autonomy and notifies the next level of recursion (as well as telling the responsible manager that it has done so).

These special signals are different in kind from the routine management signals. We call then 'algedonic'. The word means pain-and-pleasure: and it was work in neurocybernetics that taught me this answer. We rely on our bodily organs to do their jobs: but if they should fail. we get a special signal—transmitted by specially adapted neural pathways—that bring the facts to our conscious attention. The mechanism is precautionary. Clearly it involves a threat to autonomy. but the body politic cannot sustain the risk of autonomic inaction any more than we can as human beings. And remember that there is nothing covert about this. The delay factors are discussed with the managers concerned. and they are informed if the algedonic signal is transmitted. Indeed. they may be very relieved—if the problem is seen as beyond their control—to know that the signal has automatically gone.

In this way. just as in the body. a sign of special distress automatically breaks through to whatever level is required to deal with it (Figure 8). For if the management group which receives the signal fails to act within *its* appropriate time delay. the signal will go up to the level next above. Thus the signal makes it possible for a problem concerning that limestone crusher in the cement factory to reach the President's Economic Council. Let us hope that never happens: but it would be surprising if signals of distress were never received there from the Sector level.

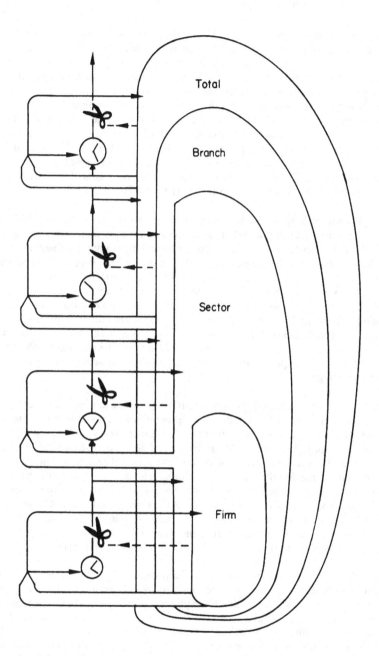

Figure 8. Cyberstride operating at four autonomous levels of recursion, with algedonic feedback (see text).

THE FACULTY OF FORESIGHT

The real-time control system I have so briefly described is founded on the following elements: a cybernetic model of any viable system; a cybernetic analysis of the real-life systems appropriate to each level of recursion, and their iconic representation; a design of a large number of interlocking homeostats; the provision of a national communications network capable of operating now on a daily basis and eventually on the basis of continuous input; variety engineering throughout the system to incorporate filtration on the human brain's scale; and the Cyberstride computer program suite capable of monitoring inputs, indexical calculations, taxonomic regulation, short-term forecasting by Bayesian probability theory, autonomic exception reporting, and algedonic feedback. It makes quite a package, and it exists. It represents a system of here-and-now management of the economy that is not based on historical records, but on an immediate awareness of the state of affairs and the *projection* of that awareness into the short-term future.

Let us call this whole thing the NOW system. Then clearly we also need the FUTURES system. What are we doing all this for? If government is not to be merely the management of perpetual crisis, it needs to look ahead. Party-political programmes are supposed to be all about the kind of society the people want, and the government is supposed to be dedicated to achieving that. In practice, perpetual crisis drives out mandated intentions. It even happens (dare I say?) that entire sets of electoral policies become reversed when power is granted. This can be only because government has no arrangements for realistic normative planning. It has a political theory, but it does not understand the system it is manipulating. It is just laughable to say, for example: 'the theory is all right, but the trade unions (or the City, or the banks, or the people themselves) will not operate the theory'. The unions, the City, the banks and the people are all elements of the total system that the government claims to be able to govern.

Thus I introduce what I have to say about long-range planning in terms of understanding systems and how they respond; and I do so in deliberate contrast to the many schools of thought that base their conception of inventing the future simply on forecasting it. My objection to that approach is twofold. In the first place I do not believe that we *can* forecast the future—and that is a fairly strong objection. The future, I reckon, is known only to God; and it seems to me that the class of men who have always come nearest to perceiving his intentions are the science fiction writers. They have usually been very close to scientific reality. The people who run society, who are famous for being 'realistic' and 'responsible', turn out to be outrageously irresponsible just because they are so unrealistic. Their unrealism consists in a refusal to notice what science is actually doing, and a refusal to think through the inevitable *systemic* consequences of the policies they underwrite.

These were the reasons why I was determined to provide the Chilean government with an instrument for investigating the systemic consequences of alternative courses of action. For there really are *choices* to be made. When you read that car prices in Chile have gone up by 900% in a single year, what is your response? Is this the inevitable result of Marxist dogma, is it just what you expect from nationalization, is it a measure of inflation, or what? To whom does it occur that it may be the result of a deliberate *choice* between economic desiderata? Thus are we all brainwashed by the consumer society, in which the motor car is an absolute god.

The second reason why I object to the forecasting approach to long-range planning is that it assumes that there is 'a future' out there, lying in wait for us. This is not true, surely, except in so far as larger systems beyond our own—and in which we acquiesce—take a stranglehold on us. I have already suggested that this may doom the Chilean experiment. The real freedom we have is to change our structures and our policies so that the future is different from the future we should have encountered had we not made those changes. And this is where understanding dynamic systems becomes the task. The fact is that we need not to forecast but to experiment.

Experimentation is not easily or perhaps justifiably done when we are talking of social institutions. Scientists undertake social experiments on animal populations, which they try to use as models of human populations—but the discrepancies may be very wide. Probably the best experimental tool available is the computer simulation. According to this approach, one programmes a computer to represent the dynamic social situation, and then experiments on that. If one asks how such a model could possibly be validated—he learns that the model can be fed with historic data—on the basis of which it ought to simulate the appropriate historic outcome. That is at least a start in a demonstration of validity.

I introduce the topic of dynamic systems simulation in this way, calling it an experimental tool, because I consider there to be a great deal of misunderstanding on the subject. If we experiment on a model, putting in possible policies and reading off possible outcomes, then of course we appear to be making predictions. Some people have been causing a great deal of public disquiet with some such predictions about the ecosystemic future of the planet. Personally, I do not mind their doing so—because I believe the public ought to be thoroughly disquieted on this score. But we must make methodological distinctions here. In so far as these models make predictions, it is vital that projections of the input variables be correctly made. There is the rub because specialists disagree quite fundamentally about the trends that have been built into some of those models. Clearly, if it is taken as input that fossil fuel will run out by a certain date, then predictions for the ecosystem incorporating this input will be falsified if that date turns out to be wrong. But suppose our objective is not to make predictions, but to make experiments to find out how the ecosystem works. That is a different matter. We should put in a whole range of possible dates for the exhaustion of fossil fuel, and find out what difference they made to total performance and by when. After that, we should have a good idea what policy to adopt towards research into novel sources of energy. And that policy would not be the fruit of predictions that might well be falsified; it would be the embodiment of our understanding as to where the system's vulnerability lies.

My belief is that government planning should be based on this same idea. If we make a dynamic model of the economy, concentrating our power of resolution on the areas in which our decisions appear most unsure or most frightening, then we shall learn how the system operates. The first task is to identify the crucial parameters, which (because complex systems are richly interactive and internally reverberating) are not always the parameters assumed to be critical. It is quite characteristic of cybernetic studies to obtain results that are counter-intuitive. Therein lies their value. The next task is to discover how those parameters may best be manipulated, which (because political dealing is a complicated business too) may be in roundabout ways rather than by direct intervention.

What matters about a dynamic system. if you want to understand how it behaves, is not so much noticing the sore points themselves, nor resolving the apparently insoluble politics of applying remedies to those sore points—all of which turn out to be unacceptable remedies for some segment of the population. What matters is to change the structure of the system. so that homeostatic equilibrium is restored and the sore points disappear. That involves variety engineering: it is likely to mean the redesign of institutions, the addition of informational feedbacks, and the calculated change of time-lags in various rates of flow. Economists, perhaps. would not recognize those three cybernetic prescriptions as counting towards the solution of what are regarded as economic problems. But are *all* our problems economic? I think there is a prior set of problems about the regulation of society (which it falls to governments to solve), which may well have economic causes and consequences. but which are themselves about effective organization.

Returning to the Chilean story. then. we wanted to create a facility for normative planning. suitable for all levels of recursion, embodying dynamic system simulation. Now the task of inventing a fresh computer compiler for this purpose was outside our time-scale. A number of compilers exists, and we chose to use the Dynamo compiler in its latest version (5). The choice was made on the grounds of its elegance and its relatively long existence— meaning that it is very well debugged. The choice has been criticized. and will be again; because this is the very compiler used in the work that I referred to as making predictions about the planet using inputs that many ecologists regard as insecure. To me. that is like blaming the pornographic content of a book on the English language in which it is written. My defence of the compiler says nothing about my concurrence or otherwise with ecological predictions, any more than hearing my defence of English would tell you my views on pornography.

For the record. then. we again formed two teams—one in Santiago. and the other in London. These teams were organized differently from the two Cyberstride teams. and had no members in common; and this simulations pair operated in a different way. Instead of members of the London team taking program suites out to Santiago to be developed. as happened with Cyberstride. a member of the Chilean team came to London to learn a cybernetic skill. Moreover. whereas all the Cyberstride runs using actual data were undertaken on the Santiago computers. the simulation runs for a long time were undertaken on computers in London. In this way dynamic systems models for the Chilean futures system were originally developed. but by now the whole of the work is being done in Santiago.

There is much that is new about these models. but for obvious reasons I shall not discuss their content. What is worth remarking upon is the status of the information fed into them. As I said just now, models of this type are often criticized on the grounds that their inputs are suspect. Now this is not surprising; because. as I also said before. economic information at the national level is usually about a year out of date. But Cyberstride produces information that is *immediate*. Then there is a question about the interface between the real-time control system and the futures system. If absolutely current information can be used continuously to update our models of the world, a new era dawns in national planning. Well.....at any rate it happens just like that in the brain. We should indeed be foolish to choose between the alternatives open to us as men on the strength of knowing what our circumstances were like last year.

A DECISION MACHINE: THE OPSROOM

And now we reach the final question. How do we 'get it all together'. How is so much sophisticated science to be made available to those who bear the brunt? In most countries, this is a function for the civil service. Those people constitute the ultimate filter. The ministerial briefing stands, however responsibly, between the minister and all those urgent facts of the NOW system, all those experiments in foresight of the FUTURES system.

I wanted ministers to have a direct experience, an immediate experience, an experimental experience. And what goes for ministers goes also, at another level of recursion, for managers — whether the managers of the social economy, or (at yet other levels of recursion) of enterprises or of plants. Above all, if 'participation' has any meaning, no-one must be disbarred because of an inadequate grasp of jargon, of figurework, of high-level rituals. As I told you before, the workers themselves must have access to the whole of this. Let me put the point before you in two contrasting ways.

When I first expounded the cybernetic model of any viable system (which I have not expounded today) to President Allende, I did so on a piece of paper lying between us on the table. I drew for him the entire apparatus of interlocking homeostats, in terms of the neurophysiological version of the model—since he is by profession a medical man. It consists of a five-tier hierarchy of systems. I worked up through the first, second, third and fourth levels. When I got to the fifth, I drew an histrionic breath—all ready to say: 'And *this*, compañero presidente, is *you*'. He forestalled me. 'Ah', he said, with a broad smile, as I drew the topmost box: 'at last—the people'.

I do not care what political outlook any of us may have: that story ought to convey a profound message. It deeply affected me, and it affects this work. The second perception of the same point that I give you comes from that *Litany* written by the folklore singer Angel Parra, which I quoted at the outset. This is what his song says on the subject (my translation):

> *Equal* I say to the Minister
> Selling promises forlorn
> Since all of us are hostage
> For that baby to be born.

Society can no more afford the alienation of the people from the processes of government than it can afford their alienation from science.

And is this really a political question any more, once we say that all of us are men? The fact is that no man, worker or minister, has more neurological jellyware than anyone else— although he may make marginally better use of his endowment. We have seen how that man, minister or worker, can be saved from drowning in a inundation of statistics and reports—through variety engineering, and the deployment of computers as quasi-intelligent machines. But how does the filtered information get into his head?

The answer to this lies in the *operations room*. If the connotation of that phrase reminds some people of a wartime headquarters, the allusion is quite deliberate. For in the opsroom real-time information is laid out, quite graphically, for immediate decision; and in the opsroom a synoptic view of the whole battle is made plain, so that the total system can be encompassed by human powers of foresight. We used every scrap of relevant scientific knowledge in designing the place—neurocybernetic knowledge of brain processes, knowledge from applied and group psychology, knowledge from ergonomics.

The opsroom looks like a film set for a futuristic film. But it is not science fiction; it is science fact. It exists, and it works; it exists and it works for the worker as well as the minister. [Photographs of this opsroom are reproduced as a plate section at the back of the dust jacket of this book.] There are seven chairs in there, because seven is the maximum creative group. There are various screens in there, all using iconic representations of information, because those are the sort the human brain can best handle.

The central screen—central in that all the others are referred to it—is a picture of the viable system (Photograph 3). It is eight feet high and four feet wide, and it is set up according to the recursion theorem, for whatever group happens to be using the room. The operations involved are marked in the circles: the current molecular indexical levels for the taxonomic triple-index in each element are shown by iconic descriptions in the square boxes. The total square in each case stands for potentiality; then the green level is actuality, and the red level is capability. You can see how easy it is, if you remember the explanation about their ratios, to get an immediate grasp of the relative levels of Productivity and Latency in each case.

There are a great many interlocking homeostats operating here, which can be discussed as people come to understand the cybernetic laws that govern their behaviour. This is not readily understood from a still photograph, and in fact this screen is animated. There are no arrows to be seen, therefore: just moving lines. Scientists often suppose that to mark a line with an arrow makes it clear that the total system so encumbered with arrows is actually dynamic. Not so: people read the arrows as indicating directional, but still static relationships. Besides, the most critical loops here operate at differential speeds (they can be changed)—which tells the brain a great deal about the relative lags in the system.

In the top third of the diagram, three boxes may be noted. The lower of these controls the NOW system, and the central one controls the FUTURES system. The top box (the boss or 'the people'?) monitors their interaction, to which attention is drawn in the animation by a constant movement in the big yellow circle.

The Cyberstride exception reports flow on the horizontal red lines; and when they exist an Exception Screen is lit, giving details. An algedonic signal is indicated by flashing red arrows on the vertical axis (in the photograph, such a signal may be seen emanating from the middle element); and any algedonic activity lights the Algedonic Screen.

Shown in Photograph 4 are the two screens I have just mentioned. On the left is the Exception Screen, showing two alerting signals from Cyberstride, together with a first indication of the kind of warning coming through. On the right is the Algedonic Screen, showing signals from two different levels of recursion below—each marked by a red light flashing at a different speed. As I said, attention veers to these two real-time inputs because of the clues given on the main screen first described. Obviously both these screens are currently set up by hand, whereas they could be set by direct electronic output from the computer. But I would like to repeat that this is simply an annoyance due to component shortages; it does not represent a gap in the total cybernetic system.

This, then, is the real-time input to the opsroom—its sensing devices spreading out over three thousand miles of country, and its quasi-intelligent filtration continuously reducing an immense informational variety to human proportions. Then what will our seven-man team of creative thinkers want to do next? For make no mistake: the opsroom is a decision machine, in which men and equipment act in symbiotic relationship to amplify their respective powers in one new synergy of enhanced intelligence. They have to start talking and deciding on their actions. For this purpose, they will need background information; and I need hardly explain that there are no files, libraries of reports, or minutes of the last meeting *here*. Paper is banned from this place. The answer is Datafeed. (Photograph 5).

It consists of three data screens, as you can see, and a huge index screen. Each of the data screens in supported by five carousel projectors, each carrying eighty slides of iconic information. So we can choose three out of twelve-hundred presentations—one out of four-hundred on each screen. But it is obvious that twelve-hundred slides cannot be listed on the index screen above, however huge. How shall we get at our treasure-trove of supportive information? It is again a problem in variety engineering: select three from twelve-hundred. Of course, one could have a catalogue, and a decimal keyboard. That would have requisite variety. However, experience teaches that unskilled people will not usually agree to operate such devices. They see them as calling for a typing skill, and want to insinuate a girl between themselves and the machinery. Indeed, this fact has held up the development of on-line conversational computing very seriously indeed. We are faced with an ergonomic problem. It is vital that the occupants interact directly with the machine, and with each other.

In a creative conversation, men become very animated. They seize pieces of paper, and draw on them; they snatch the pencil, and change the drawing: 'no, no, it is like *that*'. The solution to the ergonomic problem takes note of all these things. We produced special chairs which swivel through 270 degrees of arc, in the arms of which are mounted panels containing large knobs of different shapes (clearly visible in Photograph 1). By thumping one of the three knobs in the top row, a screen is selected—and an index automatically appears on the control screen. The index is catalogued by the use of five symbols, which are repeated in the second row of knobs. By pressing the appropriate combination of knobs, the item selected from the first index appears on the control screen, in the form of a second index which lists the actual slides. So a second combination procures the required presentation.

The variety engineering says: there are $2^5 = 32$ ways of combining five knobs; and if that is done twice, $2^{10} = 32 \times 32 = 1024$ alternatives are made available. That is enough selection power to handle 400 slides on each screen, with plenty to spare for control engineering purposes. (Four buttons would yield only $2^8 = 256$ alternatives.) One of the two knobs in the bottom row allows one man out of the seven to seize control of Datafeed with a thump, and the other releases the control when he says '*thump*—that's what I mean'. There is no finicky skill involved in working this apparatus—and people seem to take to it very quickly indeed. As to all that thumping: I wanted to make the dramatic act of using the equipment an effective part of the creative conversation, just like seizing the pencil, or banging the table.

Thus it is that when real-time inputs indicate the need for supportive information, the decision-takers may select on the three screens (for example, as in Photograph 5) the iconic flowchart that contains the relevant input, a photograph of the plant concerned, and some indexical information. If an expansion or explanation of that information is available, for example the history of a Latency Index may well be supported by an investment plan for realizing that latency, then a direct clue is given on the screen as to how to key that new slide into place (such a clue is visible on Screen C). In the close-up of Datafeed (Photograph 6), the picture of the plant has been replaced with a list of products.

All this supportive information is semi-permanent. It must in principle be updated, but not too often. As to its adequacy, remember that all sixteen carousel magazines can easily be changed, so we have a new set (of 1200 slide capacity) for each level of recursion. It is enough. In any case, there are two more back-projection screens in the opsroom to allow special presentations to be made. So far I have spoken about the NOW system, but certainly Datafeed supports the FUTURES system too. The relationship between the two is very clear on the huge main screen, where its coruscating homeostat is a constant reminder of the need to balance investment between what is and what will be. And that FUTURES system, with its simulation capability, has its own screen (Photograph 7). This is the flowchart of a typical *Dynamo* simulation—though not a very complicated one. The two points I want to make about it are unfortunately not communicated in this static picture.

The whole raison d'etre for simulations is to *work with them*. They do not sit there 'making forecasts', as I said. The output of the model shown is a projection made by a computer of how the major variables will vary over the next ten years—if nothing changes—and that projection is illuminated on one of the spare screens. To understand how the economic system works, the people in the room need two facilities, neither of which is available on an ordinary flowchart. First, they must be able to *alter* the structure in front of them. That is easily done in the computer: attendant scientists can change a few equations on request, and produce a new read-out in a few minutes. But how do you alter the flowchart? The answer to that is to use flexible magnets, and we did. However, to decide *how* to alter the flowchart you must understand the flows—and therefore we wanted to animate this screen. The problem was how to animate a flowchart that you wish continually to reconstruct. The British suppliers of the animated equipment solved that problem; and I wish I could show you the flow-lines on this model moving, and how readily its structure can be changed.

Indeed, we could spend all day in the opsroom together without exhausting its meaning as a new tool of management, and a new route to worker participation. This is the first one ever built on these cybernetic principles, and it is only a beginning.

The room and its furnishings were designed and made in Chile. The optical system and control logic for Datafeed were designed and built in England, and both the animated screens were created by another British manufacturer. I have described such a room as this over many years, and once wrote: 'It is not the operational research, technology or experience that is lacking to produce the first (such) control centre. It is the managerial acceptance of the idea, plus the will to see it realized' (3). I finally found both the acceptance and the will—on the other side of the world.

THE INCONCLUSION

This has been a very long lecture, but it deals with a very large subject : how the science of effective organization, which we call cybernetics, joins hands with the pursuit of effective freedom, which we call politics. What a new—and what a vital—issue those words betoken. Where have I heard them before?

> 'the cybernetics of men,
> as you, Socrates,
> often call politics...'

You can tell from that name that I am quoting; and we seem to be up against a time-lag of two thousand years. But now we are doing something about it. Now we have some cybernetic tools.

What I have been able to tell you today, however, is plainly incomplete; please bear in mind that this whole thing began just sixteen months ago. Therefore, although the system exists, it is—in a proper academic sense—unproven. I expect that it, like any other infant, will be slapped on the wrist (if not worse) and told to toe the line—if not worse.

For during that period of sixteen months, various attempts have been made to overthrow the Chilean democracy. I have seen that, from fairly deep inside. Scientifically too, during that period, I have been told a hundred times that it would take more than twenty years to do what has now *been* done—during that period.

We have to take note that innovation, whether political or scientific, does not favour those who hold the real power. And if either kind of innovation stands to favour ordinary folk, and both these do, then it will be opposed.

For this reason, I am not naming here my many colleagues and collaborators. They know my feelings of esteem and affection for their ability, their dedication, and their friendship. What any of them asks of me that I can do, he should consider done.

For this reason also, I commend my compatriots here today to watch, more avidly than many doubtless have, what happens next in Chile. There will be lessons there for Britain, I believe; and for humanity.

So now good-bye.

I remember Richard Godman in this very place.

Requiescas in pace.

REFERENCES

1. Norbert Wiener. *Cybernetics*, John Wiley. New York. 1948.
2. W. Ross Ashby. *Design for a Brain*, Chapman and Hall. London. 1954.
3. Stafford Beer. *Brain of the Firm*, Allen Lane. The Penguin Press. London. 1972.
4. P. J. Harrison and C. R. Stevens. 'A Bayesian Approach to Short-term Forecasting'. *Operational Research Quarterly*, Vol. 22. No. 4, December, 1971.
5. Jay W. Forrester. *World Dynamics*, Wright-Allen Press. Cambridge. Mass.. 1971.

I promised a further note
when you had read that story
                but for the perspicuous
                it is probably redundant.

The Goodman Lecture
was delivered in February 1973.

On the 11th September
Salvador Allende
that marvellous man
died in a bloody business.

Throughout June and July .
I had been in Chile.
My last meeting with the President
July 26th
was very strained—

                it was obviously probable
                by then
                and evident to us both
                that we would not meet again
                in the presidential palace
                La Moneda
                in those circumstances.

                La Moneda
                is now a shell.

I have written and broadcast much
since then
about the assassination
of a poor country
by the rich world.

All that experience
is not part of this story

                or perhaps
                I do not want
                to say much more
                about it
                yet

COLOUR CODE : YELLOW
Narrative

or perhaps
the whole story
                is implied
by this very book
    . . .

At any rate
I would invite
those who care
to read again
pages 423 to 429
with which I have not subsequently tampered
and to reflect
on what I
and you
have since learned.

Here is an undoctored quotation from page 424
        I take advantage
        only of this technique
        of spacing :

*It appears to me that the government did not
anticipate the full vindictiveness with which
the rich world would react to its actions,
which I emphasize have—so far—been
perfectly legal.*

*At any rate, a true resolution of the very
potent conflicts in Chilean society is not
discernible within the mounting instability,
and may be long postponed.*

*But I consider that this is largely a phenomenon
of the cybernetics of international power :
you could say that the Chilean people have not
been given a chance.*

*They are being systematically isolated behind
those beautiful Andes mountains, and are in a
state of seige.*

COLOUR CODE : YELLOW
Narrative

To pick on some words :

       vindictiveness

       perfectly legal

       very potent conflicts

       the cybernetics of international power

STET
as the printers say :

let it stand.

And now
I would like to end this message
in a personal way
       as I began it
       and have tried to keep it going
       in these personal bits.

First of all—some thanks.

Betty Johnson typed
       often several times
the exceedingly overwritten scripts
of all but the last two Arguments of Change
which were done by Sallie my wife.

I thank them both so much
invariably done
with minutes to spare

       aeroplanes to catch
       deadlines. . . . .

I thank also
all those who commissioned the Arguments
all those who listened to them
all those who published them
       and gave permission
       for their use here

and you
who got this far.

COLOUR CODE : YELLOW
Narrative

It would have been possible
        you may have thought
to take apart the Arguments of Change
and to reassemble them
        you might have preferred that
into a great big theory
about how the world should be run.

This was never on the cards.

The trouble is that
I don't know
how the world should be run.

All I can do
is to share an experience.

All I can say is
this is how it was.

        Here are various approaches
        to various issues.

        The many-faceted 'thing' in the centre
            is elusive
            and adaptable

        but it is certainly not
        a big fat theory.

        Somewhere in all this
        is the metamessage
            to do with insight
            and to do with hope.

        Naturally
        I hope you got the message
        and maybe
        learned a new skill

        but not a new creed.

COLOUR CODE : YELLOW
Narrative

So now for the strange thing
　　　　　which for the perspicuous
　　　　　is probably redundant.

I think I may have got the message myself.
I can never re-enter these three years
because I have come out of them
on the other side.

　　　　　I do not wish to retract anything I have said.

　　　　　But I do feel quite different.

I hope that my children
and their children's children
to whom this message was dedicated

and yours too

can handle all their metathreats.

　　　　　In love and peace

Stafford Beer.

COLOUR CODE : YELLOW
Narrative

READER'S GUIDE TO *PLATFORM FOR CHANGE*
Jon Li

TABLE OF CONTENTS OF THE READER'S GUIDE

HOW TO READ *PLATFORM FOR CHANGE*

1. The author's own statement in the prelims is the most straightforward version of what this book is about.

2. Read the Thesis (pp. 379–91), and then grapple with the graphic of the Thesis (390–1). Now you will be able to see Stafford's big picture, and as you fill in the pieces reconstruct it into your own way of thinking.

3. Take a look at the table of platforms below, and see if there are any that seem particularly interesting. Each platform has a different tone, because it has a different audience and context. They vary so much that any two will give you completely different views on how to do systems analysis.

4. If you want to skip around, then it will help to start with the narrative before a particular platform. It will help you to understand Stafford's attitude and expectations for that piece.

INTRODUCTION

Problems. You have problems on your mind.

The world used to work. Things that used to work most of the time are going wrong more and more.

Like a paved road with pot holes, institutions are falling apart, especially our public institutions—the structures that are supposed to hold our society together. Change seems to continue, and not for the better. Money is a real problem. It is more expensive all the time. For organizations, how to maintain the status quo is enough to break the bank. Did we not use all the tricks we could in last year's budget? Where can we get more money? How are we ever going to do even as much as we did last year? The parts of the puzzle no longer seem to fit together.

Platform for Change argues that we need to rethink *all* of our social institutions. It provides an intellectual context for re-creating society.

But the book asks a lot of the reader—to follow a new logic, to create a new model using as a metaphor anything that is organic rather than anything that is mechanical, to think meta rather than higher like a hierarchy, dynamic rather than static, and evolving, learning and adapting rather than locked in concrete.

Whether you work in a large firm, or a public institution, you should find *Platform*'s insights apply to a wide variety of settings. It was written from the perspective of a management scientist who knows a lot about viable organizations.

Platform says: call it a *system*, and then look at a dynamic *synthesis* model that is present–future oriented.

Platform asks you to expand your thinking. Do not give up your analytical tools, but please take a look at the bigger picture. Synthesize your idea about the problem you are dealing with. Create a model of the world surrounding your problem. Make the model big enough that your problem is small. Identify what impacts on your problem. Can you change an impact so that your problem disappears?

Platform has many observations about management and organizations that will challenge your thinking. Although it is over two decades old, most of the concerns still ring true. And the call to use *science* to help reformulate our social institutions has its own logic.

At the heart of *Platform* is the idea that computers offer citizens and managers profound new power to deal with information. The biggest change since the book was first published is the astronomical increase in computer number crunching.

But are the public policy judgements any better as a consequence? The results are grim.

Platform builds a logic for using science to create new tools for managing large, complex social institutions—especially the firm, and the larger economy. The goal is to design viable systems.

The most difficult idea in *Platform* is about money: that it deals with cost but not benefit (see Key concept No. 10 below).

Platform concludes with the tension of an explosive, real-life political tragedy—a report of work in progress for the Allende administration, to use modern science to manage the economy of Chile. The Chile experience empirically confirmed the power of the tools. The world has changed a lot since *Platform* was published 20 years ago. The Berlin Wall is down, and the Soviet empire has vanished. And the world has grown even more complex, complicated and confusing. But the book is even more timely and relevant today because it is about today's choices and how they can affect the future.

TABLE OF *PLATFORMS*

Each of these statements was developed by Stafford to address a particular audience, in a particular setting. Each has a unique tone appropriate to the context. Usually they include the basic components of the message: the megathreats, overwhelming complexity, systems and metalanguage, using science to examine issues of organization and society, and using computers to manage information.

Homo Gubernator pp. 21–37
The Pierre Teilhard de Chardin Association of Great Britain and Ireland,
Central Hall, Westminster, London

Operational research as revelation pp. 55–69
President's Inaugural Address, Operational Research Society,
London

Health and quiet breathing pp. 85–93
Lunch Talk, Hospital Centre,
London

Management in cybernetic terms pp. 103–17
Prepared for UNESCO, the United Nations Educational, Social and Cultural
Organization

The cybernetic cytoblast: management itself pp. 133–51
Chairman's Address, International Cybernetics Congress,
Imperial College, London

Questions of metric pp. 161–74
President's Address, joint meeting: Operational Research Society and Institute of
Management Science,
Imperial College, London

The law and the profits pp. 191–212
Frank Newsam Memorial Lecture,
Police College, Bramshill

Managing modern complexity pp. 219–41
US House Committee on Science and Astronautics,
Washington, DC

The software milieu pp. 263–71
Management Today

Dynamics of decision pp. 277–97
Dinner Talk, British Institute of Management,
Savoy Hotel, London

The liberty machine pp. 307–21
Conference on Ecological Systems, American Society for Cybernetics,
Washington, DC

Science and the mass media pp. 329–35
BBC Radio,
London

Renascence pp. 345–68

The surrogate world we manage pp. 397–416
President's Address, Society for General Systems Research,
Philadelphia, Pennsylvania

Fanfare for effective freedom: cybernetic praxis in government pp. 421–52
Richard Goodman Memorial Lecture,
Brighton Polytechnic, Moulsecoomb, Brighton

KEY CONCEPTS

1. The world is in trouble. It is not just the threat of the bomb or plutonium terrorists, or pollution or over-population. It is all of those and more. The world seems to be growing ever more complex, and society's institutions (our governments and economies) seem less and less able to cope with the problems. Increasing complexity means more variety and increasing uncertainty—especially about how the larger social environment will respond in the future. Stafford calls the larger problem 'complexification', a word he got from Teilhard de Chardin.

2. We need to learn to use science. We need to invoke *science*—defined as the organized body of human knowledge about the world and its workings. Science offers the means:
   (a) to measure and manipulate complexity through mathematics;
   (b) to design complex systems through general systems theory;
   (c) to devise viable organizations through cybernetics;
   (d) to work effectively with people through behavioural science;
   (e) to apply all this to practical affairs through operations research.
   The problem must be looked at in a new way that is not limited by the blinders of particular scientific disciplines, but which encourages interdisciplinary capabilities from the depositories of knowledge of physical, biological and social systems.
   Cybernetics is the name of the science of how organizations can effectively manage information, using biological criteria for the question of viability.

3. Arguments of change, not for change. While this book was written a decade before *Future Shock* by Alvin Toffler, it starts with the fundamental idea that society is now in a state of continuous change. This does not mean that any particular outcome is inevitable. It does mean that current institutions were designed to adapt to a different set of problems than we are now confronting, and the risk of organizational failure, even species extinction, is great.

4. Esoteric boxes. Modern organizations are self-defined structures which have survived in part because they adapt as little as possible to outside influences. Each has its own rules, and procedures for allocating and using resources for some purpose. Each esoteric box is locked into its own particular established course of action.

5. Data vs. information. Part of the problem is endless data. It has become pollution—swamping out whatever might be important. The issue has become: what data is actually useful, and how can it be identified? Stafford's idea is that information is what changes us: information is a new fact that is so significant that it forces an organization to rethink its current course of action, and then divert its course based on re-evaluated options.

6. Requisite variety. Variety is a measure of complexity. Additional choices multiply current options, often exponentially, which means exploding complexity. An organization is a structural device for a large number of people to work together and reduce proliferating variety. Ross Ashby developed the Law of Requisite Variety: in order to manage complexity, an individual or an organization must meet or preferably exceed the variety it must confront in its environment, if it is to survive and accomplish its purpose.

7. Metalanguage. The current language of organizations (hierarchy, data) needs to be reconceptualized, because many issues in the current language have become undecidable. A higher level of logic allows discussion of systemic problems, unaddressable in an organization's daily operational language. The language of general systems theory was specifically designed to allow communication about organizational adaptation, restructuring and evolution. An organization is a system with identifiable boundaries and subsystems which have defined roles, and which is attempting to survive in a dynamic, unstable environment. One of the interesting things about general systems theory (there are many interesting things) is that it is inherently decentralizing because the logic and the language encourage individuals to synthesize and integrate their own experience and points of view as legitimate and useful.

8. Synthesis vs. analysis. A key idea of the metalanguage concept is that the world has spent too much time in dissection, division and analysis. One way to tie together the above seven ideas is to create a metalanguage to string together esoteric boxes, and then re-create them to accommodate exploding complexity.

9. Computers. The biggest real change in two decades since Stafford first published *Platform* is the astronomical increases in computing power. Chip miniaturization has led to the inexpensive personal computer, local networks to tie them together, and the Internet to give people access to computer information around the world. Evolving applications, such as modelling and graphics, have made new uses possible. But what is useful? If there were a thousand pieces of data to choose from, it will not be easier to find the important data if the situation has evolved and there are now a million peces of data.

Platform is about figuring out what is important, and so is even more relevant as the world grows more complex and the noise of insignificant data grows louder.

10. Eudemony (u' de mo ne). This is an old English word from the Greek. It means well-being, closer to prosperity than ecstasy. Actually, the purpose of *Platform* is to introduce eudemony into our vocabulary, as a unit of measure which is a metalanguage into our vocabulary, as a unit of measure which is a metalanguage to the metric of money, which is a constraint. Money is a useful tool but it is inadequate as a mechanism for evaluating relative social worth. Maybe money worked when life was not so dynamic, but the issues around us have grown so large in scale (like planetary destruction and species extinction) that monetary statements no longer translate into terms that most people can wrestle with. If you think of the concept of eudemony as a system, and *Platform* as its environment, then eudemony becomes the throbbing heart of *Platform*'s living, dynamic ideas.

KEY WORDS INDEX
(Speeches/platforms in parentheses)

PLATFORM AS A THEORETICAL CONTEXT FOR BEER'S VIABLE SYSTEM MODEL (VSM) CONSTRUCT

At this stage in Stafford's distinguished career (1994), his hallmark is his Viable System Model (VSM), his crowning achievement his work in Chile for Allende, and his new idea Team Syntegrity.

For those interested in Stafford's VSM, *Platform* is a puzzle, because it is almost as though VSM does not exist. VSM's recursive structure with multiple feedback links is barely alluded to as such, except as a theoretical necessity. Serious students of Stafford's ideas will find that *Platform* offers his conceptual metalanguage which surrounds his VSM ideas, structures and proscriptions. (Jon Li has read *Brain of the Firm* and *The Heart of Enterprise*, and is still confused by some of the VSM.)

One way to understand *Platform* is that the speeches or platforms represent opportunities for Stafford to put on a public face and preach to an audience intelligent enough to be expected to follow a whole speech of cascading new ideas—crescendoing new ideas. After a while, common themes come out. More likely, they are explained in a significantly different way that helps the reader begin to fathom the multidimensionality of the problems that confront us as people living on this planet. Stafford's version of Chardin's idea is that comlexification forces us to create metalanguage to describe these difficult problems as a step towards constructive institutional transformation. But Stafford leaves no doubt that he is talking about revolutionary change of our social structure. What he really cares about is doing judo on large institutions and their myths, manipulating their management concept at least 90% and asking everyone in the organization to help decide what is important enough to do *from now on*.

People working with VSM will be a lot more effective after they have worked their way through *Platform* because it will give them the opportunity to clarify their own informational and organizational biases, independent of the object of study.

WHY JON LI IS THE AUTHOR OF THIS READER'S GUIDE

Jon Li is a political economist who has been writing about applied general systems theory since 1975, and the ideas in *Platform for Change* since 1976. Jon has worked in county mental health administration, for the California legislature as a consultant on health and welfare policy, and in video production. Jon is involved in setting up the Davis Community Network, a residential citywide computer network linked to Internet. Jon recently convinced the Davis City Council to run a 3 year planning process to revise the City General Plan; with over 200 citizen volunteers on 14 committees; with issues ranging from housing, transportation, land use and open space (state mandated) to economics, health and social services, and computers (which are not required elements of the City General Plan). Jon's theory goal of applying general systems theory is to convince the California legislature to set up similar citywide generalist committees in every city in California, and then hold a decentralized state constitutional convention. Jon is usually seen around Davis on his bicycle.

Platform for Change is Jon Li's favorite book. Why is that? Because he can read so much between the lines that he can get lost in a paragraph and forget the topic. Jon Li has read *Platform for Change* nine times and finds it thought provoking each re-read. He knows the book well enough to keep the different speeches/platforms in perspective, along with the thesis, the metalanguage and the explanation—all in one picture in his brain. If you look at the system dynamic in the prelims, Stafford's book is a favorite system to analyze. Jon Li considers it the bible for bureaucrats.

CONCLUSION

In a discussion about social change, parameters include immediate and short-term goals and further goals, identifying means to achieve ends, and tactics to accomplish a strategy.

A higher level of analysis is to characterize evolutionary vs. revolutionary change. Two hundred years of US legislative compromise suggests that often the final agreement creates new problems with the same old basic structure. At some point in time, old institutions become obsolete, impossible to maintain, and finally die. The concept paradigm shift has become popularized to signify a radical departure from previous structures and standards to a whole new way of doing things. The new world is unrecognizable from the eyes of the old world.

Platform for Change is an argument for applied general systems theory as a superior method of scientific problem-solving. In addition to the traditional scientific tools of analysis and dissection, general systems theory offers a theoretical overview which helps an individual to integrate and synthesize fragments into a dynamic whole.

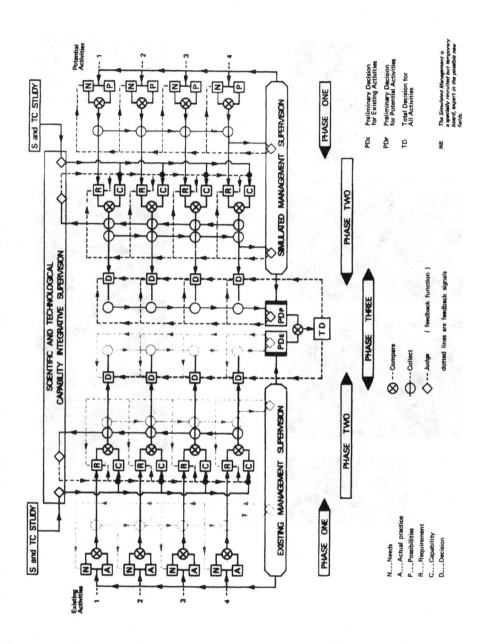

S and TC STUDY

S and TC STUDY

Potential Activities
1
2
3
4

SCIENTIFIC AND TECHNOLOGICAL
CAPABILITY INTEGRATIVE SUPERVISION

SIMULATED MANAGEMENT SUPERVISION

EXISTING MANAGEMENT SUPERVISION

Existing Activities
1
2
3
4

PHASE ONE

PHASE TWO

PHASE THREE

PHASE TWO

PHASE ONE

N---Needs
A---Actual practice
P---Possibilities
R---Requirement
C---Capability
D---Decision

PDe   Preliminary Decision
       for Existing Activities

PDe   Preliminary Decision
       for Potential Activities

TD   Total Decision for
       All Activities

NB.   The Simulated Management is
       a specially recruited but temporary
       board, expert in the possible new
       fields.

⊗ ---Compare

⊕ ---Collect

◇ ---Judge   (feedback function)

dotted lines are feedback signals

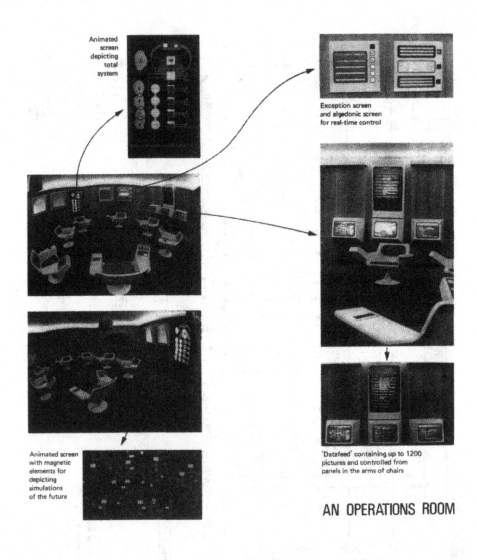

Animated
screen
depicting
total
system

Exception screen
and algedonic screen
for real-time control

Animated screen
with magnetic
elements for
depicting
simulations
of the future

'Datafeed' containing up to 1200
pictures and controlled from
panels in the arms of chairs

AN OPERATIONS ROOM